1b

HOLT McDOUGAL

¡Avancemos!

HOLT McDOUGAL

a division of Houghton Mifflin Harcourt

1b

HOLT McDOUGAL

¡Avancemos!

Celebraciones

Cultura INTERACTIVA Explora las celebraciones del mundo hispano

Agosto: Feria de Málaga C2

Septiembre: Día de la Independencia C4

Octubre: El 12 de Octubre C6

Noviembre: ¡Día de los Muertos! C8

Diciembre: Las Navidades C10

Enero: ¡Año Nuevo! C12

Febrero: ¡Carnaval! C14

Marzo: Las Fallas C16

Abril: Semana Santa C18

Mayo: ¡Cinco de Mayo! C20

Junio: Inti Raymi C22

Julio: Día de Simón Bolívar C24

El Día de los Muertos,
Santiago Sacatepéquez, Guatemala

New Year's Eve, Madrid, Spain

Online at CLASSZONE.COM

Cultura INTERACTIVA *pp. C2–C3, C4–C5, C6–C7, C8–C9, C10–C11, C12–C13, C14–C15, C16–C17, C18–C19, C20–C21, C22–C23, C24–C25*

Antes de avanzar

Parte 1 **Un rato con los amigos** 2
  Repaso: ¿Qué te gusta hacer? 2
  Repaso: Mis amigos y yo 3
  Práctica de vocabulario 4
  Práctica de gramática 6
  Repaso: Subject pronouns and **ser** 6
  Repaso: Gustar with nouns and infinitives 8
  Repaso: Present tense of **-ar** verbs 10

Parte 2 **¡Vamos a la escuela!** 12
  Repaso: En la clase 12
  Repaso: En la escuela 13
  Práctica de vocabulario 14
  Práctica de gramática 16
  Repaso: The verb **tener** 16
  Repaso: The verb **estar** 18
  Repaso: The verb **ir** 19

Parte 3 **Comer en familia** 20
  Repaso: El desayuno, El almuerzo 20
  Repaso: La familia 21
  Práctica de vocabulario 22
  Práctica de gramática 25
  Repaso: Present tense of **-er** and **-ir** verbs . . . 25
  Repaso: Stem-changing verbs: **e → ie** 27

Parte 4 **En el centro** 28
  Repaso: En la tienda de ropa 28
  Repaso: En el restaurante 29
  Práctica de vocabulario 30
  Práctica de gramática 32
  Repaso: Direct object pronouns 32
  Repaso: Stem-changing verbs: **o → ue** 34
  Repaso: Stem-changing verbs: **e → i** 35

Repaso de Partes 1 a 4 36

¿Recuerdas?
- Definite and indefinite articles *p. 5*
- Noun-adjective agreement *p. 7*
- Telling time *p. 14*
- Numbers before nouns *p. 15*
- **del** *p. 18*
- **al** *p. 19*
- Possessive adjectives *p. 22*
- Giving dates *p. 23*
- Comparatives *p. 24*
- The verb **hacer** *p. 26*
- **ir a** + infinitive *p. 30*

UNIDAD 5

Ecuador
¡Bienvenido a nuestra casa!

Cultura INTERACTIVA   Explora la cultura de Ecuador 38

Lección 1

Tema: **Vivimos aquí** 40

VOCABULARIO

Describing a house, Household items, Furniture . .   42

Práctica 45

Telehistoria escena 1 46

GRAMÁTICA

Ser or **estar** 48

Práctica 49

Telehistoria escena 2 52

Ordinal numbers 54

Práctica 55

TODO JUNTO

Telehistoria completa 58

Juegos y diversiones: ¡Dibújalo! 61

Lectura: Vivir en Ecuador 62

Conexiones: Las ruinas de Ingapirca 64

En resumen 65

Repaso de la lección 66

Cultura
- **Explora Ecuador**
  p. 38
- **Casas ecuatorianas**
  p. 51
- **Sitios geográficos**
  p. 57
- **Vivir en Ecuador**
  p. 62

 ¿Recuerdas?
- stem-changing verbs:
  o → ue *p. 45*
- location words *p. 49*
- colors *p. 50*
- clothing *p. 55*

 Did you get it?
Student Self-Check
*pp. 45, 47, 51, 53,
57, 60*

Online at CLASSZONE.COM

Cultura INTERACTIVA
*pp. 38–39
96–97*

Animated Grammar
*pp. 48, 54, 65
76, 82, 93*

@HomeTutor VideoPlus
*pp. 46, 52, 58
74, 80, 86*

 **Video/DVD**

Vocabulario
pp. 42–44, 70–72
Telehistoria
*pp. 46, 52, 58
74, 80, 86*

Una casa tradicional con jardín, Quito, Ecuador

Una fiesta de cumpleaños, Quito, Ecuador

Lección 2

Tema: **Una fiesta en casa** **68**

VOCABULARIO

Planning a party, chores **70**

Práctica **73**

Telehistoria escena 1 . . . . **74**

GRAMÁTICA

More irregular verbs **76**

Práctica **77**

Telehistoria escena 2 . . . . **80**

Affirmative **tú** commands **82**

Práctica **83**

TODO JUNTO

Telehistoria completa **86**

Juegos y diversiones: Mímica **89**

Lectura cultural: Bailes folklóricos de Ecuador y Panamá **90**

Proyectos culturales: Arte textil de Ecuador y Panamá **92**

En resumen **93**

Repaso de la lección **94**

Cultura

- **Fiestas de Quito** *p. 77*
- **Los textiles de Otavalo** *p. 85*
- **Bailes folklóricos de Ecuador y Panamá** *p. 90*
- **Arte textil de Ecuador y Panamá** *p. 92*
- **¡Así celebramos!** *p. 96*

 ¿Recuerdas?

- **tener que** *p. 75*
- interrogative words *p. 79*
- expressions of frequency *p. 81*
- direct object pronouns *p. 83*

 PARA Y PIENSA **Did you get it?**
Student Self-Check
pp. 73, 75, 79, 81, 85, 88

UNIT 5 WRAP-UP

Comparación cultural **Lectura y escritura: ¡Así celebramos!** **96**

Repaso inclusivo ♻ **Unidades 1–5** **98**

Entre dos ¿? **288**

¡AvanzaRap! DVD Sing and Learn

UNIDAD 6 República Dominicana

Mantener un cuerpo sano

Cultura INTERACTIVA Explora la cultura de la República Dominicana **100**

Lección 1

Tema: **¿Cuál es tu deporte favorito?** **102**

VOCABULARIO

Sports **104**

Práctica **107**

Telehistoria escena 1 . . . . **108**

GRAMÁTICA

The verb **jugar** **110**

Práctica **111**

Telehistoria escena 2 . . . . **114**

The verbs **saber** and **conocer** **116**

Práctica **117**

TODO JUNTO

Telehistoria completa **120**

Juegos y diversiones: Memoria **123**

Lectura: Un club de deportes **124**

Conexiones: La bandera dominicana . . . **126**

En resumen **127**

Repaso de la lección **128**

Cultura

- **Explora la República Dominicana** *p. 100*
- **La Serie del Caribe** *p. 112*
- **El arte representativo** *p. 119*
- **Un club de deportes** *p. 124*

 ¿Recuerdas?

- numbers from 200 to 1,000,000 *p. 107*
- **gustar** with nouns *p. 109*
- comparatives *p. 113*

 Did you get it?

Student Self-Check *pp. 107, 109, 113, 115, 119, 122*

Online at CLASSZONE.COM

Cultura INTERACTIVA
pp. 100–101 158–159

Animated Grammar
pp. 110, 116, 127 138, 144, 155

@HomeTutor VideoPlus
pp. 108, 114, 120 136, 142, 148

Video/DVD

Vocabulario
pp. 104–106, 132–134

Telehistoria
pp. 108, 114, 120 136, 142, 148

Un partido en la escuela, Santo Domingo,
República Dominicana

Un día en la Playa Caribe, Juan Dolio,
República Dominicana

Lección 2

Tema: *La salud* **130**

VOCABULARIO

Staying healthy, Parts of the body **132**

Práctica **135**

Telehistoria escena 1 . . . . **136**

GRAMÁTICA

Preterite of regular **-ar** verbs **138**

Práctica **139**

Telehistoria escena 2 . . . . **142**

Preterite of **-car, -gar, -zar** verbs **144**

Práctica **145**

TODO JUNTO

Telehistoria completa **148**

Juegos y diversiones: Simón dice **151**

Lectura cultural: Dos atletas de alta velocidad . **152**

Proyectos culturales: Gestos y refranes **154**

En resumen **155**

Repaso de la lección **156**

Cultura
- **La artista y su estilo** *p. 141*
- **El Festival del Merengue** *p. 147*
- **Dos atletas de alta velocidad** *p. 152*
- **Gestos y refranes** *p. 154*
- **Deportes favoritos** *p. 158*

♻ *¿Recuerdas?*
- **gustar** with nouns *p. 137*
- stem-changing verbs **o → ue** *p. 137*
- telling time *p. 139*

 Did you get it?
Student Self-Check
pp. 135, 137, 141, 143, 147, 150

UNIT 6 WRAP-UP

Comparación cultural — **Lectura y escritura: Deportes favoritos** **158**

Repaso inclusivo ♻ **Unidades 1–6** **160**

Entre dos ¿? **290**

¡AvanzaRap!
DVD
Sing and Learn

UNIDAD 7 Argentina

¡Una semana fenomenal!

Cultura INTERACTIVA Explora la cultura de Argentina . . . 162

Lección 1

Tema: En el cibercafé 164

VOCABULARIO

Sending e-mails, Talking about when
events occur 166

Práctica 169

Telehistoria escena 1 170

GRAMÁTICA

Preterite of regular **-er** and **-ir** verbs 172

Práctica 173

Telehistoria escena 2 176

Affirmative and negative words 178

Práctica 179

TODO JUNTO

Telehistoria completa 182

Juegos y diversiones: ¿Qué letra? 185

Lectura: Un cuestionario sobre
las computadoras 186

Conexiones: El lenguaje 188

En resumen 189

Repaso de la lección 190

Cultura

- **Explora Argentina** p. 162
- **El lunfardo** p. 173
- **Las playas de Mar del Plata** p. 181
- **Un cuestionario sobre las computadoras** p. 186

 ¿Recuerdas?

- affirmative **tú** commands p. 171
- telling time p. 173
- foods and beverages p. 175
- preterite of regular **-ar** verbs p. 180

 Did you get it?

Student Self-Check
pp. 169, 171, 175, 177, 181, 184

Online at CLASSZONE.COM

Cultura INTERACTIVA
pp. 162–163
220–221

Animated Grammar
pp. 172, 178, 189
200, 206, 217

@HomeTutor VideoPlus
pp. 170, 176, 182
198, 204, 210

 **Video/DVD**

Vocabulario
pp. 166–168, 194–196

Telehistoria
pp. 170, 176, 182
198, 204, 210

La Casa Rosada, Buenos Aires, Argentina

El Parque de la Costa, El Tigre, Argentina

Lección 2

Tema: *Un día en el parque de diversiones* 192

VOCABULARIO

Making a phone call, Places of interest 194

Práctica 197

Telehistoria escena 1 198

GRAMÁTICA

Preterite of **ir, ser,** and **hacer** 200

Práctica 201

Telehistoria escena 2 204

Pronouns after prepositions 206

Práctica 207

TODO JUNTO

Telehistoria completa 210

Juegos y diversiones: Categorías 213

Lectura cultural: Museos excepcionales 214

Proyectos culturales: Nombres y apellidos 216

En resumen 217

Repaso de la lección 218

UNIT 7 WRAP-UP

Comparación cultural — **Lectura y escritura: ¿Conoces un lugar divertirdo?** 220

Repaso inclusivo ♲ **Unidades 1–7** 222

Entre dos ¿? 292

Cultura
- **El puerto de La Boca** *p. 203*
- **La comida argentina** *p. 209*
- **Museos excepcionales** *p. 214*
- **Nombres y apellidos** *p. 216*
- **¿Conoces un lugar divertido?** *p. 220*

 ¿Recuerdas?
- noun-adjective agreement *p. 199*
- places around town *p. 205*
- stem-changing verbs: **e → i** *p. 209*

 Did you get it?
Student Self-Check
pp. 197, 199, 203, 205, 209, 212

¡AvanzaRap!
DVD
Sing and Learn

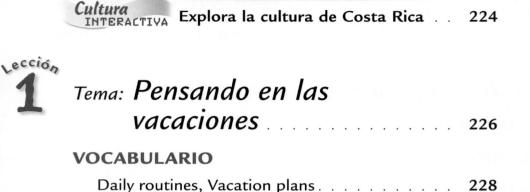

UNIDAD 8 Costa Rica
Una rutina diferente

Cultura INTERACTIVA Explora la cultura de Costa Rica . . 224

Lección 1

Tema: **Pensando en las vacaciones** 226

VOCABULARIO
Daily routines, Vacation plans 228
Práctica 231
Telehistoria escena 1 232

GRAMÁTICA
Reflexive verbs 234
Práctica 235
Telehistoria escena 2 238
Present progressive 240
Práctica 241

TODO JUNTO
Telehistoria completa 244
Juegos y diversiones: Tu rutina diaria 247
Lectura: Mi viaje a Costa Rica 248
Conexiones: ¡Vamos al museo! 250
En resumen 251
Repaso de la lección 252

Cultura
- Explora Costa Rica *p. 224*
- El paisaje de Costa Rica *p. 237*
- El uso de *usted, tú* y *vos p. 243*
- Mi viaje a Costa Rica *p. 248*
- ¡Vamos al museo! *p. 250*

 ¿Recuerdas?
- preterite of **hacer** *p. 231*
- direct object pronouns *p. 233*
- parts of the body *p. 235*
- chores *p. 241*
- houses *p. 242*
- telling time *p. 245*

 Did you get it?
Student Self-Check
pp. 231, 233, 237, 239, 243, 246

 **Online** at CLASSZONE.COM

Cultura INTERACTIVA
pp. 224–225 282–283

Animated Grammar
pp. 234, 240, 251 262, 268, 279

@HomeTutor VideoPlus
pp. 232, 238, 244 260, 266, 272

 **Video/DVD**
Vocabulario *pp. 228–230, 256–258*
Telehistoria *pp. 232, 238, 244 260, 266, 272*

Una familia habla de las vacaciones,
San José, Costa Rica

Una tienda de artesanías y recuerdos,
San José, Costa Rica

Lección 2

Tema: ¡Vamos de vacaciones! . . . 254

VOCABULARIO

Discussing vacation and leisure activities 256

Práctica 259

Telehistoria escena 1 260

GRAMÁTICA

Indirect object pronouns 262

Práctica 263

Telehistoria escena 2 266

Demonstrative adjectives 268

Práctica 269

TODO JUNTO

Telehistoria completa 272

Juegos y diversiones: El mercado 275

Lectura cultural: Mercados en
Costa Rica y Uruguay 276

Proyectos culturales: Postres en
Costa Rica y Uruguay 278

En resumen 279

Repaso de la lección 280

Cultura

• **El transporte** *p. 264*
• **El café** *p. 271*
• **Mercados en Costa Rica y Uruguay** *p. 276*
• **Postres en Costa Rica y Uruguay** *p. 278*
• **¡De vacaciones!** *p. 282*

 ¿Recuerdas?

• family *p. 263*
• numbers from 200 to 1,000,000 *p. 264*
• **gustar** with an infinitive *p. 267*
• present progressive *p. 269*
• classroom objects *p. 271*

 Did you get it?
Student Self-Check
pp. 259, 261, 265, 267, 271, 274

UNIT 8 WRAP-UP

Comparación cultural   Lectura y escritura:
¡De vacaciones! 282

Repaso inclusivo ♻ Unidades 1–8 284

Entre dos ¿? 294

¡AvanzaRap!
DVD
Sing and Learn

Recursos

Expansión de vocabulario

    Unidad 5 . . . . **R2**

    Unidad 6 . . . . **R3**

    Unidad 7 . . . . **R4**

    Unidad 8 . . . . **R5**

Para y piensa   Self-Check Answers **R6**

Resumen de gramática. **R9**

Glosario

    Español-inglés. **R18**

    Inglés-español. **R28**

Índice **R37**

Créditos **R45**

¡Avancemos!

About the Authors

Estella Gahala

Estella Gahala received degrees in Spanish from Wichita State University, French from Middlebury College, and a Ph.D. in Educational Administration and Curriculum from Northwestern University. A career teacher of Spanish and French, she has worked with a wide variety of students at the secondary level. She has also served as foreign language department chair and district director of curriculum and instruction. Her workshops and publications focus on research and practice in a wide range of topics, including culture and language learning, learning strategies, assessment, and the impact of current brain research on curriculum and instruction. She has coauthored twelve basal textbooks. Honors include the Chevalier dans l'Ordre des Palmes Académiques and listings in *Who's Who of American Women, Who's Who in America,* and *Who's Who in the World.*

Patricia Hamilton Carlin

Patricia Hamilton Carlin completed her M.A. in Spanish at the University of California, Davis, where she also taught as a lecturer. Previously she earned a Master of Secondary Education with specialization in foreign languages from the University of Arkansas and taught Spanish and French at the K–12 level. Patricia currently teaches Spanish and foreign language/ESL methodology at the University of Central Arkansas, where she coordinates the second language teacher education program. In addition, Patricia is a frequent presenter at local, regional, and national foreign language conferences. In 2005, she was awarded the Southern Conference on Language Teaching's Outstanding Teaching Award: Post-Secondary. Her professional service has included the presidency of the Arkansas Foreign Language Teachers Association and the presidency of Arkansas's DeSoto Chapter of the AATSP.

Audrey L. Heining-Boynton

Audrey L. Heining-Boynton received her Ph.D. in Curriculum and Instruction from Michigan State University. She is a professor of Education and Romance Languages at The University of North Carolina at Chapel Hill, where she teaches educational methodology classes and Spanish. She has also taught Spanish, French, and ESL at the K–12 level. Dr. Heining-Boynton served as the president of ACTFL and the National Network for Early Language Learning. She has been involved with AATSP, Phi Delta Kappa, and state foreign language associations. In addition, she has presented both nationally and internationally and has published over forty books, articles, and curricula.

Ricardo Otheguy

Ricardo Otheguy received his Ph.D. in Linguistics from the City University of New York, where he is currently professor of Linguistics at the Graduate Center. He is also director of the Research Institute for the Study of Language in Urban Society (RISLUS) and coeditor of the research journal *Spanish in Context.* He has extensive experience with school-based research and has written on topics related to Spanish grammar, bilingual education, and Spanish in the United States. His work has been supported by private and government foundations, including the Rockefeller Brothers Fund and the National Science Foundation. He is coauthor of *Tu mundo: Curso para hispanohablantes,* and *Prueba de ubicación para hispanohablantes.*

Barbara J. Rupert

Barbara Rupert completed her M.A. at Pacific Lutheran University. She has taught Level 1 through A.P. Spanish and has implemented a FLES program in her district. Barbara is the author of CD-ROM activities for the *¡Bravo!* series. She has presented at many local, regional, and national foreign language conferences. She has served as president of both the Pacific Northwest Council for Languages (PNCFL) and the Washington Association for Language Teaching, and was the PNCFL representative to ACTFL. In 1996, Barbara received the Christa McAuliffe Award for Excellence in Education, and in 1999, she was selected Washington's "Spanish Teacher of the Year" by the Juan de Fuca Chapter of the AATSP.

John DeMado, Creative Consultant

John DeMado has been a vocal advocate for second-language acquisition in the United States for many years. He started his career as a middle/high school French and Spanish teacher, before entering the educational publishing profession. Since 1993, Mr. DeMado has directed his own business, John DeMado Language Seminars. Inc., a company devoted exclusively to language acquisition issues. He has authored numerous books in both French and Spanish that span the K–12 curriculum. Mr. DeMado wrote and performed the ¡*AvanzaRap*! songs for Levels 1 and 2.

Carl Johnson, Senior Program Advisor

Carl Johnson received degrees from Marietta College (OH), the University of Illinois, Université Laval, and a Ph.D. in Foreign Language Education from The Ohio State University, during which time he studied French, German, Spanish, and Russian. He has been a lifelong foreign language educator, retiring in 2003 after 27 years as a language teacher (secondary and university level), consultant, and Director of Languages Other Than English for the Texas Department of Education. He has completed many publications relating to student and teacher language proficiency development, language textbooks, and nationwide textbook adoption practices. He also served as president of the Texas Foreign Language Association, Chair of the Board of the Southwest Conference on Language Teaching, and president of the National Council of State Supervisors of Foreign Languages. In addition, he was named Chevalier dans l'Ordre des Palmes Académiques by the French government.

Rebecca L. Oxford, Learning Strategy Specialist

Rebecca L. Oxford received her Ph.D. in educational psychology from The University of North Carolina. She also holds two degrees in foreign language from Vanderbilt University and Yale University, and a degree in educational psychology from Boston University. She leads the Second Language Education and Culture Program and is a professor at the University of Maryland. She has directed programs at Teachers College, Columbia University; the University of Alabama; and the Pennsylvania State University. In addition, she initiated and edited *Tapestry*, a series of student textbooks used around the world. Dr. Oxford specializes in language learning strategies and styles.

Contributing Writers

Louis G. Baskinger
New Hartford High School
New Hartford, NY

Jacquelyn Cinotti-Dirmann
Duval County Public Schools
Jacksonville, FL

Consulting Authors

Dan Battisti
Dr. Teresa Carrera-Hanley
Bill Lionetti
Patty Murguía Bohannan
Lorena Richins Layser

❋ Teacher Reviewers

Middle School Reviewers

Mary Jo Aronica
Lincoln Hall Middle School
Lincolnwood, IL

Suzanne M. Auffray
The Overlake School
Redmond, WA

Elizabeth M. Bossong
Vestal High School
Vestal, NY

Zahava Frymerman
G. W. Carver Middle School
Miami, FL

Ana Johnson
Rising Star Middle School
Fayetteville, GA

Sharon Larracoechea
North Junior High
Boise, ID

Deborah Tomkinson
James Madison Middle School
Titusville, FL

Elizabeth L. Torosian
Lowell Community Charter Public
  School
Lowell, MA

Heather T. Walker
Chester Middle School
Chester, VA

Mari Zimmerman
James C. Wright Middle School
Madison, WI

High School Reviewers

Sue Arandjelovic
Dobson High School
Mesa, AZ

Susan K. Arbuckle
Mahomet-Seymour High School
Mahomet, IL

Kristi Ashe
Amador Valley High School
Pleasanton, CA

Shaun A. Bauer
Olympia High School, *retired*
Orlando, FL

Sheila Bayles
Rogers High School
Rogers, AR

Robert L. Bowbeer
Detroit Country Day Upper School
Beverly Hills, MI

Hercilia Bretón
Highlands High School
San Antonio, TX

Adrienne Chamberlain-Parris
Mariner High School
Everett, WA

Mike Cooperider
Truman High School
Independence, MO

Susan B. Cress
Sheridan High School
Sheridan, IN

Michèle S. de Cruz-Sáenz, Ph.D.
Strath Haven High School
Wallingford, PA

Lizveth Dague
Park Vista Community High School
Lake Worth, FL

Parthena Draggett
Jackson High School
Massillon, OH

Rubén D. Elías
Roosevelt High School
Fresno, CA

Phillip Elkins
Lane Tech College Prep High School
Chicago, IL

Maria Fleming Alvarez
The Park School
Brookline, MA

Michael Garber
Boston Latin Academy
Boston, MA

Marco García
Derry University Advantage Academy
Chicago, IL

David Gonzalez
Hollywood Hills High School
Hollywood, FL

Raquel R. González
Odessa Senior High School
Odessa, TX

Neyda Gonzalez-Droz
Ridge Community High School
Davenport, FL

Becky Hay de García
James Madison Memorial
  High School
Madison, WI

Fatima Hicks
Suncoast High School, *retired*
Riviera Beach, FL

Gladys V. Horford
William T. Dwyer High School
Palm Beach Gardens, FL

Pam Johnson
Stevensville High School
Stevensville, MT

Richard Ladd
Ipswich High School
Ipswich, MA

Patsy Lanigan
Hume Fogg Academic Magnet
  High School
Nashville, TN

Kris Laws
Palm Bay High School
Melbourne, FL

Kristen M. Lombardi
Shenendehowa High School
Clifton Park, NY

Elizabeth Lupafya
North High School
Worcester, MA

David Malatesta
Niles West High School
Skokie, IL

Patrick Malloy
James B. Conant High School
Hoffman Estates, IL

Brandi Meeks
Starr's Mill High School
Fayetteville, GA

Kathleen L. Michaels
Palm Harbor University High School
Palm Harbor, FL

Linda Nanos
Brook Farm Business Academy
West Roxbury, MA

Nadine F. Olson
School of Teaching and Curriculum
   Leadership
Stillwater, OK

Pam Osthoff
Lakeland Senior High School
Lakeland, FL

Nicholas Patterson
Davenport Central High School
Davenport, IA

Carolyn A. Peck
Genesee Community College
Lakeville, NY

Daniel N. Richardson
Concord High School, *retired*
Concord, NH

Rita E. Risco
Palm Harbor University High School
Palm Harbor, FL

Miguel Roma
Boston Latin Academy
West Roxbury, MA

Lauren Schultz
Dover High School
Dover, NH

Nona M. Seaver
New Berlin West Middle/High
   School
New Berlin, WI

Susan Seraphine-Kimel
Astronaut High School
Titusville, FL

Mary Severo
Thomas Hart Middle School
Pleasanton, CA

Clarette Shelton
WT Woodson High School, *retired*
Fairfax, VA

Maureen Shiland
Saratoga Springs High School
Saratoga Springs, NY

Irma Sprague
Countryside High School
Clearwater, FL

Mary A. Stimmel
Lincoln High School
Des Moines, IA

Karen Tharrington
Wakefield High School
Raleigh, NC

Alicia Turnier
Countryside High School
Clearwater, FL

Roberto E. del Valle
The Overlake School
Redmond, WA

Todd Wagner
Upper Darby High School, *retired*
Drexel Hill, PA

Ronie R. Webster
Monson Junior/Senior High School
Monson, MA

Cheryl Wellman
Bloomingdale High School
Valrico, FL

Thomasina White
School District of Philadelphia
Philadelphia, PA

Jena Williams
Jonesboro High School
Jonesboro, AR

Program Advisory Council

Louis G. Baskinger
New Hartford High School
New Hartford, NY

Linda M. Bigler
James Madison University
Harrisonburg, VA

Flora Maria Ciccone-Quintanilla
Holly Senior High School
Holly, MI

Jacquelyn Cinotti-Dirmann
Duval County Public Schools
Jacksonville, FL

Desa Dawson
Del City High School
Del City, OK

Robin C. Hill
Warrensville Heights High School
Warrensville Heights, OH

Barbara M. Johnson
Gordon Tech High School, *retired*
Chicago, IL

Ray Maldonado
Houston Independent School
   District
Houston, TX

Karen S. Miller
Friends School of Baltimore
Baltimore, MD

Dr. Robert A. Miller
Woodcreek High School
   Roseville Joint Union High School
   District
Roseville, CA

Debra M. Morris
Wellington Landings Middle School
Wellington, FL

Maria Nieto Zezas
West Morris Central High School
Chester, NJ

Rita Oleksak
Glastonbury Public Schools
Glastonbury, CT

Sandra Rosenstiel
University of Dallas, *retired*
Grapevine, TX

Emily Serafa Manschot
Northville High School
Northville, MI

La Telehistoria

Hi! My name is Alicia. My family and I live in Miami, Florida. My favorite thing to do is play soccer. At the Pan-American Youth Games, my team took second place. I made a lot of great friends from all over the world. I also met Trini Salgado, the best soccer player ever!

I got a T-shirt like hers, but I never got her to autograph it. She is always traveling to different countries, so maybe I can send my shirt to some of my soccer friends to try to get it signed.

Follow along in the *¡Avancemos!* Telehistoria to find out what happens to Alicia's T-shirt as it travels from country to country.

SALGAD
10

Trini Salgado

En Parque de l

Próximo Sábado, 15 de Jun

Sandra-San Antonio ✓
Pablo-México ✓
Rodrigo-Puerto Rico ✓
Maribel-España ✓
Manuel-Ecuador ✓
Mario-República ✓
Dominicana ✓
Florencia-Argentina ✓
Jorge-Costa Rica ✓

Level 1a

1 San Antonio

Sandra

2 Mexico

Pablo

3 Puerto Rico

Rodrigo

4 Spain

Maribel

Level 1b

5 Ecuador

Manuel

6 Dominican Republic

Mario

7 Argentina

Florencia

8 Costa Rica

Jorge

Key Words to Know

el autógrafo autograph

la camiseta T-shirt

el jugador (la jugadora) de fútbol soccer player

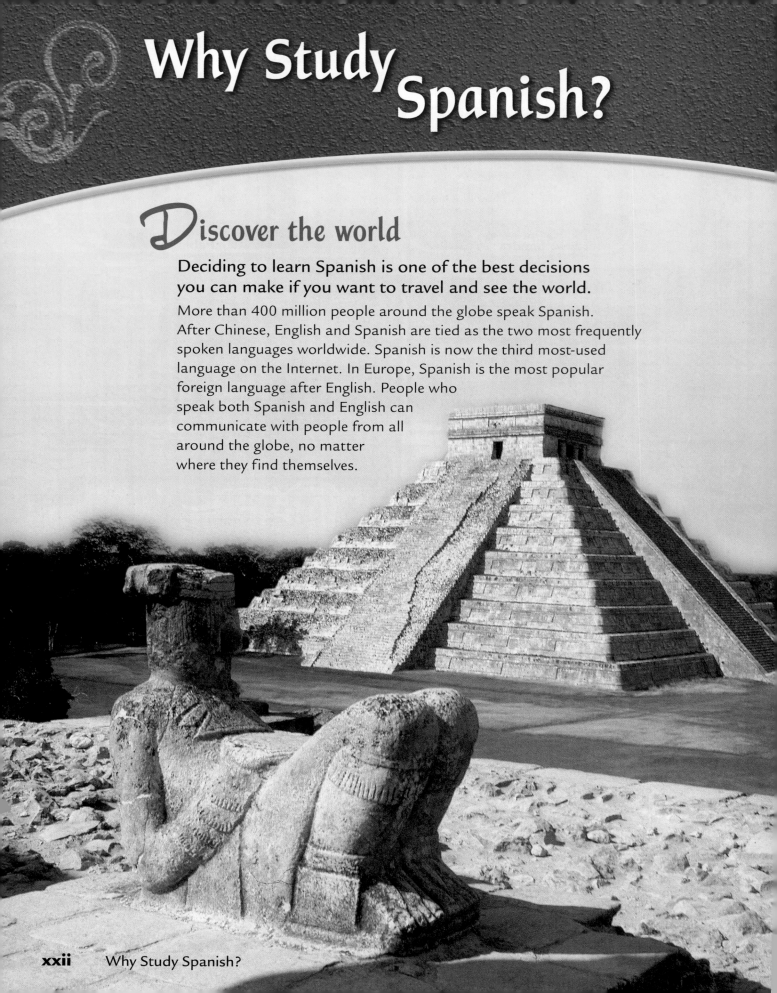

Why Study Spanish?

Discover the world

Deciding to learn Spanish is one of the best decisions you can make if you want to travel and see the world.

More than 400 million people around the globe speak Spanish. After Chinese, English and Spanish are tied as the two most frequently spoken languages worldwide. Spanish is now the third most-used language on the Internet. In Europe, Spanish is the most popular foreign language after English. People who speak both Spanish and English can communicate with people from all around the globe, no matter where they find themselves.

Explore your community

Inside the United States, Spanish is by far the most widely spoken language after English.

There are currently over 30 million Spanish speakers in the U.S. When you start to look and listen for it, you will quickly realize that Spanish is all around you—on the television, on the radio, and in magazines and newspapers. You may even hear your neighbors speaking it. Learning Spanish will help you communicate and interact with the rapidly growing communities of Spanish speakers around you.

 # Experience a new perspective

Learning a language is more than just memorizing words and structures.

When you study Spanish, you learn how the people who speak it think, feel, work, and live. Learning a language can open your eyes to a whole new world of ideas and insights. And as you learn about other cultures, you gain a better perspective on your own.

 # Create career possibilities

Knowing Spanish opens many doors.

If you speak Spanish fluently, you can work for international and multinational companies anywhere in the Spanish-speaking world. You can create a career working as a translator, an interpreter, or a teacher of Spanish. And because the number of Spanish speakers in the U.S. is growing so rapidly, being able to communicate in Spanish is becoming important in almost every career.

What is Vocabulary?

Building Your Spanish Vocabulary

Vocabulary is a basic building block for learning a foreign language. By learning just a few words, you can start to communicate in Spanish right away! You will probably find that it is easier to understand words you hear or read than it is to use them yourself. But with a little practice, you will start to produce the right words in the right context. Soon you will be able to carry on conversations with other Spanish speakers.

How Do I Study Vocabulary?

First Steps

· Read all of the new words in **blue** on the Vocabulary presentation page in your textbook.

· Point to each word as you say it out loud.

Be Creative

· Make flashcards with your new vocabulary words. You could also draw pictures of the words on the back of the flashcards.

· Group vocabulary words by theme. Add other words that fit the categories you've learned.

· Imagine a picture of the word.

· Create a rhyme or song to help you remember the words.

Make It Personal

· Use vocabulary words to write original sentences. Make them funny so you'll be sure to remember!

· Label everyday items in Spanish.

· Create reminders for difficult words. Put note cards inside your locker door, or on your mirror at home.

· See it, and say it to yourself! For example, if you are learning colors and clothing words, think of the Spanish word to describe what your friends are wearing.

el cuaderno

Practice Makes Perfect

· Say your vocabulary words out loud and repeat each word several times.

· Write each word five times, keeping its meaning in mind.

· Use Spanish words with your classmates outside of class—if you're having lunch in the cafeteria, use the words you know for food. Greet your classmates in the hallway in Spanish!

Create Your Own System

· Practice a little bit every day. Many short sessions are better than one long one.

· Focus on the words that are the hardest for you.

· Find a buddy. Quiz one another on the vocabulary words.

· Keep a vocabulary notebook and update it regularly.

· Use the study sheets in the back of your workbook to review vocabulary.

What is Grammar?

Some people think of grammar as the rules of a language, rules that tell you the "correct" way to speak a language. For instance, why do you say *big red house,* not *red big house*? Why do you say *how much money do you have* instead of *how many money*? If English is your first language, you probably don't think about the rule. You make the correct choice instinctively because it *sounds right*. Non-native speakers of English have to learn the rules. As you begin your study of Spanish, you will need to learn the grammar rules of Spanish.

Why Should I Study Grammar?

Grammar helps you to communicate.

For instance, using the past tense or future tense makes it clear when something happens. (*I did my homework* versus *I will do my homework*.) Using subject pronouns lets you know who is performing the action. (*I gave the book to her* versus *She gave the book to me*.) Using correct grammar when speaking Spanish will help you communicate successfully with native speakers of Spanish.

How Do I Study Grammar?

Read the English Grammar Connection before each grammar explanation.

Think about how you use the same type of grammar in English. Understanding your own language will help you to better understand Spanish.

> **English Grammar Connection:** A **verb tense** is the form of the verb that shows *when* an action is happening. The **present tense** shows that an action is happening *now*. The Spanish present-tense verb form **estudiamos** can be expressed in English in three different ways: *we study, we are studying,* or *we do study.*
>
> We **study** Spanish.   **Estudiamos** español.
>
>   ↑   ↑
>
> **present-tense verb**   **present-tense verb**

Practice the new forms that you are learning.

Completing the practice activities in your student book and workbook will help you to learn the correct way to say things.

Use the Spanish you know as often as you can.

After all, that's how you learned to speak English, by hearing and speaking it every day.

What Is Culture?

To communicate with people from Spanish-speaking countries in a meaningful way, you need to know something about their culture. Vocabulary and grammar will help you learn what words to say and how to put them together, but culture will give you a better understanding of "how, when, and why to say what to whom."

What exactly is culture?

Culture includes . . .

- Art
- History
- Traditions
- Relationships
- Music
- Holidays
- Food
- Architecture
- Pastimes

    and more!

How can I learn about another culture?

- Read the **Comparación cultural** information to find out more about the cultures that you are studying.
- Think about the answers to the questions in the **Comparación cultural.**
- Think about the perspectives and practices that shape and influence the culture.
- Compare your own culture with the cultures you are studying.

El mundo

OCÉANO ÁRTICO

Mar de Siberia
Oriental

Mar de Beaufort

Bahía
de
Baffin

GROENLANDIA
(DINAMARCA)

RUSIA

Alaska
(EE.UU.)

Mar de Bering

Bahía
de
Hudson

Mar del
Labrador

CANADÁ

OCÉANO ATLÁNTICO

ESTADOS UNIDOS

REP. DOMINICANA

ISLAS
BAHAMAS

PUERTO RICO (EE.UU.)

SAN CRISTÓBAL Y NEVIS

Golfo de
México

HAITÍ

ANTIGUA Y BARBUDA

Islas Hawai
(EE.UU.)

CUBA

GUADALUPE (FRANCIA)

MÉXICO

JAMAICA

DOMINICA

BELICE

Mar Caribe

MARTINICA (FRANCIA)

SANTA LUCÍA

SAN VICENTE Y GRANADINAS

ISLAS
MARSHALL

OCÉANO PACÍFICO

GUATEMALA

GRANADA

BARBADOS

EL SALVADOR

PANAMÁ

TRINIDAD Y TOBAGO

HONDURAS

NICARAGUA

COSTA
RICA

VENEZUELA

GUAYANA
FRANCESA
(FRANCIA)

NAURU

KIRIBATI

COLOMBIA

ISLAS
SALOMÓN

ISLAS
TUVALU

Islas Galápagos
(Ecuador)

ECUADOR

GUYANA

SURINAM

SAMOA

BRASIL

VANUATÚ

Samoa
Americana
(EE.UU.)

PERÚ

FIDJI

TONGA

BOLIVIA

NUEVA
CALEDONIA
(FRANCIA)

PARAGUAY

NUEVA
ZELANDA

CHILE

URUGUAY

ARGENTINA

Islas Malvinas
(R.U.)

ISLANDIA

OCÉANO ÁRTICO

Mar de Kara

Mar de Barents

Mar de Laptev

Mar de
Noruega

SUECIA   FINLANDIA

NORUEGA

ESTONIA
LETONIA
LITUANIA

BIELORRUSIA

1	DINAMARCA	9	ESLOVENIA
2	HOLANDA	10	CROACIA
3	BÉLGICA	11	BOSNIA Y HERZEGOVINA
4	LUXEMBURGO	12	SERBIA Y MONTENEGRO
5	SUIZA	13	ALBANIA
6	REPÚBLICA CHECA	14	MACEDONIA
7	ESLOVAQUIA	15	BULGARIA
8	HUNGRÍA		

RUSIA

Mar del
Norte

REINO
UNIDO

IRLANDA

POLONIA

ALEMANIA

60°N

Lago
Baikal

Mar de
Ojotsk

UCRANIA

AUSTRIA

MOLDAVIA

KAZAKSTÁN

MONGOLIA

FRANCIA

ANDORRA

RUMANIA

Mar Negro

ITALIA

GEORGIA

Mar Caspio

UZBEKISTÁN

KIRGUISTÁN

COREA
DEL NORTE

Mar de
Japón

ESPAÑA

PORTUGAL

GIBRALTAR
(R.U.)

GRECIA

MALTA

TURQUÍA

ARMENIA

AZERBAIYÁN

TURKMENISTÁN

TADJIKISTÁN

CHINA

COREA
DEL SUR

JAPÓN

MARRUECOS

Islas Canarias
(Esp.)

TÚNEZ

Mar Mediterráneo

CHIPRE
LÍBANO

SIRIA

IRAQ

IRÁN

AFGANISTÁN

ISRAEL

JORDANIA

EGIPTO

BAHREIN

KUWAIT
QATAR

E.Á.U

PAQUISTÁN

NEPAL

BHUTÁN

BANGLADESH

30°N

Trópico de Cáncer

SAHARA
OCCIDENTAL

ARGELIA

LIBIA

ARABIA
SAUDITA

OMÁN

INDIA

MYANMAR

TAIWÁN

OCÉANO
PACÍFICO

CABO
VERDE

MAURITANIA

MALÍ

NÍGER

CHAD

ERITREA

YEMEN

LAOS

TAILANDIA

VIETNAM

FILIPINAS

GUAM
(EE.UU.)

SENEGAL

GAMBIA

GUINEA

BURKINA
FASO

BENIN

NIGERIA

SUDÁN

JIBUTI

CAMBOYA

Mar
Arábigo

Golfo
de
Bengala

Mar de
China

MICRONESIA

GUINEA
BISSAU

COSTA
DE
MARFIL

TOGO

GHANA

REP. CENTRO-
AFRICANA

CAMERÚN

ETIOPÍA

SOMALIA

ISLAS
MALDIVAS

SRI
LANKA

BRUNEI

PALAU

SIERRA
LEONA

LIBERIA

GUINEA
ECUATORIAL

GABÓN

CONGO

REP. DEM.
DEL CONGO

UGANDA

KENIA

RUANDA

MALAYSIA

Ecuador 0°

SANTO TOMÉ
Y PRÍNCIPE

CABINDA
(ANGOLA)

BURUNDI

TANZANÍA

SEYCHELLES

SINGAPUR

INDONESIA

PAPUASIA
NUEVA GUINEA

ANGOLA

ZAMBIA

MALAWI

COMORES

TIMOR
ORIENTAL

MOZAMBIQUE

NAMIBIA

ZIMBABWE

BOTSWANA

MADAGASCAR

MAURICIO

OCÉANO ÍNDICO

Trópico de Capricornio

AUSTRALIA

SUAZILANDIA

SUDÁFRICA

LESOTHO

30°S

N

O   E

S

0   1,000   2,000 millas

0   1,000   2,000 kilómetros

60°S

ANTÁRTIDA

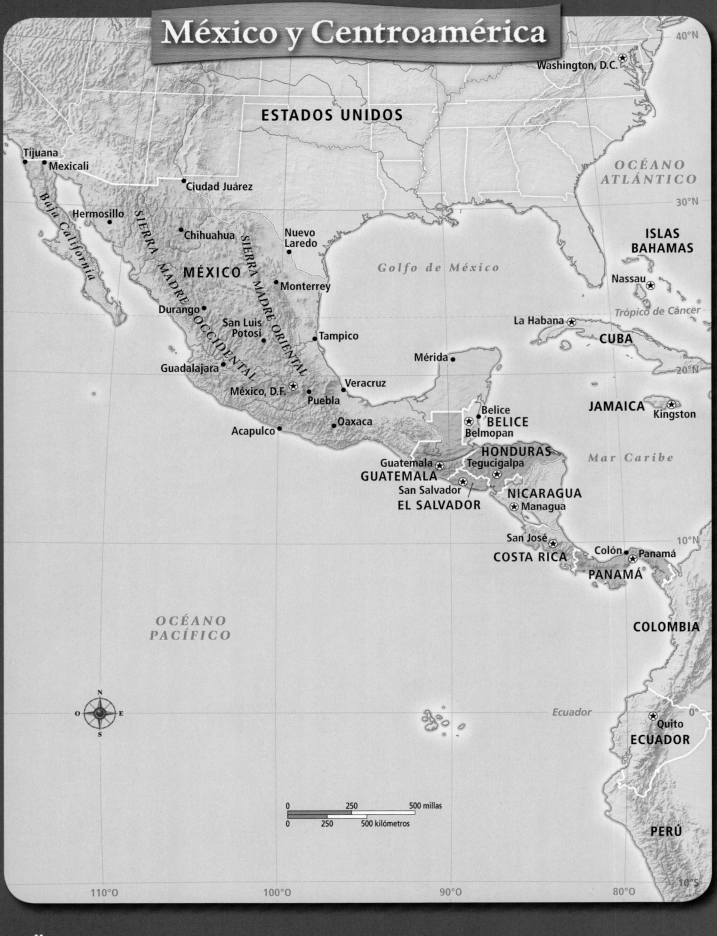

México y Centroamérica

ESTADOS UNIDOS

Washington, D.C.

Tijuana
Mexicali

Ciudad Juárez

*OCÉANO
ATLÁNTICO*

Hermosillo

Baja California

Chihuahua

Nuevo
Laredo

**ISLAS
BAHAMAS**

Nassau

MÉXICO

SIERRA MADRE OCCIDENTAL

SIERRA MADRE ORIENTAL

Monterrey

Golfo de México

Trópico de Cáncer

Durango

San Luis
Potosí

La Habana

CUBA

Guadalajara

Tampico

Mérida

20°N

México, D.F.

Veracruz

JAMAICA

Kingston

Puebla

Belice

Acapulco

Oaxaca

BELICE
Belmopan

Mar Caribe

Guatemala

HONDURAS
Tegucigalpa

GUATEMALA

San Salvador

NICARAGUA

EL SALVADOR

Managua

COSTA RICA

San José

Colón

Panamá

10°N

PANAMÁ

*OCÉANO
PACÍFICO*

COLOMBIA

Ecuador

Quito

0°

ECUADOR

0   250   500 millas
0   250   500 kilómetros

PERÚ

10°S

110°O   100°O   90°O   80°O

40°N

30°N

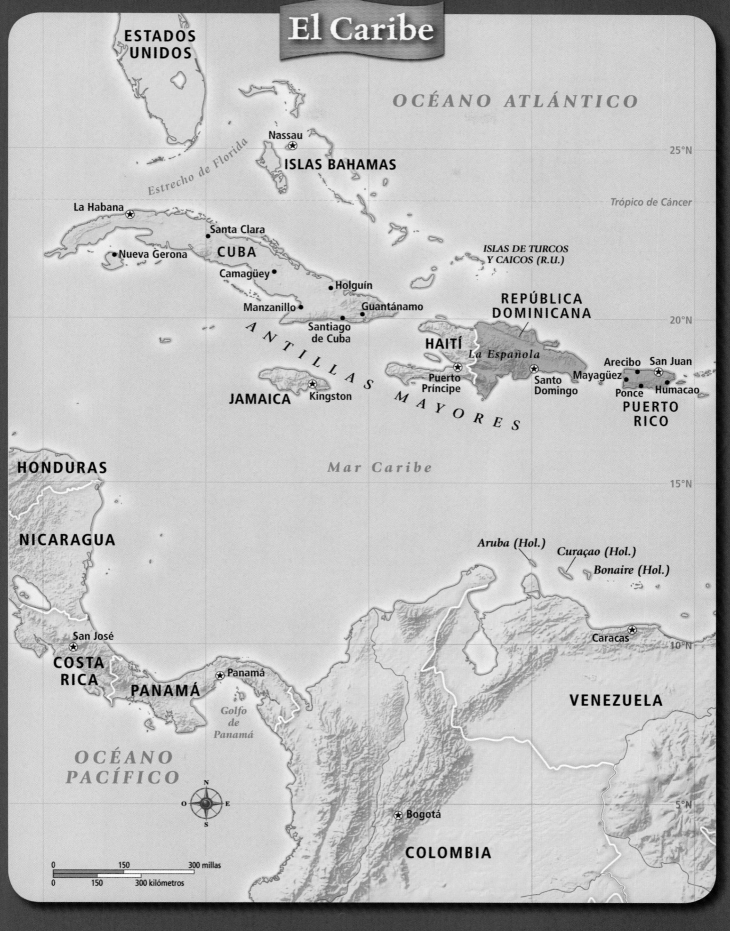

El Caribe

ESTADOS UNIDOS

OCÉANO ATLÁNTICO

Estrecho de Florida

Nassau

ISLAS BAHAMAS

25°N

Trópico de Cáncer

La Habana

Santa Clara

Nueva Gerona

CUBA

Camagüey

Holguín

Manzanillo

Guantánamo

Santiago de Cuba

ISLAS DE TURCOS Y CAICOS (R.U.)

REPÚBLICA DOMINICANA

HAITÍ

La Española

20°N

Arecibo

San Juan

Mayagüez

Ponce

Humacao

PUERTO RICO

Puerto Príncipe

Santo Domingo

A N T I L L A S

M A Y O R E S

JAMAICA

Kingston

Mar Caribe

15°N

HONDURAS

NICARAGUA

Aruba (Hol.)

Curaçao (Hol.)

Bonaire (Hol.)

San José

Caracas

10°N

COSTA RICA

Panamá

PANAMÁ

Golfo de Panamá

VENEZUELA

OCÉANO PACÍFICO

N
O   E
S

5°N

Bogotá

COLOMBIA

| 0 | 150 | 300 millas |
| 0 | 150 | 300 kilómetros |

Sudamérica

Mar Caribe

TRINIDAD Y TOBAGO
Puerto España

Barranquilla
Cartagena
Maracaibo
Lago Maracaibo
Caracas
Río Orinoco

OCÉANO ATLÁNTICO

VENEZUELA

Georgetown
Paramaribo

Medellín
Manizales
Bogotá
GUYANA
SURINAM
Cayena

COLOMBIA

GUAYANA FRANCESA (FRANCIA)

Cali

Otavalo
Quito
Río Negro
Ecuador 0°

ECUADOR
Río Amazonas

Guayaquil
Cuenca

Río Madeira
Río Tapajós
Río Xingú
Río Tocantins

PERÚ

Trujillo

BRASIL

10°S

Callao
Lima

C
O
R
D
I
L
L
E
R
A

Lago Titicaca

BOLIVIA
La Paz
Cochabamba
Santa Cruz
Sucre

Brasilia

Río São Francisco

OCÉANO PACÍFICO

Islas Galápagos
(Ecuador)

Bogotá
COLOMBIA

Quito
ECUADOR
PERÚ

0   200   400 millas
0   200   400 kilómetros

D
E

L
O
S

GRAN CHACO
PARAGUAY

20°S

CHILE
Salta
Asunción

San Miguel de Tucumán
Resistencia

Trópico de Capricornio

Córdoba

30°S

Valparaíso
Mendoza
Rosario
URUGUAY

Santiago
Buenos Aires
Montevideo

OCÉANO ATLÁNTICO

ARGENTINA
La Plata

Concepción

A
N
D
E
S

P
A
M
P
A
S

Mar del Plata

OCÉANO PACÍFICO

Temuco

Bahía Blanca

P
A
T
A
G
O
N
I
A

N
O   E
S

0   250   500 millas
0   250   500 kilómetros

40°S

Estrecho de Magallanes
Islas Malvinas (R.U.)

Tierra del Fuego
Cabo de Hornos

50°S

100°O   90°O   80°O   70°O   60°O   50°O   40°O   30°O   20°O

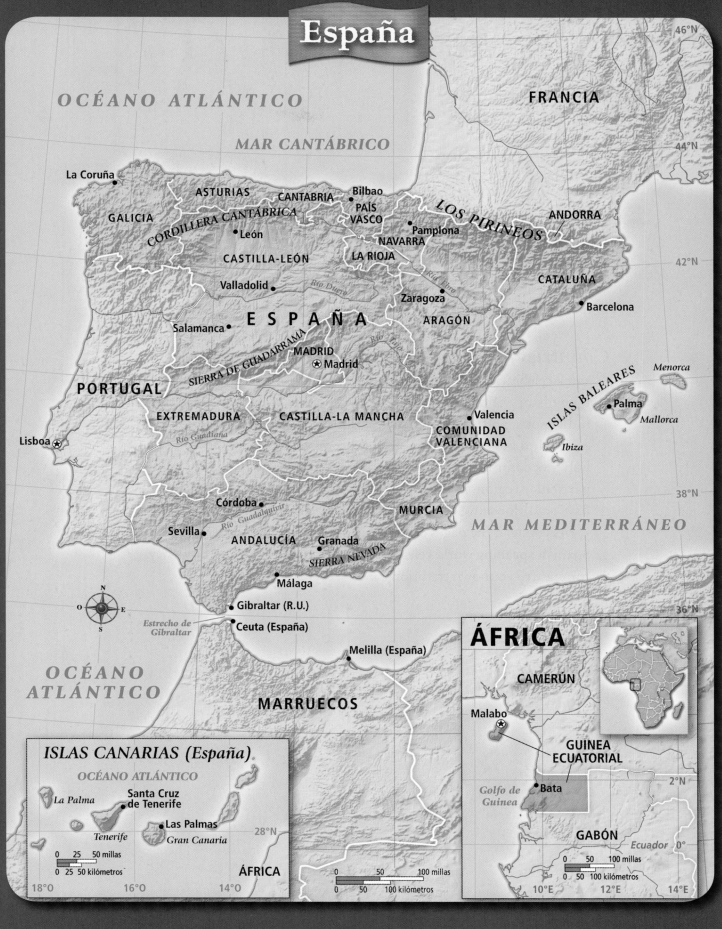

España

OCÉANO ATLÁNTICO

FRANCIA

MAR CANTÁBRICO

La Coruña

ASTURIAS CANTABRIA Bilbao

GALICIA CORDILLERA CANTÁBRICA PAÍS VASCO

León

NAVARRA

Pamplona

LOS PIRINEOS

ANDORRA

CASTILLA-LEÓN LA RIOJA

Valladolid

Río Duero

Río Ebro

CATALUÑA

Zaragoza

Barcelona

ESPAÑA

ARAGÓN

Salamanca

MADRID

SIERRA DE GUADARRAMA

Río Tajo

Madrid

PORTUGAL

EXTREMADURA

CASTILLA-LA MANCHA

Río Guadiana

ISLAS BALEARES

Menorca

Palma

Mallorca

Valencia

COMUNIDAD VALENCIANA

Ibiza

Lisboa

Córdoba

Río Guadalquivir

MURCIA

MAR MEDITERRÁNEO

Sevilla

ANDALUCÍA

Granada

SIERRA NEVADA

Málaga

Gibraltar (R.U.)

Ceuta (España)

N
O E
S

Estrecho de Gibraltar

OCÉANO ATLÁNTICO

Melilla (España)

MARRUECOS

ÁFRICA

CAMERÚN

Malabo

GUINEA ECUATORIAL

Golfo de Guinea

Bata

GABÓN

Ecuador

2°N

0°

10°E 12°E 14°E

0 50 100 millas
0 50 100 kilómetros

ISLAS CANARIAS (España)

OCÉANO ATLÁNTICO

La Palma

Santa Cruz de Tenerife

Tenerife

Las Palmas

Gran Canaria

28°N

0 25 50 millas
0 25 50 kilómetros

18°O 16°O 14°O

ÁFRICA

0 50 100 millas
0 50 100 kilómetros

46°N

44°N

42°N

38°N

36°N

Las celebraciones

The following lessons about holidays are provided for your personal enjoyment. You may choose to read them on your own, or your teacher may present them throughout the year.

Countries in the Spanish-speaking world often share the same celebrations and holidays. The celebrations are a result of a long history of traditions that reflect the mix of primarily Spanish, indigenous, and African cultures. Holidays celebrating religious events and beliefs are often similar between countries. Other holidays commemorate events or people that are important to a particular region. Many holidays, though celebrated on the same day, have traditions and customs that differ between countries.

As you read the pages of Celebraciones, you will discover how the Spanish-speaking world celebrates important holidays and how they compare to your own traditions.

Contenido

Agosto: Feria de Málaga C2

Septiembre: Día de la Independencia C4

Octubre: El 12 de Octubre C6

Noviembre: ¡Día de los Muertos! C8

Diciembre: Las Navidades C10

Enero: ¡Año Nuevo! C12

Febrero: ¡Carnaval! C14

Marzo: Las Fallas C16

Abril: Semana Santa C18

Mayo: ¡Cinco de Mayo! C20

Junio: Inti Raymi C22

Julio: Día de Simón Bolívar C24

FERIA DE MÁLAGA

La Feria de Málaga celebrates King Ferdinand and Queen Isabella's triumphant entrance into the coastal city of Málaga on August 19, 1487. The pair claimed the city for the crown of Castile, an event this Spanish city has been celebrating for over 500 years. The *Feria de Málaga* now lasts for nine days and takes place in two parts of the city. Each day at noon the downtown fills with fairgoers. In the *Real,* a separate fairground, participants in *flamenco* dress or riding clothes ride on horseback or in horse-drawn carriages, or stroll, in a tradition known as *el paseo.* This daytime *feria* unfolds against a backdrop of music, singing, and dancing and ends at 6:00 p.m., when everyone goes home to rest. The celebration starts again at night in the *Real* and continues into the early morning hours. For this nightly *feria,* people gather in public and private *casetas,* to enjoy concerts, theatrical presentations, music, dance, and food. The last night of the *feria* ends with a city-sponsored concert followed by a spectacular fireworks display.

Feria de caballos More than a thousand riders and over a hundred horse-drawn carriages and carts participate in *el paseo.*

Música callejera Musicians play in the streets during the *feria.* Here a *panda,* or group, plays *verdiales,* traditional music that features guitars, tambourines, and tiny cymbals.

Una caseta offers free samples of *paella,* a rice and seafood dish that is a regional specialty from the coastal cities of Spain.

Bailando flamenco Fairgoers perform folkloric dances such as *flamenco* and *sevillanas* in the streets, plazas, and *casetas,* wherever there is music.

Una entrada a la feria Riders pass in front of one of the decorative entrances to a street in the historic downtown of Málaga.

Vocabulario para celebrar

los caballos	horses
las carretas	horse-drawn carriages
las casetas	small houses or tents
la feria	fair
el paseo	a walk, stroll, or ride

Comparación cultural

1. Does your town or city celebrate its beginnings or inauguration as a community, or is there a special "town day"? What events take place during the celebration?

2. What events in your community or region are similar to those of the *Feria de Málaga*? Describe them and then compare them to the *Feria de Málaga*.

DÍA DE LA INDEPENDENCIA

El *Día de la Independencia* falls in September for many of the Spanish-speaking countries in the Americas. Mexico celebrates on September 15 and 16, with the *Grito de la Independencia,* music, fireworks, and parades. The first *Grito* occurred at dawn on September 16, 1810, when Padre Miguel Hidalgo de Costilla called to the people of Dolores to rise up against the Spanish crown. That rebellion led to the Mexican War of Independence.

Just two days later, on September 18, 1810, Chile declared its independence from Spain. Today Chile celebrates the date during a week of *fiestas patrias* that include parades, rodeos, dance competitions, and special foods.

Eleven years later, on September 15, 1821, a large part of Central America also proclaimed its independence from Spain, becoming El Salvador, Nicaragua, Guatemala, Costa Rica, and Honduras. These countries celebrate their independence on the 14 and 15 with a focus on students: parades, assemblies, and sports competitions.

México

El Grito de la Independencia On the night of September 15, the president of Mexico commemorates *el Grito* by ringing a bell, proclaiming *¡Que viva México!*, and waving the Mexican flag from a balcony above the Zócalo. Crowds gather below to participate in the *Grito*.

Fiestas patrias Costa Rican schoolchildren, dressed in colors of their country, dance in a parade.

Costa Rica

Guatemala

El recorrido de la antorcha Runners carrying a flaming torch start in Guatemala and end in Costa Rica. All along the route, uniformed schoolchildren wait expectantly for the torch to pass.

Vocabulario para celebrar

la antorcha	torch
la banda	band
las fiestas patrias	patriotic holidays
el grito	shout
el recorrido	run, journey
proclamar	to declare

Comparación cultural

1. Compare the way your town or city celebrates Independence Day with the celebrations in Mexico and Central America. How are they similar? Are there any differences?

2. How do you celebrate Independence Day? Do you participate in community events or have a special tradition?

El 12 de Octubre

El 12 de Octubre has many different meanings in the Spanish-speaking world. For some people it is *el Día de Colón*, the day Christopher Columbus arrived in the Americas. For some, it is *el Día de la Hispanidad*, a day to celebrate one's connection with all other Spanish-speaking people, regardless of their country. And for others, it is *el Día de la Raza*, a day when indigenous people come together as a community and celebrate their heritage. Other Spanish speakers celebrate their mixed heritage of indigenous, African, and European cultures. How you celebrate depends very much on you and your family's origin and on the community where you live. For all Spanish-speaking groups, *el 12 de octubre* marks a key turning point in the lives and cultures of the people in Spain and those living in the Americas.

Vocabulario para celebrar

Cristóbal Colón	Christopher Columbus
el Día Nacional	National Day
la hispanidad	the cultural community of Spanish speakers
la raza	race

México

Día de la Raza Indigenous groups gather in Mexico City dressed in their community's traditional outfits, some wearing pre-Columbian clothing and headdresses.

See these pages come alive!

Cultura INTERACTIVA
ClassZone.com *See these pages come alive!*

Chile
Día de la Raza A woman from the Pehuenche indigenous community gathers with other indigenous groups in downtown Santiago.

Nueva York
Día de la Hispanidad High school students carry flags representing all the American countries as they march in a parade down Fifth Avenue.

España
Día Nacional de España The Spanish government celebrates with a parade in Madrid.

Comparación cultural

1. How do you celebrate October 12 in your community or school? Is it similar to or different from the celebrations in Spanish-speaking countries? How so?

2. What does October 12 mean to you? Which of the Spanish names for the holiday has the most meaning for you? How would you rename the holiday to celebrate your heritage?

Celebraciones **C7**

¡Día de los Muertos!

Estados Unidos

Las mojigangas People parade through the Pilsen-Little Village neighborhood of Chicago. Some carry *mojigangas*, giant papier-mâché puppets typically carried in Mexican processions.

On Día de los Muertos families visit the cemeteries and gravesites of their loved ones. They clean the sites and leave flowers and candles and, in many countries, they bring entire meals with special drinks and traditional breads to share with the deceased. Displays are set up next to the gravesite that include flowers, hand-crafted skeletons, colorful paper cutouts, candy skulls, personal items, and photos. Family members pass the night sharing food and conversation as they keep vigil for their ancestors.

The celebration of *Día de los Muertos* spans two days, November 1 and 2. Also known as *Día de los Difuntos*, the traditions originate in the centuries-old religious holiday *Día de Todos los Santos*. In the Americas, this holiday coincided with pre-Columbian festivals that celebrated the harvest, the new year, and honored the dead. The mix of cultures and traditions resulted in the celebration *Día de los Muertos*.

México

Las calaveras A display of dressed-up skulls and skeletons on a street in Mexico City

Ecuador

El pan de muertos This bread is made only for *Día de los Muertos.* In Ecuador, these breads are called *guaguas de pan.* *Guagua* is the Quechua word for "baby" and refers to the bread's shape. The *guaguas* are served with *colada morada,* a warm, purple-colored drink made from blueberries and raspberries.

México

El papel picado These tissue paper cutouts are a common holiday decoration. To celebrate *Día de los Muertos,* the cutouts form images of skeletons.

Guatemala

Los barriletes Guatemalans celebrate by flying *barriletes,* or colorful kites, to which they attach messages for the deceased. The town of Santiago Sacatepéquez celebrates with a *barrilete* contest.

Vocabulario para celebrar

las calaveras	skulls
el cementerio	cemetery
los difuntos	deceased
el esqueleto	skeleton
el pan de muertos	special bread made for *Día de los Muertos*
el papel picado	paper cutouts
los santos	saints

Comparación cultural

1. Does your family or community have a special day or specific traditions to remember the deceased? How are they similar to or different from the traditions of *Día de los Muertos*?

2. Centuries ago in Europe, the night of October 31, before All Saint's Day, was known as "All Hallowed's Eve." According to ancient beliefs, on this night the dead join the world of the living. Today we call this night Halloween. How would you compare the celebrations of Halloween and *Día de los Muertos*?

Celebraciones   **C9**

Las Navidades

Las Navidades are celebrated throughout the Spanish-speaking world with family gatherings and special meals. Celebrations start in mid-December and, in some countries, extend to January 6.

Many families gather the night of December 24, or *la Nochebuena,* to share a special meal of traditional foods and drinks that vary depending on the country. *Tamales, empanadas,* and *buñuelos* are served in many countries. In Spain, there is turkey, or *pavo,* and *turrón.* In Argentina and Chile, where it is summer, people eat cold foods and salads.

The tradition of giving and receiving gifts also forms a part of *las Navidades.* In some countries, families exchange gifts at midnight on *la Nochebuena,* while in others children receive gifts the morning of December 25, and in other countries the gifts appear the morning of January 6. Often gifts are given primarily to children.

Panamá

Un desfile navideño The holiday parade in Panama City takes place in mid-December.

México

La noche de rábanos On the night of December 23, elaborate carvings made from radishes, or *rábanos,* are on display in Oaxaca's central plaza. The figures include people, animals, and even entire scenes. This unique tradition has been celebrated for over 100 years.

Argentina

Las empanadas Dancers dress as *empanadas* in Buenos Aires. These meat-filled pies are especially enjoyed during *las Navidades.*

Perú

El Día de los Reyes Magos In Peru, Argentina, the Dominican Republic, Paraguay, and Spain, children receive presents on January 6 from *los Reyes Magos*. In anticipation, children leave out a snack for the Three Kings, carrots or grass for the camels, and a pair of empty shoes for the gifts.

España

Un desfile navideño Circus elephants take part in Madrid's holiday parade on January 5. In Spain, parades on January 5 or 6 celebrate the arrival of *los Reyes Magos*.

Vocabulario para celebrar

la Nochebuena	Christmas Eve
los Reyes Magos	Three Kings
la rosca de reyes	sweet bread eaten on January 6
el turrón	almond nougat candy
los villancicos	seasonal Christmas songs

Comparación cultural

1. Do you and your family celebrate a holiday in December? If so, compare the traditions of your family to the traditions of *las Navidades*.
2. What special meals and foods do you associate with certain holidays? Describe the foods you traditionally enjoy on a holiday you celebrate.
3. What time of the year do you give or receive gifts and for what reason?

¡Año Nuevo!

El Año Nuevo celebrates the arrival of the New Year and *la Nochevieja* says goodbye to the old. In much of the Spanish-speaking world, traditions include making a toast, exchanging a kiss or hug, or eating twelve grapes—one for each stroke of midnight—to ensure your wishes come true for the New Year. Other good luck traditions include wearing yellow or red, eating a tablespoon of lentils, or carrying a suitcase around the block if you hope to take a trip. To wish someone a happy New Year, say *¡Feliz año nuevo!* or *¡Próspero año nuevo!*

On *Nochevieja*, there are also traditions for saying goodbye to the old year. Some people dress in masks representing *el año viejo*. Others build satirical figures called *los años viejos* that represent famous people or politicians. Adorned with poems or messages that poke fun at *el año viejo*, and filled with shavings and firecrackers, these figures are lit on fire at midnight, to burn and explode on street corners, as a final *despedida*, or farewell, to the old year.

Perú

La buena suerte In Lima, people believe touching a Chinese Lion brings happiness, good luck, and prosperity in the New Year. Ten percent of Peru's population is of Chinese descent.

España

La medianoche In Madrid, people gather in the Puerta del Sol, holding bags of 12 grapes as they wait for the 12 strokes of midnight from the Puerta del Sol clock, the city's official timekeeper.

Colombia

Paseo de los años viejos In Popayán, families and neighbors take their *año viejo* figures out for a final ride before the *Nochevieja* celebration. Later on, at midnight, they will burn the figures.

Guatemala

Baile de los Gigantes In Antigua, people celebrate the New Year with the folkloric "Dance of the Giants." These giant heads, or *cabezudos,* are similar to costumes used since the medieval period in Spain.

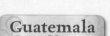

Vocabulario para celebrar

el Año Nuevo	New Year
el brindis	toast
las doce uvas	twelve grapes
las lentejas	lentils
la medianoche	midnight
la Nochevieja	New Year's Eve

Comparación cultural

1. How do you celebrate the New Year? Does your family or community have any special traditions? Are any of the traditions similar to the ones in Spanish-speaking countries? How are they similar or different?

2. If you were to build an *año viejo* representing the past year, what figure or event would you portray? Explain your choice.

¡Carnaval!

Carnaval marks a period of festivity prior to the beginning of Lent. Lent was, and for some still is, a 40-day period of solemnity and fasting with the removal of meat from the diet being a key feature. You can see the word *carne* (meat) in *Carnaval*; traditionally, this was the last chance to eat meat before the Lenten fast. Today, *Carnaval* often resembles a lively, multi-day party.

Falling in either February or March, *Carnaval* is typically celebrated during the five days that precede Ash Wednesday, the first day of Lent. In some countries, *Carnaval* lasts longer, overlapping other local celebrations. In many regions, traditions such as throwing water and eggs can start over a month before the actual holiday. The planning for the next year's parades, parties, and dance groups often starts as soon as the current *Carnaval* ends!

España

Disfraces Elaborate costumes are central to the *Carnaval* celebration. This costume, entitled "África soy yo," appeared in Las Palmas, in the Canary Islands.

Carnaval Revelers dance in Encarnación, site of the largest celebration in Paraguay.

Paraguay

México

Cascarones Breaking *cascarones* on the heads of friends and other party-goers is a *Carnaval* tradition. The sprinkling of confetti from these hollowed-out eggs is said to bring good luck, as seen here in Mazatlán.

Bolivia

Máscaras are a *Carnaval* tradition dating back to medieval Spain. This masked dancer is from the parade in Oruro, where some 40,000 folkloric dancers and musicians participate.

Bailarines folklóricos Dancers from the Mestizaje dance group perform in Barranquilla. The Colombian government proclaimed this city's *Carnaval* celebration, which combines indigenous, African, and European traditions, a National Cultural Heritage. UNESCO declared it a "Masterpiece" for its cultural uniqueness.

Colombia

Vocabulario para celebrar

los bailarines	dancers
la banda	musical band
Carnaval	Carnival
los cascarones	confetti-filled eggs
el disfraz	costume
las máscaras	masks

Comparación cultural

1. The ways in which *Carnaval* is celebrated in the Spanish-speaking world differ depending on the region. Why do you think the celebrations have evolved differently?

2. Compare the traditions of *Carnaval* to any holiday that you celebrate. Which one(s) are similar? How are they similar?

Las Fallas

Las Fallas is a weeklong festival in March that engulfs the city of Valencia, Spain. Tens of thousands of visitors from all over the world come to the city to experience *Las Fallas,* a week of pageants, music, flowers, and creative displays. Each day, the deafening explosions of thousands of firecrackers, *la mascletà,* fills the city at 2:00 p.m. and each night's celebration ends in fireworks.

The main characters of the celebration are the *ninots,* gigantic figures built of wood, plaster, and cardboard. The largest are up to several stories tall. Neighborhood organizations build these enormous figures during the preceding year. Then, during the week of *Las Fallas,* they display them in intersections, parks, and plazas throughout the city. The public visits the more than 400 *fallas* and votes for their favorite one. On the last night at midnight, all but the favorite are burned in enormous bonfires. Then one final, brilliant display of fireworks explodes over the city.

Los ninots These gigantic figures poke fun at well-known people or current events from the preceding year.

Las falleras During the festival, women dress in traditional outfits that include lace dresses, veils, jewelry, and colorful sashes.

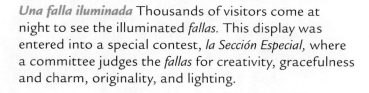

La Cremà At midnight on the last night, the *fallas* are burned throughout the city. At the same time there are huge displays of colorful fireworks, which include explosions of roman candles and thousands of firecrackers.

Una falla iluminada Thousands of visitors come at night to see the illuminated *fallas*. This display was entered into a special contest, *la Sección Especial,* where a committee judges the *fallas* for creativity, gracefulness and charm, originality, and lighting.

Vocabulario para celebrar

La Cremà	burning of the *fallas*
las fallas	displays of figures
los falleros	celebrants of *Las Fallas*
los fuegos artificiales	fireworks
la mascletà	rhythmic explosion of large and small firecrackers
los ninots	large papier-mâché figures
quemar	to burn

Comparación cultural

1. Fireworks are a major part of *Las Fallas*. Does your community or region have fireworks displays? When and for what reasons?

2. Are there any other traditions in the festival of *Las Fallas* that are similar to traditions you follow in your community? What are they? Are they part of a specific celebration or season?

Semana Santa

La Semana Santa is one holiday during the year where in most Spanish-speaking countries entire towns, businesses, schools, and government close for at least four days, Thursday through Sunday. People that have relocated to other places often go back to their hometowns. Others take advantage of the long break to go to the countryside or beach. Entire communities come together for *Semana Santa* celebrations. In some places, religious processions fill the streets each day of the week from Palm Sunday to Easter; in others, Thursday and Friday are the most important days. Most *Semana Santa* traditions are hundreds of years old and originated in Spain, but many now have a unique twist due to the mix of cultures in each country.

México

Vestidos blancos Girls from San Miguel de Allende dress in white for the procession on *Viernes Santo*. In this town, the celebrations extend for two weeks, ending on *el Domingo de Pascua* with an explosion of papier-mâché figures in the center of town.

El Salvador

Alfombras de aserrín Rugs traditionally made of colored sawdust or sand, flowers, and fruits cover the streets where processions will pass in Sonsonate. Artisans also now use modern industrial paints and sprays.

Ecuador

La fanesca Ecuadorians eat *fanesca*, a bean and grain soup with a fish base, only during *Semana Santa*. The soup is traditionally served with *bolitas de harina* (fritters), *plátano verde* (fried green plantain), fresh cheese, and *ají*, a spicy sauce.

Perú

Decoraciones de flores Flowers fill the city of Tarma for the *Semana Santa* celebrations. In preparation for the processions that begin on Thursday, arches and rugs made of flowers decorate the streets and remain on display until Sunday.

Vocabulario para celebrar

las alfombras	rugs
las flores	flowers
las procesiones	processions
Semana Santa	Holy Week

México

Una procesión Young boys carry streamers during the processions in Cadereyta.

Comparación cultural

1. What holidays do you celebrate with special parades or processions? What kinds of decorations do people use?

2. In what kind of event would most of the people in your community participate? Compare the event to *Semana Santa*.

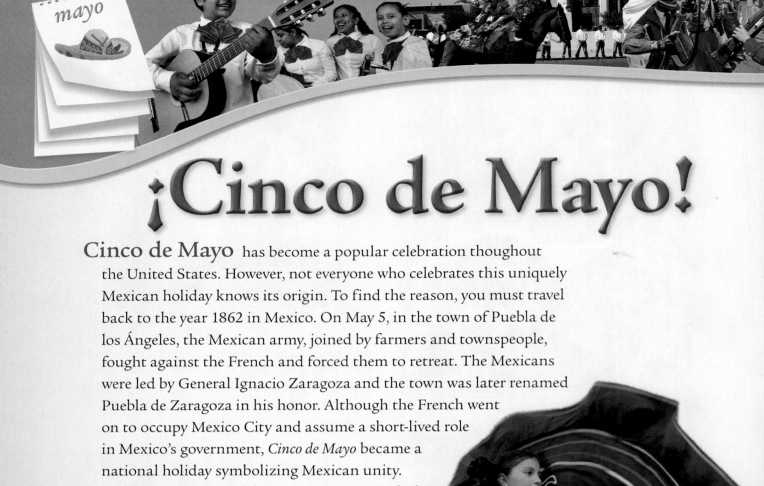

¡Cinco de Mayo!

Cinco de Mayo has become a popular celebration thoughout the United States. However, not everyone who celebrates this uniquely Mexican holiday knows its origin. To find the reason, you must travel back to the year 1862 in Mexico. On May 5, in the town of Puebla de los Ángeles, the Mexican army, joined by farmers and townspeople, fought against the French and forced them to retreat. The Mexicans were led by General Ignacio Zaragoza and the town was later renamed Puebla de Zaragoza in his honor. Although the French went on to occupy Mexico City and assume a short-lived role in Mexico's government, *Cinco de Mayo* became a national holiday symbolizing Mexican unity.

A *Cinco de Mayo* celebration in Mexico includes dancing, music, and reenactments of the battle. In many parts of the U.S. where there is a large Mexican or Mexican-American community, you will often find *Cinco de Mayo* celebrations.

Los Ángeles

Mariachis y bailarines Folkloric dancers and musicians perform throughout the day in the Plaza Olvera during the *Cinco de Mayo* celebrations.

México

Reconstrucción de la batalla
A reenactment of the historic battle in Puebla commemorates Mexico's victory over the French.

Vocabulario para celebrar

los bailarines	dancers
la batalla	battle
el ejército	army
los franceses	French
los músicos	musicians
la reconstrucción	reenactment

Washington, D.C.

Bailarín folklórico A dancer performs in a traditional Mexican costume at the White House.

Comparación cultural

1. Do you know of a *Cinco de Mayo* celebration in your community or region? If so, how or where is it celebrated?

2. What important battles or historic events are celebrated in your community or state? How are they celebrated? Are they local or national holidays? Compare one of these holiday celebrations with the *Cinco de Mayo* celebrations.

Inti Raymi

Inti Raymi, or the "Festival of the Sun," falls on June 21 or 22, the date of the southern hemisphere's winter solstice, the shortest day of the year. Indigenous communities throughout the Andean highland countries of South America celebrate the winter solstice with ceremonies designed to bring the Sun back and shorten the longest night. Incan in origin, *Inti Raymi* honored the sun as the source of light, heat, and life, and celebrated the start of a new planting season. The name *Inti Raymi* comes from the Quechua language: *inti* means "sun" and *raymi* means "festival." The largest festival takes place in Cuzco, Peru, the ancient capital of the Incan civilization and empire. In Cuzco, *Inti Raymi* has grown into a major tourist attraction. Thousands of people visit the city to enjoy the performances by folkloric groups and to watch the theatrical presentation of the Incan ceremony, the focal point of the celebration.

Perú

Presentación cultural de Inti Raymi
In Cuzco, professional actors and actresses interpret the roles of the Incan emperor and others.
Above: A woman carries offerings.
Right: The Incan emperor passes through the streets of Cuzco to the ruins of the Incan fortress, Sacsayhuaman.

Ecuador

Indígenas ecuatorianas A dance group from the Paktarinmi cultural organization forms a "sacred circle" with grains of corn, a pre-Incan rite. In Ecuador, which lies on the equator, this date is considered the summer solstice, rather than the winter.

Vocabulario para celebrar

el aymara   language of indigenous group from Bolivia and Peru

los incas   Incas, an ancient South American people

el quechua   language common to many South American indigenous groups and adopted and spread by Incas

el sol   sun

Bolivia

Los aymaras In the pre-Columbian ruins of Tihuanaku, an Aymara priest blows on a shell to celebrate the winter solstice, which marks the new year. The Aymara are one of two dominant indigenous groups in Bolivia, comprising 25 percent of the population. The other group, Quechua, makes up 30 percent.

Comparación cultural

1. In North America, June 21 is the summer solstice, or the longest day of the year, and December 21 is the winter solstice, or the shortest day of the year. What important holidays or events occur during this time of year?

2. In ancient civilizations, the appearance of the sun and moon were important events that helped mark the passing of time and the seasons. If you were to celebrate the winter or summer solstice, what would you include in your celebration?

Día de Simón Bolívar

Simón Bolívar, known as *El Libertador,* envisioned a united South America, a union for which he fought, but never attained. Despite this, he was instrumental in bringing about much of South America's independence from Spain and became one of its most revered leaders. His birthday is a national holiday in Venezuela, Ecuador, and Bolivia, and many cities and towns have plazas or monuments in his honor.

Born on July 24, 1783, in Caracas, Venezuela, Simón Bolívar strongly believed in freedom from Spanish rule and worked toward that goal as a political leader, writer, and military commander. With his troops, he liberated present-day Venezuela, then Colombia. He was then named president of Gran Colombia, a federation comprised of what is now Venezuela, Colombia, Panama, and Ecuador. He went on to lead his troops into Peru, aiding in the final defeat of Spain. For two more years, Bolívar maintained his leadership, writing the constitution of Bolivia, a country named in his honor. By 1827, his dream of unification dissolved amidst growing rivalries between the South American military leaders. Three years later Bolívar died, on December 17, 1830.

Colombia

Monumento a Simón Bolívar This monument marks the location of the Battle of Boyacá, where Bolívar's forces defeated the Spanish resulting in the liberation of Gran Colombia. To celebrate the anniversary of the battle, students form the colors of the Colombian flag.

Bolívares Venezuela's currency carries both Bolívar's name and image.

Venezuela

Ecuador

Líder de la Batalla de Pichincha Each year, the city of Quito commemorates the Battle of Pichincha, where Simón Bolívar sent troops under the command of Antonio José de Sucre to defeat the Spanish in one of the crucial battles in the fight for independence.

Simón Bolívar (1830), José Gil de Castro
José Gil de Castro, renowned painter of Chilean society and of the independence leaders, painted this portrait of Bolívar in the early 1800s.

Venezuela

Vocabulario para celebrar

la batalla   battle
la independencia
          independence
El Libertador
          the liberator

Plaza de Bolívar This statue of Bolívar is located in the Plaza Bolívar, the historic, political, and commercial center of Caracas.

Comparación cultural

1. What famous leader in U.S. history would you compare with Simón Bolívar? Why? What do both leaders have in common?

2. What U.S. holidays are in honor of famous leaders? How are they celebrated? What other ways do we honor our important leaders?

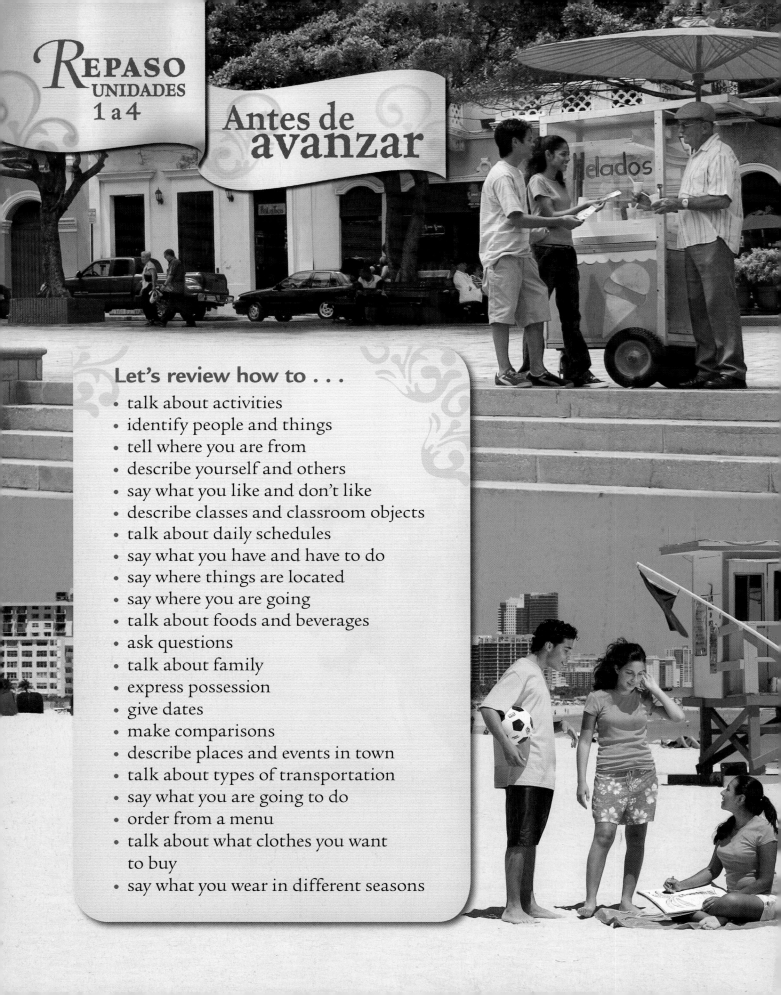

Let's review how to . . .

- talk about activities
- identify people and things
- tell where you are from
- describe yourself and others
- say what you like and don't like
- describe classes and classroom objects
- talk about daily schedules
- say what you have and have to do
- say where things are located
- say where you are going
- talk about foods and beverages
- ask questions
- talk about family
- express possession
- give dates
- make comparisons
- describe places and events in town
- talk about types of transportation
- say what you are going to do
- order from a menu
- talk about what clothes you want to buy
- say what you wear in different seasons

Parte 1 Un rato con los amigos

Repaso: ¿Qué te gusta hacer?

andar en patineta

correr

descansar

dibujar

escuchar música

practicar deportes

leer un libro

hablar por teléfono

jugar al fútbol

mirar la televisión

montar en bicicleta

estudiar

pasear

pasar un rato con los amigos

tocar la guitarra

Las actividades

alquilar un DVD
comprar
contestar
enseñar
escribir correos electrónicos
hacer la tarea
llegar
necesitar
preparar la comida
trabajar
usar la computadora

¿Te gusta...?

Me gusta...
No me gusta...

Para beber y comer

el agua (fem.)	el jugo
la fruta	las papas fritas
la galleta	la pizza
el helado	el refresco

Los días de la semana

¿Qué día es hoy?	lunes
el día	martes
hoy	miércoles
mañana	jueves
la semana	viernes
	sábado
	domingo

Repaso: Mis amigos y yo

alta

baja

grande

pequeño

joven

viejo

pelo rubio

pelirroja

pelo castaño

¿Cómo eres?

artístico(a)   organizado(a)
atlético(a)   perezoso(a)
bueno(a)   serio(a)
cómico(a)   simpático(a)
desorganizado(a)   trabajador(a)
estudioso(a)
inteligente   bonito(a)
malo(a)   guapo(a)

Las personas

el (la) amigo(a)   el hombre
la chica   el (la) maestro(a)
el chico   la mujer
el (la) estudiante

Práctica de VOCABULARIO

1 | ¿Comer o beber?

Use **bebo** to indicate that the item is something you drink or **como** to indicate that it is something you eat.

1. la galleta
2. el agua
3. el jugo
4. las papas fritas

5. el helado
6. el refresco
7. la fruta
8. la pizza

2 | Le gusta...

The people below are doing their favorite activities. Identify what each person likes to do.

modelo: jugar al fútbol

1.
2.
3.

4.
5.
6.

7.
8.
9.

3 | ¿Alta o baja?

**Hablar
Escribir**

Look at the pictures and choose the correct word to describe each person.

1. ¿alta o baja?

2. ¿atlético o artístico?

3. ¿joven o vieja?

4. ¿cómico o serio?

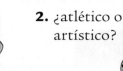

5. ¿perezosa o trabajadora?

6. ¿grande o pequeño?

4 | ¿Cómo son?

**Hablar
Escribir**

Complete each sentence with **chico(a)(os)(as), hombre,** or **mujer** and the
correct indefinite article.

> **modelo:** Mariela es _____ muy cómica.
> Mariela es una chica muy cómica.

1. Enrique es _____ muy inteligente.
2. La señorita Cabral es _____ muy organizada.
3. Clara es _____ muy simpática.
4. Esteban y Javier son _____ muy atléticos.
5. El señor Ramírez es _____ muy trabajador.
6. Victoria y Tania son _____ muy estudiosas.

♻ ¿RECUERDAS?

The definite articles **el, la, los,** and **las**
as well as the indefinite articles **un, una,
unos,** and **unas** match their nouns in
gender and number.

El chico es **un** ami**go.**

5 | ¿Qué te gusta hacer?

Hablar

Ask a partner whether he or she likes to do the following activities. What do
both of you like to do? Are there activities that neither of you likes to do?

> **modelo:** alquilar un DVD

Ⓐ ¿Te gusta alquilar un DVD?

Ⓑ Sí, me gusta alquilar un DVD. (No, no me gusta alquilar un DVD.)

1. preparar la comida
2. dibujar
3. hacer la tarea
4. correr
5. pasear

6. escribir correos electrónicos
7. jugar al fútbol
8. escuchar música
9. hablar por teléfono
10. montar en bicicleta

Práctica de GRAMÁTICA

♻ REPASO Subject Pronouns and *ser*

Use **ser** with **subject pronouns** to identify or describe a person or to say where he or she is from.

Singular			Plural		
yo	soy	*I am*	nosotros(as)	somos	*we are*
tú	eres	*you are*	vosotros(as)	sois	*you are*
usted	es	*you are*	ustedes	son	*you are*
él, ella	es	*he, she is*	ellos(as)	son	*they are*

familiar → tú ... vosotros(as) ← *familiar*

formal → usted

Nosotros somos amigos.   ***We are*** *friends.*

• Use **tú** with a friend, a family member, or someone younger.

• Use **usted** with a person you don't know, someone older, or someone for whom you want to show respect.

---

6 | ¿Tú o usted?

Hablar
Escribir

Use **tú** or **usted(es)** to indicate the subject pronouns that you would use to talk to the following people.

> **modelo:** el señor Blanco
> usted

1. Sara, una buena amiga

2. la señora Paz

3. unos amigos en México

4. el maestro de español

5. Pepe, un chico joven

6. el señor y la señora Ríos

---

7 | ¿De dónde somos?

Hablar
Escribir

Choose the correct form of **ser** to tell where these people are from.

1. Yo (es / soy) de Paraguay.

2. Él (eres / es) de Honduras.

3. Nosotros (son / somos) de Estados Unidos.

4. Ustedes (soy / son) de Colombia.

5. Ellas (son / es) de Bolivia.

6. Tú (eres / son) de Guatemala, ¿no?

Antes de avanzar

8 | ¿Cómo son las personas?

Escribir

Write sentences describing the people in the pictures.

modelo: Emilia
Emilia es alta.

1. Paco

2. nosotros

3. las chicas

4. Tito

5. Octavio y Mónica

6. Celia

7. Ignacio

♻ ¿RECUERDAS?

Adjectives agree in gender and number with the nouns they describe.

Esperan**za** es guap**a.** Los chic**os** también son guap**os.**

Some adjectives have the same form for masculine and feminine, but they still agree in number with the noun they modify.

Mart**a** es inteligent**e** y jove**n.** Artur**o** y Marta son inteligent**es** y jóven**es.**

9 | ¿Cómo somos?

**Hablar
Escribir**

Ask a partner to describe himself or herself. How are the two of you alike? How are you different? Write a summary of your similarities and differences.

Ⓐ ¿Cómo eres?

Ⓑ Soy organizado y atlético...

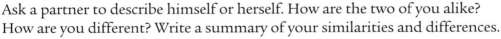

Alonzo es organizado.
Yo soy desorganizada.
Alonzo y yo somos inteligentes...

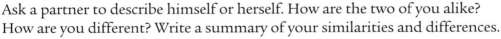

♻ REPASO Gustar with Nouns and Infinitives

Use **gustar** to talk about things and activities that people like.

To talk about things people like, use **gustar** + **noun**. If what is liked is singular, use **gusta**.

(A mí) **Me gusta el libro.**	(A nosotros) **Nos gusta el libro.**
(A ti) **Te gusta el libro.**	(A vosotros) **Os gusta el libro.**
(A usted, él, ella) **Le gusta el libro.**	(A ustedes, ellos, ellas) **Les gusta el libro.**

If what is liked is plural, use **gustan.**

Me gustan los libros.   **Nos gustan las papas fritas.**

To talk about activities, use **gusta** + **infinitive.**

Les gusta dibujar.

10 | A Sarita le gusta...

**Hablar
Escribir**

Sarita is emphatic about her likes and dislikes. What does she say about the following things and activities? Use **¡Me gusta...!** or **¡Me gustan...!** if Sarita likes it. Use **¡No me gusta...!** or **¡No me gustan...!** if she doesn't like it.

modelo: los jugos ☺
            ¡Me gustan los jugos!

1. el agua ☹   **4.** las galletas ☹
2. las papas fritas ☺   **5.** jugar al fútbol ☹
3. mirar la televisión ☺   **6.** montar en bicicleta ☺

11 | ¿A quién...?

**Hablar
Escribir**

Give the correct phrase with **gustar** to tell what people like and don't like.

modelo: A él _____ andar en patineta.
            A él le gusta andar en patineta.

1. A mí no _____ estudiar.
2. A Andrés _____ los refrescos.
3. A nosotros _____ escribir correos electrónicos.
4. A ti _____ leer un libro.
5. A ellos no _____ jugar al fútbol.
6. A nosotras _____ las papas fritas.
7. A Luisa no _____ el helado.
8. A ustedes _____ las galletas.

12 | Las comidas que me gustan

Hablar

Ask a partner whether he or she likes the following foods and drinks.
Which foods do you both like? Are there foods that neither of you likes?

A ¿Te gusta el agua?

B Sí, me gusta el agua. (No, no me gusta el agua.)

1.

2.

3.

4.

5.

6.

13 | Lo que nos gusta

**Hablar
Escribir**

Ask five classmates about foods and activities they like. Make a chart like the
one below to record their answers. Then write a summary of your findings.
Don't forget to include yourself!

yo ¿Qué les gusta hacer?

Alicia Me gusta practicar deportes.

Lalo Me gusta hablar por teléfono.

yo ¿Qué comidas les gustan?

Alicia Me gusta el helado.

Lalo Me gustan las galletas.

Nombre	Actividad	Comida
yo	hablar por teléfono	las papas fritas
Alicia	practicar deportes	el helado
Lalo	hablar por teléfono	las galletas

A Lalo y a mí nos gusta hablar por teléfono. A Alicia le gusta
practicar deportes. A Lalo le gustan las galletas...

♻ REPASO Present Tense of -ar Verbs

Many infinitives in Spanish end in **-ar.** These verbs form the present tense by dropping the **-ar** and adding the appropriate ending.

habl~~ar~~ ◄— **o, as, a, amos, áis, or an**

hablar *to talk, to speak*			
yo	**hablo**	nosotros(as)	**hablamos**
tú	**hablas**	vosotros(as)	**habláis**
usted, él, ella	**habla**	ustedes, ellos(as)	**hablan**

Hablo inglés.

I speak English.
I am speaking English.
I do speak English.

¿Hablan español?

Do they speak Spanish?
Are they speaking Spanish?

14 | Después de las clases

**Leer
Escribir**

Patricia is talking about what she and her friends do after school. Complete the paragraph with the correct form of the appropriate verb.

andar   mirar   hablar

montar   pasar   tocar

A mis amigos y a mí nos gusta hacer muchas cosas después de las clases. Yo __1.__ por teléfono. Isabel __2.__ la televisión. Roberto __3.__ en patineta. Juana y Luis __4.__ en bicicleta. Los lunes, Ana María y yo __5.__ la guitarra en la escuela. Y tú, ¿ __6.__ un rato con los amigos después de las clases?

15 | Las actividades

Escuchar

Listen to the descriptions of people and match them with the appropriate activities.

a. Descansa mucho.   **e.** Dibuja mucho.
b. Usa la computadora.   **f.** Estudia mucho.
c. Toca la guitarra.   **g.** Compra muchos libros.
d. Practica deportes.   **h.** Enseña bien.

16 | Los sábados

Hablar
Escribir

Use the picture clues to tell what these people do on Saturdays.

modelo: Elvira
Elvira habla por teléfono.

1. tú

2. Juan y María

3. nosotros

4. Martín

5. ellos

6. yo

17 | ¡A jugar! Los días de la semana

Hablar

On a piece of paper, write down one activity you do each day of the week outside of school. Do not show your paper to anyone! Work with a partner. Try to guess what your partner does each day of the week.

A ¿Estudias los viernes?

B No, no estudio los viernes. Y tú, ¿practicas deportes los lunes?

18 | Un domingo típico

Escribir

Write a paragraph about some of your activities on Sundays. Use verbs from the list.

estudiar   alquilar   descansar   mirar

hablar   escuchar   practicar   ¿ ?

modelo: Descanso los domingos. Miro la televisión o alquilo un DVD. Mis amigos y yo practicamos deportes...

¡Vamos a la escuela!

Repaso: En la clase

la tiza
el pizarrón
el reloj
la ventana
el mapa
la puerta
el borrador
la mochila
la silla
el escritorio
el lápiz
el cuaderno
la calculadora
la pluma
el papel

Más vocabulario

antes de	hay...
después (de)	tarde
el examen	temprano

Los números

0 cero	10 diez	20 veinte	30 treinta
1 uno	11 once	21 veintiuno	31 treinta y uno
2 dos	12 doce	22 veintidós	40 cuarenta
3 tres	13 trece	23 veintitrés	50 cincuenta
4 cuatro	14 catorce	24 veinticuatro	60 sesenta
5 cinco	15 quince	25 veinticinco	70 setenta
6 seis	16 dieciséis	26 veintiséis	80 ochenta
7 siete	17 diecisiete	27 veintisiete	90 noventa
8 ocho	18 dieciocho	28 veintiocho	100 cien
9 nueve	19 diecinueve	29 veintinueve	

La hora

¿A qué hora es...?	la hora
¿Qué hora es?	el horario
A la(s)...	menos
Es la.../Son las...	el minuto
de la mañana	...y cuarto
de la noche	...y (diez)
de la tarde	...y media

Repaso: En la escuela

la biblioteca

el baño

la oficina del (de la) director(a)

la cafetería

el pasillo

el gimnasio

¿Cómo estás?

cansado(a)
contento(a)
deprimido(a)
emocionado(a)
enojado(a)

nervioso(a)
ocupado(a)
tranquilo(a)
triste

¿Cómo es la clase?

aburrido(a)
difícil
divertido(a)

fácil
interesante

La frecuencia

de vez en cuando
muchas veces
mucho
nunca
siempre
todos los días

¿Dónde?

al lado (de)
cerca (de)
debajo (de)
delante (de)

dentro (de)
detrás (de)
encima (de)
lejos (de)

Expresiones con *tener*

tener calor
tener frío
tener ganas de...
tener hambre
tener razón

tener sed
tener suerte

¿Cuántos años tienes?
Tengo... años.

Las clases

el arte
las ciencias
el español
la historia
el inglés
las matemáticas

Práctica de VOCABULARIO

1 | ¿Con qué frecuencia?

**Hablar
Escribir**

Complete the sentences with the most logical expressions of frequency.

1. Nosotros (siempre / nunca) hablamos español en la clase de español.
2. Tú hablas con el director (muchas veces / de vez en cuando).
3. Los maestros enseñan (de vez en cuando / todos los días).
4. El director (siempre / nunca) anda en patineta en el pasillo.
5. Dibujo en la clase de arte (muchas veces / de vez en cuando).
6. Los buenos estudiantes sacan malas notas (de vez en cuando / todos los días).

2 | ¿A qué hora es la clase de arte?

Escribir

Write what time each class meets.

modelo: La clase de arte es a las once.

`11:00`

1.

`9:20`

2.

Gramática española

`1:35`

3.

ENGLISH TODAY

`10:10`

4.

`8:30`

5.

`12:45`

6.

`2:25`

♻ ¿RECUERDAS?

- Use **Es la una** to say that it is one o'clock.
- Use **Son las...** for any other time.
- Use **y** + **minutes** for time *after* the hour.
  Son las cinco **y diez.**   *It's 5:10.*
- Use **menos** + **minutes** for time *before* the hour.
  Es la una **menos cinco.**   *It's 12:55.*
- Use **y** or **menos cuarto** for a quarter of an hour and **y media** for half an hour.
- Use **a la(s)...** to say at what time something happens.

3 | ¿Dónde?

Escuchar

Listen to the sentences and indicate the place in the school being described.

modelo: Dibujo con lápices de colores y papel. El maestro es artístico.
Es la clase de arte.

4 ¿Cuántos hay?

Escribir

You are taking inventory of the school supply closet. Write sentences telling how many of each item there are. Spell out the numbers.

1. 21

2. 68

3. 45

4. 71

5. 59

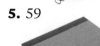

6. 31

♻ ¿RECUERDAS?

For the numbers 21, 31, and so on, use **veintiún, treinta y un,** and so on before a masculine noun and **veintiuna, treinta y una,** and so on before a feminine noun.

Hay **cuarenta y un** maestros en la escuela.

Hay **veintiuna** computadoras en la biblioteca.

5 El horario de clases

Leer
Escribir

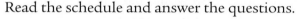

Read the schedule and answer the questions.

1. ¿A qué hora es la clase de historia?

2. ¿Qué clase hay antes de la clase de español?

3. ¿A qué hora es la clase de ciencias?

4. ¿Qué clase enseña el señor Ramírez?

5. ¿A qué hora es la clase de español?

6. ¿Qué clase hay después de la clase de historia?

Horario de Yolanda Arroyo

HORA	CLASE	MAESTRO
8:00	música	Sr. Cruz
8:55	español	Sra. Peña
9:50	ciencias	Srta. García
10:45	matemáticas	Sr. Ramírez
12:15	historia	Sr. Delgado
1:10	inglés	Sra. Oliva

6 Mi clase favorita

Escribir

Write a paragraph about your favorite class. Tell who teaches it, when it meets, the items you need for it, the classroom activities you do and how often you do them, what the class is like, how many students there are, and so on.

modelo: Me gusta mucho la clase de historia. El señor Rees enseña la clase a la una y media. Es muy interesante...

Práctica de GRAMÁTICA

♻ REPASO The Verb tener

Use the verb **tener** to talk about what you have.

tener *to have*			
yo	**tengo**	nosotros(as)	**tenemos**
tú	**tienes**	vosotros(as)	**tenéis**
usted, él, ella	**tiene**	ustedes, ellos(as)	**tienen**

Manuela **tiene** clase de arte todos los días.
*Manuela **has** art class every day.*

Use **tener** + que + **infinitive** to talk about what someone has to do.

Tenemos que **llegar** temprano.
***We have to arrive** early.*

Tener is used to form many expressions that in English would use the verb *to be*.

Ustedes **tienen** razón.   **Tengo** trece años.
You are right.   *I am thirteen years old.*

7 | ¿Qué tienen?

Hablar
Escribir

Tell what these people have on their desks at school.

1. yo

2. los estudiantes

3. la directora

4. nosotros

5. tú

6. el maestro

8 | Un día difícil

Leer
Escribir

Complete the e-mail below with the correct forms of **tener**.

> Hola, Alma.
>
> ¿Cómo estás? Yo no estoy muy bien. Mis amigos y yo __1.__ que llegar temprano a la escuela. Nosotros __2.__ que estudiar. Yo __3.__ un examen de matemáticas a las diez y media. Víctor __4.__ mucha tarea para la clase de ciencias a la una. María Elena y Cristina __5.__ un examen de ciencias a las dos menos diez. Y tú, ¿qué __6.__ que hacer hoy?
>
> Helena

9 | Expresiones

Escribir

Look at the clues and write sentences using **tener** expressions.

 modelo: nosotros
Nosotros tenemos ganas de pasear.

1. ellos

2. Rafael

3. Pepe

4. yo

5. Nadia

6. ustedes

10 | ¡Tenemos mucho que hacer!

Hablar

Ask five classmates what they have to do after school today.

A ¿Qué tienen que hacer después de las clases hoy?

B Tengo que usar la computadora.

C Tengo que estudiar.

♻ REPASO The Verb estar

Use **estar** to indicate location and say how people feel.

estar	to be		
yo	**estoy**	nosotros(as)	**estamos**
tú	**estás**	vosotros(as)	**estáis**
usted, él, ella	**está**	ustedes, ellos(as)	**están**

Los papeles **están** encima de los escritorios.
*The papers **are** on top of the desks.*

Alberto **está** contento porque no tiene mucha tarea.
*Alberto **is** happy because he doesn't have a lot of homework.*

11 | ¿Cómo están y dónde están?

Escribir

Complete each sentence with the correct form of **estar** to say how people feel or where they are.

> **modelo:** Ella _____ en la biblioteca.
> Ella está en la biblioteca.

1. Nosotros _____ cansados.

2. José y Tomás _____ en el gimnasio.

3. Gloria _____ contenta.

4. Yo _____ en la clase de español.

5. El maestro _____ ocupado.

6. Tú _____ en la clase también.

7. Daniela _____ enojada.

8. Ustedes _____ tristes.

12 | En mi escuela

Escribir

Write five sentences telling where things are located in your Spanish classroom or in your school.

> **modelo:** La biblioteca está al lado del gimnasio. El gimnasio está lejos de la oficina del director...

♻ ¿RECUERDAS?

When **de** is followed by the definite article **el,** they combine to form the contraction **del.**

La cafetería está lejos **del** gimnasio.

♻ REPASO The Verb ir

Use **ir** to talk about where someone is going.

ir *to go*			
yo	**voy**	nosotros(as)	**vamos**
tú	**vas**	vosotros(as)	**vais**
usted, él, ella	**va**	ustedes, ellos(as)	**van**

Voy a la cafetería.
I'm going to the cafeteria.

13 | ¿Adónde vas, Nicolás?

Hablar
Escribir

Read the clues below and choose the place that would best describe where each person is going. Tell where the people are going and why.

> la biblioteca   la cafetería   la clase de arte
>
> la oficina   la clase de matemáticas   el gimnasio

modelo: Nicolás: comprar jugo
Nicolás va a la cafetería para comprar jugo.

1. Luisa: hablar con el director
2. tú: dibujar
3. ustedes: tomar un examen
4. yo: practicar deportes
5. Mario y Carlos: comer
6. nosotros: estudiar

♻ ¿RECUERDAS?

When **a** is followed by the definite article **el,** they combine to form the contraction **al.**

Los estudiantes van **al** gimnasio.

14 | ¿A qué hora vas a...?

Hablar

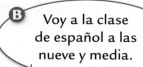

Ask a partner at what times he or she goes to various places in the school.

A ¿A qué hora vas a la clase de español?

B Voy a la clase de español a las nueve y media.

Parte 3 Comer en familia

Repaso: El desayuno

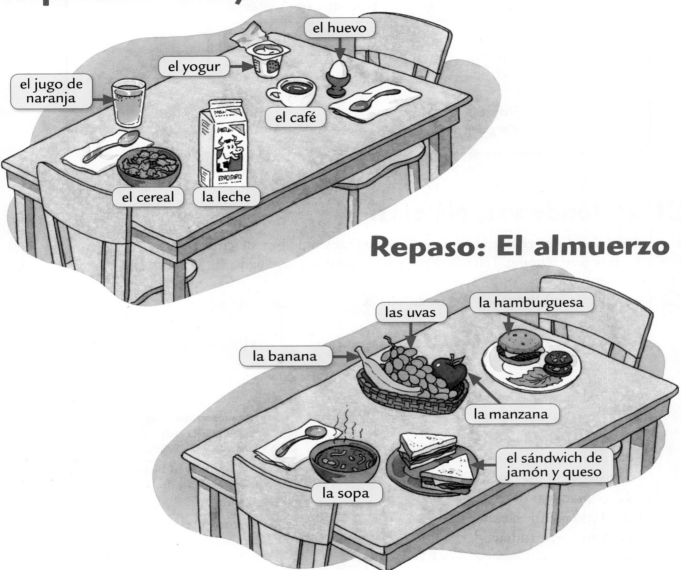

el huevo

el yogur

el jugo de naranja

el café

el cereal

la leche

Repaso: El almuerzo

las uvas

la hamburguesa

la banana

la manzana

el sándwich de jamón y queso

la sopa

Para hacer preguntas

¿Adónde?
¿Cómo?
¿Cuál(es)?
¿Cuándo?
¿Cuántos(as)...?
¿Dónde?
¿Por qué?
¿Qué?
¿Quién(es)?

Más vocabulario

la bebida   la comida
la cena   el pan

¿Cómo es la comida?

horrible
nutritivo(a)
rico(a)

Las acciones

aprender   pensar
cerrar   preferir
compartir   querer
empezar   vender
entender   vivir

Repaso: La familia

los abuelos

la abuela

el abuelo

los padres

la madre

el padre

los tíos

la tía

el tío

los hermanos

el hermano

la hermana

los primos

el primo

la prima

el perro

el gato

Más vocabulario

la hija   la madrastra
el hijo   el padrastro
los hijos

Los números

doscientos(as)	setecientos(as)
trescientos(as)	ochocientos(as)
cuatrocientos(as)	novecientos(as)
quinientos(as)	mil
seiscientos(as)	un millón (de)

Los meses

enero	mayo	septiembre
febrero	junio	octubre
marzo	julio	noviembre
abril	agosto	diciembre

La fecha

¿Cuál es la fecha?
el cumpleaños
la fecha de nacimiento
¡Feliz cumpleaños!

Práctica de VOCABULARIO

1 | ¿El desayuno o el almuerzo?

Hablar
Escribir

Tell whether each food item is for breakfast or lunch.

modelo: El jugo de naranja es para el desayuno.

1.

2.

3.

4.

5.

6.

2 | ¿Mi o mis?

Leer Choose the correct possessive adjective.

1. La familia de (mi / mis) amiga Yolanda tiene tres gatos.
2. (Nuestras / Nuestros) tías son bonitas.
3. Marcela y (sus / su) hermana van a la biblioteca.
4. ¿Cuántos años tienen (tu / tus) abuelos?
5. (Mi / Mis) hermanos son inteligentes.
6. Rolando pasa un rato con (su / sus) padres.

♻ ¿RECUERDAS?

These are the possessive adjectives.

mi(s)	nuestro(a)(s)
tu(s)	vuestro(a)(s)
su(s)	

They agree in number with the nouns they describe.

Tus primos son cómicos.

Nuestro(a) and **vuestro(a)** must also agree in gender with their nouns.

Nuestros primos son de San Diego.

3 | ¿Quiénes son?

Escuchar Listen to and answer the questions with the correct family word.

modelo: ¿Quién es el hijo de tu tía?
Es mi primo.

4 ¿Cuál es la pregunta?

Leer
Escribir

Read the sentences. Then write a logical question that each sentence would answer, using one of the interrogative words provided.

modelo: Mi padre es alto.
    ¿Cómo es tu padre?

1. Voy a la oficina del director.
2. Mi hermana tiene siete años.
3. Me gusta el jugo de naranja.
4. Necesito descansar porque estoy muy cansado.
5. Estoy muy bien.
6. Mi maestro de español es el señor Sánchez.
7. Mis abuelos llegan hoy.
8. Mis padres están en la oficina.

dónde	cuándo
cómo	por qué
adónde	quién
cuántos(as)	qué

5 Tres generaciones

Escribir

Write sentences giving the date of birth of each person in Rodrigo's family.

modelo: La fecha de nacimiento del abuelo es el trece de octubre de mil novecientos treinta y cinco.

abuelo 13/10/1935

abuela 31/05/1940

padre 17/08/1962

madre 24/04/1964

Rodrigo 01/01/1993

Ana 24/12/1998

♻ ¿RECUERDAS?

To give the date, use the following phrase: **Es el** + number + **de** + month.

Hoy **es el** diecinueve **de** septiembre.

Only the first of the month does not follow this pattern.

Es el **primero** de noviembre.

The year is expressed in **thousands** and **hundreds**.

mil cuatrocientos noventa y dos

6 | ¿Cómo son?

Look at the drawings and make comparisons using **más... que, menos... que,** and **tan... como.**

modelo: Graciela / atlético(a) / Leonardo
Graciela es más atlética que Leonardo.

1. Berta / perezoso(a) / Javier

2. el gato / pequeño(a) / el perro

3. Diego / estudioso(a) / Ricardo

4. Margarita / cómico(a) / Gustavo

5. las galletas / nutritivo(a) / las manzanas

6. Felipe / bajo(a) / Patricia

> ### ♻ ¿RECUERDAS?
>
> Use with adjectives:
> - **más... que**
> - **menos... que**
> - **tan... como**
>
> If no adjectives:
> - **más que...**
> - **menos que...**
> - **tanto como...**
>
> Irregular comparative words:
> - **mayor**
> - **menor**
> - **mejor**
> - **peor**

7 | ¿Quién, qué, dónde, cuándo...?

Use the correct interrogative words to complete these questions. You may use a word in the list more than once. Then ask a partner the questions.

> **cuál**   **cuándo**   **cuántos(as)**   **qué**   **quién**

modelo: ¿ _____ hermanos tienes?

1. ¿ _____ personas hay en tu familia?
2. ¿ _____ es más estudioso que tú?
3. ¿ _____ te gusta comer en el almuerzo?
4. ¿ _____ es mejor: el desayuno o el almuerzo?
5. ¿ _____ es tu cumpleaños?
6. ¿ _____ es tu clase favorita?

A ¿Cuántos hermanos tienes?

B Tengo tres hermanos. ¿Y tú?

Práctica de GRAMÁTICA

The endings for regular verbs that end in **-er** or **-ir** are the same except in the **nosotros(as)** and **vosotros(as)** forms.

vender *to sell*			
yo	**vendo**	nosotros(as)	**vendemos**
tú	**vendes**	vosotros(as)	**vendéis**
usted, él, ella	**vende**	ustedes, ellos(as)	**venden**

-**er** verbs = -**emos**, -**éis**

compartir *to share*			
yo	**comparto**	nosotros(as)	**compartimos**
tú	**compartes**	vosotros(as)	**compartís**
usted, él, ella	**comparte**	ustedes, ellos(as)	**comparten**

-**ir** verbs = -**imos**, -**ís**

Mario **vende** comida en la cafetería.
*Mario **sells** food in the cafeteria.*

Compartimos las uvas.
***We are sharing** the grapes.*

8 | ¿Qué escribe?

Escribir

Tell what these people do by using the correct form of the appropriate verb. Each verb should be used only once.

escribir   comer   vender   beber

compartir   correr   leer   vivir   aprender

modelo: José: correos electrónicos
José escribe correos electrónicos.

1. mis abuelos: yogur
2. tú: en el gimnasio
3. Sara: agua después de correr
4. yo: el español en la clase
5. el hombre: bicicletas y patinetas
6. ustedes: comida en la cafetería
7. nosotros: muchos libros
8. ella: cerca de la escuela

9 | En el café

The café is very busy today. Tell what these people are doing.

1. el hombre

2. mis tías

3. Fernandito

4. nosotras

5. Orlando

6. Luisa y Roberto

10 | Hago, haces...

Complete the sentences with the correct form of **hacer.**

1. ¿Qué _____ tus padres en la oficina?
2. Mi familia y yo _____ mucho los fines de semana.
3. Yo _____ la tarea de matemáticas con mi amiga.
4. ¿Qué _____ tú para llegar temprano a la escuela?
5. ¿Dónde _____ ustedes la tarea?
6. ¿Qué _____ Eva después de las clases hoy?

¿RECUERDAS?

Hacer is irregular in the **yo** form.

ha**go**	hacemos
haces	hacéis
hace	hacen

11 | ¿Qué haces?

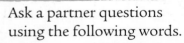

Ask a partner questions using the following words.

A ¿Aprendes más en la clase de español o en la clase de inglés?

B Aprendo más en la clase de español.

modelo: aprender más (en la clase de español o en la clase de inglés)

1. beber más (jugo o leche)
2. compartir comida más (con los amigos o con la familia)
3. escribir más (con una pluma o con un lápiz)
4. vivir (cerca o lejos de la escuela)
5. comer más (bananas o manzanas)
6. leer más (en la clase de inglés o en la clase de historia)

🔁 REPASO Stem-Changing Verbs: e → ie

Stem-changing verbs have regular present-tense **-ar**, **-er**, and **-ir** endings. For **e → ie** stem-changing verbs, the **e** in the stem changes to **ie** in all forms except **nosotros(as)** and **vosotros(as)**.

stem changes to

queer   **quie**ro

querer	*to want*
quiero	queremos
quieres	queréis
quiere	quieren

Other **e → ie** stem-changing verbs you have learned are **cerrar, empezar, entender, pensar,** and **preferir**.

Mis abuelos **prefieren** comer la cena temprano.
*My grandparents **prefer** to eat dinner early.*

12 | ¿Qué quieres comer?

Escribir

Write sentences telling what these people want to eat or drink.

1. yo

2. nosotros

3. Ignacio y Sonia

4. Alberto

5. mis hermanitas

6. tú

13 | ¿Y tú?

Escribir

Answer the questions in complete sentences.

1. ¿A qué hora empiezan las clases en tu escuela?
2. ¿Prefieres comer las uvas o las manzanas?
3. ¿Qué quieres para tu cumpleaños?
4. ¿A qué hora cierra la cafetería de tu escuela?
5. ¿Qué entiendes mejor, las ciencias o la historia?
6. ¿Qué piensas hacer mañana?

Repaso: En la tienda de ropa

negro(a)

amarillo(a)

anaranjado(a)

marrón

la camiseta

los jeans

los pantalones cortos

los calcetines

los pantalones

los zapatos

la chaqueta

el sombrero

la camisa

la blusa

el vestido

blanco(a)

rojo(a)

azul

verde

Para ir de compras	
el centro comercial	el gorro
el dinero	llevar
el dólar	nuevo(a)
el euro	pagar
feo(a)	el precio

Las estaciones
el invierno
el otoño
la primavera
el verano

Antes de avanzar

Repaso: En el restaurante

el brócoli

las verduras

el tomate

la ensalada

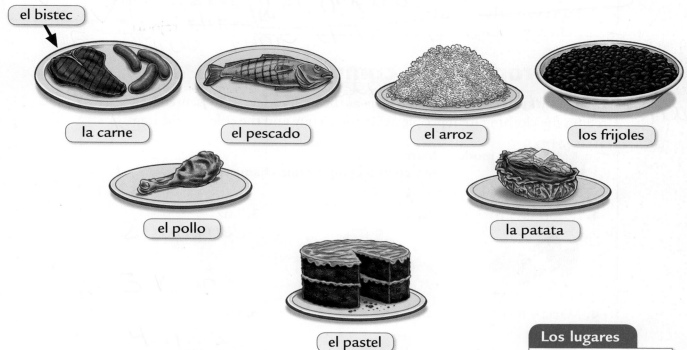

el bistec

la carne

el pescado

el arroz

los frijoles

el pollo

la patata

el pastel

Para comer

el (la) camarero(a)
costar
la cuenta
de postre
el menú
la mesa
pedir
el plato principal
la propina
servir

Las acciones

almorzar
dormir
encontrar
poder
tomar
ver
volver

El transporte

a pie
la calle
en autobús
en coche

Los lugares

el café
el centro
el cine
el parque
el teatro

Más vocabulario

el concierto
las entradas
la música rock
la película
la ventanilla

Práctica de VOCABULARIO

1 | ¿Adónde van?

Leer | Read the sentences about what people are going to do this evening. Tell where each person is going to be.

> **modelo:** La señora Molina va a comprar una blusa.
> Va a ir a la tienda.

1. Voy a jugar al fútbol con mis amigos.
2. Mis hermanos van a ver una película.
3. Vas a ir de compras en varias tiendas.
4. El señor Rivera va a pedir bistec y arroz.
5. Vamos a ver un concierto de música rock.
6. Ivana va a beber un refresco.

♻ ¿RECUERDAS?

To talk about what you are going to do, use the phrase **ir a** + **infinitive.**

Voy a comprar zapatos.

Teresa **va a ir** al concierto.

2 | ¿Qué ropa van a comprar?

Escribir | Everybody knows exactly what to buy at the mall today. Write sentences telling the clothing item people are going to buy and the color of the item.

modelo: Marco
Marco va a comprar una chaqueta negra.

1. nosotras

2. tú

3. Luz

4. María y Eva

5. usted

6. yo

3 | ¿Qué haces?

Escuchar | Listen to the questions and use words from the list to answer in complete sentences.

a pie	en coche	bistec	pastel	gorro

pantalones cortos	centro comercial	parque

4 | ¿Qué van a pedir?

Hablar
Escribir

Customers are getting ready to order at a restaurant. Look at each picture and tell what the person is going to order.

modelo: Ana
Ana va a pedir pollo y verduras.

1. la señora Ortiz

2. Ramón

3. nosotros

4. yo

5. tú

6. los chicos

5 | ¿Cómo van a la escuela?

Hablar

Ask at least five classmates how they get to school. Record your findings in a chart like the one below and then write a summary.

yo ¿Cómo van ustedes a la escuela?

Anita Voy en autobús.

Daniel Voy a pie.

A pie	En coche	En autobús
Daniel	Sara	Anita

6 | Mi color favorito

Escribir

Write about your favorite color. Tell what clothes and other items of that color you have.

modelo: Me gusta mucho el color rojo. Tengo camisetas rojas, una chaqueta roja y zapatos rojos...

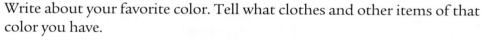

Práctica de GRAMÁTICA

Direct object pronouns can be used to replace direct object nouns.

Singular		Plural	
me	me	**nos**	us
te	you (familiar)	**os**	you (familiar)
masculine → **lo**	you (formal), him, it	**los**	you, them ← *masculine*
feminine → **la**	you (formal), her, it	**las**	you, them ← *feminine*

A **direct object pronoun** is placed directly *before* the **conjugated verb**.

Quiero los pantalones negros.
I want the black pants.

Los quiero.
I want them.

When an **infinitive** follows the **conjugated verb,** the **direct object pronoun** can be placed *before* the **conjugated verb** or be *attached* to the **infinitive**.

7 ¿Lo o la?

Leer | Choose the correct direct object pronouns to complete the sentences.

1. De postre hay un pastel. (Lo / La) comemos con helado.
2. Me gustan mucho las camisetas. (Lo / Las) compro.
3. Aquí está la cuenta. (La / Lo) pago.
4. Necesito calcetines. (Nos / Los) venden en la tienda de ropa.
5. ¿De qué hablas? No (te / nos) entiendo.
6. ¿Dónde está el camarero? ¿(Lo / La) ves?

8 ¿Qué va a comer?

Hablar
Escribir | Tell what Guillermo is going to or not going to eat, based on his preferences. Use direct object pronouns.

> **modelo:** No le gusta el brócoli.
> No va a comerlo. (No lo va a comer.)

1. Le gusta la ensalada.
2. Prefiere los tomates rojos.
3. El pescado es horrible.
4. No le gustan las verduras.
5. La pizza es rica.
6. Le gusta el pollo.
7. Los frijoles son horribles.
8. No le gusta la carne.

9 | Sí, lo tengo

Hablar

Ask a partner whether he or she has the following clothing items. His or her answers will include direct object pronouns.

A ¿Tienes un gorro negro?

B Sí, lo tengo. (No, no lo tengo.)

1.
2.
3.
4.
5.
6.

10 | ¿Qué van a hacer?

Hablar

What is everyone doing after school today? Survey five classmates to see whether they are going to do the following things. They will answer, using direct object pronouns.

modelo: tocar la guitarra

A ¿Vas a tocar la guitarra?

B Sí, voy a tocarla. (Sí, la voy a tocar.)

C No, no voy a tocarla. (No, no la voy a tocar.)

1. leer un libro
2. escribir correos electrónicos
3. comer verduras
4. hacer la tarea
5. usar la computadora
6. alquilar un DVD
7. comprar ropa
8. mirar la televisión

11 | ¿Cuándo lo llevas?

Escribir

Tell when you wear the following clothing items.

modelo: gorro
Lo llevo cuando hace frío en el invierno.

1. pantalones cortos
2. ropa formal
3. sombrero
4. chaqueta
5. jeans
6. camiseta

REPASO Stem-Changing Verbs: o → ue

Some verbs have an **o → ue** stem change in the present tense. For **o → ue** stem-changing verbs, the last **o** of the stem changes to **ue** in all forms except **nosotros(as)** and **vosotros(as).**

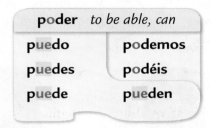

poder *to be able, can*	
puedo	podemos
puedes	podéis
puede	pueden

Carmen **puede** ir al concierto.
*Carmen **can** go to the concert.*

Other verbs you know that have this stem change are **almorzar, costar, dormir, encontrar,** and **volver.**

12 | ¿A qué hora vuelven?

Escribir

Tell when everyone is returning home today. Write out the times.

modelo: yo (4:00)
Yo vuelvo a las cuatro.

1. el camarero (10:30)
2. tú (3:50)
3. nosotros (7:00)

4. ellos (8:45)
5. Estela (6:15)
6. ustedes (5:25)

13 | No puedo...

Hablar

Ask a partner whether he or she is going to do the following activities. Your partner is going to say that he or she can't and then give a reason.

modelo: practicar deportes en el parque

A ¿Vas a practicar deportes en el parque?

B No, no puedo practicar deportes en el parque porque estoy cansado.

1. ir al concierto de música rock
2. escribir correos electrónicos
3. pagar la cuenta en el café

4. ir al cine
5. hacer la tarea
6. ir de compras

Antes de avanzar
34 treinta y cuatro

Some **-ir** verbs have an e → i stem change in the present tense. The last **e** of the stem changes to **i** in all forms except **nosotros(as)** and **vosotros(as).**

servir *to serve*	
s**i**rvo	servimos
s**i**rves	servís
s**i**rve	s**i**rven

Another verb you know with this stem change is **pedir.**

¿**Pi**des una ensalada?   ***Are you ordering** a salad?*

14 | ¿Qué sirven?

Hablar Escribir

There's a big family dinner at your house, and everybody is taking turns helping to serve the food. Tell what people are serving.

modelo: Amelia
Amelia sirve el arroz.

1. yo

2. mi padre

3. mis hermanos y yo

4. tú

5. ustedes

6. mis primos

15 | En un restaurante

Hablar

Work in a group to act out a restaurant scene. Use some of these ideas.

Ideas for the customers
• One of you can't decide what to order.
• One of you orders everything on the menu.
• One of you is a small child who doesn't want anything on the menu.

Ideas for the waiter or waitress
• You tell your customers about special dishes you are serving today.
• You tell your customers that the restaurant isn't serving any of the dishes they try to order.
• You serve your customers the wrong dishes.

Repaso de Partes 1 a 4

To review
• vocabulary
  pp. 2, 12, 20, 28

1 Listen and review vocabulary

AUDIO

Listen to the groups of words. Say what word doesn't belong in each group and why.

> **modelo:** ciencias, arte, matemáticas, calculadora
> Calculadora no es una clase.

To review
• **ser** p. 6
• **gustar** p. 8

2 Describe people and what they like

Describe the people in the pictures. Include physical traits, likes, and clothing.

> **modelo:** Leonardo
> Leonardo tiene pelo rubio. Es alto. Le gusta usar la computadora. Lleva una camiseta roja, jeans y zapatos blancos. Le gusta el cereal.

1. el señor Acevedo   **2.** la señora Robles   **3.** David

4. la señorita Fuentes   **5.** Gabriel   **6.** Paula

To review
- **tener** p. 16
- **estar** p. 18
- **ir** p. 19

3 | Tell about family

Complete each sentence with the correct form of **tener, estar,** or **ir.**

1. Yo _____ en el gimnasio.
2. Mi madre _____ un vestido amarillo.
3. Nosotros _____ al restaurante.
4. Mi hermano y yo _____ ganas de ver una película.
5. Mis primos _____ nerviosos.
6. ¿Adónde _____ tú?
7. Yo _____ al parque.
8. Nosotros _____ contentos.
9. Mi gato _____ encima de la mesa.
10. Yo _____ que hacer la tarea.

To review
- **-ar** verbs p. 10
- **-er** and **-ir** verbs p. 25

4 | Describe a shopping trip

Complete the paragraph with the correct form of the appropriate verb.

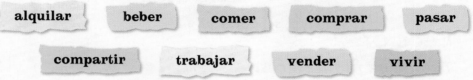

| alquilar | beber | comer | comprar | pasar |
| compartir | trabajar | vender | vivir |

Los sábados voy al centro comercial con mis hermanas Isabel y Susana. Vamos a pie porque nosotras __1.__ muy cerca del centro comercial. Mi amigo Bernardo __2.__ allí en una tienda. Él __3.__ ropa. Yo __4.__ un rato con él. A Isabel le gusta ir de compras. Muchas veces ella __5.__ una camiseta o un libro. Susana __6.__ un video. Nosotras __7.__ en un café. Isabel, Susana y yo __8.__ una pizza y __9.__ refrescos.

To review
- stem-changing verbs pp. 27, 34, 35

5 | Tell about weekend activities

Ernesto and Julio are talking about what to do tonight. Complete their conversation with the correct form of the appropriate stem-changing verb.

Ernesto: ¿ __1.__ (Encontrar / Querer) tú ir al concierto de música rock?

Julio: Sí. ¿Cuánto __2.__ (costar / cerrar) las entradas?

Ernesto: Treinta dólares. Yo __3.__ (pedir / poder) comprar las entradas ahora. Son las cuatro, y la ventanilla __4.__ (cerrar / volver) a las cinco.

Julio: Bueno. ¿A qué hora __5.__ (dormir / empezar) el concierto?

Ernesto: A las ocho. Yo __6.__ (querer / almorzar) comer en un restaurante antes del concierto. ¿Te gusta el restaurante Buen Gusto?

Julio: No. Yo __7.__ (pensar / preferir) el restaurante Camino Real. Ellos __8.__ (servir / pedir) buena comida allí.

Ernesto: Tienes razón. Yo siempre __9.__ (pedir / servir) el arroz con pollo allí. ¿Vamos al restaurante a las seis? ¿Qué __10.__ (pensar / encontrar) tú?

Julio: Muy bien. Nos vemos a las seis en el restaurante.

Ecuador

¡Bienvenido a nuestra casa!

Lección 1
Tema: **Vivimos aquí**

Lección 2
Tema: **Una fiesta en casa**

«¡Hola!
Somos Fernando y Elena.
Somos de Quito, Ecuador.»

Venezuela

Colombia

Islas Galápagos

Ecuador

Perú

Océano
Pacífico

Bolivia

Chile

Paraguay

Argentina

Uruguay

Océano
Pacífico

Otavalo

Quito

Coca

Saquisilí

Ecuador

Guayaquil

RUINAS DE
INGAPIRCA

Cuenca

Machala

Población: 13.927.650

Área: 109.483 millas cuadradas

Capital: Quito

Moneda: el dólar estadounidense,
desde *(since)* el año 2000

Idiomas: español, quechua y otras
lenguas indígenas

Comida típica: locro, fritada, llapingachos

Gente famosa: Alexandra Ayala Marín (periodista),
Gilda Holst (escritora), Julio Jaramillo (cantante),
Jefferson Pérez (atleta)

Canguil, tostado, chifles

Jóvenes ecuatorianos aplauden al equipo nacional

◄ **Nuestra pasión: el fútbol** In Ecuador, major-league soccer games are played on weekends in the cities of Quito and Guayaquil, while informal games are played at any time, in every city, town, and village. These fans of the **Selección Nacional** team hope for an appearance at the World Cup (**Copa Mundial**). *Where and when is your favorite sport played?*

El volcán Cotopaxi y la ciudad de Quito

Las montañas de los Andes Not far from the capital city of Quito lies the 19,347-foot Cotopaxi, the world's highest active volcano. The Andes mountain range, which stretches 4,500 miles north to south along the western coast of South America, has many mountains that reach 20,000 feet or more. *What mountain ranges in the United States are you familiar with?* ►

◄ **La ropa tradicional** In *Las floristas*, Camilo Egas shows indigenous women from the market town of Otavalo, north of Quito. They are wearing traditional clothing: white blouses and layered white and black skirts with red sashes, along with gold or red coral jewelry. *How do people in the United States express themselves through the clothing they wear?*

Las floristas (1916), Camilo Egas

Ecuador

Lección 1

Tema:

Vivimos aquí

¡AVANZA!

In this lesson you will learn to
- describe a house and household items
- indicate the order of things
- describe people and locations

using
- **ser** or **estar**
- ordinal numbers

♻ *¿Recuerdas?*
- stem-changing verbs: **o → ue**
- location words
- colors
- clothing

Comparación cultural

In this lesson you will learn about
- Ecuadorian artist Targelia Toaquiza
- important geographical locations
- houses and apartments for sale in Ecuador

Compara con tu mundo

This family lives in Quito, Ecuador, a city that blends modern and traditional building styles. This house has many features of traditional Spanish architecture, such as the white exterior and red-tiled roof. *Do you live in an apartment building or a house? What is your house like?*

¿Qué ves?

Mira la foto

¿Vive esta familia en un lugar tranquilo?

¿Hay más chicos o chicas?

¿Qué ropa lleva la chica? ¿Y los chicos?

Una casa tradicional con jardín
Quito, Ecuador

Presentación de VOCABULARIO

Goal: Learn about what Manuel's house is like. Then practice what you have learned to describe a house and household items. *Actividades 1–2*

♻ *¿Recuerdas?* Stem-changing verbs: **o → ue** p. 34

VIDEO
DVD

AUDIO

A ¡Hola! Me llamo Manuel. Vivo en **una casa** grande. Tiene dos **pisos.** Hay **un patio** y **un jardín** detrás de la casa.

la casa

el patio

el jardín

B A Elena y a mí nos gusta jugar **videojuegos** en **la sala**. En **la cocina** preparamos la comida y en **el comedor** comemos todos los días.

la sala

el sillón

el sofá

los videojuegos

el televisor

la alfombra

la cocina

el suelo

el comedor

C Cuando **subimos la escalera**, llegamos a mi **cuarto**. Allí me gusta estudiar, escuchar mis **discos compactos** y descansar.

subir

la escalera

Continuará...

Presentación de VOCABULARIO

D En mi cuarto tengo **un tocadiscos compactos, un radio** y otras **cosas.**

el espejo

el radio

la cómoda

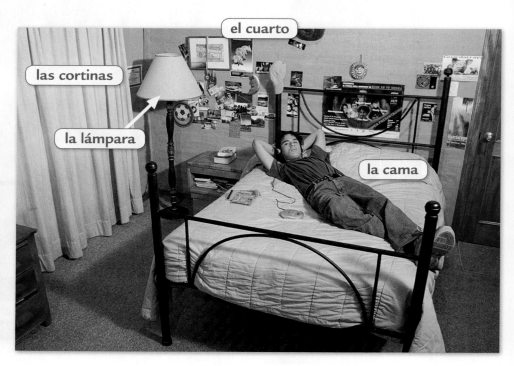

el cuarto

las cortinas

la lámpara

la cama

E Mi amigo Fernando piensa que vivir en **un apartamento** es **ideal.** Prefiere vivir en un apartamento donde puede ver el centro de Quito.

el apartamento

el primer piso

la planta baja

Más vocabulario

el armario *closet*
bajar *to descend*
el lector DVD *DVD player*
los muebles *furniture*

Expansión de vocabulario p. R2

¡A responder! Escuchar

Listen to the list of items found in a house. Point to the photo of the room in which each item is found.

@HomeTutor VideoPlus
Interactive Flashcards
ClassZone.com

Práctica de VOCABULARIO

1 | ¿Dónde encuentras...? ♻ ¿*Recuerdas?* Stem-changing verbs: **o → ue** p. 34

Hablar
Escribir

Indicate where you would find these items.

modelo: ¿sala o jardín?
Encuentro **un televisor** en **la sala.**

1. ¿cuarto o cocina?

2. ¿comedor o baño?

3. ¿cocina o sala?

4. ¿baño o patio?

5. ¿jardín o cuarto?

6. ¿comedor o sala?

2 | ¿Qué es?

Hablar
Escribir

Read the clues to identify places or things in a house.

modelo: Hay una mesa y sillas, y la familia come aquí pero no prepara
la comida aquí.
Es el comedor.

1. Son para las ventanas y las cierras en la noche.
2. La necesitas para bajar al primer piso.
3. Está en el suelo de una sala.
4. Lo usas para ver un DVD.
5. La usas para leer en la noche.
6. Lo usas para escuchar discos compactos.

Más práctica   Cuaderno *pp. 1–3*   Cuaderno para hispanohablantes *pp. 1–4*

PARA Y PIENSA

Did you get it? Name three items that can be found in . . .
1. la sala   **2.** el cuarto

 Get Help Online
ClassZone.com

VOCABULARIO en contexto

Goal: Notice the words Fernando and the Cuevas family use to talk about the rooms in their house. Then practice what you have learned to talk about rooms and other things in a house. *Actividades 3–5*

Telehistoria escena 1

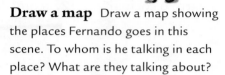
@*HomeTutor* VideoPlus
View, Read and Record
ClassZone.com

STRATEGIES

Cuando lees

Compare uses of the verb This scene contains **Voy a...** and **¿Van a...?** What do they mean? Is this different from the meaning in **¿Y vas al gimnasio?** (Unit 2, Lesson 2)?

Cuando escuchas

Draw a map Draw a map showing the places Fernando goes in this scene. To whom is he talking in each place? What are they talking about?

VIDEO
DVD

AUDIO

Sra. Cuevas   Fernando

Elena   Manuel

Mrs. Cuevas is working in the garden when Fernando arrives.

Fernando: ¿Cómo está, señora Cuevas? ¿Está Manuel?

Sra. Cuevas: ¿Qué tal, Fernando? Sí, escucha discos compactos en su cuarto...

Fernando: Ah, gracias. Voy a subir.

Sra. Cuevas: ...o está en la sala. Le gusta mucho jugar videojuegos con Elena. ¿Van a estudiar?

Fernando: Sí.

Sra. Cuevas: Bueno. ¡Ah! *(She hands him a package.)* Fernando, es para Manuel.

Fernando takes it and walks inside, where Elena and Manuel are playing videogames in the living room.

Fernando: Hola.

Manuel: *(distracted)* Hola, Fernando.

Elena: Hola, Fernando. ¿Van a estudiar aquí en la sala, en el comedor o en el cuarto de Manuel?

Fernando: *(shrugging his shoulders)* ¿Manuel?

Elena: ¡Manuel! *(She turns off the television to get his attention.)*

Manuel: ¡OK! ¿Qué tal si estudiamos en mi cuarto?

Continuará... p. 52

También se dice

Ecuador To say where Manuel is, Mrs. Cuevas uses the word **cuarto.** In other Spanish-speaking countries you might hear:
- **España** la habitación
- **Argentina, Chile** la pieza
- **México** la recámara
- **muchos países** la alcoba, el dormitorio

3 La casa de la familia Cuevas *Comprensión del episodio*

Escuchar
Leer

Read the sentences and decide who is being described in each one:
Fernando, Señora Cuevas, Manuel, or Elena.

> **modelo:** Van a estudiar.
> Manuel y Fernando van a estudiar.

1. Va a subir la escalera para ver a Manuel.
2. Le gusta mucho jugar videojuegos con Elena.
3. Habla con Fernando cuando él llega a la casa.
4. Habla con Fernando porque Manuel no escucha.

4 Las cosas que hay en la casa

Hablar

Describe these household items for a partner to guess.

una mesa   un televisor   una cómoda

un disco compacto   una cama   un radio

A Puedes encontrarlo en muchos lugares: la sala, la cocina, tu cuarto. Lo usas para escuchar música o deportes.

B Es un radio.

5 El apartamento ideal

Escribir

Write a description of an ideal apartment.

> **modelo:** El apartamento ideal es grande.
> En la sala hay...

sala

comedor

patio

cocina   baño   cuarto

PARA Y PIENSA

Did you get it? Name items Manuel may use to do the following.
1. escuchar música   **2.** estudiar   **3.** jugar videojuegos

Get Help Online
ClassZone.com

Presentación de GRAMÁTICA

Goal: Learn the differences between **ser** and **estar.** Then practice using these two verbs to describe people and locations. *Actividades 6–12*

♻ *¿Recuerdas?* Location words p. 13, colors p. 28

English Grammar Connection: Remember that there are two ways to say the English verb *to be* in Spanish: **ser** and **estar** (see pp. 6 and 18).

Ser or estar

Animated Grammar
ClassZone.com

Ser and **estar** both mean *to be.* How do you know which verb to use?

Here's how:

Use **ser** to indicate origin: where someone or something is from.

> **Soy** de Quito.
> *I'm from Quito.*

Use **ser** to describe personal traits and physical characteristics.

> Los estudiantes **son** inteligentes.
> *The students **are** intelligent.*

Ser is also used to indicate professions.

> La señora Ramírez **es** maestra.
> *Mrs. Ramírez **is** a teacher.*

Remember that you also use **ser** to identify people or things and to give the time and the date.

Use **estar** to indicate location: where someone or something is.

> Quito **está** en Ecuador.
> *Quito **is** in Ecuador.*

Estar is also used to describe conditions, such as how someone feels.

> physical: ¿Cómo **estás**?   **Estoy** bien.
> *How **are you**?*   *I'm fine.*

> emotional: **Estamos** contentos.   **Están** enojados.
> ***We are** happy.*   ***They are** angry.*

Más práctica
Cuaderno *pp. 4–6*
Cuaderno para hispanohablantes *pp. 5–7*

🎵 **Conjuguemos.com**

@HomeTutor
Leveled Practice
ClassZone.com

Práctica de GRAMÁTICA

6 | El apartamento de Fernando 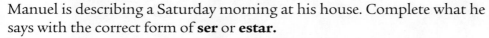 ¿*Recuerdas?* Location words p. 13

Escribir

Help Fernando describe his apartment. Use **ser** and **estar** to write sentences with the information given.

> **modelo:** el apartamento: grande / cerca de la escuela
> El apartamento es grande. Está cerca de la escuela.

1. la sala: marrón / lejos de la escalera
2. las cortinas: nuevo / delante de las ventanas
3. el cuarto: pequeño / en la planta baja
4. el sillón: blanco / cerca del sofá
5. las lámparas: feo / encima de las mesas
6. el jardín: bonito / en el patio
7. la cómoda: grande / en el cuarto
8. la alfombra: viejo / debajo del sofá

7 | Un sábado con la familia

**Leer
Escribir**

Manuel is describing a Saturday morning at his house. Complete what he says with the correct form of **ser** or **estar.**

> Los sábados yo no __1.__ cansado porque duermo mucho. Bajo a la cocina a las diez; mis padres y Elena ya __2.__ allí. Elena __3.__ mi hermana. Ella __4.__ un poco perezosa. Mi padre y yo preparamos el desayuno. La cocina __5.__ grande y amarilla. La mesa y las sillas __6.__ cerca de la ventana. Las cortinas __7.__ blancas. La alfombra __8.__ de Otavalo, en Ecuador. Después del desayuno, mi familia y yo __9.__ contentos porque vamos a jugar al fútbol. Nosotros __10.__ muy atléticos.

8 | Los amigos de Manuel

**Escuchar
Escribir**

Manuel is describing various people. Listen to his description and take notes. Then answer the questions.

1. ¿Cómo está Manuel hoy?
2. ¿De dónde es Rosa?
3. ¿Cómo es ella?
4. ¿Dónde está su casa?
5. ¿De dónde son José y Carlos?
6. ¿Cómo son ellos?
7. ¿Dónde está su apartamento?
8. ¿Cómo es su apartamento?

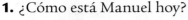

9 | En la sala

Hablar
Escribir

Look at the drawing of the living room. Then use the verbs **ser** and **estar** to form as many sentences as you can to describe the drawing.

modelo: El sofá es verde y viejo.

10 | ¡A jugar! ¿Cómo es? ♻ ¿*Recuerdas?* Colors p. 28

Hablar

In a group of three, take turns describing each drawing. Try to be the last person who can add something to the description without repeating.

 **A** Es una sala.

 **B** La mesa está cerca del sofá.

C La sala es verde...

1.

2.

11 | Mi casa

Escribir

Comparación cultural

Casas ecuatorianas

How do landscapes reflect a community's way of life? The Tigua artists from the **Ecuadorian Andes** are known for their colorful paintings, created with chicken feather brushes on sheephide. Their artwork shows the world around them: mountains, valleys, farms, and livestock. Tigua paintings, such as *Nochebuena* by Targelia Toaquiza, are typically landscapes that show scenes of community life, such as festivals, indigenous traditions, harvests, and everyday rural activities.

Nochebuena *(alrededor de 1990),* Targelia Toaquiza

Compara con tu mundo

What would a painting showing community life in your area include?

Write a description of where you live. Explain where it is and what it's like.

modelo: Mi casa está cerca de Quito. Es blanca y está al lado de una casa anaranjada. También está cerca del agua...

12 | ¿Y tú?

Hablar
Escribir

Answer the following questions in complete sentences.

1. ¿Cómo estás hoy?
2. ¿Cómo eres?
3. ¿Cuál es tu cuarto favorito en tu casa o apartamento?
4. ¿Dónde está la cocina en tu casa o apartamento?
5. ¿De dónde son las personas de tu familia?
6. ¿De qué color es tu mochila?
7. ¿Quién es tu maestro(a) favorito(a)?
8. ¿A qué hora es tu clase de español?
9. ¿Cuál es tu clase favorita?
10. ¿Cómo es tu mejor amigo(a)?

Más práctica   Cuaderno *pp. 4–6*   Cuaderno para hispanohablantes *pp. 5–7*

PARA Y PIENSA

Did you get it? Complete each sentence with the correct form of **ser** or **estar**.

1. Nosotros _____ en la cocina.
2. Voy a mi cuarto porque _____ cansado.
3. El espejo _____ de Bogotá.
4. Los jardines _____ bonitos.

Get Help Online
ClassZone.com

GRAMÁTICA *en contexto*

¡AVANZA! **Goal:** Identify the ways **ser** and **estar** are used in Manuel and Fernando's conversation about themselves and things in the house. Then use these verbs to talk about people and things in your life. *Actividades 13–15*

Telehistoria escena 2

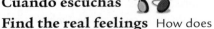

@HomeTutor VideoPlus
View, Read and Record
ClassZone.com

STRATEGIES

Cuando lees

Consider the influence of the setting
Early in this scene, you find out whether Manuel's bedroom is neat or messy. This has a big influence on the action in the scene. How and why?

Cuando escuchas

Find the real feelings How does Elena describe Manuel? Is she sincere, or is she saying the opposite of what she feels? How can you tell?

VIDEO
DVD

AUDIO

Manuel: ¡Mi cuaderno no está aquí!

Fernando: *(distracted)* Y, ¿encima de la cama? ¿Y cerca de la lámpara? ¿Y en el armario? ¿En la cómoda?

Manuel looks around, but Fernando finds the notebook on the floor.

Fernando: Manuel, ¡eres muy desorganizado! ¡Todas tus cosas están en el suelo!

Meanwhile, Elena sees the package from Alicia in the living room and calls upstairs.

Elena: ¡Manuel! ¡Manueeeel!

Manuel: *(He goes downstairs.)* ¿Qué quieres? Estoy muy ocupado.

Elena: Sí, tú eres muy estudioso.

She gives him the package. Manuel opens it, dropping the T-shirt on the floor to read the letter. He goes back to his room.

Fernando: *(reading the letter)* ¿Tienes que ir al centro de Quito? ¿A ver a Trini Salgado?

Manuel: Sí. ¡Alicia quiere el autógrafo de Trini! Es importante. Tenemos que ir.

As they leave, Fernando realizes that Manuel forgot the T-shirt.

Fernando: Manuel... ¿y la camiseta? **Continuará...** p. 58

También se dice

Ecuador When asking where Manuel's notebook is, Fernando uses the word **el armario.** In other Spanish-speaking countries you might hear:
- **España el armario empotrado**
- **muchos países el clóset**

13 | Los problemas de Manuel *Comprensión del episodio*

Escuchar
Leer

Tell whether the following sentences are true or false. Correct the false sentences.

1. Manuel es muy organizado.
2. Manuel está tranquilo.
3. Manuel no puede encontrar su calculadora.
4. Todas las cosas de Manuel están en el suelo.
5. Fernando y Manuel tienen que ir al centro comercial.
6. Quieren ver a Trini.
7. Fernando quiere el autógrafo de Trini Salgado.
8. Fernando y Manuel tienen que ir, y Manuel tiene la camiseta.

14 | Una persona importante

Escribir

Write a description of someone special in your life. Answer the following questions.

Para organizarte:

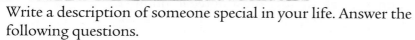

- ¿Quién es?
- ¿Cómo es?
- ¿De dónde es?
- ¿Dónde está ahora?
- ¿Cómo estás cuando pasas un rato con él o ella?

modelo: Mi madre es simpática y trabajadora. Es más alta que mi padre. Es de Seattle, Washington, pero está en Portland ahora...

15 | Mi cuarto

Hablar

Describe your room to a partner. He or she will draw it.

modelo: Mi cuarto es grande. La puerta está al lado de la cómoda. El televisor y los videojuegos están encima de la cómoda...

PARA Y PIENSA

Did you get it? Choose the correct verb in each sentence based on the Telehistoria.

1. Manuel (es / está) muy desorganizado.
2. Todas las cosas (son / están) en el suelo.
3. El cuaderno no (está / es) encima de la cama.

Get Help Online
ClassZone.com

Lección 1
cincuenta y tres **53**

Presentación de GRAMÁTICA

Goal: Learn how to use ordinal numbers. Then practice them to indicate the order of things, and to talk about the floors of a house or building. *Actividades 16–20*

♻ *¿Recuerdas?* Clothing p. 28

English Grammar Connection: In both English and Spanish, **ordinal numbers** indicate position in a series or the order of items.

in **second** place   en **segundo** lugar

Ordinal Numbers

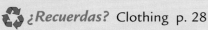

Animated Grammar
ClassZone.com

When used with a noun, an **ordinal number** must agree in number and gender with that noun.

Here's how:

Ordinal Numbers

primero(a)	*first*	**sexto(a)**	*sixth*
segundo(a)	*second*	**séptimo(a)**	*seventh*
tercero(a)	*third*	**octavo(a)**	*eighth*
cuarto(a)	*fourth*	**noveno(a)**	*ninth*
quinto(a)	*fifth*	**décimo(a)**	*tenth*

Ordinals are placed before **nouns.**

before the noun ⌐ *agrees*

Es la **primera** película de María Conchita Alonso.
*It's the **first** movie of María Conchita Alonso.*

agrees

Nuestro apartamento está en el **octavo** piso.
*Our apartment is on the **eighth** floor.*

Primero and **tercero** drop the **o** before a **masculine singular noun.**

drops the **o** ⌐
Enero es el **primer** mes del año.
*January is the **first** month of the year.*

Más práctica
Cuaderno *pp. 7–9*
Cuaderno para hispanohablantes *pp. 8–11*

@HomeTutor
Leveled Practice
ClassZone.com

Práctica de GRAMÁTICA

16 | ¿En qué piso?

Escribir

Tell on which floor each family lives.

> **modelo:** Gutiérrez (2)
> La familia Gutiérrez vive en **el segundo piso.**

1. Díaz (7)   **4.** Ponce (1)   **7.** García (3)

2. Granados (5)   **5.** Romero (9)   **8.** Martínez (8)

3. Santiago (10)   **6.** Sánchez (6)   **9.** Cabral (4)

17 | La nueva casa

Hablar
Escribir

The Icaza family is moving into a new house. Look at this to-do list. Use ordinal numbers to tell on what day the family members do things.

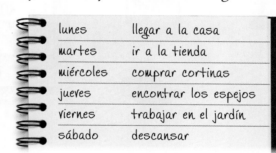

> **modelo:** El primer día ellos
> llegan a la casa.

lunes	llegar a la casa
martes	ir a la tienda
miércoles	comprar cortinas
jueves	encontrar los espejos
viernes	trabajar en el jardín
sábado	descansar

18 | La primera persona lleva... ¿Recuerdas? Clothing p. 28

Hablar

These people are standing in line. Use ordinal numbers to ask a partner what they are wearing.

A ¿Qué lleva la **primera** persona?

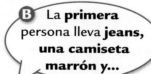

B La **primera** persona lleva **jeans, una camiseta marrón y...**

19 | Los pisos del almacén

Hablar

Ask a partner which floor of a department store you would go to for the following items.

A ¿A qué piso voy para comprar sopa?

B Necesitas ir a la planta baja para comprar sopa.

1.

2.

3.

4.

5.

6.

ALMACÉN

5	MUEBLES
4	DECORACIÓN
3	APARATOS ELECTRÓNICOS
2	ROPA DE MUJERES
1	ZAPATOS
Planta Baja	CAFETERÍA

Pronunciación La acentuación

In Spanish, just like in English, certain syllables are stressed more than others. If a word ends in a vowel, **n,** or **s,** and there is no written accent, the next-to-last syllable is stressed.

> Estoy cerca del **sillón** en la **sala** con el **reloj.**

sala	**suben**
cortinas	**apartamento**

If a word ends in a consonant other than **n** or **s,** the natural stress falls on the last syllable of the word.

mujer	**reloj**	**bajar**
ideal	**televisor**	

Words that have written accents are stressed on the syllable with the accent.

jardín	**sillón**	**lámpara**
sofá	**décimo**	

56 Unidad 5 Ecuador
cincuenta y seis

20 | Planes para las vacaciones

Escribir

Write a list of the things you would like to do on each day of your next school vacation. Use ordinal numbers.

modelo: El primer día, voy a dormir diez horas. El segundo día, voy a comer en un restaurante con mi familia...

Comparación cultural

Sitios geográficos

How does a country's location in the world make it unique? **Ecuador** is located on the equator, which divides the northern and southern hemispheres. The Mitad del Mundo monument marks the location of the equator. There you can stand with one foot in each hemisphere. Ushuaia, in the province of Tierra del Fuego in **Argentina,** is the southernmost city in the world. It is known as *la ciudad del fin del mundo* (the city at the end of the earth). Located a little over 600 miles from Antarctica, it is a common starting point for arctic explorations.

Compara con tu mundo

What geographical locations, like Key West, are important in the United States and why? Have you ever been to any of these places?

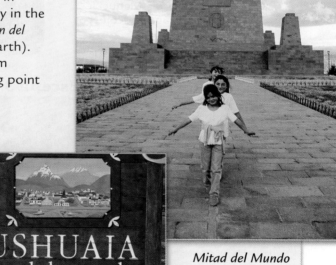

Ushuaia, Argentina

Mitad del Mundo

Más práctica   Cuaderno *pp. 7–9*   Cuaderno para hispanohablantes *pp. 8–11*

PARA Y PIENSA

Did you get it? Say that you are on the following floors.
1. sixth
2. ninth
3. second
4. third

Get Help Online
ClassZone.com

Todo junto

Goal: *Show what you know* Identify how Manuel, his mother, and Fernando use **ser** and **estar** to talk about different places in the house. Then practice these verbs and ordinal numbers to describe houses and apartments. *Actividades 21–25*

Telehistoria completa

STRATEGIES

Cuando lees

Read to know whether and where
You already know that Manuel has lost the T-shirt. Read to find out whether he finds it. If so, where?

Cuando escuchas

Notice reactions As you listen, consider the reactions of Manuel, his mother, and Fernando to the T-shirt dilemma. How does each one react? How can you tell?

Escena 1 *Resumen*
Fernando va a la casa de Manuel porque necesitan estudiar. Pero a Manuel le gusta más jugar videojuegos.

Escena 2 *Resumen*
Manuel no puede encontrar su cuaderno. Fernando piensa que Manuel es muy desorganizado.

Escena 3

 VIDEO DVD

AUDIO

Manuel: ¡Mamá! ¡La camiseta! ¿Dónde está?

Sra. Cuevas: ¿Qué camiseta?

Manuel: La camiseta de Alicia, mi amiga de Miami.

Sra. Cuevas: Ay, hijo. Aquí en el jardín no está. Tiene que estar en la casa.

Manuel: ¡Mamá! ¡Por favor!

Sra. Cuevas: Manuel, estoy ocupada.

Manuel goes back inside, where Fernando is waiting in the living room.

Manuel: ¿Dónde está? Aquí en la mesa no está.

Fernando: No está encima de la mesa. No está en tu cuarto.

Manuel: ¡No, tiene que estar aquí!

Fernando: ¿En el comedor? ¿En la cocina?

Fernando notices something next to his chair.

Fernando: Manuel, aquí hay un gato al lado del sillón.

Manuel: Sí, es Fígaro, el gato de Elena. ¿Y qué?

Fernando: El gato está encima de ¡una camiseta!

21 ¿En qué orden? *Comprensión de los episodios*

Escuchar
Leer

To describe the episodes, put the sentences in order.

a. La camiseta está debajo del gato.

b. Manuel y Elena están en la sala.

c. Fernando llega a la casa de Manuel.

d. Manuel no encuentra su cuaderno.

e. La camiseta de Alicia no está en el jardín.

f. Fernando y Manuel van a estudiar en el cuarto de Manuel.

g. Fernando habla con la señora Cuevas.

h. Manuel habla con la señora Cuevas.

22 Descríbelos *Comprensión de los episodios*

Escuchar
Leer

Answer the questions, according to the photos.

1.

a. ¿Quiénes son?

b. ¿Cómo son?

c. ¿Dónde están?

d. ¿Cómo están?

2.

a. ¿Quién es?

b. ¿Cómo es?

c. ¿Dónde está?

d. ¿Cómo está?

23 Una visita a tu casa

Hablar

> **STRATEGY Hablar**
>
> **Use graphics while you talk** For your current or ideal house or apartment, take photos, find photos in magazines or on the Internet, or make detailed drawings with objects' colors shown in each room. Use the graphics while talking with your partner.

Describe your house or apartment or your dream house to a partner.
Say what each room is like and what's in each room.

modelo: Vivo en un apartamento. Está en el décimo piso. Hay una sala grande con muchos muebles. En la sala hay un sofá negro...

24 | Integración

Leer
Escuchar
Hablar

You and your family are going to live in Quito for a year and need an apartment. Look at the rental listings and listen to the real estate agent's message. Describe which apartment is best for all of you.

Fuente 1 Lista de apartamentos

Calle Olmedo, 38 Apartamento en el centro de Quito. Cuesta 1.300 dólares al mes. Está en el tercer piso. Tiene tres cuartos con muchos armarios y dos baños. La sala es un poco pequeña pero la cocina es muy grande. Hay un patio pequeño. Está cerca de tiendas y restaurantes.

Calle de los Olivos, 45 Apartamento lejos del centro. Cuesta 1.050 dólares al mes. Está en el primer piso. Tiene cinco cuartos y tres baños. La cocina es grande y la sala es bonita. El apartamento tiene muchas ventanas y armarios grandes. No tiene patio, pero hay un parque cerca.

Calle Simón Bolívar, 76 Apartamento cerca del centro. Cuesta 1.125 dólares al mes. Está en el décimo piso y puedes ver todo el centro. Tiene dos cuartos y un baño. La sala es grande y la cocina también. También hay un patio bonito. Está cerca de los cines y los teatros.

Fuente 2 Mensaje telefónico

Listen and take notes
- ¿Cómo es el apartamento y dónde está?
- ¿Cuánto cuesta?

modelo: Quiero vivir en el apartamento de la calle... porque...

25 | Una casa increíble

Escribir

Write an ad to sell a house. Tell where the house is, what it's like, and what rooms and furniture it has.

modelo:

> **¡Casa bonita!** Está cerca del centro. Es grande y tiene cinco cuartos y cuatro baños. La escalera es muy bonita. Ya tiene muebles. En la sala hay un sofá y dos sillones.

Writing Criteria	Excellent	Good	Needs Work
Content	Your ad includes a lot of information.	Your ad includes some information.	Your ad includes little information.
Communication	Most of your ad is organized and easy to follow.	Parts of your ad are organized and easy to follow.	Your ad is disorganized and hard to follow.
Accuracy	Your ad has few mistakes in grammar and vocabulary.	Your ad has some mistakes in grammar and vocabulary.	Your ad has many mistakes in grammar and vocabulary.

Más práctica Cuaderno *pp. 10–11*   Cuaderno para hispanohablantes *pp. 12–13*

PARA Y PIENSA

Did you get it? Use **ser, estar,** and an ordinal number to complete the sentences.
1. Fígaro _____ el gato de Elena. No _____ tranquilo.
2. Fígaro vive en el _____ piso. (7)

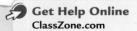
Get Help Online
ClassZone.com

Juegos y diversiones

Review vocabulary by playing a game.

¡DIBÚJALO!

The Setup

Your teacher will write lesson vocabulary words or phrases on index cards and put the cards in a pile. He or she will set up an easel with a large pad of paper and markers at the front of the room. Form two teams.

Playing the Game

A player on Team A will pick a card from the pile and draw pictures to represent the word or phrase on the card. Team A has 30 seconds from the time the player starts drawing to guess what the Spanish word or phrase is. Your teacher will be the timekeeper. Each correct guess gains the team a point.

If Team A can't guess the word in time, then Team B will get a chance to guess. If Team B guesses correctly, it gets two points.

Teams will take turns drawing.

The Winner!

The team with the most points at the end wins.

Materials

- easel with a large pad of paper
- markers
- index cards with vocabulary words
- timer

¿Es una casa?

Lectura

AUDIO

Vivir en Ecuador

The following are an apartment brochure from Quito and a real-estate ad from Guayaquil.

STRATEGY Leer

Use a checklist and explain Make a checklist showing which place—apartment or house—is more useful for a single person, a small family, and a large family. List reasons.

	el apartamento	la casa	¿Por qué?
una persona			
una familia pequeña			
una familia grande			

COMEDOR

CUARTO

COCINA

SALA

LAS CAMELIAS
COMUNIDAD RESIDENCIAL

EL QUITEÑO MODERNO
- Construcción antisísmica [1]
- Jardines comunales
- Sauna
- Gimnasio
- Portero [2] de 24 horas
- Áreas verdes y recreativas
- Cerca de tiendas, supermercados y restaurantes

¿Quieres estar cerca de todo? El Quiteño Moderno está en un lugar muy conveniente.

Desde [3] el noveno piso puedes ver todo el centro.

Apartamento de 95 metros cuadrados [4] $65.000

RESIDENCIAS
PICHINCHA
AV. EL INCA, 32
TELÉFONO 244–5502

---

[1] earthquake-proof   [2] Doorman   [3] From   [4] square

Cerro Santa Ana
Comunidad privada de 18 residencias

Aquí puedes ir de compras o al cine y en unos minutos volver a tu casa cerca del río[5] Guayas. Cerro Santa Ana es para las personas a quienes les gusta el aire puro tanto como un lugar urbano.

$130.000

Casa ultramoderna de dos pisos con acceso fácil a Guayaquil

- 4 cuartos
- 3 baños
- sala-comedor
- cocina

- oficina
- área de máquinas de lavar[6]
- 2 garajes

La casa está en un lugar tranquilo pero no está muy lejos de Guayaquil. Puedes preparar la comida en el patio y hay zonas para practicar deportes.

Cerro Santa Ana | Escalón 68 | Teléfono 231–6687

---

[5] river   [6] washing machines

PARA Y PIENSA

¿Comprendiste?

1. ¿Cómo es el apartamento y dónde está? ¿Y la casa?
2. ¿Qué puedes hacer en los dos lugares?
3. ¿Cuál es mejor para una familia, el apartamento o la casa? ¿Por qué?

¿Y tú?
Explícale a otro(a) estudiante dónde prefieres vivir y por qué.

Conexiones *Las matemáticas*

Las ruinas de Ingapirca

At one time, the Incan empire stretched from modern-day Colombia to Chile. At Ingapirca, an important settlement in Ecuador, the Incas built a majestic temple called El Templo del Sol (Temple of the Sun). Carved into a steep rocky cliff, the temple served as a fortress and place of worship.

Many Incan buildings have withstood centuries of earthquakes. The Incas used large stone blocks of different shapes for building. Often the blocks, as well as the doors and windows, were wider at the base and narrower at the top.

Look at the images below. Write two paragraphs comparing the shapes you see in the buildings to other shapes such as circles, squares, and triangles. Give the names and a description of the shapes you discuss. Make an illustration for each shape.

El Templo del Sol

Las ruinas de Sacsayhuaman, Perú

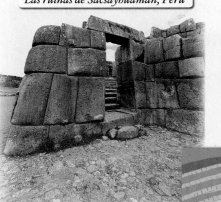

oeste ← → este

El Templo del Sol

Proyecto 1 *Las ciencias sociales*

The external walls of the buildings at Ingapirca were made of chiseled blocks that fit together so precisely that no mortar was needed to hold them. Research and report on how the Incas may have cut, transported, and fit these huge blocks without the use of iron tools or wheels.

Proyecto 2 *La historia*

Research the Incan empire and create a map showing its size. Then write a paragraph about its population, duration, and political structure.

Proyecto 3 *El lenguaje*

There are many different indigenous groups and languages in Ecuador. The most common indigenous language, Quechua, was also spoken by the Incas. Spanish and English have borrowed many words from Quechua. Use the Internet or a library to find four or five Quechua words that are used in Spanish. Write the words in Spanish, then explain what they mean in English.

LECCIÓN 1

En resumen
Vocabulario y gramática

Animated Grammar
Interactive Flashcards
ClassZone.com

Vocabulario

Describe a House

el apartamento	*apartment*	el jardín	*garden*
el armario	*closet; armoire*	(*pl.* los jardines)	
bajar	*to descend*	el patio	*patio*
la casa	*house*	el piso	*floor (of a building)*
la cocina	*kitchen*	la planta baja	*ground floor*
el comedor	*dining room*	la sala	*living room*
el cuarto	*room; bedroom*	subir	*to go up*
la escalera	*stairs*	el suelo	*floor (of a room)*
ideal	*ideal*		

Describe Household Items

la cosa	*thing*
el disco compacto	*compact disc*
el lector DVD	*DVD player*
el radio	*radio*
el televisor	*television set*
el tocadiscos compactos	*CD player*
los videojuegos	*video games*

Furniture

la alfombra	*rug*	la lámpara	*lamp*
la cama	*bed*	los muebles	*furniture*
la cómoda	*dresser*	el sillón	*armchair*
las cortinas	*curtains*	(*pl.* los sillones)	
el espejo	*mirror*	el sofá	*sofa, couch*

Ordinal Numbers

primero(a)	*first*
segundo(a)	*second*
tercero(a)	*third*
cuarto(a)	*fourth*
quinto(a)	*fifth*
sexto(a)	*sixth*
séptimo(a)	*seventh*
octavo(a)	*eighth*
noveno(a)	*ninth*
décimo(a)	*tenth*

Gramática

Ser or estar

Ser and **estar** both mean *to be*.

- Use **ser** to indicate origin.
- Use **ser** to describe personal traits and physical characteristics.
- **Ser** is also used to indicate professions.
- You also use **ser** to express possession and to give the time and the date.

- Use **estar** to indicate location.
- **Estar** is also used to describe conditions, both physical and emotional.

Ordinal Numbers

When used with a noun, an **ordinal number** must agree in number and gender with that noun.

- **Ordinals** are placed before nouns.
- **Primero** and **tercero** drop the **o** before a masculine singular noun.

Repaso de la lección

¡LLEGADA!

Now you can
- describe a house and household items
- indicate the order of things
- describe people and locations

Using
- **ser** or **estar**
- ordinal numbers

To review
- **ser** or **estar**
  p. 48

1 | Listen and understand

AUDIO

Listen to Rebeca describe her house. Then tell whether the statements are true or false.

1. La casa es muy bonita.
2. Hay un sillón en la sala.
3. En el comedor hay diez sillas.
4. El baño está detrás del comedor.
5. En el segundo piso hay tres cuartos y dos baños.
6. El cuarto de Rebeca es azul.

To review
- ordinal numbers
  p. 54

2 | Indicate the order of things

Señor Cabrera has to help the tenants of his apartment building move some furniture. Tell on what floor of the bulding these items are.

modelo: PB
Las alfombras están en la planta baja.

1. 4°

2. 5°

3. 6°

4. 3°

5. 7°

6. 1°

7. 2°

8. 8°

To review
• ser or estar
  p. 48

3 | Describe a house and household items

Joaquín is describing his house. Complete his e-mail message with the correct form of **ser** or **estar**.

> Hola, amigo. Aquí __1.__ yo en mi casa. Nuestra casa __2.__ al lado del parque. La casa __3.__ blanca y muy bonita. Ahora mi hermano y yo __4.__ en nuestro cuarto. Muchos discos compactos __5.__ en el suelo porque nosotros no __6.__ muy organizados. ¿Y tú? ¿Tú __7.__ organizado o desorganizado? El cuarto de nuestros padres __8.__ al lado de nuestro cuarto. Su cuarto __9.__ más grande que nuestro cuarto. ¿Cómo __10.__ tu casa?

To review
• ser or estar
  p. 48

4 | Describe people and locations

Describe these people and tell where they are.

modelo: Ernesto (artístico / en el parque / tranquilo)
Ernesto es artístico. Está en el parque. Está tranquilo.

1. las maestras (simpáticas / en la escuela / contentas)
2. tú (estudioso / en la biblioteca / nervioso)
3. la señora Moreno (seria / deprimida / en el pasillo)
4. nosotros (cómicos / en el teatro / emocionados)
5. mi hermano menor (malo / en su cuarto / enojado)
6. yo (inteligente / en clase / ocupado)

To review
• Comparación
  cultural pp. 40,
  51, 57

5 | Ecuador and Argentina

Comparación cultural

Answer these culture questions.

1. What are some characteristics of traditional Spanish architecture?
2. What are some features found in Tigua paintings?
3. What does Ecuador's **Mitad del Mundo** monument mark?
4. Why is Ushuaia, Argentina, known as **la ciudad del fin del mundo**?

Más práctica Cuaderno *pp. 12–23* Cuaderno para hispanohablantes *pp. 14–23*

Get Help Online
ClassZone.com

Ecuador

Lección 2

Tema:

Una fiesta en casa

¡AVANZA!

In this lesson you will learn to
- plan a party
- talk about chores and responsibilities
- tell someone what to do
- say what you just did

using
- more irregular verbs
- affirmative **tú** commands
- **acabar de** + infinitive

♻ ¿Recuerdas?
- **tener que**, interrogative words
- expressions of frequency
- direct object pronouns

Comparación cultural

In this lesson you will learn about
- a festival honoring Quito, and textiles in Otavalo
- folk dances and traditional crafts, like **tapices** and **molas**
- throwing parties in Ecuador, Argentina, and Panama

Compara con tu mundo
This photo shows a teenager's birthday party in Quito, Ecuador. In Latin America it is common to celebrate with family and perhaps a few close friends. *Where and with whom do you like to celebrate your birthday?*

¿Qué ves?

Mira la foto

¿Están en un parque las personas?

¿Elena sirve pastel o una pizza?

¿Qué muebles hay?

Una fiesta de cumpleaños
Quito, Ecuador

Presentación de VOCABULARIO

¡AVANZA! **Goal:** Learn about how Elena and others get ready for Manuel's surprise party. Then practice what you have learned to talk about how you plan a party. *Actividades 1–2*

VIDEO DVD

AUDIO

A ¡Hola! Soy Elena. Vamos a **dar una fiesta** porque es el cumpleaños de Manuel, pero es **un secreto**. Antes de **celebrar, hay que limpiar** la cocina porque está **sucia**.

limpiar la cocina

barrer el suelo

sacar la basura

lavar los platos

cortar el césped

darle de comer al perro

B Acabamos de limpiar la cocina pero **todavía** tenemos que trabajar. Toda la casa **debe** estar **limpia**.

hacer la cama

planchar la ropa

pasar la aspiradora

C Mi papá quiere **ayudar** con **los quehaceres** pero no **cocina** muy bien. Prefiere **poner la mesa.**

cocinar

poner la mesa

Continuará...

Presentación de VOCABULARIO

(continuación)

D Son las cuatro y **los invitados** van a **venir** a las cinco. Papá **pone las decoraciones** y Fernando **envuelve un regalo** para Manuel.

decorar

las decoraciones

el globo

envolver

el regalo

el papel de regalo

E Cuando Manuel llega, todos **dicen** «¡Sorpresa!» Yo **canto** «Feliz cumpleaños» y mis padres **bailan.**

la fiesta de sorpresa

los invitados

cantar

bailar

Más vocabulario

abrir *to open*	**salir** *to leave, to go out*
buscar *to look for*	**si** *if*
invitar a *to invite (someone)*	**traer** *to bring*
recibir *to receive*	
Expansión de vocabulario p. R2	

¡A responder! Escuchar

Listen to the list of activities. As you listen, act out the activities.

@HomeTutor VideoPlus
Interactive Flashcards
ClassZone.com

Práctica de VOCABULARIO

1 | La fiesta de cumpleaños

Leer

Read the clues that describe a birthday party in order to identify words from the list.

papel de regalo	invitados	globos
regalo	decoraciones	secreto

1. Las usas para decorar la casa.
2. Son las personas en la fiesta.
3. Lo abres si celebras tu cumpleaños.
4. Son decoraciones de colores.
5. Hay una fiesta de sorpresa y no debes decirlo.
6. Lo usas para envolver un regalo.

2 | ¿Qué hay que hacer?

Hablar
Escribir

Look at the photos and identify the chores that must be done.

modelo: Hay que limpiar la cocina.

1.

2.

3.

4.

5.

6.

Más práctica   Cuaderno *pp. 24–26*   Cuaderno para hispanohablantes *pp. 24–27*

PARA Y PIENSA

Did you get it? Name four things you do before having a party at your house.

Get Help Online
ClassZone.com

VOCABULARIO *en contexto*

 Goal: Identify the words Fernando and the Cuevas family use to talk about the preparations they have to do before Manuel's party. Then use what you have learned to talk about your chores and responsibilities. **Actividades 3–4**

♻ *¿Recuerdas?* **tener que** p. 16

Telehistoria escena 1

@**HomeTutor** VideoPlus
View, Read and Record
ClassZone.com

STRATEGIES

VIDEO
DVD

AUDIO

Cuando lees

Consider cultural customs How do Manuel's family and friends prepare for his birthday party? How are teenagers' birthdays usually celebrated in the United States? What are some differences and similarities?

Cuando escuchas

Listen for cognates This scene has several cognates, including **sorpresa.** Listen for them. Which ones do you recognize? How do they help you with understanding?

 Fernando

 Elena

Sr. Cuevas

Sra. Cuevas

The Cuevas family is preparing for a party. Fernando arrives with a gift.

Fernando: ¿Y los regalos? ¿Dónde...?

Sra. Cuevas: En la mesa.

Elena: Fernando, ¿qué regalo traes para Manuel?

Fernando: Un videojuego. Lo acabo de envolver.

Sr. Cuevas: Un videojuego. ¡Qué sorpresa!

Fernando: ¿Puedo ayudar?

Elena: Sí, puedes abrir la puerta a los invitados.

Fernando: Ay, prefiero preparar la comida. ¡Me gusta cocinar!

Sr. Cuevas: Bueno. Puedes ayudar en la cocina.

Guests begin to arrive, and everyone starts to wonder when Manuel is coming.

Sra. Cuevas: ¿Qué hora es? *(to Elena)* ¿Dónde está tu hermano?

Fernando: Acabo de hablar por teléfono con Manuel. Va a venir.

Continuará... p. 80

3 | Preparan una celebración *Comprensión del episodio*

Escuchar
Leer

Choose the correct answer.

1. Los regalos están
   a. en la cocina.
   b. en el comedor.
   c. en la mesa.

2. Fernando acaba de
   a. envolver el regalo.
   b. ayudar en la cocina.
   c. abrir la puerta a
     los invitados.

3. Fernando trae
   a. un DVD para Manuel.
   b. un disco compacto
     para Manuel.
   c. un videojuego para Manuel.

4. Fernando prefiere
   a. abrir la puerta a los invitados.
   b. jugar videojuegos.
   c. preparar la comida.

4 | Las obligaciones en casa ♻ *¿Recuerdas?* **tener que** p. 16

Hablar

Ask a partner whether he or she has to do these chores at home. If not, who has to do them?

A ¿Tienes que barrer el suelo?

B Sí, tengo que barrer el suelo. (No, no tengo que barrer el suelo. Mi padre tiene que hacerlo.)

1.
2.
3.

4.
5.
6.

PARA Y PIENSA

Did you get it? Complete each sentence with the appropriate vocabulary word.
1. Manuel saca _____ antes de ir a la escuela.
2. El señor Cuevas corta _____ los sábados.
3. Fernando necesita pasar _____ porque sus abuelos van a venir.

Get Help Online
ClassZone.com

Presentación de GRAMÁTICA

Goal: Learn the forms of six more irregular verbs. Then practice using these verbs to talk about parties. *Actividades 5–9*

♻ *¿Recuerdas?* Interrogative words p. 20

English Grammar Connection: Just as the English verb *to be* does not follow a pattern in the present tense (*I am, you are, he/she/it is,* etc.), **irregular verbs** in Spanish do not follow the pattern of regular or stem-changing verbs.

More Irregular Verbs

Dar, decir, poner, salir, traer, and **venir** are all irregular. How do you form the present tense of these verbs?

Here's how:

Decir has several irregular forms. Only the **nosotros(as)** and **vosotros(as)** forms are regular.

> **Dicen** que es una fiesta de sorpresa.
> *They say that it is a surprise party.*

decir	*to say, to tell*
digo	decimos
dices	decís
dice	dicen

Venir is similar to **tener,** except that the **nosotros(as)** and **vosotros(as)** forms have **-ir** endings, while **tener** uses **-er** endings.

> ¿De dónde **vienes**?
> *Where **are you coming** from?*

venir	*to come*
vengo	venimos
vienes	venís
viene	vienen

Some verbs are irregular only in the **yo** form of the present tense.

> **Doy** una fiesta.
> *I am giving a party.*

dar	*to give*	doy
poner	*to put, to place*	pongo
salir	*to leave, to go out*	salgo
traer	*to bring*	traigo

Más práctica
🔄 Conjuguemos.com
Cuaderno *pp. 27–29*
Cuaderno para hispanohablantes *pp. 28–30*

@HomeTutor
Leveled Practice
ClassZone.com

Práctica de GRAMÁTICA

5 | ¿Lo haces?

Hablar
Escribir

Tell whether you do the following things at a surprise party.

> **modelo:** salir con amigos antes de la fiesta
> (No) Salgo con amigos antes de la fiesta.

1. poner la mesa con platos bonitos
2. dar diez regalos
3. salir de la fiesta muy temprano
4. venir a la fiesta con amigos
5. traer libros de historia
6. decir «¡Feliz cumpleaños!»

6 | ¡Vamos a celebrar!

Leer
Escribir

Comparación cultural

Fiestas de Quito

How do people show pride for their community? On December 6, *quiteños* celebrate Fiestas de Quito, a festival honoring the anniversary of the founding of Quito, **Ecuador,** in 1534. The weeklong celebration includes many parades, concerts, and dances. Some residents perform *serenatas quiteñas,* musical tributes to their city. Other popular activities are fireworks displays and the Reina de Quito beauty pageant. Many young people build and decorate wooden cars to race in competitions for their age level.

Preparan los carritos de madera (wooden cars) para las fiestas.

Compara con tu mundo *Is there an event that celebrates your area or region? If so, what is it like?*

Manuel and Fernando are talking on the phone. Complete their conversation with the correct form of the appropriate verb.

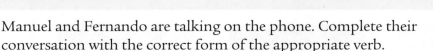

| dar | decir | salir | traer | poner | venir |

Manuel: ¿Cuándo __1.__ tú a mi casa? Tenemos que decorar los carritos para las Fiestas de Quito.

Fernando: Yo __2.__ de aquí en quince minutos y llego en media hora.

Manuel: Elena __3.__ que la carrera (*race*) empieza a las dos.

Fernando: Hay un desfile (*parade*) después. ¿Vas a traer tu guitarra?

Manuel: Sí, yo la __4.__ . Quiero tocar una serenata quiteña.

Fernando: ¡Y yo voy a cantar! ¿Qué hacemos después del desfile?

Manuel: Elena y yo __5.__ una fiesta en casa. Ahora ella prepara la ensalada y yo __6.__ la mesa.

Fernando: Bueno, llego en media hora. ¡Hasta luego!

7 | ¿A qué hora vienen?

The Cuevas family is expecting many visitors this Sunday. Use the verbs **decir** and **venir** to give the time in the morning or the afternoon people say they are coming to visit.

> **modelo:** Gilda / 6:00
> Gilda dice que viene a las seis de la tarde.

1. Sebastián y Leti / 10:30
2. nosotros / 3:15
3. el tío de Manuel / 4:00
4. yo / 1:45
5. los primos de Manuel / 11:15
6. Fernando / 11:40
7. los abuelos de Manuel / 9:30
8. tú / 5:45
9. la tía de Manuel / 5:00
10. ustedes / 1:30

8 | Una fiesta en la clase

Hablar

There's a party in your Spanish class. Ask a partner whether he or she is bringing these things to the party, and why or why not.

A ¿Traes DVDs a la fiesta?

B Sí, traigo DVDs porque quiero ver películas. (No, no traigo DVDs porque no quiero ver películas.)

1.

2.

3.

4.

5.

6.

9 | Hay que preparar ♻ ¿Recuerdas? Interrogative words p. 20

Hablar

A friend of yours is helping organize a birthday party. Ask a partner about the party preparations.

modelo: ¿cuándo? / dar la fiesta

A ¿Cuándo das la fiesta?

B Doy la fiesta el sábado.

1. ¿cuántos(as)? / venir a la fiesta
2. ¿qué? / traer a la fiesta
3. ¿dónde? / poner las decoraciones
4. ¿qué? / servir para comer y beber

5. ¿por qué? / dar la fiesta
6. ¿qué? / cantar los invitados
7. ¿qué? / decir los invitados
8. ¿cuándo? / salir los invitados

AUDIO

Pronunciación   Las letras b y v

In Spanish, the **b** and **v** are pronounced almost the same. As the first letter of a word, at the beginning of a sentence, or after the letters **m** and **n**, **b** and **v** are pronounced like the hard *b* in the English word *boy*.

Soy **B**árbara. **B**ailo la cum**b**ia en Colom**b**ia.

In the middle of a word, **b** and **v** have a softer sound, made by keeping the lips slightly apart.

Listen and repeat.

basura	**v**enir	alfom**b**ra	in**v**itar
de**b**er	toda**v**ía	glo**b**o	aca**b**ar

Bárbara **b**aila la cum**b**ia en Colom**b**ia.
De**b**es su**b**ir al octavo piso.

Más práctica   Cuaderno *pp. 27–29*   Cuaderno para hispanohablantes *pp. 28–30*

PARA Y PIENSA

Did you get it? Complete each sentence with the correct form of one of the irregular verbs you just learned.
1. Yo _____ la mesa porque los invitados van a llegar.
2. Isabel _____ que el pastel es muy rico.
3. Yo _____ los regalos a la fiesta.

⤷ **Get Help Online** ClassZone.com

GRAMÁTICA *en contexto*

¡AVANZA!

Goal: Pay attention to the irregular verbs that Manuel, his family, and his friends use to talk about what to do at his party. Then use them to talk about what you and others do at parties. *Actividades 10–12*

 ¿Recuerdas? Expressions of frequency p. 13

Telehistoria escena 2

@HomeTutor VideoPlus
View, Read and Record
ClassZone.com

STRATEGIES

Cuando lees
Predict based on visuals Predict what might happen, based on the photos. Does Manuel get the T-shirt signed? Was Manuel surprised, or did he know about the party?

Cuando escuchas
Consider two kinds of language Notice feelings based on both spoken language and body language, such as facial expressions, posture, and gestures. How does Manuel feel about Fernando's present? How do you know?

VIDEO
DVD

AUDIO

Manuel

Manuel arrives home with Alicia's T-shirt, admiring the autograph.

Manuel: ¡El autógrafo de Trini Salgado!

Elena: *(in the backyard)* ¡Allí viene Manuel!

Manuel enters the yard.

Todos: ¡Sorpresa!

Sra. Cuevas: ¡Feliz cumpleaños, hijo!

Elena: ¡Aquí viene el pastel!

Manuel blows out the candles while people clap.

Manuel: Y, ¿qué hago ahora?

Fernando: ¡Abrir los regalos! Yo los traigo.

Manuel: *(opening a gift)* ¡Qué sorpresa! ¡Un videojuego! No lo tengo. Muchas gracias, Fernando.

Fernando: Hmmm... Y, ¿qué hacemos ahora?

Sr. Cuevas: ¡A bailar todos! **Continuará...** p. 86

También se dice

Ecuador When serving the cake, Elena uses the word **el pastel**. In other Spanish-speaking countries you might hear:
• **España la tarta**
• **Puerto Rico el bizcocho**
• **muchos países el queque, la torta**

10 | Muchas sorpresas *Comprensión del episodio*

Escuchar
Leer

Answer the questions about the episode.

1. ¿Quiénes dan la fiesta?
2. ¿Quién viene?
3. ¿Quién trae los regalos?
4. ¿Quiénes dicen «¡Sorpresa!»?
5. ¿Qué recibe Manuel de Fernando?
6. ¿Qué quiere hacer el señor Cuevas?

11 | ¿Con qué frecuencia? ♻ *¿Recuerdas?* Expressions of frequency p. 13

Hablar

Talk with classmates about how often you do the following activities.

A ¿Con qué frecuencia sales con amigos?

B Salgo con amigos de vez en cuando.

C Nunca salgo con amigos.

1.
2.
3.

4.
5.
6.

12 | ¿Y tú?

Escribir

Answer the questions in complete sentences.

1. ¿Das muchas fiestas? ¿A quién(es) invitas?
2. ¿Quién pone la mesa en tu casa?
3. ¿Qué traes a tus clases?
4. ¿A qué hora sales de la casa en la mañana?
5. ¿A qué hora vienes a la escuela?
6. ¿Qué dices cuando recibes un regalo?

PARA Y PIENSA

Did you get it? Complete each sentence based on the Telehistoria with the correct form of **venir, traer,** or **decir.**

1. Elena _____ que Manuel _____ a la fiesta.
2. Fernando _____ un regalo.

Get Help Online ClassZone.com

Presentación de GRAMÁTICA

 Goal: Learn how to give affirmative **tú** commands and use **acabar de** + infinitive. Then tell someone what to do and say what you just did. **Actividades 13–18**

♻ *¿Recuerdas?* Direct object pronouns p. 32

English Grammar Connection: In both English and Spanish, **affirmative commands** are used to tell someone to do something.

Clean the kitchen!   ¡**Limpia** la cocina!

[**command**]   [**command**]

Affirmative tú Commands

Animated Grammar
ClassZone.com

Use **affirmative tú commands** with a friend or a family member.

Here's how:

Regular **affirmative tú commands** are the same as the **él/ella** forms in the present tense.

Infinitive	Present Tense	Affirmative tú Command
lavar	(él, ella) **lava**	¡**Lava** los platos!
barrer	(él, ella) **barre**	¡**Barre** el suelo!
abrir	(él, ella) **abre**	¡**Abre** la puerta!

Some verbs you know have irregular **affirmative tú commands**.

Infinitive	decir	hacer	ir	poner	salir	ser	tener	venir
Affirmative tú Command	di	haz	ve	pon	sal	sé	ten	ven

If you use an **affirmative command** with a **direct object pronoun,** attach the pronoun to the end. Add an accent when you attach a pronoun to a command of two or more syllables to retain the original stress (see p. 56).

¡**Cierra** la ventana!   *becomes* → ¡**Ciérrala**!
Close the window!   **Close** it!

¡**Pon** la mesa ahora!   *becomes* → ¡**Ponla** ahora!
Set the table now!   **Set** it now!

Más práctica   🐾 **Conjuguemos.com**
   Cuaderno *pp. 30–32*
   Cuaderno para hispanohablantes *pp. 31–34*

@HomeTutor
Leveled Practice
ClassZone.com

Práctica de GRAMÁTICA

13 | ¿Quién tiene que hacerlo?

Escribir

Manuel is always telling Elena what to do. Use commands to write what he says to her.

modelo: limpiar la cocina
   Limpia la cocina, por favor.

1. lavar los platos
2. planchar la ropa
3. venir a casa
4. barrer el suelo
5. salir temprano
6. hacer la cama

7. cortar el césped
8. ser buena
9. sacar la basura
10. traer el pastel
11. ir a la tienda
12. poner la mesa

14 | ¿Debo hacerlo? ♻ ¿Recuerdas? Direct object pronouns p. 32

Hablar

You and a partner are planning a birthday party. Ask him or her what you should do. Follow the model.

modelo: comprar el papel de regalo

 A ¿Debo comprar el papel de regalo?

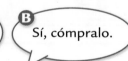 B Sí, cómpralo.

1. traer las bebidas
2. preparar la comida
3. buscar los globos
4. poner las decoraciones
5. limpiar la cocina

6. envolver los regalos
7. abrir la puerta a los invitados
8. servir el pastel
9. pasar la aspiradora
10. sacar la basura

15 | Una casa sucia

Escuchar

Elena's mother needs help cleaning their house. Listen to the situations and write the mother's commands to Elena.

16 | ¡Qué desastre!

Clara has guests coming for dinner tomorrow, but her house is a mess! Look at the drawing and give as many commands as you can to tell her what she needs to do.

modelo: Saca la basura.

Nota gramatical

When you want to say that something has just happened, use the verb phrase **acabar de + infinitive.**

Acabamos de **comprar** el pastel para la fiesta. *We just bought the cake for the party.*

Acaban de **cortar** el césped. *They just cut the grass.*

---

17 | ¿Ayudas?

Hablar

There's a long list of chores. Tell a partner what to do. Your partner will tell you that he or she just did it.

A Limpia la cocina.

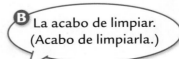
B La acabo de limpiar. (Acabo de limpiarla.)

18 | Problemas y soluciones

Hablar
Escribir

Give commands to help each person resolve his or her problem.

> modelo: Tengo hambre.
> Come un sándwich.

1. Estoy muy cansada.
2. Quiero sacar buenas notas.
3. Siempre llego tarde.
4. Tengo sed.
5. Quiero ver una película.
6. Mis padres tienen muchos quehaceres.
7. Mañana es el cumpleaños de mi amigo.
8. Mis amigos vienen a mi casa para la cena.
9. Necesito ir al centro.
10. Quiero dar una fiesta.

Comparación cultural

Los textiles de Otavalo

Why are traditional crafts important to a culture? Many tourists visit the town of Otavalo for its Saturday market to find woven sweaters, rugs, and other items. The Otavalos, an indigenous group from **Ecuador,** have practiced weaving for centuries and are famous worldwide for their textiles. Common designs include landscapes, animals, and geometric patterns. The Otavalos take pride in their heritage and have achieved economic success selling their work both locally and internationally.

Textiles en el mercado de Otavalo

Compara con tu mundo *What are some traditional U.S. crafts? Do you know anyone who makes or collects these crafts?*

Más práctica   Cuaderno *pp. 30–32*   Cuaderno para hispanohablantes *pp. 31–34*

PARA
Y
PIENSA

Did you get it? Give the affirmative **tú** command of each verb. Then say you just did it.
1. decorar la sala   2. hacer los quehaceres   3. cortar el césped

Get Help Online
ClassZone.com

Todo junto

¡AVANZA!

Goal: Show what you know Identify the affirmative **tú** commands and irregular verbs the Cuevas family uses in their discussion of after-party chores. Then say what chores need to be done, using irregular verbs and commands. *Actividades 19–23*

Telehistoria completa

@HomeTutor VideoPlus
View, Read and Record
ClassZone.com

STRATEGIES

Cuando lees
Find the key event A key event at the end of this scene causes big trouble. What is this event? Why is it important? What hints do you find earlier in the scene?

Cuando escuchas
Listen for commands What are the family members doing? Why wasn't the catastrophe at the end prevented?

Escena 1 *Resumen*
Fernando trae un regalo a la fiesta de sorpresa para Manuel y quiere ayudar a la familia. Manuel todavía no está en casa.

Escena 2 *Resumen*
Manuel llega a la fiesta con el autógrafo de Trini Salgado. Hay pastel, y él abre los regalos de los invitados.

VIDEO DVD

AUDIO

Escena 3

After the party, the family begins to clean up.

Sra. Cuevas: *(to Elena)* Pon los platos sucios allí.

Sr. Cuevas: Elena, barre el suelo, saca la basura y yo lavo la ropa.

Elena: ¿Y Manuel? ¿Por qué no ayuda?

Sra. Cuevas: Acaba de celebrar su cumpleaños. Hoy no tiene que limpiar.

Elena: *(to Manuel)* ¿Vienes a ayudar? Toma. *(She tries to hand him the broom.)*

Manuel: ¡Elena! Ahora, ¡no! Tengo que buscar la camiseta de Alicia. ¿Dónde está? ¿Mamá...?

Manuel and Elena go into the laundry room and find their father.

Elena: La camiseta de Alicia... ¿Dónde está?

Sr. Cuevas: ¡Ahh! ¡Acabo de lavarla!

19 | No es cierto *Comprensión de los episodios*

Escuchar
Leer

All of these sentences are false. Correct them to make them true.

1. El padre de Manuel dice que quiere cantar en la fiesta.
2. Fernando abre la puerta a los invitados.
3. La madre de Elena lava la ropa.
4. Manuel tiene que ayudar.
5. Los padres de Manuel tienen la camiseta de Alicia.
6. El padre de Manuel acaba de planchar la camiseta.

20 | ¡A buscar! *Comprensión de los episodios*

Escuchar
Leer

Look for the following in the episodes. Write down the information on a piece of paper.

> **modelo:** un quehacer que Fernando hace
> Fernando ayuda en la cocina.

1. un regalo que Manuel recibe
2. un quehacer que Fernando no quiere hacer
3. dos cosas que hacen con la camiseta
4. dos actividades que hacen en la fiesta
5. dos quehaceres que Elena tiene que hacer
6. un quehacer que el señor Cuevas hace

21 | ¡Qué organizados!

Hablar

STRATEGY Hablar

Combine imagination with organization Think creatively while organizing. To do this, consider questions like these: Is the party for a special occasion? Will it be inside or outside? When will it be? How many guests will there be? Is there a theme for party activities, decorations, and food?

Work in a group to plan a party. Talk about the food, the decorations, and chores. Tell another student to do something. He or she will tell you that it's just been done.

A Ve a la tienda para comprar un pastel.

B Acabo de ir a la tienda. Ya tengo el pastel. Pon la mesa.

C Acabo de poner la mesa. Barre el suelo.

22 | Integración

Leer
Escuchar
Hablar

You and a friend are appearing on a TV show, **¡Limpia ya!** Listen to the message to learn your mission, and look at the floor plan of the house. Then explain which rooms you are cleaning and what chores you are doing, and tell your friend what to do.

Fuente 1 Los planos de la casa

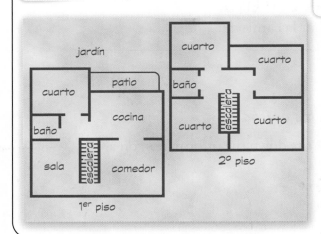

Fuente 2 Instrucciones para la misión

Listen and take notes
- ¿Qué quehaceres tienen que hacer?
- ¿Dónde tienen que hacerlos?

modelo: Yo subo al segundo piso y... Roberto, sal al jardín y...

23 | Una casa bonita y limpia

Escribir

You want to surprise your family by cleaning the house. Write a note to your brother or sister, who's not at home, asking for help. Tell him or her what to do and what you just did.

modelo: ¡Queremos una casa limpia! En el baño, acabo de sacar la basura. Barre el suelo, por favor. En la sala...

Writing Criteria	Excellent	Good	Needs Work
Content	Your note includes a lot of information.	Your note includes some information.	Your note includes little information.
Communication	Most of your note is organized and easy to follow.	Parts of your note are organized and easy to follow.	Your note is disorganized and hard to follow.
Accuracy	Your note has few mistakes in grammar and vocabulary.	Your note has some mistakes in grammar and vocabulary.	Your note has many mistakes in grammar and vocabulary.

Más práctica Cuaderno *pp. 33–34* Cuaderno para hispanohablantes *pp. 35–36*

PARA Y PIENSA

Did you get it? Give Elena three more commands for chores to do around the house.

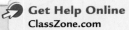
Get Help Online
ClassZone.com

Juegos y diversiones

Review vocabulary by playing a game.

The Setup

Your teacher will write lesson vocabulary words or phrases on index cards and put the cards in a pile. Form two teams.

Playing the Game

A player on Team A will pick a card from the pile and then act out the word or phrase on the card. Team A has 30 seconds to guess what the Spanish word or phrase is. Your teacher will be the timekeeper. Each correct guess gains the team a point.

If Team A can't guess the word in time, then Team B will get a chance to guess. If Team B guesses correctly, it gets two points.

Teams will take turns acting out words.

The Winner!

The team that has the most points at the end wins.

Materials

• index cards with vocabulary words
• timer

Lectura cultural

¡AVANZA! **Goal:** Read about two traditional dances of Ecuador and Panama. Then compare the two dances and talk about when you go dancing.

Comparación cultural

AUDIO

Bailes folklóricos de Ecuador y Panamá

STRATEGY Leer
Draw key aspects Draw pictures of the **sanjuanito** and the **tamborito**. Label key aspects of your drawings. Then add more details by writing captions describing each dance.

Los bailes folklóricos de Latinoamérica representan una combinación de culturas. Ayudan a formar una identidad nacional y continuar las tradiciones de las personas que viven allí. A muchas personas de Ecuador y Panamá les gusta bailar cuando celebran fiestas.

Hay muchos bailes de influencia indígena[1] en Ecuador. Uno de los bailes más populares se llama el sanjuanito. El sanjuanito tiene un ritmo alegre[2] y es una buena representación de la fusión de culturas indígenas y españolas.

Para bailar, chicos y chicas forman un círculo y muchas veces bailan con pañuelos[3] en las manos[4]. Es posible ver el baile del sanjuanito todo el año en celebraciones en casa, pero es más común durante el festival de San Juan en junio.

---

[1] indigenous [2] **ritmo...** upbeat rhythm
[3] scarves [4] hands

Ecuador

Un baile tradicional en Mitad del Mundo, Ecuador

Un baile folklórico, Ciudad de Panamá

En Panamá, es muy popular bailar salsa en fiestas o discotecas⁵, pero el baile nacional es el tamborito. El tamborito usa ritmos de influencia africana, pero también tiene orígenes indígenas y españoles.

Las personas bailan con el sonido⁶ de palmadas⁷ y tambores⁸ africanos. El tamborito es popular durante fiestas grandes y celebraciones regionales, como Carnaval. Para bailar en los festivales, las chicas llevan polleras (los vestidos tradicionales de Panamá) y los chicos llevan el dominguero (pantalones negros con una camisa blanca).

---

⁵ nightclubs   ⁶ sound   ⁷ handclaps   ⁸ drums

PARA Y PIENSA

¿Comprendiste?

1. ¿Qué influencias culturales forman el baile del sanjuanito? ¿Y el tamborito?
2. ¿Qué artículos de ropa usan para bailar en Ecuador? ¿Y en Panamá?
3. ¿En qué tipo de fiestas bailan el sanjuanito y el tamborito?

¿Y tú?

¿Te gusta bailar en fiestas? ¿Sales para bailar o bailas en casa? ¿Qué ropa llevas cuando bailas? Si no bailas, ¿quieres aprender?

Proyectos culturales

Arte textil de Ecuador y Panamá

How do different cultures express themselves through crafts?
Indigenous Otavalans are famous for the beautiful woolen textiles sold in a weekly market in Otavalo, **Ecuador.** In the San Blas Islands of **Panama,** women from the Kuna culture design and produce **molas,** which are pieces of fabric art that are traditionally sewn onto women's blouses. The crafts from both the Otavalan and the Kuna cultures are colorful, unique creations that have become representative of the people that make them.

Proyecto 1 *Tapestry design*

Ecuador Otavalan tapestries often use a design of geometric shapes and can depict people, objects of everyday life, and scenes of nature. Create a tapestry design in the Otavalan style.

Materials for making a tapestry design
Construction paper
Colored pens and
   pencils

Instructions
Think about the variety of objects the Otavalans weave. Then draw your own design using construction paper and colored pens or pencils.

Proyecto 2 *Las molas*

Panamá The Kuna women make **molas** out of several layers of colorful fabric. Make a **mola** out of paper.

Materials for making a mola
Construction paper
   (3 colors)
Piece of plain paper
Scissors
Glue

Instructions
1. Cut out a shape on plain paper to use as the pattern for your **mola.**
2. Trace the pattern onto a sheet of construction paper. Cut out the shape and set aside the sheet of paper.
3. Use scissors to trim your original pattern to make it smaller. Repeat step two on a second piece of construction paper.
4. Layer the two pieces of construction paper into a third one so that all the colors are visible.

En tu comunidad

Where can local artists in your community sell their work? What advantages would an artist have who is able to communicate with potential customers in Spanish?

Vocabulario

Plan a Party

bailar	to dance
cantar	to sing
celebrar	to celebrate
dar una fiesta	to give a party
las decor nes	decorations
decorar	to decorate
la fiesta de sorpresa	surprise party

el globo	balloon
los invitados	guests
invitar a	to invite (someone)
salir	to leave, to go out
el secreto	secret
venir	to come

Talk About Gifts

abrir	to open
buscar	to look for
envolver (ue)	to wrap
el papel de regalo	wrapping paper
recibir	to receive
el regalo	gift
traer	to bring

Talk About Chores and Responsibilities

acabar de...	to have just . . .
ayudar	to help
barrer el suelo	to sweep the floor
cocinar	to cook
cortar el césped	to cut the grass
darle de comer al perro	to feed the dog
deber	should, ought to
hacer la cama	to make the bed
lavar los platos	to wash the dishes

limpiar (la cocina)	to clean the kitchen
limpio(a)	clean
pasar la aspiradora	to vacuum
planchar la ropa	to iron
poner la mesa	to set the table
los quehaceres	chores
sacar la basura	to take out the trash
sucio(a)	dirty

Other Words and Phrases

decir	to say, to tell
hay que	one has to, one must
poner	to put, to place
si	if
todavía	still; yet

Gramática

Nota gramatical: acabar de + infinitive *p. 84*

More Irregular Verbs

Dar, decir, poner, salir, traer, and **venir** are all irregular.

decir *to say, to tell*	
digo	decimos
dices	decís
dice	dicen

venir *to come*	
vengo	venimos
vienes	venís
viene	vienen

Some verbs are irregular only in the **yo** form of the present tense.

dar	poner	salir	traer
doy	pongo	salgo	traigo

Affirmative tú Commands

Regular **affirmative tú commands** are the same as the **él/ella** forms in the present tense.

Infinitive	Present Tense	Affirmative tú Command
lavar	(él, ella) **lava**	¡Lava los platos!
barrer	(él, ella) **barre**	¡Barre el suelo!
abrir	(él, ella) **abre**	¡Abre la puerta!

There are irregular **affirmative tú commands.**

decir	hacer	ir	poner	salir	ser	tener	venir
di	haz	ve	pon	sal	sé	ten	ven

¡LLEGADA!

@HomeTutor
ClassZone.com

Now you can
- plan a party
- talk about chores and responsibilities
- tell someone what to do
- say what you just did

Using
- more irregular verbs
- affirmative **tú** commands
- **acabar de** + infinitive

To review
- more irregular verbs p. 76
- affirmative **tú** commands p. 82
- **acabar de** + infinitive p. 84

1 | Listen and understand

AUDIO

Señor Robles and his students are talking about a party. Listen to the conversation. Then match each person with the appropriate sentence.

1. La fiesta es para ella.
2. No deben hablar de la fiesta.
3. Va a traer los globos.
4. Va a ayudar a limpiar.
5. Va a poner las decoraciones.
6. Va a traer pizza.

a. Andrés
b. Carla
c. Samuel
d. el señor Robles
e. la directora
f. los estudiantes

To review
- more irregular verbs p.76

2 | Plan a party

Natalia is giving a party for her brother and is talking with a friend, Catalina. Complete their instant messages with the correct form of the appropriate verb.

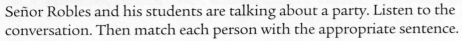

dar   poner   decir   traer   salir   venir

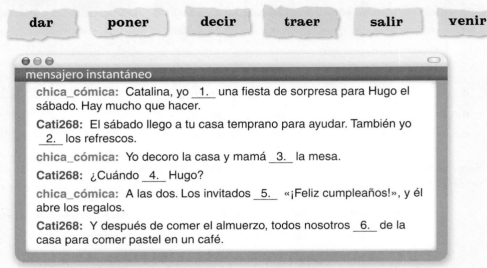

mensajero instantáneo

chica_cómica: Catalina, yo __1.__ una fiesta de sorpresa para Hugo el sábado. Hay mucho que hacer.

Cati268: El sábado llego a tu casa temprano para ayudar. También yo __2.__ los refrescos.

chica_cómica: Yo decoro la casa y mamá __3.__ la mesa.

Cati268: ¿Cuándo __4.__ Hugo?

chica_cómica: A las dos. Los invitados __5.__ «¡Feliz cumpleaños!», y él abre los regalos.

Cati268: Y después de comer el almuerzo, todos nosotros __6.__ de la casa para comer pastel en un café.

To review
- affirmative **tú** commands p. 82

3 | Tell someone what to do

Alfredo is very lazy. Use commands to write what he tells his sister to do.

> **modelo:** venir a mi cuarto
> Ven a mi cuarto.

1. traer mi mochila
2. buscar mi libro de ciencias
3. envolver el regalo para mamá

4. ponerlo en el escritorio
5. ir a la tienda
6. hacer todos mis quehaceres

To review
- **acabar de** + infinitive p. 84

4 | Talk about chores and responsibilities

Write what Fernando and others have just done.

> **modelo:** Elena
> Elena acaba de barrer el suelo.

1. mamá

2. yo

3. papá

4. ellos

5. Elena

6. Elena y yo

To review
- **las montañas** p. 39
- Comparación cultural pp. 77, 85
- Lectura cultural pp. 90–91

5 | Ecuador and Panama

Comparación cultural

Answer these culture questions.

1. What is the world's highest active volcano? Where is it located?
2. What is celebrated during **Fiestas de Quito**? How?
3. Who are the Otavalos and what are they known for?
4. How do you dance **el sanjuanito**? What instruments are used in **el tamborito**? Where are these dances popular?

Más práctica Cuaderno *pp. 35–46* Cuaderno para hispanohablantes *pp. 37–46*

Get Help Online
ClassZone.com

Panamá — Argentina
Ecuador

AUDIO

¡Así celebramos!

Lectura y escritura

WebQuest
ClassZone.com

1 **Leer** Party celebrations vary around the world. Read how María Elena, Carla, and Daniel enjoy parties and celebrations.

2 **Escribir** Using the three descriptions as models, write a short paragraph about a celebration of your own.

STRATEGY **Escribir**

Use a chart To write about a celebration, complete a chart like the one shown.

tipo de fiesta			
lugar	invitados	comida	actividades

Step 1 Complete the chart with details about the type of celebration, location, guests, food, and activities.

Step 2 Write your paragraph. Make sure to include all the information from the chart. Check your writing by yourself or with help from a friend. Make final corrections.

Compara con tu mundo

Use the paragraph you wrote to compare your celebration to a celebration described by *one* of the three students. What is similar? What is different?

Cuaderno *pp. 47–49*   Cuaderno para hispanohablantes *pp. 47–49*

Panamá

María Elena

¡Saludos desde Panamá! Me llamo María Elena. Mi familia y yo acabamos de decorar la casa para celebrar la Navidad[1]. El 24 de diciembre es muy importante en Panamá. Las familias comen la cena tarde y a las doce de la noche abren los regalos. Mis hermanos y yo siempre decoramos el árbol de Navidad[2]. También me gusta envolver regalos con papel. Quiero dar y recibir muchos regalos este año.

[1] Christmas [2] **árbol...** Christmas tree

Argentina

Carla

¡Hola! Me llamo Carla y vivo en el norte de Argentina. Todos los años celebramos un gran festival. En el festival podemos ver a los gauchos[3] con sus caballos[4], escuchar música típica y comer comida rica. Siempre llevo un vestido bonito para participar en los bailes típicos con otros chicos y chicas.

[3] Argentinean cowboys [4] horses

Ecuador

Daniel

¡Hola! Me llamo Daniel y vivo en Cuenca, Ecuador. Para la fiesta del año nuevo, muchas personas hacen figuras grandes de papel maché. Las figuras son de muchos colores y muchas veces son muy cómicas. La noche del 31 de diciembre mis padres dan una fiesta. Invitan a muchas personas. Limpiamos toda la casa, ponemos la mesa y compartimos una cena rica con nuestra familia y los otros invitados.

Repaso inclusivo
♻ Options for Review

¡AvanzaRap!
DVD
Sing and Learn

1 | Listen, understand, and compare

Escuchar

Gabriela is giving a surprise party. Listen to her phone message. Then answer the following questions.

1. ¿Qué acaba de hacer Gabriela?
2. ¿Qué sirve Gabriela?
3. ¿Qué traes tú a la fiesta?
4. ¿Dónde vive la señora Domínguez? ¿Y Jorge y Marlene?
5. ¿Qué tiene la señora Domínguez? ¿Y Jorge y Marlene?
6. ¿Qué debes hacer si los invitados llegan temprano?

Have you ever given or gone to a surprise party? How did others help prepare for the party?

2 | Give orders

Hablar

You have designed a personal robot to perform your everyday tasks for you. Your friend asks if he or she can borrow your robot for a day, but your robot only listens to you. Your friend tells you what his or her schedule is and what has to be done, and you give the commands to your robot.

Tengo que sacar la basura.

Hal, saca la basura.

3 | Plan a surprise party

Hablar

Work in a group of four to plan a surprise party for a close friend or family member. Each member of your group should take on a role: food coordinator, invitation designer, guest list creator, and activities organizer. Present your party plans to the class.

4 | Have a yard sale

Escribir

You want to earn some extra money by holding a yard sale. Make a flier to advertise what you are selling: books, personal items, clothing, and furniture. Include information such as the date, time, and location of the sale. Copy this chart on a piece of paper and use it to organize your information.

Cosas	Información

5 | Design a family home

Hablar
Escribir

Your partner has contracted you to design a floor plan for a house that will fit his or her family's personalities and lifestyles. Interview your partner to find out what his or her family is like and what they like to do. Also find out what they like and dislike about where they live now. Take notes and use the information to write a proposal. Present it to your partner.

6 | Prepare a dinner

Leer
Escribir

Your family has invited your Spanish teacher home for dinner tonight. Your parents left you this note telling you to do some dinner preparations. Read the note and write another note saying that you have just done certain tasks and make excuses as to why you can't do the other items.

Necesitamos ir a trabajar y no podemos
preparar todo. Por favor:

haz la tarea temprano
ve a la tienda para comprar el postre
prepara la ensalada
cocina el pollo y las patatas
limpia la cocina
lava los platos
saca la basura
pon la mesa

Hablamos más tarde. ¡Gracias!

6

República Dominicana

Mantener un cuerpo sano

Océano
Atlántico

Lección 1

Tema: **¿Cuál es tu deporte favorito?**

República Dominicana

Puerto Rico

Golfo de México

Cuba

Lección 2

Tema: **La salud**

México

Mar Caribe

Honduras

Nicaragua

Guatemala

Costa
Rica

«¡Hola!

Somos Mario e Isabel.
Somos de la República Dominicana.»

El Salvador

Panamá

Venezuela

Colombia

Océano Atlántico

Haití República
Dominicana   Punta
Santo   Cana
Domingo Juan
Dolio

Mar Caribe

Población: 9.507.133

Área: 18.815 millas cuadradas;
comparte la isla de La Española
con Haití

Capital: Santo Domingo

Moneda: el peso dominicano

Idioma: español

Comida típica: mangú, cazabe, la bandera

Gente famosa: Julia Álvarez (escritora), Juan Luis
Guerra (cantante), Pedro Martínez (beisbolista),
Oscar de la Renta (diseñador)

Frutas tropicales

Una familia de pescadores en una playa de Pedernales

◀ **La importancia del Mar Caribe** The white sand beaches of the Dominican Republic are popular with Dominican and international tourists. The clear blue waters and coral reefs are ideal for snorkeling and diving. *What can tourists enjoy in your area?*

El deporte nacional Baseball is considered the Dominican Republic's national sport. It can be played throughout the year because of the country's warm climate, and fans can see professional games from October through February. *What sports are popular where you live?* ▶

Juegan al deporte nacional en Santo Domingo

El Altar de la Patria en la capital

◀ **Un monumento de la Independencia** Santo Domingo's **Altar de la Patria** (Altar of the Nation) is a memorial dedicated to the heroes of the Dominican Republic's fight for freedom from Haiti in 1844. The monument's walkway contains a 32-point nautical star, considered kilometer one, from which all distances within the country are measured. *How are heroes honored in your country's capital?*

República Dominicana

1

Tema:

¿Cuál es tu deporte favorito?

¡AVANZA! **In this lesson you will learn to**

- talk about sports
- talk about whom you know
- talk about what you know

using

- the verb **jugar**
- the verbs **saber** and **conocer**
- the personal **a**

♻ *¿Recuerdas?*

- numbers from 200 to 1,000,000
- **gustar** with nouns
- comparatives

Comparación cultural

In this lesson you will learn about
- Caribbean baseball championships
- Dominican artist Juan Medina
- sports clubs in Santo Domingo

Compara con tu mundo
Baseball has been a popular pastime in the Dominican Republic since the late 1800s, especially in the southeast of the country. Most Dominican players in the U.S. major leagues come from this region. *Do you like to play or watch sports with your friends? Which is your favorite?*

¿Qué ves?

Mira la foto

¿Practican un deporte estas personas?

¿Son atléticas o perezosas?

¿Cuántas personas llevan camisetas rojas?

Un partido en la escuela
Santo Domingo, República Dominicana

Presentación de VOCABULARIO

Goal: Learn what sports Mario and Isabel like to play. Then use what you have learned to talk about sports. *Actividades 1–2*

¿*Recuerdas?* Numbers from 200 to 1,000,000 p. 21

VIDEO
DVD

AUDIO

A ¡Hola! Me llamo Mario. Soy **atleta** y mi deporte **favorito** es **el béisbol.** Hoy tenemos **un partido** con **el equipo** rojo.

el jugador

el guante

el casco

la pelota

los aficionados

el béisbol

el equipo

el campo

la jugadora

el bate

Más vocabulario

el estadio *stadium*

patinar *to skate*

Expansión de vocabulario p. R3

En la República Dominicana se dice...
In the Dominican Republic the word for *baseball game* is **el juego de pelota.**

B Acabamos de **perder** el partido, cuatro a cinco. Mi amiga Isabel y su equipo son **los ganadores.** Tal vez debo practicar otro deporte.

4 equipo azul

perder

ganar

5 equipo rojo

los campeones

C Me gusta **nadar,** pero **la piscina** está lejos de mi casa. **El voleibol** es divertido, pero prefiero el béisbol.

la natación

la piscina

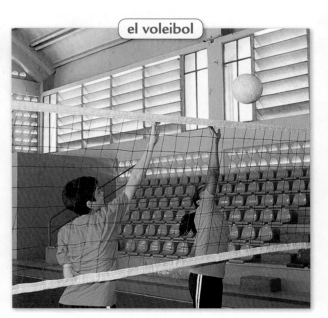

el voleibol

Continuará...

Presentación de VOCABULARIO
(continuación)

D De vez en cuando voy al **campo** para jugar al **fútbol americano,** pero es difícil **comprender las reglas.** Me gusta **el básquetbol,** pero nunca **gano.** También voy a **la cancha** de **tenis,** pero siempre hay muchas personas allí. Puedo **patinar en línea,** pero es **peligroso.** ¡Es mejor jugar al béisbol!

el fútbol americano

el básquetbol

la cancha

el tenis

la raqueta

patinar en línea

los patines en línea

¡A responder! Escuchar

Listen to the list of words associated with sports. When you hear a word associated with baseball, raise your hand.

@HomeTutor VideoPlus
Interactive Flashcards
ClassZone.com

Unidad 6 República Dominicana

Práctica de VOCABULARIO

1 | ¿Qué necesitan?

Leer | Isabel is describing the sports-related items that her friends have and/or the sports they want to play. Choose the item that each person needs.

1. Ya tiene una pelota y quiere jugar al tenis.
2. Ya tiene una pelota y un guante y quiere jugar al béisbol.
3. Tiene un casco y quiere patinar en línea.
4. Ya tiene una pelota y va a jugar al fútbol americano.
5. Quiere nadar.
6. Está en la cancha y quiere jugar al básquetbol.

casco

piscina

patines en línea

bate

pelota

raqueta

2 | La tienda de deportes ♻ *¿Recuerdas?* Numbers 200 to 1,000,000 p. 21

Hablar Escribir | The store Mundo de Deportes in Santo Domingo sells many sporting goods. Tell how much these items cost at the store.

RD$3,730

modelo: Un bate cuesta tres mil setecientos treinta pesos.

¡Atención, atletas!
En nuestra tienda, tenemos los precios más bajos.

RD$3,200

3 por RD$180

RD$2,620

RD$2,300

RD$5,475

MUNDO DE DEPORTES
Avenida 27 de febrero, 104
Santo Domingo, República Dominicana
809-555-5707

RD$435

Más práctica Cuaderno *pp. 50–52* Cuaderno para hispanohablantes *pp. 50–53*

PARA Y PIENSA

Did you get it? Say what you would need to play the following sports.
1. el básquetbol   2. el béisbol   3. el tenis

Get Help Online ClassZone.com

VOCABULARIO *en contexto*

Goal: Identify the words Isabel and Mario use to talk about sports. Then practice what you have learned to talk about sports. *Actividades 3–4*

♻ *¿Recuerdas?* **gustar** with nouns p. 8

Telehistoria escena 1

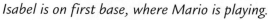

@HomeTutor VideoPlus
View, Read and Record
ClassZone.com

STRATEGIES

Cuando lees

Brainstorm before reading

Brainstorm English words for equipment used in baseball, swimming, in-line skating, tennis, football, and other sports. Which items on your list are in the Telehistoria?

Cuando escuchas

Listen for non-responses Some statements or questions don't receive responses. Listen for Mario's last questions to Isabel. Does she respond? Does Mario expect a response? Why or why not?

VIDEO
DVD

AUDIO

Isabel   Mario

Isabel is on first base, where Mario is playing.

Isabel: Hoy tu equipo va a perder el partido, Mario. Mi equipo siempre gana.

Mario: Sí, Isabel, eres muy buena jugadora de béisbol. Pero hoy nosotros vamos a ser los campeones.

Isabel: ¿Qué vas a hacer después de las clases? ¿Vamos al café?

Mario: Tengo que comprar un regalo. Es el cumpleaños de mi hermano.

Isabel: ¿Qué vas a comprar? Es un atleta. Le gusta el béisbol, ¿no?

Mario: Sí, pero tiene un bate y pelotas de béisbol.

Isabel: ¿Le gusta patinar en línea?

Mario: Sí, pero los patines en línea cuestan mucho dinero.

Isabel: ¿Le gusta el fútbol americano? ¿El tenis? La natación, ¿le gusta?

Mario: Sí, le gusta nadar pero, ¿qué puedo comprar? ¿Una piscina? ¿Agua?

Isabel's teammate hits a home run, and Mario's team loses.

Continuará... p. 114

También se dice

República Dominicana Mario uses the word **piscina** to joke about buying a swimming pool. In other Spanish-speaking countries you might hear:
• **México** la alberca
• **Argentina** la pileta

3 | ¿Quién gana? *Comprensión del episodio*

Escuchar
Leer

Complete the sentences with information from the episode.

| un bate | los campeones | ganar |

| jugadora de béisbol | patines en línea | un regalo |

1. Isabel piensa que su equipo va a _____ .
2. Mario piensa que él y su equipo van a ser _____ .
3. Isabel es una buena _____ .
4. Mario tiene que comprar _____ después de las clases.
5. El hermano de Mario no necesita _____ .
6. Mario no quiere comprar _____ porque cuestan mucho.

4 | ¿Te gustan los deportes? ♻ *¿Recuerdas?* gustar with nouns p. 8

Hablar

Ask a partner whether he or she likes the following sports.

A ¿Te gusta el fútbol?

B Sí, me gusta el fútbol. (No, no me gusta el fútbol.)

1.

2.

3.

4.

5.

6.

PARA Y PIENSA

Did you get it? Complete each sentence with the appropriate vocabulary word.
1. Cuando Isabel gana un partido, ella es _____ .
2. Al hermano de Mario le gusta nadar; su deporte favorito es _____ .
3. Mario lleva _____ porque el béisbol puede ser peligroso.

Get Help Online ClassZone.com

Presentación de GRAMÁTICA

Goal: Learn how to form the verb **jugar.** Then practice using **jugar** to talk about playing sports. *Actividades 5–11*

♻ *¿Recuerdas?* Comparatives p. 24

English Grammar Connection: There is more than one way to say the English verb *to play* in Spanish. Use **jugar** when you mean playing a sport or a game; use **tocar** when you mean playing a musical instrument or a CD.

The Verb jugar

Use **jugar** to talk about playing a sport or a game. How do you form the present tense of this verb?

Here's how:

Jugar is a stem-changing verb in which the **u** changes to **ue** in all forms except **nosotros(as)** and **vosotros(as).**

jugar	*to play*
juego	jugamos
juegas	jugáis
juega	juegan

When you use **jugar** with the name of a sport, use **jugar a + sport.**

Mi primo **juega al fútbol.**
*My cousin **plays soccer.***

Jugamos al fútbol americano.
We play football.

Juegan al béisbol en la República Dominicana.
They play baseball in the Dominican Republic.

Más práctica
Cuaderno *pp. 53–55*
Cuaderno para hispanohablantes *pp. 54–56*

↪ **Conjuguemos.com**

@HomeTutor
Leveled Practice
ClassZone.com

Práctica de GRAMÁTICA

5 | Una familia activa

Leer
Escribir

Mario's family is very athletic. Complete his description with forms of **jugar.** Then answer his question.

Mi familia practica muchos deportes. Yo __1.__ al béisbol en un equipo. Mi hermano __2.__ también. Él y mi hermana __3.__ al voleibol los sábados. Mis padres __4.__ mucho al tenis. Ellos __5.__ casi todos los días. Nosotros no __6.__ al fútbol americano, pero lo miramos en la televisión. ¿Y tú? ¿A qué deportes __7.__?

6 | ¿A qué juegan?

Escuchar
Escribir

These athletes are talking about the places where they play sports. Listen to the descriptions and write what sports these people play.

1. Elena
2. Rogelio y José
3. el equipo
4. los maestros
5. Tomás
6. la atleta

7 | En la tienda de deportes

Hablar
Escribir

Look at the drawing below and tell what sports people play, based on the items they are buying.

modelo: Jaime juega al tenis.

8 | ¿Para qué equipo?

Comparación cultural

La Serie del Caribe

How do professional athletes support their home countries? Every February, Winter League championship teams from four countries compete in baseball's *Serie del Caribe,* or Caribbean Series. Many major league ballplayers have taken part in the Winter Leagues. Miguel Tejada and David Ortiz have represented the **Dominican Republic.** Other players include Johan Santana and Miguel Cabrera for **Venezuela,** Oliver Pérez and Vinny Castilla for **Mexico,** and Carlos Beltrán and Iván Rodríguez for **Puerto Rico.**

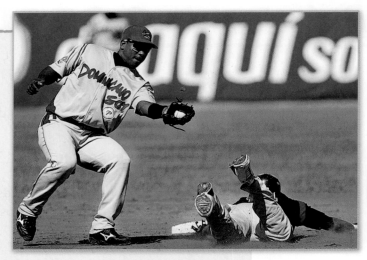

Miguel Tejada juega para el equipo de la República Dominicana durante la Serie del Caribe.

Compara con tu mundo *How does the **Serie del Caribe** compare to other sports championships you are familiar with? Can you name any athletes who have played in these championships and tell where they are from?*

Ask a partner what team each of these Winter League players plays for.

A ¿Para qué equipo juega Oliver Pérez?

B Pérez juega para el equipo de México.

9 | ¿Dónde juegas?

Ask a partner where he or she plays these sports.

1.

2.

3.

4.

5.

6.

10 ¿A qué juegas mejor? ♻ ¿Recuerdas? Comparatives p. 24

Hablar

Talk with a partner about which sports you play better than others.
Explain your answers.

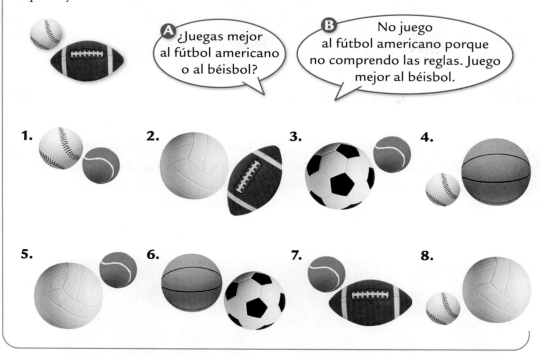

A ¿Juegas mejor al fútbol americano o al béisbol?

B No juego al fútbol americano porque no comprendo las reglas. Juego mejor al béisbol.

1.
2.
3.
4.
5.
6.
7.
8.

11 El deporte más popular

Hablar

Survey ten of your classmates to find out what sports they play.
Which sport is played by the most people?

A ¿A qué deportes juegan ustedes?

B Juego al tenis y al fútbol americano.

C Juego al béisbol.

Más práctica   Cuaderno *pp. 53–55*   Cuaderno para hispanohablantes *pp. 54–56*

PARA Y PIENSA

Did you get it? Create sentences that tell the sports each of the
following people play, using **jugar**.
1. Ana y yo / el béisbol
2. ustedes / el básquetbol
3. el hermano de Rosa / el voleibol
4. yo / el tenis

Get Help Online
ClassZone.com

GRAMÁTICA *en contexto*

¡AVANZA! **Goal:** Pay attention to the forms of **jugar** that Isabel and Mario use to talk about sports and sports equipment. Then use **jugar** to say what sports people play. *Actividades 12–13*

Telehistoria escena 2

VIDEO
DVD

AUDIO

STRATEGIES

@*HomeTutor* VideoPlus
View, Read and Record
ClassZone.com

Cuando lees

Make a mindmap for related words
Write the name of a piece of sports equipment, such as **el casco,** in the center circle. In outside circles, write as many sports as possible that use that piece of equipment.

Cuando escuchas

Listen for stressed words When Mario and Isabel talk about possible gifts, listen for the way they stress or emphasize certain words to show their preferences.

Isabel and Mario are in a sporting goods store, looking for a gift.

Isabel: Un guante de béisbol. Me gusta para tu hermano.

Mario takes the glove and puts it back on the shelf.

Isabel: Me gusta la raqueta.

He also takes the racket and puts it back. Isabel picks up a basketball.

Mario: No, una bola de básquetbol, no. Es un regalo para mi hermano; no es tu cumpleaños.

Isabel: ¿Necesita un casco?

Mario: No, pero necesito un casco para jugar al tenis.

Isabel: ¡Un partido de tenis no es peligroso!

Mario: Tú no juegas al tenis con mi hermano.

Isabel: *(laughing)* No, no juego al tenis. Pero me gusta el voleibol. ¿Tu hermano juega al voleibol?

Continuará... p. 120

También se dice

República Dominicana
Mario uses the word **bola** to talk about the ball. In other Spanish-speaking countries you might hear:
• **muchos países**
  el balón

12 | Buscan un regalo *Comprensión del episodio*

Escuchar
Leer

Tell whether each sentence is true or false. Correct the false statements.

1. Isabel piensa que un guante de béisbol es un buen regalo.
2. Mario quiere comprar una pelota de básquetbol.
3. Es el cumpleaños de Isabel.
4. Mario necesita un bate para jugar al tenis con su hermano.
5. Es peligroso cuando Mario juega al tenis con su hermano.
6. Isabel juega al tenis.

13 | Un atleta famoso

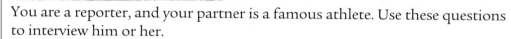

Hablar

You are a reporter, and your partner is a famous athlete. Use these questions to interview him or her.

1. ¿A qué deporte juegas?
2. ¿Dónde juegas?
3. ¿Qué necesitas hacer para ser campeón (campeona) en tu deporte?
4. ¿Qué prefieres, ser jugador(a) o aficionado(a)? ¿Por qué?
5. ¿Quién es tu atleta favorito(a)? ¿A qué deporte juega?
6. ¿Qué te gusta hacer después de un partido? ¿Qué haces cuando pierdes?

Pronunciación La letra g con a, o, u

AUDIO

Before **a, o, u,** and consonants, the Spanish **g** is pronounced like the *g* in the English word *game.*

Listen and repeat.

> Soy Gregorio.
> Me gusta jugar al
> béisbol en agosto.

ga	**go**
ganar	**tengo**
gu	**g** + consonant
guante	**reglas**

A **G**re**g**orio le **g**usta ju**g**ar al béisbol en a**g**osto.

PARA
Y
PIENSA

Did you get it? Complete each sentence based on the Telehistoria with the appropriate form of the verb **jugar.**
1. Isabel no _____ al tenis.
2. Cuando Mario y su hermano _____ al tenis, Mario necesita un casco.
3. A Isabel le gusta _____ al básquetbol.

Get Help Online
ClassZone.com

Lección 1
ciento quince **115**

Presentación de GRAMÁTICA

English Grammar Connection: There are two ways to say the English verb *to know* in Spanish: **saber** and **conocer**.

The Verbs saber and conocer

Animated Grammar
ClassZone.com

In Spanish, there are two verbs that mean *to know*. How do you form the present tense of **saber** and **conocer** and use them correctly?

Here's how: Both **saber** and **conocer** have irregular **yo** forms in the present tense.

saber	*to know*
sé	sabemos
sabes	sabéis
sabe	saben

conocer	*to know*
conozco	conocemos
conoces	conocéis
conoce	conocen

Use **saber** to talk about factual information you know.

> **Sé** cuánto cuesta el bate.
> *I **know** how much the bat costs.*

> ¿**Sabes** a qué hora empieza el partido?
> *Do you **know** what time the game begins?*

You can also use **saber** + **infinitive** to say that you know how to do something.

> Nicolás **sabe patinar** muy bien.
> *Nicolás **knows** how to skate very well.*

Use **conocer** when you want to say that you are familiar with a person or place.

> **Conozco** a tu hermano David.
> *I **know** your brother David.*

> Mi prima **conoce** Santo Domingo.
> *My cousin **knows (is familiar with)** Santo Domingo.*

You also use **conocer** to talk about meeting someone for the first time.

> Queremos **conocer** a los jugadores.
> *We want **to meet** the players.*

Más práctica
Cuaderno *pp. 56–58*
Cuaderno para hispanohablantes *pp. 57–60*

Conjuguemos.com

@HomeTutor
Leveled Practice
ClassZone.com

Práctica de GRAMÁTICA

14 | Un correo electrónico de Alicia

Leer | Alicia is writing an e-mail to Mario. Complete the e-mail by choosing the correct verb in parentheses.

> Hola, Mario:
>
> ¿Qué tal? ¿ **1.** (Sabes / Conoces) tú que Trini Salgado acaba de ganar otro partido de fútbol? Ella **2.** (sabe / conoce) jugar muy bien. Es campeona. Ella **3.** (sabe / conoce) a muchos campeones de deportes también. Yo **4.** (sé / conozco) que ella va a ir a la capital de tu país. ¿La **5.** (sabes / conoces) tú? Yo no la **6.** (sé / conozco) todavía, pero es mi jugadora favorita y tú y yo **7.** (sabemos / conocemos) que la quiero **8.** (saber / conocer). Mario, yo no **9.** (sé / conozco) dónde está la camiseta. **10.** ¿(Saben/Conocen) Isabel y tú dónde está la camiseta?
>
> Tu amiga, Alicia

Nota gramatical

When a specific person is the direct object of a sentence, use the personal **a** *after* the verb and *before* the person.

No conozco **a** Raúl.	Ayudo **a** la maestra.
I don't know Raúl.	*I am helping the teacher.*

15 | ¿Qué saben? ¿Qué conocen?

Escribir | What do these people know? Write sentences with **saber** or **conocer**.

modelo: mi madre (cuándo empieza el partido)
Mi madre sabe cuándo empieza el partido.

1. las campeonas (nadar muy bien)
2. yo (un jugador de béisbol)
3. el equipo (el estadio de fútbol)
4. tú (dónde está la cancha)
5. mis amigos y yo (la República Dominicana)
6. los jugadores (Trini Salgado)
7. yo (qué equipo va a ganar)
8. Ana (cuánto cuesta el casco)
9. tú (las ganadoras)
10. nosotros (patinar en línea)
11. ustedes (quién es el campeón)

16 | ¿Qué sabes hacer?

Hablar

Ask a partner whether he or she knows how to do the following things.

A ¿Sabes **jugar al fútbol**?

B Sí, sé **jugar al fútbol.** (No, no sé **jugar al fútbol.**)

1.

2.

3.

4.

5.

6.

---

17 | ¡A charlar!

Hablar

Work in a group of three. Use **saber** and **conocer** to talk about people, places, and things in the world of sports.

A ¿Saben jugar al voleibol ustedes?

B Sí, sé jugar al voleibol. Juego los sábados con mis hermanos.

C No, no sé jugar al voleibol. No comprendo las reglas...

1. las reglas de...
2. un lugar donde juegan al...
3. unos aficionados de...

4. el (la) atleta...
5. un lugar donde... es muy popular
6. ¿ ?

---

18 | ¿Qué saben hacer tus amigos?

Escribir

Write a paragraph about friends or other people you know and what they know how to do.

> **modelo:** Mi amigo Sean sabe tocar la guitarra. Toca todos los días...

19 | ¿Y tú?

Hablar
Escribir

Answer the following questions in complete sentences.

> **modelo:** ¿Sabes jugar a un deporte?
> Sí, sé jugar al básquetbol y al tenis.

1. ¿Sabes quién es Pedro Martínez?
2. ¿Conoces a una persona atlética? ¿Quién?
3. ¿Sabes cuánto cuestan los patines en línea?
4. ¿A qué persona famosa quieres conocer?
5. ¿Sabes cuándo es el cumpleaños de tu maestro(a) de español?
6. ¿Qué lugares conoces?
7. ¿Sabes por qué los jugadores de béisbol llevan cascos?
8. ¿Qué equipos conoces?
9. ¿Sabes dónde hay una piscina?
10. ¿Qué sabes hacer?

Comparación cultural

El arte representativo

How can artists represent the people of their country through their artwork? Juan Medina, an artist from the **Dominican Republic,** has experimented with different styles of art, combining traditional and modern techniques. Some of his paintings are inspired by his Dominican heritage, showing the history, people, and social and political issues of his country. *Vendedora de flores* shows a flower vendor. Vendors and their carts are found throughout Santo Domingo, selling everything from shaved ice to coffee to flowers to newspapers.

Compara con tu mundo *How would you represent a typical sight or activity in your community through artwork?*

Vendedora de flores
(alrededor de 1990),
Juan Medina

Más práctica   Cuaderno *pp. 56–58*   Cuaderno para hispanohablantes *pp. 57–60*

PARA Y PIENSA

Did you get it? Complete each sentence with the correct form of **saber** or **conocer.** Use the personal **a** if necessary.

1. ¿ _____ ustedes jugar al voleibol?
2. Yo _____ María muy bien porque es mi amiga.
3. Nosotros _____ que el fútbol americano puede ser peligroso.

Get Help Online
ClassZone.com

Lección 1
ciento diecinueve   **119**

Todo junto

Goal: *Show what you know* Notice how Mario and Isabel use **saber** and **conocer** to talk about people and things they know in the world of sports. Then use these verbs and **jugar** to talk about athletes and sports. *Actividades 20–24*

Telehistoria completa

@HomeTutor VideoPlus
View, Read and Record
ClassZone.com

STRATEGIES

Cuando lees

Scan for the details Before reading carefully, scan the scene for these details: Who is Trini Salgado? What is she doing today? Who is a bigger fan of Trini: Alicia or Mario's brother?

Cuando escuchas

Go for the goals While listening, consider Mario's two goals in this scene. What are they? Does he fulfill both goals during the scene?

Escena 1 *Resumen*

En un partido de béisbol, Mario habla con Isabel. Él tiene que comprar un regalo para el cumpleaños de su hermano.

Escena 2 *Resumen*

Isabel y Mario buscan un regalo en una tienda de deportes. Mario no sabe qué va a comprar.

Escena 3

VIDEO
DVD

AUDIO

Mario points to a soccer jersey.

Mario: ¡Es como la camiseta de Alicia! ¿Conoces a Trini Salgado? Ella está aquí, en Santo Domingo.

Isabel: Lo sé. ¿Alicia la conoce?

Mario: No, pero Trini es su jugadora de fútbol favorita. Alicia quiere un autógrafo en la camiseta. Y yo debo encontrar a Trini...

Vendedor: ¿Buscan a Trini Salgado? *(Mario and Isabel nod.)* ¿Saben dónde encontrar a Trini Salgado?

Mario and Isabel shake their heads, and the clerk turns up the radio.

«La jugadora de fútbol Trini Salgado va a estar en el estadio hoy a las seis de la tarde. Los primeros quinientos aficionados pueden conocer a Trini.»

Mario: ¡Vamos! *(He buys the jersey.)*

Isabel: ¿A tu hermano le gusta Trini Salgado?

Mario: No sé. ¡Pero sé que le gustan las camisetas con autógrafos de atletas importantes!

20 | ¿A quién(es) describen? *Comprensión de los episodios*

Escuchar
Leer

Tell whom these sentences describe:
Mario, Isabel, or both Mario and Isabel.

Isabel

Isabel y Mario

Mario

1. Piensa que va a ganar el partido de béisbol.
2. Su equipo de béisbol siempre gana.
3. Dice que el tenis es peligroso.
4. Va a una tienda de deportes.
5. Compra una camiseta de fútbol.
6. Dice que debe encontrar a Trini.

21 | Regalo para un atleta *Comprensión de los episodios*

Escuchar
Leer

Answer the questions, according to the episodes.

1. ¿A qué juegan Isabel y Mario?
2. ¿Qué tiene que hacer Mario después de las clases?
3. ¿Necesita un casco el hermano de Mario?
4. ¿Dónde va a estar Trini a las seis?
5. ¿Quiénes pueden conocer a Trini?
6. ¿Qué compra Mario para su hermano?

22 | Un anuncio de radio

Escribir
Hablar

STRATEGY Hablar

Use logical steps to meet the goal Use logical steps to create a radio ad, such as: (a) make a chart containing key types of information, like **qué hay en la tienda,** in column 1 and specific examples for each type in column 2; (b) choose the best examples; (c) write an exciting ad; and (d) record and present it.

Work in a group of three. Write a radio ad for a sporting goods store. Present it to the class. You should include the name of a sport and a famous athlete, what they sell in the store, and prices.

A Si quieres conocer a Trini Salgado, ven a la tienda El Deportista el sábado.

B Tenemos pelotas de fútbol, ropa... ¡y mucho más!

C El sábado, las pelotas de fútbol cuestan setecientos pesos. Puedes recibir un autógrafo de la jugadora...

23 | Integración

Leer
Escuchar
Hablar

Read the ad and listen to the sports broadcasters' commentary. Then tell which team you think will win and why.

Fuente 1 Anuncio

LA ASOCIACIÓN DOMINICANA DE BASQUETBOL PRESENTA...

¡Un partido entre dos equipos excelentes!

Los Cometas

El equipo con el mejor récord contra Los Pumas

José Luis Tejada, el centro más alto de la liga

Los Pumas

El equipo con el mejor récord de la liga: 15-1

El equipo con más puntos por partido

¿Quién va a ganar? Vas a saberlo hoy. El partido empieza a las 4:00 de la tarde en el Centro de Deportes Solimar.

Fuente 2 Comentarios

Listen and take notes
- ¿Cómo juegan los equipos?
- ¿Cómo practican antes de los partidos?

modelo: El equipo de Los... va a ganar el partido porque...

24 | Tus ideas sobre los deportes

Escribir

Do you think it's a good or bad idea for boys and girls to play on the same sports teams? Explain your answer.

modelo: Es una buena idea. Si las chicas pueden jugar al fútbol americano, deben jugar en el equipo de los chicos. Conozco a unas chicas que juegan...

Writing Criteria	Excellent	Good	Needs Work
Content	Your argument is supported with many reasons.	Your argument is supported with some reasons.	Your argument is supported with few reasons.
Communication	Your argument is organized and easy to follow.	Your argument is somewhat organized and easy to follow.	Your argument is disorganized and hard to follow.
Accuracy	Your argument has few mistakes in grammar and vocabulary.	Your argument has some mistakes in grammar and vocabulary.	Your argument has many mistakes in grammar and vocabulary.

Más práctica Cuaderno *pp. 59–60* Cuaderno para hispanohablantes *pp. 61–62*

PARA Y PIENSA

Did you get it? Fill in the paragraph with the correct form of **saber** or **conocer**.

Trini Salgado _____ jugar al fútbol muy bien. Alicia y sus amigos la _____ , y ellos _____ que ella va a estar en el estadio en Santo Domingo.

Get Help Online ClassZone.com

Juegos y diversiones

Review sports vocabulary by playing a game.

MEM⚙RIA

The Setup

Your teacher will write vocabulary words on index cards and make corresponding picture cards. He or she will attach the pairs of cards to a bulletin board in random order, blank side up. Form two teams.

Playing the Game

Players from the two teams will take turns choosing two cards. The cards are flipped to reveal their contents. Players use their memory of the cards that have been revealed in order to match the pictures with the words that represent them.

The Winner!

The team that makes the most matches wins.

Lectura

AUDIO

Un club de deportes

This is a brochure for a sports club in Santo Domingo.

STRATEGY Leer

Make a mind map Make a mind map of the sports club in Santo Domingo, showing everything the club offers. Add circles! Highlight the features you like most.

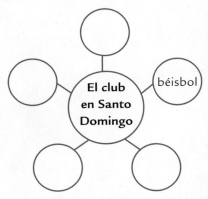

El club en Santo Domingo

béisbol

Palacio de los Deportes

¿Eres atlético?
¿Te gusta practicar deportes?
Si la respuesta es sí, ven al Palacio de los Deportes.

¿Te gusta nadar?
Tenemos una piscina olímpica.

¿Te gusta jugar al tenis?
Tenemos cinco canchas de tenis.

¿Te gusta jugar al béisbol?
Tenemos un campo de béisbol.

¿Te gusta jugar al básquetbol?
Tenemos dos canchas de básquetbol.

¿Quieres comer después de jugar?
Tenemos un café que sirve comidas y bebidas ricas y nutritivas.

Palacio de los Deportes

Para nuestros socios [1]...

Si no sabes practicar los siguientes deportes, tenemos clases de...

- natación
- tenis
- artes marciales
- ejercicios aeróbicos

Si quieres jugar con otras personas, hay equipos de...

- básquetbol
- béisbol
- voleibol

Horas

lunes a viernes	6:00 de la mañana a 9:00 de la noche
sábado	7:00 de la mañana a 6:00 de la tarde

Membresías [2]
Hay membresías personales y familiares [3]. Puedes pedir la lista de los precios.

Dirección [4]
Calle Mella, 100
Santo Domingo

Teléfono
(809) 583-1492

[1] members   [2] memberships   [3] family   [4] address

PARA Y PIENSA

¿Comprendiste?

1. ¿A qué puedes jugar en el Palacio de los Deportes?
2. ¿Qué puedes hacer si no sabes nadar?
3. Si quieres jugar con un equipo, ¿a qué puedes jugar?

¿Y tú?

Si eres socio(a) de un club de deportes, compara tu club con el Palacio de los Deportes. Si no, ¿quieres ser socio(a) del Palacio de los Deportes? Explica.

Conexiones   *Las ciencias sociales*

La bandera dominicana

The colors and symbols of the Dominican flag reflect the country's long struggle for independence from France, Spain, and Haiti. It was not until 1844 that the Dominican Republic finally gained its independence.

On the Dominican flag, blue stands for liberty (**libertad**), red for the fire and blood of the fight for independence (**independencia**), and white for faith and sacrifice (**sacrificio**).

Write a description of the coat of arms (**el escudo de armas**). Research and explain the symbolism of the laurel branch (**rama de laurel**) and the palm branch (**rama de palma**).

El simbolismo de la bandera dominicana

Libertad

Sacrificio

Independencia

El escudo de armas

Rama de palma

Rama de laurel

Proyecto 1 *La historia*

Research and write about the Dominican struggle for independence from 1800 to 1844. Include specific facts such as dates, countries that were involved, and important people.

Proyecto 2 *El arte*

Flags combine geometric shapes, colors, symbols, and mottos. Design a flag for your school and explain the meaning of each element you use. Include a motto and labels in Spanish.

Proyecto 3 *La educación física*

In many countries, people fly their flag and sing their national anthem at sporting events. Write a paragraph about the role of flags and anthems in sports. Why do you think this tradition started?

El equipo nacional de voleibol femenino en los Juegos Panamericanos de 2003

En resumen
Vocabulario y gramática

Vocabulario

Sports

el básquetbol	basketball
el béisbol	baseball
el fútbol americano	football
nadar	to swim
la natación	swimming
patinar	to skate
patinar en línea	to in-line skate
el tenis	tennis
el voleibol	volleyball

Sports Equipment

el bate	bat
el casco	helmet
el guante	glove
los patines en línea	in-line skates
la pelota	ball
la raqueta	racket

Talk About Sports

comprender las reglas	to understand the rules
favorito(a)	favorite
ganar	to win
el partido	game
peligroso(a)	dangerous
perder (ie)	to lose

Locations and People

los aficionados	fans	el equipo	team
el (la) atleta	athlete	el estadio	stadium
el campeón (pl. los campeones), la campeona	champion	el (la) ganador(a)	winner
		el (la) jugador(a)	player
el campo	field	la piscina	swimming pool
la cancha	court		

Gramática

Nota gramatical: The personal **a** *p. 117*

The Verb jugar

Jugar is a stem-changing verb in which the **u** changes to **ue** in all forms except **nosotros(as)** and **vosotros(as).**

jugar	to play
juego	jugamos
juegas	jugáis
juega	juegan

When you use **jugar** with the name of a sport, use **jugar a** + **sport.**

The Verbs saber and conocer

Both **saber** and **conocer** mean to know and have irregular **yo** forms in the present tense.

saber	to know	conocer	to know
sé	sabemos	conozco	conocemos
sabes	sabéis	conoces	conocéis
sabe	saben	conoce	conocen

- Use **saber** to talk about factual information you know. You can also use **saber** + **infinitive** to say that you know how to do something.
- Use **conocer** when you want to say that you are familiar with a person or place. You also use **conocer** to talk about meeting someone for the first time.

Repaso de la lección

¡LLEGADA!

@HomeTutor
ClassZone.com

Now you can
- talk about sports
- talk about whom you know
- talk about what you know

Using
- the verb **jugar**
- the verbs **saber** and **conocer**
- the personal **a**

To review
- the verb **jugar**
  p. 110
- the verbs **saber**
  and **conocer**
  p. 116
- the personal **a**
  p. 117

1 | Listen and understand

AUDIO

Listen to Tina's interview with Sergio Martínez, a famous athlete.
Then choose the correct answers.

1. Sergio es jugador de...
   a. fútbol americano.
   b. béisbol.
2. También Sergio sabe jugar...
   a. al voleibol.
   b. al tenis.
3. Sergio dice que el fútbol
   americano es un poco...
   a. aburrido.
   b. peligroso.

4. Sergio no conoce a...
   a. muchos de sus aficionados.
   b. muchos jugadores.
5. Sergio...
   a. corre mucho.
   b. nada mucho.
6. Sergio sabe...
   a. patinar en línea.
   b. dibujar bien.

To review
- the verb **jugar**
  p. 110

2 | Talk about sports

Write what sports these people play and what equipment they use.

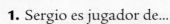

modelo: Adriana
Adriana juega al béisbol con un bate.

1. tú

2. Horacio y Mercedes

3. Santiago

4. nosotros

5. yo

6. ustedes

To review
· the verbs **saber** and **conocer** p. 116

3 | Talk about whom and what you know

Complete the e-mail message with the correct form of **saber** or **conocer**.

Hola, Norma.
Yo no __1.__ qué voy a hacer el sábado. Quiero jugar al tenis. Yo __2.__ a una chica que juega muy bien. Se llama Ana. ¿Y tú? ¿ __3.__ jugar al tenis? ¿Por qué no jugamos el sábado con Ana? Nosotras __4.__ un parque con muchas canchas. ¿Tú __5.__ el Parque Miraflores? Está cerca de mi casa. ¿Tú __6.__ dónde está la calle Olmeda? Allí está el parque. Hablamos esta noche.
Hasta luego,
Estela

To review
· the personal **a** p. 117

4 | Talk about sports

Write sentences describing the importance of sports in your daily life. Use the personal **a,** if needed.

modelo: ver / mis atletas favoritos en la televisión
(No) Veo a mis atletas favoritos en la televisión.

1. comprender / las reglas de muchos deportes
2. invitar / mis amigos a los partidos de fútbol americano
3. practicar / dos o tres deportes
4. mirar / muchos deportes en la televisión
5. ayudar / mis amigos a aprender las reglas de fútbol
6. conocer / muchos jugadores de mi equipo favorito

To review
· **El deporte nacional** p. 101
· **Altar de la Patria** p. 101
· Comparación cultural pp. 112, 119

5 | Dominican Republic and Venezuela

Comparación cultural

Answer these culture questions.

1. When is professional baseball played in the Dominican Republic?
2. What does the **Altar de la Patria** monument commemorate?
3. What is the **Serie del Caribe**? Which countries participate?
4. What is featured in Juan Medina's painting *Vendedora de flores*?

Más práctica   Cuaderno *pp. 61–72*   Cuaderno para hispanohablantes *pp. 63–72*

Get Help Online
ClassZone.com

Lección **2**

Tema:
La salud

In this lesson you will learn to
- talk about parts of the body
- make excuses
- say what you did
- talk about staying healthy

using
- the verb **doler**
- preterite of **-ar** verbs
- preterite of **-car, -gar, -zar** verbs

♻ *¿Recuerdas?*
- **gustar** with nouns
- stem-changing verbs: **o → ue**
- telling time

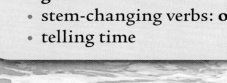

Comparación cultural

In this lesson you will learn about
- artist Amaya Salazar and a merengue festival
- gestures and sayings
- famous athletes and outdoor sports in the Dominican Republic, Honduras, and Venezuela

Compara con tu mundo
These teens are playing on a beach in the Dominican Republic. Beaches are popular places to do a variety of activities, from surfing to a simple game of catch. *What outdoor activities do you like to do to stay healthy?*

¿Qué ves?
Mira la foto
¿Hace frío?

¿Llevan camisas o camisetas los dos chicos?

¿Qué hacen Isabel y Mario?

Un día en la Playa Caribe
Juan Dolio, República Dominicana

Presentación de VOCABULARIO

¡AVANZA!

Goal: Learn about what Mario and Isabel do to stay healthy. Then use what you have learned to talk about parts of the body. *Actividades 1–2*

VIDEO DVD

AUDIO

A Soy Isabel. En **la playa** Mario y yo siempre usamos **bloqueador de sol**. Si no lo usamos, **tomar el sol** puede ser malo para **la piel**.

la playa

el mar

tomar el sol

el bloqueador de sol

B En la República Dominicana hay muchas actividades que son buenas para **la salud**. Yo **camino**, pero también puedes **hacer esquí acuático** o **bucear**. A Mario le gusta **levantar pesas**.

caminar

hacer esquí acuático

bucear

levantar pesas

C Si hacemos actividades en la playa, usamos bloqueador de sol en todo el cuerpo: la nariz, las orejas, los brazos, las piernas...

la cabeza

la oreja

el ojo

la nariz

la boca

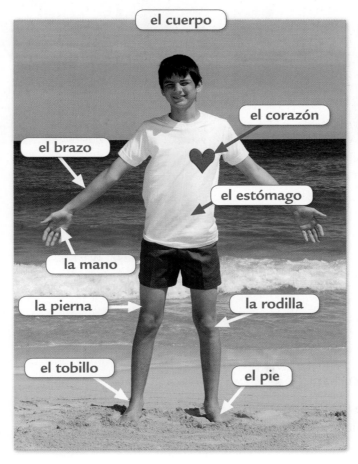

el cuerpo

el corazón

el brazo

el estómago

la mano

la pierna

la rodilla

el tobillo

el pie

Continuará...

Lección 2
ciento treinta y tres **133**

D Mario es **fuerte** pero ahora está **herido. Le duele** mucho **el tobillo.**

fuerte

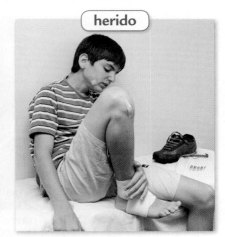

herido

E Yo soy muy **sana** pero de vez en cuando estoy **enferma.**

sana

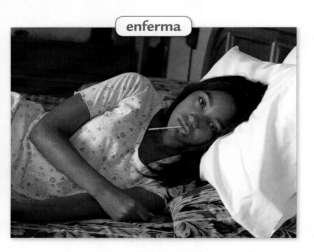

enferma

Más vocabulario

anoche *last night*	**Lo siento.** *I'm sorry.*
ayer *yesterday*	**¿Qué hiciste (tú)?** *What did you do?*
comenzar *to begin*	**¿Qué hicieron ustedes?** *What did*
terminar *to end*	*you do?*
Expansión de vocabulario p. R3	

¡A responder! Escuchar

Stand up. Listen to the professional athlete talk about what hurts. Point to each part of the body as it is mentioned.

@HomeTutor VideoPlus
Interactive Flashcards
ClassZone.com

Práctica de VOCABULARIO

1 | Las partes del cuerpo

Hablar
Escribir

Identify the parts of the body indicated in the photos.

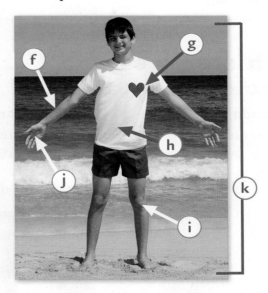

2 | ¿Qué usas?

Hablar
Escribir

Tell what parts of the body you use when you do these activities.

la boca	las manos	los ojos	los pies

los brazos	la cabeza	las piernas	¿ ?

modelo: nadar

Cuando nado, uso los brazos, las piernas, las manos y los pies.

1. caminar   **6.** patinar

2. comer   **7.** jugar al fútbol

3. bucear   **8.** bailar

4. dibujar   **9.** mirar la televisión

5. levantar pesas **10.** hacer esquí acuático

Más práctica   Cuaderno *pp. 73–75*   Cuaderno para hispanohablantes *pp. 73–76*

PARA Y PIENSA

Did you get it?
1. Name three parts of your face.
2. Name three parts of your leg.

Get Help Online
ClassZone.com

VOCABULARIO *en contexto*

¡AVANZA! **Goal:** Notice the words Isabel and Mario use to talk about what happens to Mario. Then use **doler** to say what hurts and make excuses. *Actividades 3–4*

♻️ *¿Recuerdas?* **gustar** with nouns p. 8, stem-changing verbs: **o → ue** p. 34

Telehistoria escena 1

@*HomeTutor* VideoPlus
View, Read and Record
ClassZone.com

STRATEGIES

Cuando lees
Draw and label Draw an outline of a body. Label the body parts that Mario and Isabel mention in this scene. Which others do you know?

Cuando escuchas
Listen for the action This scene has a lot of action. Listen to what happens to Mario. What does Isabel do and say in response? Will they go to their planned destination?

Mario

Isabel

Mario and Isabel get on their bicycles.

Mario: ¡Tenemos que ser los primeros aficionados en el estadio!

Isabel: Mario, ¿sabes montar en bicicleta?

Mario: Sí, sí, ¡es fácil!

Isabel: ¡Necesitas el casco!

Mario wobbles on his bicycle and crashes into a fruit cart.

Mario: ¡No estoy herido!

Isabel: Pero, ¿y el tobillo? ¿Y la pierna?

Mario: Soy fuerte y sano...

Isabel: Y la cabeza, ¿Mario? ¡Tienes la piel muy roja! ¡La nariz! Abre la boca. ¿Puedes caminar?

Mario: Sí. Me duele un poco el pie... pero puedo caminar.

Isabel: No, no debes caminar.

Mario: Pero... ¡Y Trini Salgado!

Isabel: ¿Trini Salgado? ¡Un autógrafo no es importante! Vamos... **Continuará...** p. 142

También se dice

República Dominicana Mario uses the common phrase **es fácil** to describe riding a bike. In other Spanish-speaking countries you might hear:
- **Puerto Rico** **es un guame**
- **España** **está tirado**
- **muchos países** **es pan comido, es coser y cantar**

3 | Un accidente Comprensión del episodio

Escuchar
Leer

Match phrases from the two columns to form sentences about the episode.

1. Van en bicicleta porque
2. Mario piensa que
3. Mario no debe caminar
4. Mario tiene
5. La salud de Mario es

a. la piel muy roja.
b. más importante que un autógrafo.
c. montar en bicicleta es fácil.
d. quieren ser los primeros en el estadio.
e. porque está herido.

Nota gramatical   **¿Recuerdas?** gustar with nouns p. 8

When you want to say what hurts, use **doler (ue).** This verb functions like **gustar.**

agrees *agrees*

Me duele la cabeza. *My head hurts.*   **Le duelen los brazos.** *His arms hurt.*

With **doler,** you use a definite article with parts of the body.

---

4 | ¿Quieres ir a la playa?   **¿Recuerdas?** Stem-changing verbs: o → ue p. 34

Hablar

Ask a partner whether he or she wants to do these beach activities.
Your partner will say that he or she can't because something hurts.

A ¿Quieres tomar el sol en la playa?

B Lo siento, pero no puedo. Me duele la piel.

1.

2.

3.

4.

5.

6.

PARA Y PIENSA

Did you get it? Complete each sentence based on the Telehistoria with the correct **doler** phrase.

Get Help Online
ClassZone.com

1. A Mario _____ la cabeza.   2. También a él _____ el pie y la pierna.

Presentación de GRAMÁTICA

¡AVANZA!

Goal: Learn how to form the preterite of **-ar** verbs. Then practice using the verbs to say what you did and talk about staying healthy. *Actividades 5–10*

♻ *¿Recuerdas?* Telling time p. 14

English Grammar Connection: The **preterite** is a tense used to express an action completed at a definite time in the past. This tense is usually referred to as the past tense in English. In English, regular verbs in the past tense end in *-ed*.

You **lifted** weights yesterday.
> past tense

Usted **levantó** pesas ayer.
> preterite

Preterite of Regular -ar Verbs

Animated Grammar
ClassZone.com

Use the preterite tense to talk about actions completed in the past. How do you form the **preterite** of regular **-ar** verbs?

Here's how: To form the **preterite** of a regular **-ar** verb, add the appropriate preterite ending to the verb's stem.

nadar *to swim*	
nad**é**	nad**amos**
nad**aste**	nad**asteis**
nad**ó**	nad**aron**

Notice that the **yo** and **usted/él/ella** forms have an accent over the final vowel.

Nadé en el mar.
I swam in the sea.

Mariana **patinó.**
Mariana skated.

The **nosotros(as)** form is the same in the preterite as in the present tense. Use the context to determine the tense of the verb.

Caminamos en la playa anoche.
We walked on the beach last night.

Más práctica
Cuaderno *pp. 76–78*
Cuaderno para hispanohablantes *pp. 77–79*

🎵 **Conjuguemos.com**

@HomeTutor
Leveled Practice
ClassZone.com

Práctica de GRAMÁTICA

5 | ¿Cuándo terminaron? ♻ *¿Recuerdas?* Telling time p. 14

Hablar
Escribir

Yesterday Isabel and others took walks. What does she say about when they finished their walks?

11:30 **modelo:** mi madre
　　　Mi madre terminó a las once y media.

1. yo **10:45**

2. Mario y un amigo **12:20**

3. tú **1:15**

4. Carlota **9:50**

5. ustedes **10:10**

6. nosotros **3:40**

7. mis hermanas **1:55**

8. mi padre **9:30**

6 | Una playa en la República Dominicana

Leer
Escribir

Fernando and his family went to the beach yesterday. Complete his description of what they did. Write the appropriate preterite form of the correct verb in parentheses.

Ayer mi familia y yo __1.__ (decorar / pasar) un rato en la playa de Boca Chica. Mis padres __2.__ (invitar / celebrar) a mis abuelos también. Mi madre __3.__ (trabajar / preparar) sándwiches y yo __4.__ (limpiar / ayudar) con las bebidas. Mis hermanos __5.__ (usar / bucear) en el mar y yo __6.__ (tomar / usar) el sol. Después, toda la familia __7.__ (nadar / ganar). Y tú, ¿ __8.__ (caminar / nadar) en el mar ayer?

7 | Un sábado activo

Escribir

Use words from each column to tell what people did last Saturday.

modelo: Ramón nadó en el mar.

Ramón	tomar	en el mar
yo	nadar	la cocina
mis padres	trabajar	en la sala
nosotros	limpiar	en la oficina
el perro	hablar	por teléfono
el señor Méndez	descansar	el sol
tú	celebrar	un cumpleaños

8 | En la playa

**Hablar
Escribir**

Look at the illustration below and tell what people did at the beach last weekend.

modelo: Carolina nadó en el mar.

9 | ¿Lo hiciste?

Hablar

Talk with a partner about what you did last week.

A ¿Montaste en bicicleta?

B Sí, monté en bicicleta en el parque. (No, no monté en bicicleta.)

1.    **2.**    **3.**

4.    **5.**    **6.**

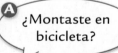

10 | Durante el fin de semana

Hablar

Work in a group of three. Talk about what you did last weekend.

| comprar un almuerzo sano | caminar en la playa |

| levantar pesas | mirar la televisión | trabajar |

| nadar en una piscina | estudiar | ¿ ? |

A ¿Compraron ustedes un almuerzo sano?

B Sí, compré una ensalada.

C No, mis amigos y yo compramos papas fritas.

Comparación cultural

La artista y su estilo

How do artists reflect a distinctive style in their painting? Bright pastel colors, glowing light, and abstract images that reveal hidden figures are common elements in Amaya Salazar's work. This painter from the **Dominican Republic** is also a sculptor and muralist. Many consider her paintings to have a magical or dreamlike quality. What images can you find hidden in this painting of a tropical forest?

Bosque escondido *(2005)*, *Amaya Salazar*

Compara con tu mundo *How would you describe the style, colors, and images used by your favorite artist? How does his or her work compare to that of Amaya Salazar?*

Más práctica   Cuaderno *pp. 76–78*   Cuaderno para hispanohablantes *pp. 77–79*

PARA Y PIENSA

Did you get it? Complete each sentence with the preterite form of the verb in parentheses.

1. Ayer mis amigos y yo _____ en el mar. (bucear)
2. Tú _____ el sol mucho y ahora tu piel está roja. (tomar)
3. José y Ricardo _____ pesas para ser más fuertes. (levantar)

Get Help Online
ClassZone.com

GRAMÁTICA *en contexto*

¡AVANZA! **Goal:** Pay attention to how Mario and Isabel use the preterite to tell the doctor about Mario's accident. Then use the preterite of regular **-ar** verbs to talk about past actions. *Actividades 11–13*

Telehistoria escena 2

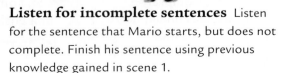
@*HomeTutor* VideoPlus
View, Read and Record
ClassZone.com

STRATEGIES

VIDEO
DVD

AUDIO

Cuando lees

Read for excuses Read the conversation involving Mario, Isabel, and the doctor. What excuse does Mario use to avoid admitting his fault in the crash?

Cuando escuchas

Listen for incomplete sentences Listen for the sentence that Mario starts, but does not complete. Finish his sentence using previous knowledge gained in scene 1.

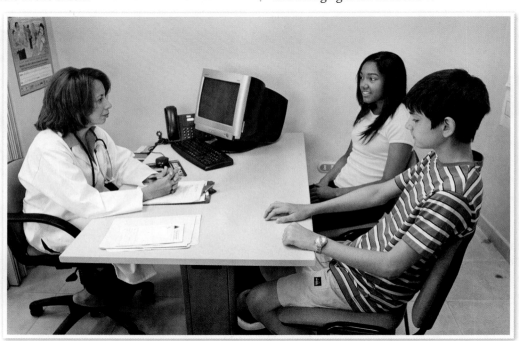

Isabel takes Mario to the doctor's office.

Doctora: ¿Mario Álvarez? ¿Está usted enfermo?

Isabel: Le duelen la pierna y la cabeza. Lo ayudé a caminar.

Doctora: *(to Mario)* ¿Qué hiciste?

Isabel: Pues, montó en su bicicleta... ¡cerca de unas frutas!

Mario: Monté en mi bicicleta...

Doctora: ¿Llevaste un casco?

Isabel: Sí, ¡pero Mario piensa que es Lance Armstrong!

Mario: Isabel, ¡el señor de las frutas caminó delante de mi bicicleta!

Isabel: Y allí... ¡Pum!

Doctora: Mario, ¿sabes montar en bicicleta?

Mario: Sí, es fácil.

Doctora: ¿Te gustó?

Mario: Ahora estoy herido, ¡pero me gustó!

Doctora: *(to Isabel)* Para la salud de tu amigo, no más bicicletas, ¡por favor! **Continuará...** p. 148

11 | Hablan con la doctora *Comprensión del episodio*

Escuchar
Leer

Tell whether these sentences about the episode are true or false. Correct the false statements.

1. A Mario le duelen la cabeza y los brazos.
2. El señor de las frutas caminó detrás de Mario.
3. Mario llevó casco.
4. La doctora piensa que Mario es Lance Armstrong.
5. A Mario le gustó montar en bicicleta.
6. Ahora Isabel está herida.

12 | De vacaciones con tu familia

Escribir

You and your family are on vacation at the beach. Write a postcard to a friend telling what you and members of your family did yesterday.

modelo:

Playa Caribe

¡Hola! ¡Estamos en la República Dominicana!

Ayer yo buceé en el mar. Mi hermana tomó el sol ...

República Dominicana
© Tarjetas Postales, S.A.

13 | ¿Qué hicieron tú y tus amigos?

Hablar
Escribir

Describe what you and your friends did recently.

1. ¿Alquilaron ustedes un DVD interesante?
2. ¿Con quién hablaste por teléfono ayer?
3. ¿Qué hiciste tú en la biblioteca ayer?
4. ¿Dónde escucharon ustedes buena música?
5. ¿Qué miraste en la televisión anoche?
6. ¿Qué hicieron ustedes en el centro comercial?

PARA Y PIENSA

Did you get it? Create sentences using each verb in the preterite tense.
1. Isabel y Mario / llevar cascos
2. Mario / no montar en bicicleta muy bien
3. el señor de las frutas / caminar delante de Mario

Get Help Online
ClassZone.com

Presentación de GRAMÁTICA

¡AVANZA! **Goal:** Learn how to form the preterite of verbs ending in **-car, -gar,** and **-zar.** Then use these verbs to say what people did. *Actividades 14–19*

English Grammar Connection: The spelling of some verbs in English changes in the past tense when *-ed* is added: for example, *admit → admitted, stop → stopped, picnic → picnicked.* Spanish also has verbs that change their spelling in the preterite.

Preterite of -car, -gar, -zar Verbs

Animated Grammar
ClassZone.com

There is a spelling change in the preterite of regular verbs that end in **-car, -gar,** or **-zar.** How do you write the verb forms that have a change in spelling?

Here's how:

Regular verbs that end in **-car, -gar,** or **-zar** have a spelling change in the **yo** form of the preterite. This change allows these words to maintain their original sound.

bus**c**ar	c	*becomes* →	**qu**	(yo) bus**qu**é
ju**g**ar	g	*becomes* →	**gu**	(yo) ju**gu**é
almor**z**ar	z	*becomes* →	**c**	(yo) almor**c**é

Busqu**é** el bloqueador de sol. Él **buscó** las toallas.
*I **looked for** the sunscreen. He **looked for** the towels.*

Jugu**é** al béisbol. Ellas **ju**g**aron** al fútbol.
*I **played** baseball. They **played** soccer.*

Almorc**é** a la una. ¿A qué hora **almor**z**aste** tú?
*I **ate lunch** at one o'clock. What time **did you eat lunch**?*

Más práctica
  Cuaderno *pp. 79–81*
  Cuaderno para hispanohablantes *pp. 80–83*

Conjuguemos.com

@HomeTutor
Leveled Practice
ClassZone.com

Práctica de GRAMÁTICA

14 | La agenda de Isabel

Escribir

Look at Isabel's planner. Complete what she says she did last week.
Follow the model.

> **modelo:** «_____ a las cuatro el martes.»
> «Practiqué el piano a las cuatro el martes.»

lunes	martes	miércoles	jueves	viernes	sábado
3:00 jugar al béisbol	3:30 pagar las entradas	3:00 tocar la guitarra con Roberto	5:00 practicar el piano	4:00 practicar el piano	10:00 nadar
5:00 practicar el piano	4:00 practicar el piano	5:00 buscar un vestido nuevo	7:00 estudiar	8:00 llegar a la fiesta	11:00 limpiar la casa
8:00 estudiar	7:00 comenzar un libro nuevo		9:00 sacar la basura		12:30 practicar el piano
					1:00 almorzar con Luz María
					7:30 alquilar un DVD

domingo
3:00 jugar al béisbol
5:00 practicar el piano
8:00 estudiar

1. «_____ a la una el sábado.»
2. «_____ a las ocho el viernes.»
3. «_____ a las siete el martes.»
4. «_____ a las tres y media el martes.»
5. «_____ a las tres el miércoles.»
6. «_____ a las cinco el miércoles.»
7. «_____ a las tres el domingo.»
8. «_____ a las nueve el jueves.»

15 | Ayer...

**Hablar
Escribir**

Isabel is talking about what she and the people she knows did yesterday.
Choose the correct verbs from the list and conjugate them in the preterite to
complete the sentences.

| pagar | sacar | empezar |
| tocar | almorzar | jugar |

Mis clases __1.__ a las ocho de la mañana. A las doce, yo __2.__ en la
cafetería con mis amigos. Yo __3.__ treinta pesos por una hamburguesa
y papas fritas. Después de las clases, mis amigos y yo __4.__
al béisbol en el parque. Más tarde, yo __5.__ la basura. Mi hermano
__6.__ la guitarra.

16 | Muchas preguntas

**Escuchar
Escribir**

Mario wants to know what you did yesterday. Listen to his questions and write your answers.

> **modelo:** ¿Pagaste el almuerzo?
> Sí, pagué el almuerzo. (No, no pagué el almuerzo.)

17 | Me duele...

Hablar

Ask a partner why he or she didn't do these things today. Your partner will answer by saying that something hurts.

> **modelo:** sacar una buena nota

A ¿Por qué no sacaste una buena nota?

B No saqué una buena nota porque me duele la cabeza.

Estudiante A

1. jugar al ¿?
2. practicar deportes
3. almorzar mucha comida
4. tocar la guitarra
5. llegar temprano a clase
6. ¿?

Estudiante B

los pies
el estómago
las piernas
la mano
la cabeza
¿?

AUDIO

Pronunciación **La letra g con e, i**

Before **e** and **i**, the **g** in Spanish is pronounced like the Spanish **j**, or **jota**.

Listen and repeat.

Soy Regina. Tengo una cámara digital.

ge →	inteligente	Argentina
	Jorge	general
gi →	gimnasio	digital
	página	Sergio

Jorge corre en el gimnasio.
Regina tiene una cámara digital.

---

18 | ¿Por qué?

Hablar
Escribir

Use words from the list to explain each statement below.

modelo: Tengo que hacer la tarea.
No la empecé.

| pagar la cuenta | sacar una mala nota | tocar la guitarra |

| no almorzar | jugar al fútbol | no buscar | no empezar |

1. Estoy cansada.
2. Me duelen las manos.
3. No tengo dinero.

4. No encuentro mi chaqueta.
5. Estoy enojado.
6. Tengo hambre.

19 | Un día en el festival

Escribir

Comparación cultural

El Festival del Merengue

El Festival del Merengue

How do music and dance reflect the culture of a country? Merengue is a lively style of music and dance that many consider a symbol of the **Dominican Republic.** Musicians use instruments such as the *güiro,* maracas, accordion, saxophone, and drums to play its characteristic rhythm. The Festival del Merengue takes place every summer in Santo Domingo. The ten-day event includes music, parades, arts and crafts fairs, cart races, and a wide variety of Dominican foods.

Compara con tu mundo *Do you know of any similar festivals in your area? Have you attended one, or would you like to?*

You went to the merengue festival. Write about your day there.

pistas: llegar, tocar, almorzar, comenzar, escuchar, bailar

modelo: El festival comenzó a las diez y...

Más práctica   Cuaderno *pp. 79–81*   Cuaderno para hispanohablantes *pp. 80–83*

PARA Y PIENSA

Did you get it? Complete each sentence with the preterite form of the appropriate verb: **comenzar, jugar, llegar,** or **practicar.**

1. Yo _____ a casa temprano.
2. ¿Ustedes _____ al tenis ayer?
3. El partido _____ a las siete.
4. Yo _____ deportes anoche.

Get Help Online
ClassZone.com

Todo junto

Goal: *Show what you know* Pay attention to the doctor's advice to Mario. Then use the preterite of regular **-ar** verbs and verbs ending in **-car, -gar,** and **-zar** to talk about your health. *Actividades 20–24*

Telehistoria completa

@**HomeTutor** VideoPlus
View, Read and Record
ClassZone.com

STRATEGIES

Cuando lees

Find the topics While reading, find at least two or three topics in this scene. One is the doctor's suggestions for Mario's health. What other topics can you identify?

Cuando escuchas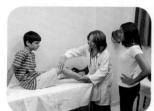

Listen for the implied meaning Listen for the unstated meaning to answer these questions: Will Mario ever get Trini's autograph? Is Mario strong and healthy now?

Escena 1 *Resumen*
Mario está herido y no puede ir con Isabel al estadio para ver a Trini Salgado.

Escena 2 *Resumen*
Isabel ayuda a Mario a caminar. A él le duelen la pierna y la cabeza. Ellos hablan con una doctora.

VIDEO
DVD

AUDIO

Escena 3

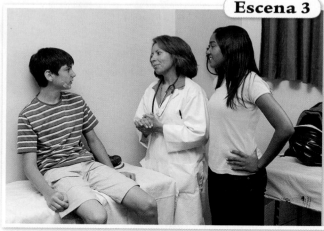

Doctora: El tobillo está bien. ¿Te duele la rodilla?

Mario: No. *(The doctor touches Mario's knee, and he yelps.)* Un poco.

Doctora: No puedes jugar al fútbol, y no puedes jugar al béisbol por cuatro semanas.

Mario: ¿Puedo levantar pesas?

Doctora: Levantar pesas, sí, con los brazos. Con las piernas, no...

Isabel: Muchas gracias, doctora. Adiós.

The doctor leaves. Mario turns to Isabel.

Mario: ¡Ay, el autógrafo para Alicia! Comencé a...

Isabel: Sí, Mario, lo siento. Comenzaste a buscar a Trini, pero ¿qué podemos hacer? *(They stand to leave.)*

Isabel: ¿Vamos a la playa mañana? El mar es bueno para los enfermos.

Mario: ¡No estoy enfermo!

20 | ¡A completar! *Comprensión de los episodios*

Escuchar
Leer

Complete the sentences to describe what happened in the episodes.

1. Isabel y Mario quieren ser los primeros...
2. Mario no está enfermo, pero...
3. Isabel y Mario buscaron a Trini Salgado porque...
4. El señor de las frutas...
5. A Mario le duele la rodilla y no puede...
6. Mario puede levantar pesas, pero...

21 | ¿Qué pasó? *Comprensión de los episodios*

Escuchar
Leer

Answer the questions about the episodes.

1. ¿Qué buscaron Isabel y Mario?
2. ¿Qué llevó Mario?
3. ¿Le gustó a Mario montar en bicicleta?
4. ¿Qué le duele a Mario?

22 | ¿Qué hiciste para la salud?

Hablar

> **STRATEGY Hablar**
> **Draw a Venn diagram for similarities and differences** While talking,
> make a Venn diagram. In one circle list healthy things *you* did that your partner
> did not. In the other circle, list what *your partner* did that you did not. In the
> overlap, list what *you both* did.

Talk with a partner about the healthy activities you did last month. Explain
what benefits the activities have for your health, where you did them, and
with whom.

caminar   jugar al ¿ ?   practicar deportes

levantar pesas   nadar   almorzar bien

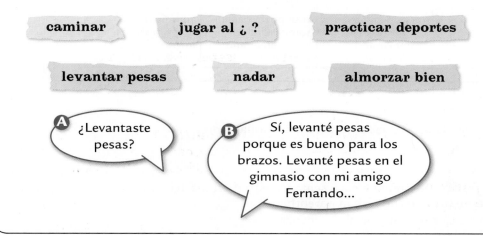

A ¿Levantaste pesas?

B Sí, levanté pesas porque es bueno para los brazos. Levanté pesas en el gimnasio con mi amigo Fernando...

23 | Integración

Leer
Escuchar
Hablar

Read the article and listen to the radio interview. Then compare what you did last week to stay healthy to what these people did.

Fuente 1 Artículo del periódico

Ricardo, ¿qué hiciste para ganar?

Ricardo Núñez es el campeón olímpico de natación. Él nos explicó cómo ganó el año pasado. Es un atleta muy trabajador. «Yo soy una persona muy seria. Practico todos los días. Este fin de semana nadé por dos horas el sábado y el domingo levanté pesas en el gimnasio por tres horas». Para él, la comida es muy importante. «Ayer preparé un desayuno muy sano... cereal, jugo de naranja y pan. Hoy almorcé una ensalada y sopa de pollo». Núñez también tiene que descansar. «También descanso. Ayer alquilé una película muy buena... una película de natación».

Fuente 2 Entrevista de radio

Listen and take notes
- ¿Qué deportes practicó la chica?
- ¿Qué almorzó?

modelo: Durante la semana yo...

24 | Un poema diamante

Escribir

Write a diamond poem about something that makes you feel healthy.

Para organizarte: **modelo:**
- *el nombre del lugar o de la actividad* ———————> la playa
- *una descripción* ——————————————> agua bonita
- *tres cosas que hiciste* ————> tomé el sol, caminé, miré el agua
- *otra descripción* ———————————> agua tranquila
- *otro nombre* ————————————> el mar Caribe

Writing Criteria	Excellent	Good	Needs Work
Content	Your poem includes most of the required elements.	Your poem includes some of the required elements.	Your poem includes few of the required elements.
Communication	Most of your poem is organized and easy to follow.	Parts of your poem are organized and easy to follow.	Your poem is disorganized and hard to follow.
Accuracy	Your poem has few mistakes in grammar and vocabulary.	Your poem has some mistakes in grammar and vocabulary.	Your poem has many mistakes in grammar and vocabulary.

Más práctica   Cuaderno *pp. 82–83*   Cuaderno para hispanohablantes *pp. 84–85*

**PARA
Y
PIENSA**

Did you get it? Complete each sentence based on the Telehistoria with the preterite form of the verb in parentheses.
1. Mario _____ a buscar a Trini. (comenzar)
2. Isabel y Mario no la _____. (encontrar)

Get Help Online
ClassZone.com

Juegos y diversiones

Review parts of the body by playing a game of Simon Says.

The Setup

Everyone in your class will stand up.

Playing the Game

Your teacher will say **Simón dice** before giving a command. You must act out what the teacher says. If you don't know what to do or you do the wrong thing, you sit down. If your teacher does not say **Simón dice** before giving the command, you should not do anything. If you act out that command by mistake, you sit down.

The Winner!

The last student standing wins.

Simón dice: Levanta la mano derecha.

Lectura cultural

¡AVANZA! **Goal:** Read about two world-class athletes from the Dominican Republic and Venezuela. Then compare them and talk about the sports you play.

Comparación cultural

AUDIO

Dos atletas de alta velocidad

STRATEGY Leer

Chart the data In a chart, record the following data for Félix and for Daniela.

	país	deporte	medallas	año(s) que ganó
Félix				
Daniela				

Latinoamérica tiene una gran historia de deportes y de atletas ganadores. Algunos[1] practican su deporte día y noche, en las calles y pistas[2] que están muy lejos de los aficionados y cámaras de televisión.

Félix Sánchez es uno de los atletas más dominantes en los 400 metros de vallas[3]. Estadounidense de nacimiento, Sánchez decidió representar a la República Dominicana, el país de sus padres, en competiciones internacionales. En los Juegos Olímpicos del 2000 en Sydney, Australia, Félix Sánchez llegó en cuarto lugar. Para tener motivación, Sánchez prometió[4] llevar el brazalete que llevó en Sydney hasta[5] ganar una medalla de

[1] Some   [2] tracks   [3] hurdles   [4] promised   [5] until

República Dominicana

Félix Sánchez con la bandera dominicana

Venezuela

oro[6]. Lo llevó por cuatro años. En los Juegos Olímpicos del 2004, ganó la primera medalla de oro para la República Dominicana y se hizo[7] héroe nacional. Después de ganar, el triunfante Sánchez caminó delante de los aficionados con la bandera[8] dominicana en las manos.

Muchas personas montan en bicicleta pero pocos van tan rápido como la ciclista venezolana Daniela Larreal. Ella ganó tres medallas de oro en los Juegos Bolivarianos en el 2001. En el 2003, se hizo campeona de la Copa Mundial[9] de Ciclismo de Pista. En agosto del 2005, ella ganó otra medalla de oro en los Juegos Bolivarianos. Llegó a los 500 metros con un tiempo de 35,56 segundos. «Qué rico es volver a estar en unos Bolivarianos y ganar nuevamente otra medalla», comentó la campeona.

Daniela Larreal y su medalla de oro

---

[6] gold   [7] became   [8] flag   [9] **Copa...** World Cup

PARA Y PIENSA

¿Comprendiste?
1. ¿Qué deporte practica Félix Sánchez? ¿Y Daniela Larreal?
2. ¿Qué ganó Sánchez? ¿Y Larreal?
3. Haz una comparación de los dos atletas. ¿Qué hacen? ¿De dónde son?

¿Y tú?
¿Practicas un deporte? ¿Cuál? ¿Ganaste medallas?

Proyectos culturales

Gestos y refranes

How can gestures and proverbs facilitate communication? When you speak, you communicate with more than just words. When you move your hands, face, or body while you speak, you are using gestures. You can also use gestures to communicate without words. Some gestures are universally understood, yet others are only understood within one language or cultural group. **Refranes,** or proverbs, are short, well-known sayings that express a basic truth or idea. Like gestures, some **refranes** are unique to one language, while others are similar in many languages.

¡En absoluto!
To show "No way!" start with your forearms crossed. Uncross your arms quickly and straighten them completely.

¡Qué loco!
To show that someone is being silly, place your finger against your temple and rotate your wrist back and forth.

¡Mucha gente!
To show that a place is crowded with people, bunch the fingers of both your hands together and then straighten your fingers. Repeat.

¡Ojo!
To show "Watch out!" use your finger to point to your eye. Tug lightly on the skin below your eye.

Proyecto 1 *Los gestos*

With a partner, practice using gestures common in Spanish-speaking countries.

Instructions
1. Study the photos that illustrate some of the gestures used in Spanish-speaking countries.
2. Make one of the gestures on the page and have your partner say its meaning aloud. Take turns.

¡En absoluto!

Proyecto 2 *Los refranes*

Illustrate one of these **refranes** and explain what it means.
1. El que busca, encuentra.
2. Quien va a Sevilla pierde su silla.
3. Donde una puerta se cierra, otra se abre.

Materials for illustrating los refranes
Colored pens or pencils
Paper

Instructions
On a piece of paper, draw the **refrán** that you selected.

En tu comunidad

It is important to understand the meanings of gestures in different cultures. Why would this be especially useful in the business world?

En resumen
Vocabulario y gramática

Animated Grammar
Interactive Flashcards
ClassZone.com

Vocabulario

Talk About Staying Healthy

enfermo(a)	*sick*	levantar pesas	*to lift weights*
fuerte	*strong*	la salud	*health*
herido(a)	*hurt*	sano(a)	*healthy*

Parts of the Body

la boca	*mouth*	la nariz	*nose*
el brazo	*arm*	(*pl.* las narices)	
la cabeza	*head*	el ojo	*eye*
el corazón (*pl.* los corazones)	*heart*	la oreja	*ear*
		el pie	*foot*
el cuerpo	*body*	la piel	*skin*
el estómago	*stomach*	la pierna	*leg*
la mano	*hand*	la rodilla	*knee*
		el tobillo	*ankle*

Outdoor Activities

el bloqueador de sol	*sunscreen*	hacer esquí acuático	*to water-ski*
bucear	*to scuba-dive*	el mar	*sea*
caminar	*to walk*	la playa	*beach*
		tomar el sol	*to sunbathe*

Make Excuses

doler (ue)	*to hurt, to ache*
Lo siento.	*I'm sorry.*

Other Words and Phrases

anoche	*last night*
ayer	*yesterday*
comenzar (ie)	*to begin*
terminar	*to end*
¿Qué hiciste (tú)?	*What did you do?*
¿Qué hicieron ustedes?	*What did you do?*

Gramática

Nota gramatical: The verb **doler** p. 137

Preterite of Regular -ar Verbs

To form the **preterite** of a regular **-ar** verb, add the appropriate preterite ending to the verb's stem.

nadar to swim	
nadé	nadamos
nadaste	nadasteis
nadó	nadaron

Preterite of -car, -gar, -zar Verbs

Regular verbs that end in **-car, -gar,** or **-zar** have a spelling change in the **yo** form of the preterite.

bus**car**	c	*becomes* →	qu	(yo)	bus**qué**
ju**gar**	g	*becomes* →	gu	(yo)	ju**gué**
almor**zar**	z	*becomes* →	c	(yo)	almor**cé**

Repaso de la lección

¡AvanzaRap!
DVD
Sing and Learn

¡LLEGADA!

Now you can
- talk about parts of the body
- make excuses
- say what you did
- talk about staying healthy

Using
- the verb **doler**
- preterite of regular **-ar** verbs
- preterite of **-car, -gar, -zar** verbs

To review
- preterite of regular **-ar** verbs p. 138
- preterite of **-car, -gar, -zar** verbs p. 144

1 | Listen and understand

AUDIO

Listen to Elisa describe a day at the beach. Then write whether or not she did the following activities.

modelo: usar bloqueador de sol
Elisa usó bloqueador de sol.

1. tomar el sol
2. bucear
3. caminar
4. almorzar

5. jugar al voleibol
6. descansar
7. tocar la guitarra
8. cantar

To review
- the verb **doler** p. 137

2 | Talk about parts of the body

Explain why these people are going to the nurse's office at school.

modelo: Andrés
A Andrés le duele la cabeza.

1.  Esteban

4. usted

2. Amalia y Patricio

5. nosotros

3.  yo

6. tú

To review
• preterite of regular **-ar** verbs p. 138

3 | Talk about staying healthy

Everyone in Guillermo's family is healthy. Complete the paragraph with the correct form of the appropriate verb to say what his family members did yesterday.

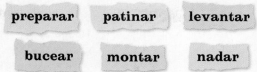

preparar   patinar   levantar

bucear   montar   nadar

A mi familia y a mí nos gusta ser sanos. Ayer mi hermano Marcos y yo __1.__ pesas antes de jugar al fútbol. Mi papá __2.__ en la piscina, y mi mamá y mi tía __3.__ en el mar. Mi hermana Carlota __4.__ una ensalada para todos nosotros. Después del almuerzo, yo __5.__ en bicicleta y mis hermanos __6.__ en línea en el parque.

To review
• preterite of **-car, -gar, -zar** verbs p. 144

4 | Say what you did

Read what Carolina did yesterday and then write whether or not you did the same thing.

modelo: Carolina sacó la basura.
Yo también saqué la basura. (Yo no saqué la basura.)

1. Llegó tarde a la escuela.
2. Tocó la guitarra.
3. Comenzó a leer un libro.
4. Practicó deportes.
5. Jugó al voleibol.
6. Almorzó a las doce y media.
7. Pagó la cuenta en un restaurante.
8. Empezó la tarea.

To review
• Beaches p. 101
• Comparación cultural pp. 141, 147
• Lectura cultural pp. 152–153

5 | Dominican Republic and Venezuela

Comparación cultural

Answer these culture questions.

1. What are beaches in the Dominican Republic known for?
2. What are some common themes of Amaya Salazar's artwork?
3. What can you see and do at Santo Domingo's **Festival del Merengue**?
4. Where are Félix Sánchez and Daniela Larreal from and what sports do they play? What competitions have they participated in?

Más práctica   Cuaderno *pp. 84–95*   Cuaderno para hispanohablantes *pp. 86–95*

Get Help Online
ClassZone.com

República Dominicana

Honduras

Venezuela

AUDIO

Deportes favoritos

Lectura y escritura

WebQuest
ClassZone.com

1 **Leer** Choices of favorite sports vary around the world. Read what Felipe, Gloria, and Agustín say about their favorite sports.

2 **Escribir** Using the three descriptions as models, write a short paragraph about your favorite sport.

STRATEGY **Escribir**

Use a sports chart
To write about your favorite sport, complete a chart like the one shown.

Categoría	Detalles
nombre del deporte	
lugar	
participantes	
equipo necesario	
ropa apropiada	

Step 1 Complete the chart with information about your sport. Include details about where it is played, who participates, what equipment is needed, and what clothes should be worn.

Step 2 Write your paragraph. Make sure to include all the information from your chart. Check your writing by yourself or with help from a friend. Make final corrections.

Compara con tu mundo

Use the paragraph you wrote to compare your favorite sport to a sport described by *one* of the three students. How are they similar? How are they different?

Cuaderno *pp. 96–98*   Cuaderno para hispanohablantes *pp. 96–98*

República Dominicana

Felipe

¡Hola! Me llamo Felipe y vivo en Punta Cana, cerca del mar. Ayer pasé el día en la playa con mis amigos. Después de nadar un rato, jugamos un partido de voleibol con ocho jugadores. Mi equipo comprende las reglas pero ayer no ganó el partido. El voleibol es mi deporte favorito porque puedo jugar con mis amigos y no es peligroso.

Honduras

Gloria

¿Qué tal? Me llamo Gloria y vivo en La Ceiba, el lugar perfecto para practicar deportes acuáticos. Mi deporte favorito es el rafting. Uno de los mejores ríos para practicar rafting en Honduras es el río Cangreja. La semana pasada, mis hermanos y yo alquilamos una balsa[1] para navegar el río. Es una actividad muy divertida.

[1] raft

Venezuela

Agustín

¡Hola! Me llamo Agustín. Soy aficionado de los deportes. Me gusta mucho el béisbol, pero me gusta más el básquetbol porque soy alto y tengo las piernas y los brazos largos[2]. También me gusta correr y saltar[3]. Mis amigos y yo jugamos casi todos los días en una cancha cerca de mi casa en Caracas.

[2] long   [3] to jump

Repaso inclusivo
♻ Options for Review

¡*AvanzaRap!*
DVD
Sing and Learn

1 | Listen, understand, and compare

Escuchar

Listen to a sports broadcast from the Dominican Republic. Then answer the following questions.

1. ¿Qué tiempo hace en el campo?
2. ¿A qué juega Mariano Sandoval?
3. ¿De dónde es Sandoval?
4. ¿Cómo juega él?
5. ¿Por qué dice Sandoval que es un buen jugador?

Have you ever excelled at something? Who influenced you and how?

2 | Be a sports commentator

Hablar

You have been asked to present a student's view on sports for a Spanish-language channel on television. Prepare a commentary on your favorite sport. Include when and where it is played, why it is important to you, and information on teams and/or athletes. You may want to videotape your commentary or present it live to the class.

3 | Talk with the school nurse

Hablar

Role-play a conversation with the school nurse. You decide to go to the nurse's office. Tell your partner what hurts and name three activities that you did recently. He or she will make a connection between the activities and your injuries and make some recommendations for getting better. Your conversation should be at least three minutes long.

¿Qué te duele?

Me duele la cabeza.

4 | Write a Web article

Escribir

Write a Web article about the sports and activities that visitors to your area can participate in. Mention at least three activities for each season of the year and explain where people should go to take part in these activities. Be sure to mention what the weather is like during different times of the year. Copy this chart on a piece of paper and use it to organize your information. Your article should be at least seven sentences long.

Estación	Actividades	Lugares

5 | Plan a class reunion

Hablar
Escribir

Work in a group of four to plan your ten-year class reunion in Punta Cana, Dominican Republic. Plan how long the reunion will be, what activities people can participate in, and what food will be served. Create an invitation and present it to the class. After looking at all of the invitations, vote for the plan that you want to use for your class reunion.

6 | Compare classes

Leer
Escribir

Silvia is in her second year of high school. Read her report cards from last year and this year. Write a paragraph about what she studied and did during her first year and the classes she has and activities she does now. Then compare her grades and give possible reasons for why her grades are different from one year to the next. Your paragraph should have at least six sentences.

Escuela Secundaria de Santo Domingo

Silvia Ibáñez
Primer año

Clase	Nota final
Matemáticas – Álgebra I	A
Arte	B
Inglés I	B
Ciencias Naturales	C
Literatura	A
Música	B

Actividades extracurriculares:
Equipo de natación
Equipo de voleibol

Escuela Secundaria de Santo Domingo

Silvia Ibáñez
Segundo año

Clase	Nota final
Ciencias – Biología	B
Historia	A
Música	A
Matemáticas – Geometría	A
Literatura	B
Inglés II	A

Actividades extracurriculares:
Banda musical (trompeta)
Equipo de voleibol

7 Argentina

¡Una semana fenomenal!

Lección 1

Tema: **En el cibercafé**

Lección 2

Tema: **Un día en el parque de diversiones**

Bolivia

Océano Pacífico

Paraguay

Argentina

Rosario **Uruguay**

Chile

★
Buenos Aires

Mar del Plata

Océano Atlántico

• *Ushuaia*

«**¡Hola!**
Somos Florencia y Mariano.
Vivimos en Argentina.»

Población: 40.482.000

Área: 1.068.302 millas cuadradas, el país hispanohablante más grande del mundo

Capital: Buenos Aires

Moneda: el peso argentino

Idioma: español

Comida típica: asado, matambre, dulce de leche

Gente famosa: Norma Aleandro (actriz), Jorge Luis Borges (escritor), César Milstein (biólogo), Mercedes Sosa (cantante)

◄ **Modernidad y tradición** Buenos Aires is often called "Paris of the Americas," in part due to its European-style architecture mixed with modern elements, such as **El Obelisco** (Obelisk) in the Plaza de la República. At 400 feet across, the Avenida 9 de Julio leading up to the plaza is considered the widest avenue in the world. *What landmarks does your community have?*

El Obelisco en la Plaza de la República, Buenos Aires

La identidad nacional y el gaucho **Los gauchos** are considered cultural icons in Argentina. They lead an independent and simple life, raising cattle on the plains (**las pampas**). *How do **gauchos** compare to the cowboys of the western United States?* ►

Gauchos y sus caballos en un bosque petrificado cerca de Sarmiento, Argentina

El Barrio de San Telmo, Buenos Aires

◄ **Un baile muy popular** On Sundays in Barrio de San Telmo, you can see **tango** dancers and hear the accordion-like instrument **el bandoneón.** Most agree that the now-famous **tango** originated in working-class neighborhoods of Buenos Aires at the end of the 19th century. *What are some popular dances in the U.S.?*

UNIDAD 7
Argentina

Lección 1

¡AVANZA!

Tema:

En el cibercafé

In this lesson you will learn to
- talk about technology
- talk about a series of events
- say what you did
- talk about indefinite or negative situations

using
- preterite of regular **-er** and **-ir** verbs
- affirmative and negative words

♻ ¿Recuerdas?
- affirmative **tú** commands
- telling time
- foods and beverages
- preterite of regular **-ar** verbs

Comparación cultural

In this lesson you will learn about
- the use of **lunfardo** in Argentina
- the city of Mar del Plata
- protecting your computer

Compara con tu mundo
These teens are drinking a tea-like beverage called **mate**. Drinking **mate** involves a special cup, often made out of a dried, decorated gourd, with a metal or wood straw, called a **bombilla**. *Does your region have a special beverage or food? What is it?*

¿Qué ves?

Mira la foto

¿Son amigos estas personas?

¿Tienen sed o tienen hambre?

¿Qué hace la chica de la blusa roja?

La Casa Rosada
Buenos Aires, Argentina

Presentación de VOCABULARIO

¡AVANZA!

Goal: Learn about how Florencia and her friends use the computer to send photos. Then practice what you have learned to talk about how you and others use the computer. *Actividades 1–2*

VIDEO DVD

AUDIO

A ¡Hola! Me llamo Florencia. **Anteayer** pasé un rato con mis amigos Mariano y Luciana. **Tomamos fotos** delante de la Casa Rosada.

tomar fotos

abril

		1	2	3	4
la semana pasada					
5	6	7	8	9	10	11
12	13	14	15 ayer	16 (hoy)	17	18
19	20 anteayer	21	22	23	24	25
26	27	28	29	30		

B Hoy, Mariano y yo estamos en la biblioteca. Aquí **navegamos por Internet,** usamos **el mensajero instantáneo** y **mandamos** correos electrónicos. Quiero mandar las fotos que tomé anteayer.

el sitio Web

el mensajero instantáneo

mandar correos electrónicos

¡Hola, Alicia!
Anteayer pasé un rato con mis amigos Mariano y Luciano en el centro de Buenos Aires. Tomamos fotos delante de la Casa Rosada, la residencia del presidente de Argentina. ¿Te gustan las fotos?
Florencia

la cámara digital

Más vocabulario

el año pasado *last year*
entonces *then, so*
luego *later, then*
más tarde *later on*

Expansión de vocabulario p. R4

Continuará...

Presentación de VOCABULARIO

(continuación)

C Es fácil mandarlas y no cuesta **nada.** Primero **conecto a Internet.** Cuando **estoy en línea,** escribo un correo electrónico con las fotos. **Por fin,** pongo **la dirección electrónica** de mi amiga y **hago clic en el icono** para mandarlas.

la dirección electrónica

la pantalla

el teclado

hacer clic en

el ratón

quemar un disco compacto

FoToS

¡A responder! Escuchar

Florencia bought a new computer. Listen to the list of words. Raise your hand if the word names part of her computer.

@HomeTutor VideoPlus
Interactive Flashcards
ClassZone.com

Práctica de VOCABULARIO

1 | El mundo digital

Leer Match the phrases to form logical sentences about computers.

1. Florencia toma fotos
2. Conectamos a Internet
3. Hago clic
4. Mariano navega
5. Uso el ratón
6. Voy a quemar

a. por Internet en la biblioteca.
b. con su cámara digital.
c. un disco compacto.
d. para estar en línea.
e. en el icono para abrir un sitio Web.
f. para hacer clic en los iconos.

2 | ¿Para qué usas...?

Hablar Escribir Tell how you use each item pictured below.

escribir en la computadora

buscar una película

mandar correos electrónicos

mirar fotos

hacer clic   tomar fotos   hablar con amigos

Cinelux
Con lluvia o con sol
9:00   11:00   4:00
El pueblo fantasma
1:00   3:00   7:00

modelo: Uso **el sitio Web** para **buscar una película.**

1.

2.

mensajero instantáneo
De Mariano:
¿Cómo estás?
¿Hablaste con Laura?
Aa *I* U
Enviar mensaje

3.

Crear correo nuevo
Enviar correo   Editar correo
De   Gilberto@superestrella.com
A
ce
Tema

4.

5.

6.

Más práctica   Cuaderno *pp. 99–101*   Cuaderno para hispanohablantes *pp. 99–102*

PARA Y PIENSA

Did you get it? 1. Name three parts of a computer.
2. Name three things you can do on the Internet.

Get Help Online ClassZone.com

VOCABULARIO en contexto

 ¡AVANZA!

Goal: Pay attention to the words Florencia uses to put events in order. Then practice these words to talk about a series of events. *Actividades 3–5*

 **¿Recuerdas?** Affirmative **tú** commands p. 82

Telehistoria escena 1

@HomeTutor VideoPlus
View, Read and Record
ClassZone.com

STRATEGIES

Cuando lees
List related words This conversation includes several expressions for time-sequencing, such as **luego.** While reading, list them and add any others you know.

Cuando escuchas
Listen for sequences Listen for places Alicia's T-shirt has been. Write the names of cities, states, and countries, using arrows for sequencing.

VIDEO DVD

AUDIO

Florencia

Mariano

Florencia: ¡Mariano! Mira, tengo un correo electrónico de Alicia.

Mariano: ¿Qué dice, Florencia? No puedo ver la pantalla.

Florencia: Alicia quiere el autógrafo de Trini Salgado en su camiseta.

Mariano: ¡Qué bárbaro tener el autógrafo de una jugadora de fútbol famosa como Trini Salgado!

Florencia: Alicia mandó la camiseta a Sandra, una amiga que vive en Texas. Después, Sandra la mandó a un amigo de Puebla, en México, pero tampoco la encontró.

Mariano: ¿Y entonces?

Florencia: Luego, su amigo de México mandó la camiseta a Puerto Rico. Más tarde, sus amigos mandaron la camiseta a España, y entonces a Ecuador y a la República Dominicana. Y por fin, anteayer la mandaron aquí a Buenos Aires. ¡Porque Trini está aquí!

Continuará... p. 176

También se dice

Argentina Mariano uses the phrase **¡Qué bárbaro!** to say *Cool!* In other Spanish-speaking countries you might hear:
• **Perú, Chile, Ecuador** **¡Qué bacán!**
• **México** **¡Qué padre!**
• **España** **¡Qué guay!**
• **muchos países** **¡Qué chévere!**

3 | ¿Adónde la mandaron? *Comprensión del episodio*

Escuchar
Leer

Use the words in the list to indicate the order of the places where Alicia's T-shirt was sent.

modelo: Primero, Alicia mandó la camiseta de Miami a Texas. Luego...

| entonces | más tarde | luego | por fin |

4 | ¿En qué orden?

Escuchar

Listen to the description of how Florencia took pictures and sent them to her friends. Then indicate the correct order of the drawings.

a.

b.

c.

d.

e.

f.

5 | ¿Cómo lo hago? ♻ *¿Recuerdas?* Affirmative tú commands p. 82

Hablar

Ask a partner how to do various things on the computer.

A ¿Cómo uso una cámara digital?

B Toma fotos. Luego ponlas en la computadora y míralas en la pantalla.

| mandar fotos |

| usar el mensajero instantáneo | mandar un correo electrónico |

| navegar por Internet | usar una cámara digital | ¿? |

PARA Y PIENSA

Did you get it? Put the following sentences in order.
a. Más tarde, Trini va a Puerto Rico y a España.
b. Luego, Trini está en Puebla, México.
c. Por fin, Trini está en Buenos Aires.
d. Primero, Trini llega a San Antonio.

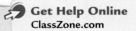
Get Help Online
ClassZone.com

Presentación de GRAMÁTICA

¡AVANZA!

Goal: Learn about the preterite forms of **-er** and **-ir** verbs. Then practice using these verbs to say what you and others did. *Actividades 6–11*

♻ *¿Recuerdas?* Telling time p. 14, foods and beverages pp. 2, 20, 29

English Grammar Connection: Remember that the **preterite** is a tense used to express an action completed at a definite time in the past (see p. 138). In English, regular verbs in the past tense end in *-ed*.

Preterite of Regular -er and -ir Verbs

Animated Grammar
ClassZone.com

Regular **-er** and **-ir** verbs follow a pattern similar to regular **-ar** verbs in the **preterite.** How do you form the **preterite** of regular **-er** and **-ir** verbs?

Here's how:

In the preterite, **-er** and **-ir** verb endings are identical.

vender *to sell*	
vend**í**	vend**imos**
vend**iste**	vend**isteis**
vend**ió**	vend**ieron**

escribir *to write*	
escrib**í**	escrib**imos**
escrib**iste**	escrib**isteis**
escrib**ió**	escrib**ieron**

The **yo** forms and the **usted/él/ella** forms take accents.

> **Vendí** la computadora.
> *I **sold** the computer.*

> Tomás **escribió** un correo electrónico.
> *Tomás **wrote** an e-mail.*

The **nosotros(as)** form of regular **-ir** verbs is the same in both the present and the preterite. Use context clues to determine the tense of the verb.

> **Salimos** a las ocho **anoche.**
> *We **left** at eight o'clock **last night.***

← The word **anoche** tells you that **salimos** is in the preterite tense.

Más práctica
Cuaderno *pp. 102–104*
Cuaderno para hispanohablantes *pp. 103–105*

Conjuguemos.com

@HomeTutor
Leveled Practice
ClassZone.com

Práctica de GRAMÁTICA

6 | ¿Cuándo volvieron? ♻ ¿Recuerdas? Telling time p. 14

Hablar
Escribir

Mariano and his friends went out yesterday. Tell when they returned home, according to the time they left and how long they were out.

> **modelo:** Mariano / 4:00 (dos horas)
> Mariano salió a las cuatro y volvió a las seis.

1. Mariano y yo / 8:30 (siete horas)
2. usted / 9:20 (dos horas)
3. yo / 6:40 (una hora)
4. Florencia y Ana / 10:05 (cuatro horas)
5. tú / 1:15 (tres horas)
6. Florencia / 2:45 (seis horas)

7 | Mariano y su familia

Leer
Escribir

Complete Mariano's e-mail by using the correct preterite form of the appropriate verb.

> Yo te **1.** (escribir / correr) un correo electrónico ayer y mandé unas fotos. ¿Tú las **2.** (vivir / recibir)? Mi familia y yo **3.** (perder / salir) a un restaurante. Mis padres **4.** (comer / deber) churrasco, el bistec de Argentina. De postre mi hermana y yo **5.** (abrir / compartir) un pastel y mi padre **6.** (subir / beber) un café. Luego nosotros **7.** (volver / ver) a casa.

Comparación cultural

El famoso Carlos Gardel

El lunfardo

How do slang words develop? Lunfardo is a variety of slang that originated among the immigrant populations of Buenos Aires, **Argentina,** during the early 20th century. Many words were influenced by other languages, especially Italian, while others were created by reversing the syllables of Spanish terms. For example, *amigos* became *gomías* and *pizza* became *zapi*. Lunfardo appeared in many tango lyrics, such as those popularized by Carlos Gardel. His music helped introduce *lunfardo* to the general public. Many people in Argentina still use some of these words in their informal speech, often in a playful or humorous manner.

Compara con tu mundo *What slang terms do you know that mean "Great!"? Would your teachers, parents, and grandparents use different terms?*

8 | En el cibercafé

Look at the drawing and tell what people did yesterday at the cybercafé.

modelo: Horacio barrió el suelo.

Sara

el Sr. López

Horacio

nosotros

los Sres. González

tú

las hermanas

AUDIO

Pronunciación   La combinación qu

You already know that **c** before **a, o, u,** and consonants makes the sound of the English *k*. To make this sound before **e** and **i** in Spanish, use **qu.**

Listen and repeat.

¿Quién tiene que hacer los quehaceres?

que	→	queso	pequeño
		raqueta	quemar
qui	→	tranquilo	quince
		quiero	equipo

¿Quieres ir al parque?

9 | La semana pasada

Hablar

Talk with a partner about the activities he or she did last week.

salir   barrer   beber   correr

recibir   comer   escribir

A ¿Saliste con tus amigos la semana pasada?

B Sí, salí con mis amigos al cine. (No, no salí con mis amigos.)

1.

2.

3.

4.

5.

6.

10 | Una encuesta ♻ *¿Recuerdas?* Foods and beverages pp. 2, 20, 29

Hablar

Take a survey of what your classmates ate and drank yesterday. Report your findings to the class.

11 | Ayer y hoy

Hablar

Ask a partner questions using the following words.

A ¿Qué aprendiste en la escuela ayer?

B Aprendí unas fechas importantes en la clase de historia.

modelo: qué / aprender en la escuela ayer

1. qué / comer antes de las clases hoy
2. a qué hora / salir de tu casa hoy
3. qué / beber antes de las clases hoy
4. qué / escribir ayer
5. a qué hora / volver a casa ayer
6. qué / vender en la cafetería ayer

Más práctica  Cuaderno *pp. 102–104*   Cuaderno para hispanohablantes *pp. 103–105*

PARA Y PIENSA

Did you get it? Fill in the preterite form of the verb in parentheses.
1. Anteayer yo _____ la cena con mi amiga Teresa. (comer)
2. ¿ _____ tú muchos regalos para tu cumpleaños? (recibir)

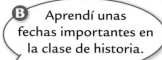
Get Help Online
ClassZone.com

GRAMÁTICA *en contexto*

Goal: Listen to Florencia and Mariano talk about what happened the day before. Then use the preterite of **-er** and **-ir** verbs to describe what you did recently. *Actividades 12–13*

Telehistoria escena 2

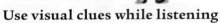

@HomeTutor VideoPlus
View, Read and Record
ClassZone.com

STRATEGIES

Cuando lees
Locate and practice key phrases
Read the scene, finding phrases about the Internet and writing or receiving e-mails. Repeat each one (aloud or to yourself) until you know it and can use it in conversation.

Cuando escuchas
Use visual clues while listening
While listening to the video, search for visual clues that tell you where Trini is going to be. How do the characters' movements keep them from finding out?

VIDEO
DVD

AUDIO

Mariano: Florencia, ¿ahora qué va a pasar con la camiseta de Alicia?

Florencia: Anoche cuando volví a casa, recibí otro correo electrónico de Alicia.

Florencia takes a printout of the e-mail from her bag.

Florencia: Aquí está. Compartimos muchas ideas anoche. Escribió que debemos buscar a Trini en el estadio.

Mariano: Pero, ¿cuándo?

Florencia: No sé. No recibí mucha información. Tenemos que navegar por Internet para buscar la fecha y la hora. ¿Salimos para el cibercafé?

As they leave, Florencia leaves her camera on the table in the restaurant.

Continuará... p. 182

12 | ¿Qué necesitan saber? *Comprensión del episodio*

Escuchar
Leer

Answer the questions about the episode.

1. ¿Qué recibió Florencia anoche?
2. ¿Quiénes compartieron ideas?
3. ¿Quién escribió que deben buscar a Trini en el estadio?
4. ¿Cómo van a buscar información Florencia y Mariano sobre la fecha y la hora?
5. ¿Adónde van ellos después?

13 | ¿Pasaste una semana fenomenal?

Leer

Take this magazine quiz to see if you had a great week. Be prepared to share your results with the class.

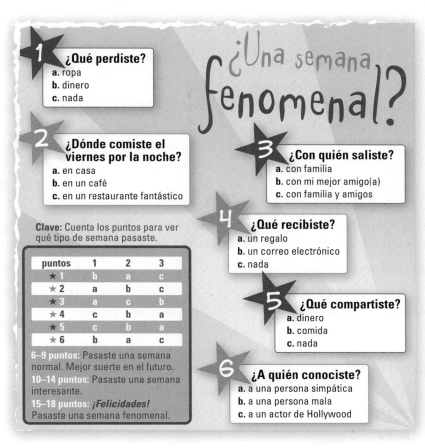

¿Una semana fenomenal?

1 ¿Qué perdiste?
a. ropa
b. dinero
c. nada

2 ¿Dónde comiste el viernes por la noche?
a. en casa
b. en un café
c. en un restaurante fantástico

3 ¿Con quién saliste?
a. con familia
b. con mi mejor amigo(a)
c. con familia y amigos

4 ¿Qué recibiste?
a. un regalo
b. un correo electrónico
c. nada

5 ¿Qué compartiste?
a. dinero
b. comida
c. nada

6 ¿A quién conociste?
a. a una persona simpática
b. a una persona mala
c. a un actor de Hollywood

Clave: Cuenta los puntos para ver qué tipo de semana pasaste.

puntos	1	2	3
★1	b	a	c
★2	a	b	c
★3	a	c	b
★4	c	b	a
★5	c	b	a
★6	b	a	c

6–9 puntos: Pasaste una semana normal. Mejor suerte en el futuro.

10–14 puntos: Pasaste una semana interesante.

15–18 puntos: *¡Felicidades!* Pasaste una semana fenomenal.

PARA Y PIENSA

Did you get it? Complete each sentence with the preterite form of the appropriate verb: **salir, compartir,** or **recibir.**
1. Florencia _____ un correo electrónico de Alicia.
2. Alicia y Florencia _____ muchas ideas.
3. Florencia y Mariano _____ para el cibercafé.

Get Help Online
ClassZone.com

Presentación de GRAMÁTICA

¡AVANZA!

Goal: Learn how to use affirmative and negative words. Then practice them to talk about indefinite or negative situations. **Actividades 14–19**

♺ **¿Recuerdas?** Preterite of regular **-ar** verbs p. 138

English Grammar Connection: A **double negative** is the use of two **negative words** to express a negative idea. Double negatives are considered incorrect in English. In Spanish, they are often required.

There's **nobody** at the door.   **No** hay **nadie** en la puerta.

Affirmative and Negative Words

Animated Grammar
ClassZone.com

Use an **affirmative** or a **negative** word when you want to talk about an indefinite or negative situation.

Here's how:

Affirmative Words		Negative Words	
algo	*something*	**nada**	*nothing*
alguien	*someone*	**nadie**	*no one, nobody*
algún/alguno(a)	*some, any*	**ningún/ninguno(a)**	*none, not any*
o... o	*either . . . or*	**ni... ni**	*neither . . . nor*
siempre	*always*	**nunca**	*never*
también	*also*	**tampoco**	*neither, not either*

Alguno(a) and **ninguno(a)** must match the gender of the noun they replace or modify. They have different forms when used before masculine singular nouns.

alguno *becomes* → **algún**   **ninguno** *becomes* → **ningún**

¿Conoces **algún** sitio Web cómico?   No conozco **ningún** sitio Web cómico.
*Do you know **any** funny Web sites?*   *I do **not** know **any** funny Web sites.*

If a verb is preceded by **no**, words that follow must be negative. A double negative is required in Spanish when **no** precedes the verb.

No queremos **nada.**   **No** me gusta **ninguna** cámara digital.
*We do **not** want **anything.***   *I do **not** like **any** digital cameras.*

However, if the negative word comes before the verb, there is no need to use **no.**

Mi padre **nunca** usa la computadora.   **Nadie** navega por Internet ahora.
*My father **never** uses the computer.*   ***No one** is surfing the Web now.*

Más práctica
    Cuaderno *pp. 105–107*
    Cuaderno para hispanohablantes *pp. 106–109*

@HomeTutor
Leveled Practice
ClassZone.com

Práctica de GRAMÁTICA

14 | ¡Qué negativa!

Hablar
Escribir

Florencia doesn't want to do anything today. Complete the conversation with affirmative and negative words.

Mariano   Florencia

Mariano: ¿Quieres ver __1.__ película en el cine Rex?
Florencia: No, no quiero ver __2.__ película en el cine Rex.

Mariano: ¿Quieres comprar __3.__ en la tienda?
Florencia: No, no quiero comprar __4.__ en la tienda.

Mariano: ¿Quieres pasar un rato con __5.__ ?
Florencia: No, no quiero pasar un rato con __6.__ .

Mariano: ¿Quieres practicar __7.__ deporte?
Florencia: No, no quiero practicar __8.__ deporte.

15 | ¡Inventa la pregunta!

Hablar
Escribir

Create a logical question for each of the following answers.

modelo: No, no tengo nada.
¿Tienes algo?

1. No, no me gusta ningún libro.
2. No, nadie tiene pluma.
3. No, no tengo ninguna clase ahora.
4. No, no quiero hacer nada hoy.
5. No como ni brócoli ni tomates.
6. No, no hay nadie en la casa ahora.
7. No, no juego a ningún deporte.
8. No, no conozco a nadie en la clase de matemáticas.
9. No, no hay nada en la pantalla.
10. No, no tengo ninguna dirección electrónica en mi computadora.

16 | El domingo pasado

Hablar

Ask a partner whether he or she did these things last Sunday. He or she will say no.

A ¿Comiste pizza y papas fritas?

B No, no comí ni pizza ni papas fritas.

1. beber algunos refrescos
2. usar el mensajero instantáneo con alguien
3. recibir algo especial de un amigo
4. tomar algunas fotos con una cámara digital
5. salir con alguien
6. escribir algún correo electrónico
7. vender algo
8. quemar algún disco compacto

17 | ¿Y tú? ♻ *¿Recuerdas?* Preterite of regular **-ar** verbs p. 138

Hablar
Escribir

Answer the questions about what you did. Explain your answers whenever possible.

modelo: ¿Aprendiste algo en la clase de español la semana pasada?
Sí, aprendí algo la semana pasada. Aprendí el vocabulario nuevo.
(No, no aprendí nada.)

1. ¿Estudiaste con alguien anteayer?
2. ¿Comiste algunas galletas anoche?
3. ¿Perdiste algo el año pasado?
4. ¿Compraste algo la semana pasada?
5. ¿Ayudaste a alguien el sábado pasado?
6. ¿Practicaste algún deporte ayer?
7. ¿Escribiste algo anoche?
8. ¿Compartiste algo con alguien ayer?

18 ¿Qué hay en la playa?

Hablar

Comparación cultural

Las playas de Mar del Plata

What features and attractions are most popular for tourists? Mar del Plata is a city in **Argentina** with miles of beaches along the Atlantic Ocean. It is a popular destination for Buenos Aires residents and other tourists during the summer, especially between December and February. Visitors can participate in a variety of activities such as sunbathing, surfing, scuba diving, and fishing.

Las playas de Mar del Plata

Compara con tu mundo *During the summer months, what are popular destinations in your area? What are common activities in these places?*

Ask a partner about the photo. Use affirmative and negative words.

A ¿Hay alguien con un sombrero en la playa?

B No, no hay nadie con un sombrero. ¿Hay algo azul?

19 Algún día

Hablar
Escribir

Add the appropriate negative or affirmative word in each sentence. Then finish the sentence so that it is true for you.

modelo: _____ día voy a ir a...
Algún día voy a ir a España.

1. No tengo _____ clase...
2. No estudio _____ en...
3. En mi familia no hay _____ muy...
4. Quiero hacer _____ el sábado con...
5. No hago _____ divertido cuando...
6. En mi clase de español hay _____ estudiantes muy...
7. No tengo _____ libro de...
8. Conozco a _____ ...

Más práctica   Cuaderno *pp. 105–107*   Cuaderno para hispanohablantes *pp. 106–109*

PARA Y PIENSA

Did you get it? Write the opposite of these sentences.
1. Siempre recibo algunos correos electrónicos.
2. Nadie escribe nada con el mensajero instantáneo.
3. A Beatriz le gusta navegar por Internet y estar en línea.

Get Help Online
ClassZone.com

Todo junto

Goal: Show what you know Notice the affirmative and negative words used to talk about Trini in Buenos Aires. Then use these words and the preterite of **-er** and **-ir** verbs to talk about past actions. *Actividades 20–24*

Telehistoria completa

STRATEGIES

Cuando lees
Notice the information exchange
While reading, notice the information exchange. What does the waiter tell Mariano and Florencia? How does he help them solve their problem?

Cuando escuchas
Practice what you hear Listen to how the speakers emphasize negative expressions (**no, nada, nadie, ni... ni**). After listening, say these sentences with proper emphasis. Remember this for future communication.

 **Escena 1** *Resumen*
Florencia recibe un correo electrónico de Alicia porque Trini Salgado va a estar en Buenos Aires. Sus amigos mandan la camiseta a Argentina.

 **Escena 2** *Resumen*
Alicia escribe que Trini va a estar en el estadio. Pero Florencia y Mariano tienen que navegar por Internet para buscar más información.

VIDEO DVD

AUDIO

Escena 3

Florencia: ¡Señor, por favor! ¿Tiene usted mi cámara?

Camarero: Sí, sí, tranquila. Aquí está. ¿Qué pasa? ¿Necesitan algo?

Mariano: No, nada. Gracias. Queremos ir al estadio para ver a Trini Salgado, pero no sabemos ni la fecha ni la hora. Nadie sabe cuándo va a llegar ella.

Florencia: Usted tampoco sabe, ¿no?

Camarero: No sé nada del estadio, pero sé que Trini Salgado va a estar en el Parque de la Costa en El Tigre, el sábado.

Florencia: ¿Sí? ¿Cómo lo sabe?

Camarero: Mira, allí dice. *(He points to a poster in the restaurant's window.)*

Mariano: ¡Florencia! Nadie encontró a Trini... ni en Estados Unidos... ni en Puerto Rico... tampoco en España. Pero ahora, tú vas a tener el autógrafo.

20 | ¿Estás seguro(a)? *Comprensión de los episodios*

Escuchar
Leer

Tell if these sentences are true or false. Correct the false sentences, using affirmative or negative words.

1. Florencia recibió algo de Alicia.
2. No van a buscar a nadie en el estadio.
3. El camarero no tiene nada de Florencia.
4. El camarero sabe algo de Trini en el estadio.
5. Nadie encontró a Trini en Estados Unidos.
6. También la encontraron en España.

21 | ¿Lo sabes? *Comprensión de los episodios*

Escuchar
Leer

Answer the questions about the episodes.

1. ¿Cuándo mandaron la camiseta a Argentina? ¿Por qué?
2. ¿Qué recibió Florencia cuando volvió a casa?
3. ¿Con quién compartió ideas Florencia?
4. ¿Qué perdió Florencia?
5. ¿Alguien sabe cuándo Trini va a llegar al estadio?
6. ¿Qué no saben Florencia y Mariano?

22 | Los reporteros

Hablar

STRATEGY Hablar

Choose an interesting topic Decide with your partner whether to talk about something interesting that actually occurred or something amazing that you can pretend happened. That way, whatever you choose to talk about in your interview will be of interest to listeners.

You are a reporter. Interview a partner about something that happened at school.

A Estamos aquí en la cafetería. Alguien habló con el director de la escuela y ya no sirven refrescos. ¿Qué piensas, Víctor?

B ¡No me gusta! No hay nada bueno para beber. Ayer bebí leche...

23 | Integración

Leer
Escuchar
Hablar

Read the Web page and listen to the radio program. Then tell where you prefer to go after school and why.

Fuente 1 Página Web

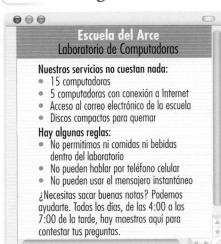

Escuela del Arce
Laboratorio de Computadoras

Nuestros servicios no cuestan nada:
- 15 computadoras
- 5 computadoras con conexión a Internet
- Acceso al correo electrónico de la escuela
- Discos compactos para quemar

Hay algunas reglas:
- No permitimos ni comidas ni bebidas dentro del laboratorio
- No pueden hablar por teléfono celular
- No pueden usar el mensajero instantáneo

¿Necesitas sacar buenas notas? Podemos ayudarte. Todos los días, de las 4:00 a las 7:00 de la tarde, hay maestros aquí para contestar tus preguntas.

Fuente 2 Programa de radio

Listen and take notes
- ¿Qué lugar buscó Raquel?
- ¿Qué hay allí?
- ¿Qué pasó allí?

modelo: Después de las clases prefiero ir al... porque...

24 | Teclados y ratones

Escribir

Write an article for a computer magazine. Tell how you used technology yesterday and how you use the computer in your daily life.

modelo: Me gusta usar la computadora. Ayer navegué por Internet, pero no escribí ningún correo electrónico. Siempre uso el mensajero instantáneo para...

Writing Criteria	Excellent	Good	Needs Work
Content	Your article includes a lot of information.	Your article includes some information.	Your article includes little information.
Communication	Most of your article is organized and easy to follow.	Parts of your article are organized and easy to follow.	Your article is disorganized and hard to follow.
Accuracy	Your article has few mistakes in grammar and vocabulary.	Your article has some mistakes in grammar and vocabulary.	Your article has many mistakes in grammar and vocabulary.

Más práctica   Cuaderno *pp. 108–109*   Cuaderno para hispanohablantes *pp. 110–111*

PARA Y PIENSA

Did you get it? Answer the following questions negatively.
1. ¿Perdió algo Mariano?
2. ¿Recibió Florencia la fecha o la hora?
3. ¿Le escribió Mariano algún correo electrónico a Alicia?

 Get Help Online
ClassZone.com

Juegos y diversiones

Review vocabulary by playing a game.

¿Qué letra?

The Setup

Your teacher will prepare cards with vocabulary words and phrases, one letter per card. For each round, he or she will have a student attach the cards for a word or phrase to a bulletin board. Each word of a phrase will be on a separate line on the board.

Materials
• index cards

Playing the Game

Three players will try to guess the word or phrase in each round of play. They will take turns asking if a certain letter is in the word or phrase. The student who attached the cards to the board will be in charge of flipping the cards when a letter is guessed correctly.

If the guessed letter is in the word or phrase, the player gets a chance to guess what the word or phrase is. If the player asks for a letter that is not in the word or phrase, then it's the next player's turn.

The Winner!

The player who guesses the most words correctly wins.

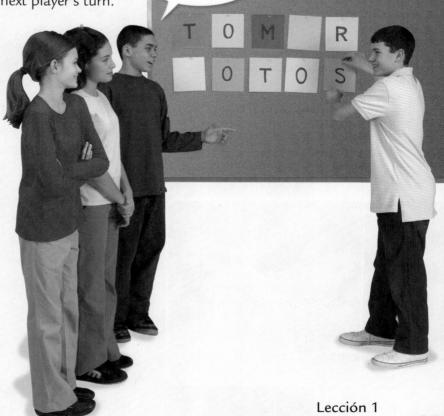

¿Hay una S?

T O M   R
  O T O S

Lectura

¡AVANZA!

Goal: Take this virus-protection questionnaire. Then talk about computer viruses and how you protect your computer.

AUDIO

Un cuestionario sobre las computadoras

Cuestionario: Protección para tu PC ⊗

STRATEGY Leer

Use a cause-and-effect chart
Make a cause-and-effect chart for computer viruses.

 www.antivirus.ar

```
┌─────────────────┐
│ software pirata │
└─────────────────┘
         │
         ▼
    ┌──────────┐
    │ un virus │
    └──────────┘
         │
         ▼
┌─────────────────┐
│ perder archivos │
└─────────────────┘
     │      │
     ▼      ▼
┌──────┐ ┌──────┐
│      │ │      │
└──────┘ └──────┘
```

Cuestionario: Protección para tu PC

¿Qué pasa cuando un virus infecta tu computadora? El virus funciona como un borrador. Puede destruir tus archivos [1]. Puede afectar tu acceso a Internet y el sistema del correo electrónico. Otras personas pueden ver tus datos [2] personales. ¿Conoces las medidas [3] básicas que debes tomar como protección contra [4] los virus? Toma este cuestionario para saber.

1. ¿Cuál de los siguientes *no* es un método típico de propagación de los virus?

A. programas que se descargan [5] de Internet
B. archivos adjuntos [6] a correos electrónicos
C. la provisión de datos personales en un sitio Web no seguro [7]
D. software pirata

---

[1] files [2] information [3] measures [4] against
[5] are downloaded [6] attached [7] secure, safe

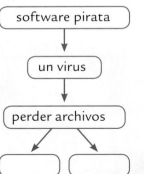

186 Unidad 7 Argentina
ciento ochenta y seis

www.antivirus.ar

Cuestionario: Protección para tu PC

Centro de Protección

Introducción
Protege tu equipo
Recursos

2. Cierto o falso: Después de instalar software antivirus, la computadora está completamente protegida[8].
   A. cierto
   B. falso

3. ¿Qué es un firewall de Internet?
   A. una contraseña[9] segura
   B. un artículo de asbesto que protege la computadora de las llamas[10]
   C. un candado[11] que puedes poner en la computadora para impedir acceso no autorizado
   D. software o hardware que ayuda a proteger la computadora contra ataques como los virus

HAZ CLIC

Respuestas correctas ⊗

1. *C:* la provisión de datos personales en un sitio Web no seguro
2. *B:* falso
3. *D:* software o hardware que ayuda a proteger la computadora contra ataques como los virus

[8] protected   [9] password   [10] flames   [11] padlock

PARA Y PIENSA

¿Comprendiste?
1. ¿Por qué son peligrosos los virus?
2. ¿Cuáles son los métodos típicos de propagación de los virus?
3. ¿Cómo se llama el software o hardware que ayuda a proteger la computadora contra ataques como los virus?

¿Y tú?
¿Qué medidas antivirus tomas cuando usas la computadora?

Conexiones *El lenguaje*

Los juegos de lenguaje

Jeringozo is a language game played by children in Argentina. To say a word in **jeringozo,** divide the word into syllables. After each one, add a syllable consisting of **p** and the vowel sound of the original syllable. For example:

tarde

tar + *pa* | de + *pe* = tar*pa*de*pe*
(Pronounced tárpa-dépe)

mesa

me + *pe* | sa + *pa* = me*pe*sa*pa*
(Pronounced mépe-sápa)

If a syllable has more than one vowel, the stressed vowel is used: **bueno** = **bue*pe*nopo** *(buépe-nópo).* Accents are omitted when writing in **jeringozo.** Try saying and writing the following words in **jeringozo:**

Argentina   **semana**   **durante**   **favorito**

Now that you have mastered it, try saying **República Dominicana**!

El juego de jeringozo

¡Hopolapa, apamipigapa!

¡Buepenospo dipiaspa!

Proyecto 1 *Las ciencias sociales*

Can you think of a game children play in English that is similar to **jeringozo**? Describe the game. How do you think these language games are invented? What purpose do they serve?

Proyecto 2 *La geografía*

Children in Chile play a variation of **jeringozo.** Look at the map of South America on page xxiv. Examine the location and geographical features of Argentina and Chile. Write a paragraph about how you think geography affects the cultures of these two countries. Why would they have cultural similarities? Why might they also have cultural differences?

Proyecto 3 *Las ciencias*

The word *Argentina* comes from *argentum,* the Latin word for silver. It has this name because Spanish explorers hoped to find silver there. Research and write about this valuable metal. What characteristics does it have that make it desirable?

Espuelas de plata (Silver spurs)

En resumen
Vocabulario y gramática

Animated Grammar
Interactive Flashcards
ClassZone.com

Vocabulario

Talk About Technology

la cámara digital	digital camera	navegar por Internet	to surf the Internet
conectar a Internet	to connect to the Internet	la pantalla	screen
la dirección (pl. las direcciones) electrónica	e-mail address	quemar un disco compacto	to burn a CD
estar en línea	to be online	el ratón (pl. los ratones)	mouse
hacer clic en	to click on	el sitio Web	Web site
el icono	icon	el teclado	keyboard
mandar	to send	tomar fotos	to take photos
el mensajero instantáneo	instant messaging		

Talk About Events

anteayer	the day before yesterday
el año pasado	last year
entonces	then, so
luego	later, then
más tarde	later on
por fin	finally
la semana pasada	last week

Talk About Negative or Indefinite Situations

algo	something	ni... ni	neither . . . nor
alguien	someone	ningún / ninguno(a)	none, not any
algún / alguno(a)	some, any	o... o	either . . . or
nada	nothing	tampoco	neither, not either
nadie	no one, nobody		

Gramática

Nota gramatical: ningunos(as) *p. 180*

Preterite of Regular -er and -ir Verbs

In the preterite, **-er** and **-ir** verb endings are identical.

vender	to sell
vend**í**	vend**imos**
vend**iste**	vend**isteis**
vend**ió**	vend**ieron**

escribir	to write
escrib**í**	escrib**imos**
escrib**iste**	escrib**isteis**
escrib**ió**	escrib**ieron**

Affirmative and Negative Words

Affirmative Words		Negative Words	
algo	something	nada	nothing
alguien	someone	nadie	no one, nobody
algún/alguno(a)	some, any	ningún/ninguno(a)	none, not any
o... o	either . . . or	ni... ni	neither . . . nor
siempre	always	nunca	never
también	also	tampoco	neither, not either

Alguno(a) and **ninguno(a)** must match the gender of the noun they replace or modify. They have different forms when used before masculine singular nouns.

Repaso de la lección

 ¡LLEGADA!

@HomeTutor
ClassZone.com

Now you can
- talk about technology
- talk about a series of events
- say what you did
- talk about indefinite or negative situations

Using
- preterite of regular -er and -ir verbs
- affirmative and negative words

To review
- preterite of regular -er and -ir verbs p. 172
- affirmative and negative words p. 178

AUDIO

1 | Listen and understand

Listen to Diana talk to Ramiro about her computer. Then write whether the statements are true or false.

1. Diana piensa que hay algún problema con su computadora.
2. Diana recibió correos electrónicos ayer.
3. A Diana y a sus amigos les gusta usar Internet.
4. Ramiro no encontró ningún problema con la computadora.
5. Diana recibió fotos de sus amigos ayer.
6. Diana no quemó ningún disco compacto anteayer.

To review
- preterite of regular -er and -ir verbs p. 172

2 | Talk about a series of events

Complete the e-mail message with the correct preterite form of the appropriate verb.

abrir	recibir	comer	salir
compartir	subir	envolver	volver

> Hola, Inés. ¿Qué tal? La semana pasada celebré mi cumpleaños. Primero mi familia y yo __1.__ a comer en un restaurante. De primer plato mi hermana __2.__ pescado. Nunca como mucha carne, entonces yo __3.__ un bistec grande con mi padre. Más tarde nosotros __4.__ a casa y cuando yo __5.__ las escaleras, vi una sorpresa: ¡unos regalos! Entonces yo los __6.__ : un videojuego de mi hermana y una cámara de mi madre. Después mi padre me explicó que él no __7.__ su regalo con papel. ¡De mi padre, yo __8.__ un perro! ¡Qué bárbaro!

To review
• preterite of regular **-er** and **-ir** verbs p. 172

3 | Say what you did

Write what these people did last week. Then write whether or not you did that activity.

modelo: el señor Cruz / a casa tarde.
El señor Cruz volvió a casa tarde.
Yo no volví a casa tarde.
(Yo también volví a casa tarde.)

barrer   recibir

beber   correr

aprender   escribir

volver   perder

comer

1. tú / un correo electrónico
2. mis amigos y yo / una pizza
3. Marta / refrescos
4. el jugador / el partido
5. Paca y Teresa / al parque
6. usted / el suelo
7. Isabel / regalos
8. mis hermanos / español

To review
• affirmative and negative words p. 178

4 | Talk about indefinite or negative situations

Juan and Juana are siblings who are very different. Read what Juan says and then write Juana's responses. Use affirmative or negative words.

modelo: **Conozco algunos sitios Web muy interesantes.**
No conozco ningún sitio Web muy interesante.

1. Siempre recibo correos electrónicos de mis amigos.
2. No mandé nada por Internet anteayer.
3. No hay ningún problema con mi computadora.
4. Los sábados quemo un disco compacto o navego por Internet.
5. Ayer tomé fotos de alguien.
6. Nunca uso cámaras digitales.

To review
• **gauchos** p. 163
• Comparación cultural pp. 164, 173, 181

5 | Argentina

Comparación cultural

Answer these culture questions.

1. What do **gauchos** do?
2. What is **mate** and how is it served?
3. What is **lunfardo**? Give an example of a **lunfardo** word.
4. When and why do many people go to Mar del Plata, Argentina?

Más práctica   Cuaderno *pp. 110–121*   Cuaderno para hispanohablantes *pp. 112–121*

Get Help Online
ClassZone.com

Argentina

Tema:

Un día en el parque de diversiones

¡AVANZA!

In this lesson you will learn to
- talk on the phone
- say where you went, how it was, and what you did
- extend invitations

using
- **¡Qué** + adjective!
- preterite of **ir, ser,** and **hacer**
- pronouns after prepositions

♻ *¿Recuerdas?*
- noun-adjective agreement
- places around town
- stem-changing verbs: **e → i**

ENTRADA

Comparación cultural

In this lesson you will learn about
- family names
- artist Benito Quinquela Martín and Argentinean cuisine
- places to visit in Argentina, Bolivia, and Nicaragua

Compara con tu mundo
El Parque de la Costa is near Buenos Aires. With over 50 rides, it is the largest amusement park in South America. *Have you visited an amusement park? What rides do you like? If you haven't, would you like to go?*

¿Qué ves?

Mira la foto

¿Están delante del cine los amigos?

¿Tiene Mariano una mochila o una chaqueta?

¿Qué tiene Florencia en las manos?

Online
SPANISH CLASSZONE.COM

Featuring...

Cultura INTERACTIVA

Animated Grammar

@HomeTutor

And more...
- **Get Help Online**
- **Interactive Flashcards**
- **Review Games**
- **WebQuest**
- **Conjuguemos.com**
- **¡AvanzaRap!**

El Parque de la Costa
El Tigre, Argentina

Argentina
ciento noventa y tres **193**

Presentación de VOCABULARIO

¡AVANZA!

Goal: Learn about Mariano's trip to the amusement park with his friends. Then practice what you have learned to talk on the phone about where you like to go with your friends. *Actividades 1–2*

VIDEO
DVD

AUDIO

A Voy a **llamar** a Florencia para invitarla a hacer algo este **fin de semana.**

llamar

el teléfono celular

Mariano

Florencia

Más vocabulario

dejar un mensaje *to leave a message*
la llamada *phone call*
¿Está...? *Is . . . there?*
No, no está. *No, he's/she's not here.*
Expansión de vocabulario p. R4

Sí, me encantaría. *Yes, I would love to.*
Un momento. *One moment.*

B

Mariano: ¿Aló? **¿Puedo hablar con** Florencia?

Florencia: Hola, Mariano. Soy yo, Florencia.

Mariano: Hola, Florencia. **¿Quieres acompañarme al zoológico? Te invito.**

Florencia: Lo siento. No me gusta mucho ir al zoológico.

Mariano: **¿Te gustaría** ir a **la feria** del libro el sábado?

Florencia: **¡Qué lástima!** El sábado no puedo, pero **me gustaría** hacer algo el domingo.

Mariano: Voy a ir al **parque de diversiones con** Luciana. ¿Quieres ir?

Florencia: **¡Claro que sí!** Hasta el domingo.

el zoológico

la feria

el acuario

el museo

Continuará...

C Hola, Florencia. Hola, Luciana. Vamos a comprar **los boletos.**
Primero quiero **subir a la vuelta al mundo.**

el parque de diversiones

la vuelta al mundo

el boleto

D No voy a subir a **la montaña rusa** porque **tengo miedo.** Luciana y yo
preferimos **los autitos chocadores.** Son más divertidos.

la montaña rusa

¡Qué miedo!

los autitos chocadores

¡Qué divertido!

¡A responder! Escuchar

Mariano invites Luciana to go to the museum. Listen to her responses
to his invitation. Make a thumbs-up sign if she accepts or a thumbs-
down sign if she declines.

@HomeTutor VideoPlus
Interactive Flashcards
ClassZone.com

Práctica de VOCABULARIO

1 | Conversaciones por teléfono

Leer | Complete the phone conversations.

1. ¿Quieres acompañarme a la feria?
   a. ¿Aló?
   b. ¡Claro que sí!
   c. Tienes una llamada.

2. ¿Puedo hablar con Julieta?
   a. No, no está.
   b. Sí, me encantaría.
   c. ¡Qué lástima!

3. ¿Está Manuel?
   a. ¿Puedo hablar con él?
   b. Te invito.
   c. Un momento.

4. ¿Aló?
   a. Un momento.
   b. ¿Puedo hablar con Rafael?
   c. ¿Puedo dejar un mensaje?

5. No, no está.
   a. ¡Claro que sí!
   b. Me gustaría dejar un mensaje.
   c. ¿Te gustaría ir a la feria?

6. ¿Te gustaría ir al museo?
   a. ¡Qué miedo!
   b. Lo siento, pero no puedo.
   c. ¿Quieres dejar un mensaje?

2 | Los boletos

Hablar
Escribir

Mariano has tickets for amusement park rides and for other places. Look at each ticket and tell what it is for.

modelo: El boleto es para **la feria del libro.**

1.    **2.**    **3.**

4. 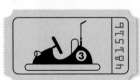   **5.**    **6.**

Más práctica   Cuaderno *pp. 122–124*   Cuaderno para hispanohablantes *pp. 122–125*

PARA Y PIENSA

Did you get it?
1. Name two amusement park rides.
2. Name four places that might require you to buy tickets.

Get Help Online
ClassZone.com

VOCABULARIO *en contexto*

Goal: Listen to Florencia and Mariano talk about the things they see at an amusement park. Then use **Qué** + adjective to describe the different activities you do. *Actividades 3–4*

♻ *¿Recuerdas?* Noun-adjective agreement p. 7

Telehistoria escena 1

STRATEGIES

Cuando lees
Map the scene Draw a map of the park, using arrows and the initials **M, L,** and **F** for the characters' changing locations. Then use location expressions, such as **cerca de...,** to write sentences describing where they are.

Cuando escuchas
Link words and visual images
Match the location expressions you hear with visual images. For example, when you hear **la montaña rusa,** visualize the roller coaster.

VIDEO DVD

AUDIO

Luciana Mariano Florencia

Florencia: *(muttering to herself)* ¿Dónde está Mariano? Tengo que llamarlo a su teléfono celular.

Mariano is also at the amusement park, with his friend Luciana.

Mariano: *(answering phone)* Hola, Florencia. Sí, Luciana y yo estamos en el Parque de la Costa. Compramos nuestros boletos.

Florencia: Yo también. ¿Pueden ver la montaña rusa?

Mariano: Sí, pero estamos más cerca de la vuelta al mundo.

Florencia: Ahora veo la vuelta al mundo. Ustedes deben estar cerca.

Mariano: Sí, sí. Veo la montaña rusa, pero no te veo.

Florencia and Mariano both walk backward, looking for each other.

Luciana: ¿Por qué no encontramos a Florencia delante de los autitos chocadores?

As she says this, Mariano and Florencia suddenly bump into each other.

Continuará... p. 204

También se dice

Argentina To say that he and Luciana are near the Ferris wheel, Mariano uses the words **la vuelta al mundo.** In other Spanish-speaking countries you might hear:
• **España** **la noria**
• **México** **la rueda de la fortuna**
• **Puerto Rico** **la estrella**
• **Perú, Colombia y otros países** **la rueda de Chicago**

@HomeTutor VideoPlus
View, Read and Record
ClassZone.com

Unidad 7 Argentina
198 ciento noventa y ocho

3 | ¿Dónde están? *Comprensión del episodio*

Escuchar
Leer

Match the phrases to form logical sentences about the episode.

1. Florencia y Mariano hablan por
2. Florencia, Luciana y Mariano están
3. Luciana y Mariano compran
4. Todos pueden ver
5. Mariano y Luciana están

a. la montaña rusa.
b. sus boletos.
c. cerca de la vuelta al mundo.
d. teléfono celular.
e. en el parque de diversiones.

Nota gramatical **¿Recuerdas?** Noun-adjective agreement p. 7

To express *How* + **adjective,** use **Qué** + **adjective** in the masculine singular form.

¡**Qué** divertido!   ¡**Qué** aburrido!
How fun!   *How boring!*

Use the feminine form only when a feminine noun is being described.

---

4 | Invitaciones

Hablar

You are in Argentina with your Spanish class. Invite a classmate to various places and attractions. He or she will give an opinion and accept or decline your invitation.

A ¿Te gustaría subir a la montaña rusa?

B ¡Qué peligroso! No, no me gustaría.

Diversiones en Argentina

¿Te gustaría conocer Argentina? Visita las atracciones de este país interesante y divertido.

PARA Y PIENSA

Did you get it? Describe the following, using **Qué** + an adjective.
1. Ir al parque es divertido.
2. La pantalla es pequeña.
3. El museo es interesante.
4. Las fotos son grandes.

Get Help Online
ClassZone.com

Presentación de GRAMÁTICA

¡AVANZA!

Goal: Learn about the irregular preterite forms of **ir**, **ser**, and **hacer**. Then practice these forms to say where you went and what you did, and tell how it was. *Actividades 5–10*

English Grammar Connection: Irregular verbs do not follow the pattern of regular verbs. In English, irregular verbs in the past tense do not end in *-ed*.

She **went** to the aquarium.

Ella **fue** al acuario.

irregular verb

irregular verb

Preterite of ir, ser, and hacer

Animated Grammar
ClassZone.com

Ir, ser, and **hacer** are irregular in the preterite tense. How do you form the preterite of these verbs?

Here's how: The preterite forms of **ir** and **ser** are exactly the same.

ir *to go* / ser *to be*	
fui	fuimos
fuiste	fuisteis
fue	fueron

Use context clues to determine which verb is being used.

Fuimos a la feria.
We went to the fair.

¡**Fue** un día divertido!
It was a fun day!

Like **ir** and **ser,** the preterite forms of **hacer** have no accents.

hacer *to do, to make*	
hice	hicimos
hiciste	hicisteis
hizo	hicieron

*Notice that the **c** becomes **z** before **o**.*

¿Qué **hiciste** ayer?
*What **did you do** yesterday?*

Él **hizo** la tarea.
*He **did** homework.*

Más práctica
Cuaderno *pp. 125–127*
Cuaderno para hispanohablantes *pp. 126–128*

Conjuguemos.com

@HomeTutor
Leveled Practice
ClassZone.com

Práctica de GRAMÁTICA

5 | Muchísimas llamadas

Leer
Escribir

On Saturday and Sunday Florencia, Mariano, and Luciana made 40 phone calls. Complete Mariano's description with the correct preterite forms of **hacer**. Then answer questions 7 and 8.

> El fin de semana pasado, mis amigas y yo __1.__ 40 llamadas por teléfono. ¡Qué bárbaro! Luciana __2.__ cinco llamadas el sábado. Luciana y Florencia __3.__ el mismo *(same)* número de llamadas el domingo. Yo __4.__ dos más que ellas el domingo. Una persona en el grupo __5.__ ocho llamadas cada *(each)* día. Florencia __6.__ dos más que Luciana el sábado. ¿Cuántas llamadas __7.__ cada persona? ¿Cuántas llamadas __8.__ tú el fin de semana pasado?

6 | ¿Cómo fue el día?

Hablar
Escribir

Many people went out yesterday. Tell where they went and whether it was fun or boring.

modelo: nosotros / parque de diversiones /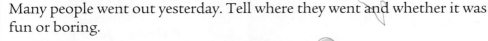
Fuimos al parque de diversiones. Fue divertido.

1. yo / museo / 😊   **4.** Florencia / centro / 😊

2. ustedes / acuario / ☹   **5.** tú / zoológico / 😊

3. mis amigos y yo / cine / ☹   **6.** mis padres / feria / ☹

7 | Fueron a diferentes lugares

Escuchar
Escribir

Listen to the descriptions and answer the questions.

1.

2.

3.

a. ¿Quiénes fueron?   **a.** ¿Quiénes fueron?   **a.** ¿Quiénes fueron?
b. ¿Qué hicieron?   **b.** ¿Qué hicieron?   **b.** ¿Qué hicieron?
c. ¿Cómo fue?   **c.** ¿Cómo fue?   **c.** ¿Cómo fue?

8 | ¿Qué hicieron?

Hablar

Ask a partner what the people in the drawing did.

A ¿Qué hicieron Rafaela y Julio?

B Fueron al museo.

la señorita Quiroga

Luisito y su abuelo

Teo

Rafaela y Julio

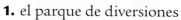
ustedes

Leonardo

9 | ¡Qué divertido!

Hablar

Talk with a partner about where you went and what you did last weekend.

A ¿Fuiste al centro?

¿Qué hicieron ustedes allí?

B Sí, fui al centro con mi familia.

Fuimos al cine y...

Estudiante A

1. el parque de diversiones
2. el centro
3. el museo
4. la playa
5. el zoológico
6. el estadio
7. el restaurante
8. ¿?

Estudiante B

ir de compras
mirar...
hacer esquí acuático
subir a...
pasar un rato
comer
pasear
¿?

10 | ¿Cuándo fuiste?

Hablar Escribir

Tell when you last went to the following places, and one thing that you did there.

| hoy | ayer | el año pasado |

| anoche | la semana pasada | anteayer | ¿ ? |

modelo: la playa
Fui a la playa el año pasado. Tomé el sol.

1. el parque
2. la cafetería
3. la biblioteca
4. la piscina
5. el cine
6. el centro comercial
7. el gimnasio
8. la oficina del (de la) director(a)
9. la clase de matemáticas
10. un restaurante

Comparación cultural

El puerto de La Boca

How do paintings reflect a city's character? People from Buenos Aires, **Argentina,** are called *porteños,* meaning "people of the port." This reflects the essential role of the port in the nation's development. La Boca, the city's first port, is a famous neighborhood of Buenos Aires known for its brightly colored buildings. The artist Benito Quinquela Martín grew up in La Boca in the early 20th century, during the height of the port's development. His paintings capture the neighborhood's color and port activities.

Compara con tu mundo *What are some port cities in the United States? Have you visited any of them?*

Día de trabajo (1948),
Benito Quinquela Martín

Más práctica   Cuaderno *pp. 125-127*   Cuaderno para hispanohablantes *pp. 126-128*

PARA Y PIENSA

Did you get it? Complete the following sentences with the correct preterite form of **hacer** and **ir** or **ser.** Then tell whether you used **ir** or **ser.**
1. Nosotros _____ la tarea; _____ muy fácil.
2. Yo _____ a la playa. _____ esquí acuático.
3. ¿ _____ ellos al parque? ¿Y qué _____ allí?

Get Help Online
ClassZone.com

Lección 2
doscientos tres **203**

GRAMÁTICA en contexto

¡AVANZA!

Goal: Notice how Mariano, Florencia, and Luciana use the preterite tense to talk about what they and others did. Then use **ir, ser,** and **hacer** in the preterite to ask about what others did. *Actividades 11–12*

♻ *¿Recuerdas?* Places around town p. 29

Telehistoria escena 2

@HomeTutor VideoPlus
View, Read and Record
ClassZone.com

STRATEGIES

Cuando lees
Identify verb forms in context
Identify preterite-tense forms of **ir** in this scene. For each, find out where the character(s) went and why.

Cuando escuchas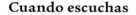
Sort out the speakers In this scene, characters use **dice que...** to report what another person says. Listen for who reports what was said. What information do they report?

VIDEO
DVD

AUDIO

Luciana: ¡Ay! Che, Mariano, ¿adónde fuiste?

Mariano: Yo fui a ver dónde podemos encontrar a Trini. Sé dónde está.

Luciana: ¿Cómo lo sabes?

Mariano: Fue el señor de la ventanilla. Él dice que Trini fue a la vuelta al mundo.

Florencia: Mariano, ¡qué bárbaro! ¡Vamos!

They start to walk. Florencia stops to speak to someone, then catches up.

Florencia: El señor dice que Trini y sus amigos fueron a comer.

Mariano: ¿Trini fue a comer? ¡Ay, no! ¿Qué podemos hacer? Tenemos que ir a buscarla.

They reach the food court but don't see Trini.

Luciana: Fuimos a la vuelta al mundo, fuimos al restaurante. ¿Dónde está Trini? Nunca la vamos a encontrar.

Continuará... p. 210

También se dice

Argentina Luciana uses the word **che** to greet Mariano in a friendly way. In other Spanish-speaking countries you might hear:
• **México cuate**
• **España tío(a), colega**
• **Colombia llave**
• **Puerto Rico, Venezuela y otros países pana**

Unidad 7 Argentina
204 doscientos cuatro

11 | Fueron a buscarla *Comprensión del episodio*

Escuchar Leer

Answer the questions about the episode.

1. ¿Quién habló con el señor de la ventanilla?
2. ¿Quién fue a la vuelta al mundo?
3. ¿Quién habló con otro señor en el parque?
4. ¿Qué dice el señor?
5. ¿Por qué fueron al restaurante los chicos?
6. ¿Quién dice que nunca van a encontrar a Trini?

12 | ¡A jugar! Adivina ♻ *¿Recuerdas?* Places around town p. 29

Hablar

Work in a group of three. Give clues about what you did so your partners can guess where you went.

| un partido de... | el cine | el centro comercial | la playa |

| el museo | el parque de diversiones | un concierto | ¿ ? |

A Compré bloqueador de sol y nadé en el mar.

B ¿Fuiste a la piscina?

C ¿Fuiste a la playa?

Pronunciación Las letras **LL** y **Y**

AUDIO

The letter combination **ll** in Spanish sounds like the English *y* in *yet*. The **y** has the same sound unless it stands alone or is at the end of a word, in which case the **y** is pronounced like the *ee* in the English word *see*.

Listen and repeat.

llamar	tobillo	rodilla	ella	galleta
yo	ayer	playa	mayo	desayuno
y	hay	muy	hoy	

Yo me llamo Marco y ella es Yolanda.

Hoy voy a la playa de Marbella. Es muy bonita.

PARA Y PIENSA

Did you get it? Ask Mariano the questions to which he would provide these statements as answers. Use **ir, ser,** and **hacer.**

1. Florencia, Luciana y yo fuimos al restaurante.
2. Yo hablé con el señor de la ventanilla.
3. El día fue divertido.

Get Help Online
ClassZone.com

Presentación de GRAMÁTICA

¡AVANZA!

Goal: Learn what pronouns are used after prepositions. Then practice them to give and accept or decline invitations. **Actividades 13–18**

♻ **¿Recuerdas?** Stem-changing verbs: **e → i** p. 35

English Grammar Connection: Prepositions (such as *at, for, in, on,* and *with* in English) link a noun or a **pronoun** with another word in a sentence. In both English and Spanish, some of the pronouns that follow these prepositions are different from the subject pronouns.

I have a ticket. The ticket is **for me.**   **Yo** tengo un boleto. El boleto es **para mí.**

Pronouns After Prepositions

Animated Grammar
ClassZone.com

Use **pronouns** after **prepositions** like **a, con, de,** and **para.**

Here's how: **Pronouns** that follow prepositions are the same as the subject pronouns in all forms except **mí** (**yo**) and **ti** (**tú**).

Pronouns After Prepositions	
mí	**nosotros(as)**
ti	**vosotros(as)**
usted, él, ella	**ustedes, ellos(as)**

La montaña rusa está **detrás de mí.**   El teléfono celular está **cerca de ti.**
*The roller coaster is **behind me.***   *The cellular phone is **near you.***

When you use **mí** and **ti** after the preposition **con,** they combine with **con** to form the words **conmigo** and **contigo.**

¿Vas al museo **conmigo**?   Sí, voy **contigo.**
*Are you going to the museum **with me**?*   *Yes, I'm going **with you.***

♻ **¿Recuerdas?** You use these pronouns with verbs like **gustar** to emphasize or clarify which person you are talking about (see p. 8).

A **él** le **gusta** ir al zoológico.   *He likes to go to the zoo.*
A **ella** le **gusta** ir al zoológico.   *She likes to go to the zoo.*
A **usted** le **gusta** ir al zoológico.   *You like to go to the zoo.*

Más práctica
Cuaderno *pp. 128–130*
Cuaderno para hispanohablantes *pp. 129–132*

@HomeTutor
Leveled Practice
ClassZone.com

Práctica de GRAMÁTICA

13 | ¿A quién le gusta?

Hablar
Escribir

Look at the photos and tell who likes to do each activity a lot. Be sure to use the correct pronouns.

modelo: tú
A ti te gusta nadar.

1. ellas

2. nosotros

3. yo

4. ustedes

5. él

6. ella

14 | Invitaciones para ella

Escribir

It's sunny today, so Luciana wants to do something outdoors. Her friends invite her to go to various places. Write her responses, using pronouns.

modelo: ¿Quieres ir al cine con nosotros?
No, no quiero ir al cine con ustedes.

1. ¿Te gustaría ir a la playa conmigo?
2. ¿Quieres comprar ropa para ti en el centro comercial?
3. ¿Quieres tomar fotos de nosotros en el parque?
4. ¿Te gustaría ir al Café Internet con Mariano y Florencia?
5. ¿Puedes preparar la comida para mí y para mi hermano?
6. ¿Puedo ir al zoológico contigo?

15 | Te invito

Have phone conversations to invite a classmate to go to these places. Your partner will say that he or she is going with someone else.

modelo: mis tíos

A ¿Aló? ¿Puedo hablar con Ana?

Bien. ¿Te gustaría ir al museo conmigo?

B Hola, Laura. Soy yo. ¿Cómo estás?

Lo siento, pero no puedo ir contigo. Voy a ir con mis tíos.

1. él

2. ellas

3. mi hermano

4. ellos

5. mis padres

6. ella

16 | ¿Y tú?

Answer the questions. Use pronouns in your answers.

1. ¿Te gustaría subir a una montaña rusa con tus amigos?

2. ¿Tienes miedo cuando no hay nadie contigo?

3. ¿Qué hay delante de ti ahora?

4. ¿A qué museo te gustaría ir con los estudiantes de tu clase?

5. ¿Qué te gusta hacer con tus amigos durante el fin de semana?

6. ¿Cómo contestas el teléfono cuando hay una llamada para ti?

17 | En un restaurante ♻ ¿*Recuerdas?* Stem-changing verbs e → i p. 35

Escribir

Comparación cultural

La comida argentina

What factors influence a country's cuisine? In the late 18th century, many *estancias,* or ranches, were developed on the sprawling grasslands, or *pampas,* of **Argentina.** More beef is eaten per person in Argentina than in any other country. Some people may have *bife,* or steak, twice a day. A traditional weekend activity of many Argentines is an *asado,* or outdoor barbecue with family and friends. Steakhouses, known as *parrillas,* are also common. Argentinean cuisine is not limited to meat, however. Because of Argentina's many Italian immigrants, dishes such as pizza and pasta are also popular.

Compara con tu mundo
What has influenced the common foods available in your area? Has the land or cultural background of your area had an impact?

Un gaucho prepara bife en una estancia.

Restaurante Mirasol

~~~~ Parrilla ~~~~
Bife de chorizo $11,00
Bife de lomo $12,00
~~~~ Pastas ~~~~
Ravioles de ricota $9,00
Canelones $9,00
~~~~ Pizzas ~~~~
Cuatro quesos
Vegetariana *(espinaca y tomates)*
mediana: $11,50   grande: $15,00

Write about a trip to this restaurant. Tell who goes with you, what they order, and why.

> **modelo:** Mis padres y mi hermano van conmigo al Restaurante Mirasol.
> Mi padre pide el bife de chorizo porque a él le gusta la carne...

18 | Una entrevista

Hablar

Use the following phrases to ask a partner questions. He or she will use a pronoun to answer.

> **modelo:** ¿Dejas mensajes cómicos para...?

A ¿Dejas mensajes cómicos para **tus amigos?**

B Sí, dejo mensajes cómicos para **ellos.**

1. ¿Adónde vas con...?
2. ¿Qué te gusta hacer con...?
3. ¿De qué color son los ojos de...?
4. ¿Cuándo es el cumpleaños de...?
5. ¿Qué haces para el cumpleaños de...?
6. ¿Qué compartes con...?

Más práctica   Cuaderno *pp. 128-130*   Cuaderno para hispanohablantes *pp. 129-132*

PARA Y PIENSA

Did you get it? Complete the sentences with the correct pronoun according to the hint in parentheses.
1. ¿Te gustaría ir con _____ ? (Simón y yo)
2. El boleto es para _____ . (tú)
3. Quiero ir con _____ . (mis amigos)

Get Help Online
ClassZone.com

Lección 2
doscientos nueve   **209**

Todo junto

¡AVANZA!

Goal: *Show what you know* Pay attention to the different characters and their roles in this scene. Then practice using the preterite forms of **ir, ser,** and **hacer** and prepositions after pronouns to tell a friend what activities you did. *Actividades 19–23*

Telehistoria completa

@HomeTutor VideoPlus
View, Read and Record
ClassZone.com

STRATEGIES

Cuando lees

Recall and reason As you read, recall the previous scenes to understand how hard the teenagers have tried to find Trini Salgado. Analyze why another woman shows up at the information booth.

Cuando escuchas

Compare characters' approaches Listen for how Florencia assigns tasks and compare it with how the announcer calls for Trini. What differences do you hear in their approaches to making something happen?

Escena 1 *Resumen*

Florencia va al parque de diversiones para buscar a Trini Salgado, pero primero necesita encontrar a Mariano y a su amiga, Luciana.

Escena 2 *Resumen*

Los amigos van a la vuelta al mundo y al restaurante para buscar a Trini Salgado, pero no la encuentran.

VIDEO
DVD

AUDIO

Escena 3

Luciana: *(eyeing a food stand)* Empanadas, ¡qué ricas! Voy a comprar unas.

Florencia: Gracias, Luciana. ¿Por qué no compras un refresco para mí, y unas empanadas para nosotros dos? Y Mariano, ¿te gustaría venir conmigo a buscar a Trini a los autitos chocadores?

Luciana speaks with a manager, who makes an announcement over the loudspeaker.

(crackling) «Atención, por favor, señorita Trini Salgado, por favor, la esperan en la puerta, señorita Trini Salgado».

Florencia y Mariano: ¡Vamos!

A woman, not the famous soccer player, arrives at the booth.

Mujer: Señor, ¡yo soy Trini Salgado!

Florencia: ¿Trini Salgado? ¿La jugadora de fútbol?

Mujer: *(confused)* ¿La jugadora de fútbol?

19 | ¡No es cierto! *Comprensión de los episodios*

Escuchar
Leer

Correct the errors in these sentences.

1. Luciana y Mariano compraron boletos para el zoológico.
2. Luciana y Mariano hablaron por teléfono.
3. Florencia habló con el señor de la ventanilla.
4. Luciana fue a comprar hamburguesas y un café.
5. Florencia invitó a Mariano a acompañarla a la montaña rusa para buscar a Trini.
6. Los amigos encontraron a Trini Salgado, la jugadora de fútbol.

20 | ¿Qué pasó? *Comprensión de los episodios*

Escuchar
Leer

Tell what happened in the episodes. Mention at least two things for each photo.

1.

2.

3.

21 | Unas llamadas telefónicas

Hablar

> **STRATEGY Hablar**
> **Expand and use the list** The list contains an open topic, signified by ¿ ?
> Expand the list by including three or four new ideas of your own. Use as many
> ideas as possible during the phone conversation, making them understandable
> to your partner.

Have phone conversations with a partner, using the ideas in the list.
Share your best conversation with the class.

Para organizarte:
- Invita a la persona al parque de diversiones o a otro lugar.
- Habla sobre adónde fuiste y qué hiciste durante la semana pasada.
- ¿ ?

A ¿Aló?

B Buenas tardes. ¿Puedo hablar con Andrew, por favor?

22 | Integración

Leer
Escuchar
Hablar

Read the note and listen to the phone message. Decide which invitation you want to accept. Leave messages for Álvaro and Carlos with your response.

Fuente 1 Nota

> 3 P.M.
>
> Llamó Álvaro. Ayer fue a la ventanilla del zoológico y compró dos boletos. Tienen una exhibición con elefantes y gorilas de África. Quiere saber si te gustaría ir con él mañana, a la una y media de la tarde. Álvaro te invita; no necesitas dinero. Llámalo a su casa, y si no está allí, deja un mensaje en su teléfono celular.

Fuente 2 Mensaje telefónico

Listen and take notes
• ¿Qué hizo Carlos anteayer?
• ¿Qué quiere hacer mañana? ¿Cuál es el problema?

modelo: Hola,... Me gustaría...
(Hola,... Lo siento...)

23 | Una carta para un(a) amigo(a)

Escribir

Write a letter about where you went and what you did last week. Also include an invitation.

modelo: ¿Sabes qué? La semana pasada fui a la feria con mis amigos. Compré helados para ellos y...

Writing Criteria	Excellent	Good	Needs Work
Content	Your letter includes a lot of information.	Your letter includes some information.	Your letter includes little information.
Communication	Most of your letter is organized and easy to follow.	Parts of your letter are organized and easy to follow.	Your letter is disorganized and hard to follow.
Accuracy	Your letter has few mistakes in grammar and vocabulary.	Your letter has some mistakes in grammar and vocabulary.	Your letter has many mistakes in grammar and vocabulary.

Más práctica   Cuaderno *pp. 131–132*   Cuaderno para hispanohablantes *pp. 133–134*

PARA
Y
PIENSA

Did you get it? Create sentences using the preterite form of each verb and the correct pronoun after each preposition.
1. Florencia / hacer / una llamada a (Mariano)
2. Las empanadas / ser / para (Florencia y Mariano)
3. Mariano / ir / con (Florencia) a los autitos chocadores

Get Help Online
ClassZone.com

Juegos y diversiones

Review vocabulary by playing a game.

The Setup

Your teacher will prepare index cards with questions on them. Form pairs.

Playing the Game

A player will get an index card with a question on it. It is this player's task to get a partner to guess what the question is by giving as many clues as possible without using any of the key words in the question. Your teacher will be the judge and scorekeeper.

If the first player uses any of the key words in the question as he or she gives clues, then the pair is disqualified. If the second player can't guess the question within 30 seconds, another pair will get a chance to play.

The Winners!

The pair that comes up with the correct question the fastest wins.

Materials

• index cards
• timer

Lectura cultural

Comparación cultural

AUDIO

Museos excepcionales

STRATEGY Leer

Compare museums Make a table to compare the two museums by name (**nombre**), location (**ubicación**), focus (**enfoque**), and exhibits (**exhibiciones**).

	1.	2.
nombre		
ubicación		
enfoque		
exhibiciones		

Argentina

¿Qué imaginas cuando piensas en un museo? Muchas personas imaginan cuartos formales con obras[1] de arte. Hay museos en Latinoamérica que celebran su cultura y también dan una experiencia diferente, sin[2] tantas restricciones como un museo tradicional.

El Museo al Aire Libre[3] no tiene ni puertas ni paredes[4], pero es uno de los museos más populares de Buenos Aires. Está en el corazón de La Boca, una sección de Buenos Aires cerca del mar, en una calle pequeña que se llama el Caminito. Allí viven muchos artistas argentinos en sus famosas casas multicolores.

---

[1] works   [2] without   [3] Open-air   [4] walls

El Museo al Aire Libre en Buenos Aires, Argentina

El Museo de Instrumentos Musicales en La Paz, Bolivia

El Caminito sirve como un marco[5] natural para diversas obras de arte: pinturas[6], esculturas y murales. Es posible caminar por la calle, ver obras de arte, comer en cafés, escuchar música y mirar a personas que bailan el tango.

La cultura boliviana, especialmente la música, tiene dos orígenes: indígena[7] y español. En el centro de La Paz, Bolivia, la calle Jaén tiene varios museos de arte donde puedes ver obras indígenas. El Museo de Instrumentos Musicales es un poco diferente de los otros. En este museo interactivo, ¡puedes tocar algunos de los instrumentos! Allí hay exhibiciones de instrumentos precolombinos, instrumentos de viento y tambores[8]. Puedes tocar instrumentos como el charango, una guitarra pequeña de influencia española.

---

[5] frame   [6] paintings   [7] indigenous   [8] drums

PARA Y PIENSA

¿Comprendiste?

1. ¿Dónde está el Museo al Aire Libre? ¿Y el Museo de Instrumentos Musicales?
2. ¿Qué hay en los dos museos?
3. ¿Por qué no es tradicional el museo de Buenos Aires? ¿Y el museo de La Paz?

¿Y tú?

¿Alguna vez fuiste a un museo? ¿Con quién? ¿Te gustaría visitar el Museo al Aire Libre o el Museo de Instrumentos Musicales? ¿Por qué?

Proyectos culturales

Nombres y apellidos

How do last names show family ties across generations? In English-speaking countries, people traditionally inherit one last name, from their father. In Spanish-speaking countries, many people inherit two last names (**apellidos**); the first is the father's, the second is the mother's. Look at the chart to see how this works. Which names represent the father and which ones represent the mother?

Alejandro García Montoya

Guadalupe Saavedra Alderete

Lorenzo Robledo Trujillo

Esperanza Landa Córdoba

Gregorio García Saavedra

Margarita Robledo Landa

Marisol Antonia García Robledo

Proyecto 2 Photo album

Make a photo album of your immediate family or one you know. Use two last names to label the people in your photos.

Materials for photo album
Photos or copies of photos
Construction paper
Glue or tape
Cardboard and cord or ribbon

Instructions
1. Make a page for each person you want to include in your album, using construction paper. Label the page with his or her name or write a caption below each photo. Use the two last names. You may include the date of birth or words that describe the person's interests and personality.
2. Make a cover for your family album. Punch holes in the cover and pages. Bind them together with cord or ribbon.

Proyecto 1 Family tree

Make a family tree of your family or a family you know.

Instructions for family tree
Draw a family tree chart like the one above to show how the family names of you, your parents, and grandparents would change using the Spanish tradition of two last names.

En tu comunidad

If you know any native speakers of Spanish, ask them about their own last names. Do they have two surnames? If so, do they ordinarily use both of them?

Lección 2

En resumen
Vocabulario y gramática

Animated Grammar

Interactive Flashcards
ClassZone.com

Vocabulario

At the Amusement Park

los autitos chocadores	bumper cars
el boleto	ticket
la montaña rusa	roller coaster
subir a	to ride
¡Qué divertido!	How fun!
¡Qué miedo!	How scary!
tener miedo	to be afraid
la vuelta al mundo	Ferris wheel

Places of Interest

el acuario	aquarium
la feria	fair
el museo	museum
el parque de diversiones	amusement park
el zoológico	zoo

Make a Phone Call

dejar un mensaje	to leave a message
la llamada	phone call
llamar	to call (by phone)
el teléfono celular	cellular phone

Extend Invitations

¿Quieres acompañarme a...?	Would you like to come with me to . . . ?
¿Te gustaría...?	Would you like . . . ?
Te invito.	I'll treat you. / I invite you.

Other Words and Phrases

con	with
el fin de semana	weekend

Talk on the Phone

¿Aló?	Hello?
¿Está...?	Is . . . there?
No, no está.	No, he's / she's not.
¿Puedo hablar con...?	May I speak with . . . ?
Un momento.	One moment.

Accept

¡Claro que sí!	Of course!
Me gustaría...	I would like . . .
Sí, me encantaría.	Yes, I would love to.

Decline

¡Qué lástima!	What a shame!

Gramática

Nota gramatical: ¡**Qué** + adjective! *p. 199*

Preterite of ir, ser, and hacer

Ir, ser, and **hacer** are irregular in the preterite tense. The preterite forms of **ir** and **ser** are exactly the same.

ir *to go* / ser *to be*	
fui	fuimos
fuiste	fuisteis
fue	fueron

hacer *to do, to make*	
hice	hicimos
hiciste	hicisteis
hizo	hicieron

Pronouns After Prepositions

Pronouns that follow prepositions are the same as the subject pronouns except **mí (yo)** and **ti (tú).**

Pronouns After Prepositions	
mí	nosotros(as)
ti	vosotros(as)
usted, él, ella	ustedes, ellos(as)

The preposition **con** combines with **mí** and **ti** to form the words **conmigo** and **contigo.**

@HomeTutor
ClassZone.com

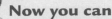
¡LLEGADA!

¡*AvanzaRap!*
DVD
Sing and Learn

Now you can
- talk on the phone
- say where you went, how it was, and what you did
- extend invitations

Using
- ¡**Qué** + adjective!
- preterite of **ir, ser,** and **hacer**
- pronouns after prepositions

To review
- ¡**Qué** + adjective! p. 199
- pronouns after prepositions p. 206

AUDIO

1 Listen and understand

Listen to the conversations. On a separate piece of paper, write **sí** or **no** to tell whether or not each invitation is accepted.

To review
- ¡**Qué** + adjective! p. 199

2 Extend invitations

Jaime is asking Laura to go out with him. Write his invitations and her responses.

modelo: no / horrible
Jaime: ¿Quieres acompañarme a la feria?
Laura: No. ¡Qué horrible!

1. sí / interesante

2. sí / bonito

3. no / aburrido

4. sí / divertido

5. no / peligroso

6. sí / bueno

To review
• pronouns after prepositions
  p. 206

3 | Talk on the phone

Complete the conversation with **con** or **para** and the correct pronoun.

—¿Bueno?

—¿Está Manuel?

—Sí, soy yo.

—Manuel, soy Guillermo. ¿Te gustaría ir al acuario __1.__ ? Te invito. Ya tengo un boleto __2.__ , y si quieres acompañarme, puedo comprar un boleto __3.__ .

—Lo siento, Guillermo, pero no puedo ir __4.__ . Carlos y Beatriz quieren ir al museo y voy __5.__ . ¿Por qué no vienes __6.__ ? Vamos a salir a las diez.

—Mi hermano también quiere ir. Voy a hablar __7.__ para ver si puede.

—Está bien. Hasta luego.

To review
• preterite of **ir, ser,** and **hacer** p. 200

4 | Say where you went, how it was, what you did

Luisa is talking with Gregorio. Read Gregorio's answers and then write Luisa's questions. Use the verbs **ir, ser,** and **hacer.**

modelo: Hice muchas cosas el sábado. (¿Qué?)
         ¿Qué hiciste el sábado?

1. El viernes fui al cine. (¿Adónde?)
2. La película fue muy interesante. (¿Cómo?)
3. Lucas fue conmigo. (¿Quién?)
4. Hicimos algo muy divertido después. (¿Qué?)
5. Fuimos al nuevo café. (¿Adónde?)
6. La comida fue buena. (¿Cómo?)

To review
• Comparación cultural pp. 192, 203, 209
• Lectura cultural pp. 214–215

5 | Argentina and Bolivia

Comparación cultural

Answer these culture questions.

1. Where is El Parque de la Costa and what can you do there?
2. To whom does the term **porteños** refer and why?
3. What foods are popular in Argentina and why? What is an **asado**?
4. Describe what you can find on **el Caminito** in Buenos Aires and **calle Jaén** in La Paz.

Get Help Online
ClassZone.com

Más práctica Cuaderno *pp. 133–144* Cuaderno para hispanohablantes *pp. 135–144*

Nicaragua

Bolivia

Argentina

AUDIO

¿Conoces un lugar divertido?

Lectura y escritura

WebQuest
ClassZone.com

① **Leer** People like to go to different places to have fun. Read about the places that Luis, Liliana, and Eva visited.

② **Escribir** Using the three descriptions as models, write a short paragraph about a place you recently visited.

> **STRATEGY** **Escribir**
> **Make an activity timeline** Make a timeline of your activities. What did you do first, second, third, and so on? Use the timeline to guide your writing.
>
> Primero   Segundo   Tercero

Step 1 Complete the timeline, showing what you did first, second, third, and so on.

Step 2 Write your paragraph, including all the activities on your timeline. Check your writing by yourself or with help from a friend. Make final corrections.

Compara con tu mundo

Use the paragraph you wrote to compare your visit to a visit described by *one* of the three students. Are the activities similar? In what ways are they different?

Cuaderno *pp. 145–147*   Cuaderno para hispanohablantes *pp. 145–147*

Bolivia

Luis

¿Qué tal? Soy Luis y vivo en La Paz, en las montañas de los Andes. Anteayer mis amigos y yo hicimos algo divertido. Primero fuimos al Paseo el Prado, una calle divertida. Allí caminamos y miramos los restaurantes y las tiendas. Por fin llegamos a la Plaza del Estudiante. Encontramos a otros amigos allí. Hizo buen tiempo, entonces hablamos y paseamos en la plaza. ¡Qué bonito!

Argentina

Liliana

¡Hola! Me llamo Liliana y soy de Buenos Aires. Ayer mi hermana y yo fuimos a un parque de diversiones cerca de mi casa. Primero nosotras subimos a la montaña rusa, pero a mí no me gustó. ¡Qué miedo! Me gustaron más los autitos chocadores. Más tarde comimos unas hamburguesas. Luego miramos un espectáculo de láser[1]. Volvimos a casa en la noche, cuando cerró el parque. ¡Qué bárbaro!

[1] **espectáculo...** laser show

Nicaragua

Eva

Me llamo Eva y soy de Managua. El jueves pasado mis padres y yo fuimos a Masaya, el centro folklórico de Nicaragua. Todos los jueves, en el Mercado Nacional de Artesanías[2] celebran las Verbenas de Masaya: un festival folklórico de danza y música. Los artistas llevan trajes[3] de muchos colores. ¡Tomé unas fotos fabulosas! Después compramos artesanías y comimos comidas típicas de Nicaragua. ¡Fue muy divertido!

[2] **Mercado...** National Handicraft Market   [3] costumes

Repaso inclusivo
♻ Options for Review

¡*AvanzaRap!*
DVD
Sing and Learn

1 | Listen, understand, and compare

Escuchar

Listen to the phone conversation. Then answer the following questions.

1. ¿Quién llama a Jaime?
2. ¿Quién contesta el teléfono en la casa de Jaime?
3. ¿Adónde fue Jaime?
4. ¿Quiere dejar un mensaje Teresa?
5. ¿Qué quiere hacer Teresa hoy? ¿Con quién?
6. ¿Cuál es el número del teléfono celular de Jaime?

Who do you like to do things with on the weekends? Where do you go?

2 | Write a computer guide

Escribir

While working at your summer job in a cybercafé, you are asked to create a guide for Spanish-speaking customers. Include the café's name, location, hours, and prices. Explain what kinds of computers the café has and what customers are able to do there, and give step-by-step instructions for those who are unfamiliar with Internet activities. Your guide should have illustrations and at least eight sentences.

3 | Talk with a fellow passenger

Hablar

You are on a plane returning home after a long weekend trip. You strike up a conversation with the teen sitting next to you. Find out as much as you can about him or her: name, age, where he or she is from, where he or she is going, and what he or she is going to do there. Your partner will also ask where you went and what you did there. Your conversation should be at least two minutes long.

¿Adónde fuiste?

Fui a Chicago.

4 | Present a trip

Hablar

Prepare a presentation about the last trip or outing that you took. Make a poster out of your own photos or magazine clippings and give your poster a title. Use it as a visual cue while you talk about where you went and with whom, when and how you got there, and what you did. Copy this chart on a piece of paper and use it to organize your information. Your presentation should be at least two minutes long.

¿Adónde?	
¿Con quién?	
¿Cuándo?	
¿Cómo?	
¿Qué?	

5 | Create a TV ad

Hablar

Work with a partner. Use the Internet to research an amusement park in a Spanish-speaking country. Then write the script for a TV ad for the park, mentioning the name, days and hours of operation, prices, and rides, including any special facts or features. Also tell people how they can get there from the nearest city. Record the ad or present it to the class.

6 | Give advice to another teen

Leer Escribir

You run an advice column on the Web for other teens. Read this e-mail that a student sent to you and write a response, telling him what to do. Use affirmative **tú** commands, **deber,** and **tener que** in your response. Your e-mail should include at least six pieces of advice.

Hola. Soy estudiante del primer año de español. Tengo un problema y necesito tu ayuda. Me gusta aprender el español, pero muchas veces saco malas notas en los exámenes. La clase es interesante y escucho a la maestra, pero no entiendo nada. ¿Qué debo hacer?

Muchas gracias.

Estudiante nervioso

UNIDAD 8

Costa Rica

Una rutina diferente

Lección 1

Tema: **Pensando en las vacaciones**

Lección 2

Tema: **¡Vamos de vacaciones!**

«**¡Hola!**
Somos Jorge y Susana.
Vivimos en San José, Costa Rica.»

Océano Atlántico

Golfo de México

Cuba

República Dominicana

Puerto Rico

México

Honduras

Mar Caribe

Nicaragua

Guatemala

El Salvador

Panamá

Costa Rica

Venezuela

Océano Pacífico

Colombia

Ecuador

Volcán Arenal

San José

Limón

Puntarenas

Jacó

Costa Rica

Océano Pacífico

Península de Osa

Mar Caribe

Población: 4.195.914

Área: 19.730 millas cuadradas

Capital: San José

Moneda: el colón (por Cristóbal Colón)

Idioma: español

Comida típica: gallo pinto, casado, sopa negra

Gente famosa: Óscar Arias Sánchez (político), José Figueres Ferrer (político), Claudia Poll (atleta), Francisco Zúñiga (artista)

Casado

La naturaleza: un lugar para relajarse
The active Arenal Volcano provides immense heat to the waters nearby, which creates the Tabacón hot springs. Costa Ricans and other tourists come here to relax and enjoy the health benefits of the springs' mineral water pools. *Where can people go to relax and experience nature in your area?* ▶

Las aguas termales de Tabacón y el Volcán Arenal

Un competidor de surf kayac en Puntarenas

◀ **Los deportes acuáticos** Costa Rica's Pacific coast has dozens of beaches where tourists come to sunbathe and swim. More daring water sports, especially surfing, are also very popular. Costa Rica hosted a recent World Surf Kayak Championship. *Where can people practice water sports where you live?*

Las artesanías de madera The town of Sarchí holds an annual festival for their **carretas,** or wooden oxcarts. The carts were used to transport coffee in Costa Rica in the 1800s, before the construction of the railroad. Today's **carretas** are elaborately painted by hand, often have musical wheels, and can be found in all sizes, even as miniature souvenirs. *What typical handicrafts are made in the United States?* ▶

Las carretas, artesanías típicas de Sarchí

Costa Rica

Lección

1

Tema:

Pensando en las vacaciones

¡AVANZA!

In this lesson you will learn to
- talk about a typical day
- talk about what you are doing
- talk about your daily routine while on vacation

using
- reflexive verbs
- present progressive

♻ ¿Recuerdas?
- preterite of **hacer**, chores, houses
- direct object pronouns
- parts of the body, telling time

Comparación cultural

In this lesson you will learn about
- forms of address
- vacation spots in Costa Rica

Compara con tu mundo
The tropical plants you see here are just a few of the 12,000 known plant species that populate Costa Rica's diverse landscape. *What plants and trees are native to your region?*

¿Qué ves?
Mira la foto
¿Hace sol?

¿Hay fruta o pasteles en la mesa?

¿Dónde está la familia?

Una familia habla de las vacaciones
San José, Costa Rica

Presentación de VOCABULARIO

Goal: Learn about the daily routines of Susana and Jorge and where they would like to go on vacation. Then practice what you have learned to talk about your daily routine and trips you've taken. *Actividades 1–2*

♻ *¿Recuerdas?* Preterite of **hacer** p. 200

VIDEO
DVD

AUDIO

A ¡Hola! Me llamo Susana. En los días de escuela **me acuesto** muy temprano. **Normalmente** tengo que **despertarme** a las seis. Antes del desayuno voy al baño para **lavarme la cara** y **maquillarme**.

acostarse

dormirse

despertarse

levantarse

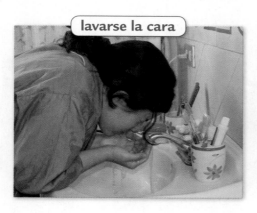
lavarse la cara

maquillarse

B **Generalmente** mi hermano Jorge **se levanta** tarde y pasa mucho tiempo en el baño. **Se afeita, se ducha** y usa **el secador de pelo** para **secarse el pelo.** Siempre usa mi **pasta de dientes** para **cepillarse los dientes.** No es fácil vivir con él.

afeitarse

el peine

el jabón

el cepillo de dientes

la pasta de dientes

el champú

la toalla

el secador de pelo

C Después de **peinarse** y **vestirse,** Jorge **se pone** una chaqueta para ir a la escuela. Está contento porque mañana vamos **de vacaciones.**

peinarse

vestirse

ponerse la chaqueta

Continuará...

D Para **las vacaciones,** mi familia y yo vamos a **hacer un viaje.**
A mí me gustaría ir a **la ciudad,** pero Jorge quiere ir al **campo.**

la ciudad

el campo

E Mamá prefiere hacer un viaje **en tren** y papá quiere hacer un viaje **en barco.**

en tren

en barco

Más vocabulario

en avión *by plane*
el hotel *hotel*
esperar *to wait (for)*
quedarse en *to stay in*
la rutina *routine*
bañarse *to take a bath*
lavarse *to wash oneself*
secarse *to dry oneself*

Expansión de vocabulario p. R5

¡A responder! Escuchar

Listen to Jorge's routine. Act out the verbs as you hear them.

@HomeTutor VideoPlus
Interactive Flashcards
ClassZone.com

Práctica de VOCABULARIO

1 | ¿Qué usas?

Leer Match each activity with the item that someone would need to do it.

1. secarse el cuerpo
2. bañarse
3. lavarse el pelo
4. secarse el pelo
5. peinarse
6. cepillarse los dientes
7. vestirse
8. maquillarse

a. el cepillo de dientes
b. la ropa
c. el champú
d. la toalla
e. el espejo
f. el jabón
g. el peine
h. el secador de pelo

2 | Las vacaciones ♻ ¿Recuerdas? Preterite of **hacer** p. 200

Hablar | Ask a partner if he or she did these things during vacation.

modelo: hacer un viaje en

A ¿Hiciste un viaje en coche?

B Sí, hice un viaje en coche el año pasado.

1. hacer un viaje en

2. hacer un viaje en

3. hacer un viaje en

4. hacer un viaje a

5. hacer un viaje a

6. hacer un viaje a

Más práctica   Cuaderno *pp. 148–150*   Cuaderno para hispanohablantes *pp. 148–151*

PARA Y PIENSA

Did you get it?
1. Name three morning activities and three nighttime activities in your daily routine.
2. Name three ways to travel.

Get Help Online
ClassZone.com

VOCABULARIO *en contexto*

Goal: Identify the words Susana uses to talk about what she would like to do on vacation. Then use the words to talk about being on vacation. **Actividades 3–4**

♻ **¿Recuerdas?** Direct object pronouns p. 32

Telehistoria escena 1

VIDEO
DVD

AUDIO

@HomeTutor VideoPlus
View, Read and Record
ClassZone.com

STRATEGIES

Cuando lees
Group the travel expressions While reading, group the scene's expressions for vacation destinations and modes of transportation. What are some other destinations and modes of transportation?

Cuando escuchas
Understand the interruption Notice the interruption. Who interrupts whom? What is each person doing at the time? What is the response? How do you think the parents feel when they arrive?

Susana · Jorge · Papá · Mamá

Susana reads about vacations as she waits for her brother so they can leave for school.

Susana: *(daydreaming)* Voy a hacer un viaje con mi familia. Podemos ir en avión, en barco...

Jorge: *(yelling from the other room)* ¡Susana!

Susana: *(ignoring him)* ¿Voy al campo o a la ciudad? El año pasado mi familia y yo fuimos al campo. Pero yo generalmente prefiero...

Jorge: ¡Susana! ¿Qué haces?

She goes to the kitchen. Jorge is sitting calmly at the table, shaking an empty milk carton.

Jorge: Susana, ¿dónde está la leche?

Susana: ¡Mamá, papá!

Their parents come running into the kitchen.

Mamá: Susana, ¿qué?

Susana: Mi hermano es imposible. ¡Me voy a quedar en un hotel!

Continuará... p. 238

Unidad 8 Costa Rica
232 doscientos treinta y dos

3 | Las vacaciones de Susana *Comprensión del episodio*

Answer the questions about the episode.

1. ¿Qué va a hacer Susana?
2. ¿Con quién quiere ir de vacaciones?
3. ¿Cómo pueden hacer el viaje?
4. ¿Adónde pueden ir de vacaciones?
5. ¿Adónde fueron el año pasado?
6. ¿Quién es Jorge?
7. ¿Cómo es Jorge?

4 | En el hotel ♻ *¿Recuerdas?* Direct object pronouns p. 32

Hablar

You are on vacation and lost your suitcase. Tell a partner the items you don't have. He or she will tell you if they are available at the hotel, based on the sign.

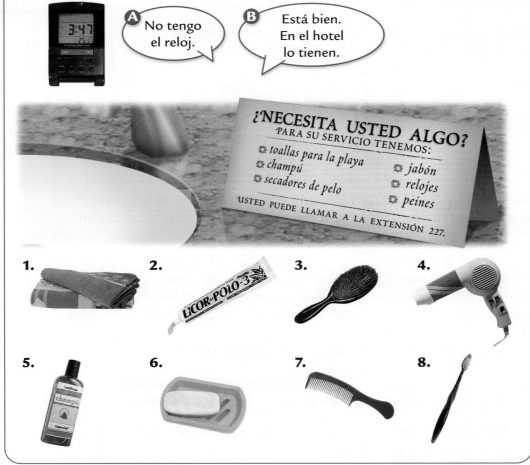

A No tengo el reloj.

B Está bien. En el hotel lo tienen.

¿NECESITA USTED ALGO?
PARA SU SERVICIO TENEMOS:
❋ toallas para la playa
❋ champú
❋ secadores de pelo
❋ jabón
❋ relojes
❋ peines
USTED PUEDE LLAMAR A LA EXTENSIÓN 227.

1.
2.
3.
4.
5.
6.
7.
8.

PARA Y PIENSA

Did you get it? Complete each sentence with the most logical word, based on the Telehistoria: **la ciudad, unas vacaciones,** or **un hotel.**

1. Susana quiere tomar _____ .
2. Susana no quiere ir al campo; prefiere ir a _____ .
3. Susana quiere quedarse en _____ para estar lejos de Jorge.

Get Help Online ClassZone.com

Presentación de GRAMÁTICA

Goal: Learn how to form and use reflexive verbs. Then use these verbs to describe the daily routines of yourself and others. **Actividades 5–10**

♻️ *¿Recuerdas?* Parts of the body p. 133

English Grammar Connection: Reflexive verbs and **reflexive pronouns** show that the subject of a sentence both does and receives the action of the verb. The reflexive pronouns in English end in -*self* or -*selves*.

She **dried herself** with a towel.   Ella **se secó** con una toalla.

Reflexive Verbs

Animated Grammar
ClassZone.com

Use **reflexive pronouns** with **reflexive verbs** when the subject in a sentence is the same as its object.

Here's how:

lavar**se**	*to wash oneself*
me lavo	**nos** lavamos
te lavas	**os** laváis
se lava	**se** lavan

Many verbs can be used with or without reflexive pronouns. When there is no reflexive pronoun, the person doing the action does not receive the action.

reflexive

Anita **se lava.**
Anita washes herself.

not reflexive

Anita **lava** los platos.
Anita washes the dishes.

Do *not* use possessive adjectives with **reflexive verbs.** Use the **definite article** instead.

Anita **se lava la** cara.   *Anita is washing her face.*

When an infinitive follows a conjugated verb, the **reflexive pronoun** can be placed before the **conjugated verb** or attached to the **infinitive.**

Me voy a **acostar** a las once.   *I'm going to go to bed at eleven.*

or Voy a **acostarme** a las once.

Some verbs have different meanings when used reflexively.

dormir   *to sleep* → **dormirse**   *to fall asleep*
poner   *to put* → **ponerse**   *to put on (clothes)*

Más práctica
  Cuaderno *pp. 151–153*
  Cuaderno para hispanohablantes *pp. 152–154*

🔄 **Conjuguemos.com**

@HomeTutor
Leveled Practice
ClassZone.com

Práctica de GRAMÁTICA

5 | ¡Se lavan! ♻ ¿Recuerdas? Parts of the body p. 133

**Hablar
Escribir**

Tell what these people wash.

1. tú

2. nosotros

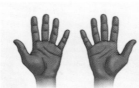

3. Jorge

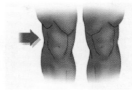

4. yo

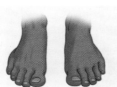

5. ustedes

6. los chicos

6 | ¿La mañana o la noche?

**Hablar
Escribir**

Tell when people do these activities: in the morning or at night.

    modelo: levantarse

        Las personas se levantan en la mañana.

1. ponerse los calcetines   **4.** peinarse

2. acostarse   **5.** vestirse

3. despertarse   **6.** dormirse

7 | ¿Qué hacen primero?

**Hablar
Escribir**

Explain the logical order in which the following people do these activities.

    modelo: yo (dormirse / acostarse)

        Primero me acuesto y luego me duermo.

1. mi familia y yo (despertarse / levantarse)

2. tú (vestirse / ducharse)

3. mis amigas (maquillarse / bañarse)

4. usted (secarse / ponerse la ropa)

5. mi padre (afeitarse / secarse la cara)

6. yo (cepillarse los dientes / acostarse)

8 | Lorena y Napoleón

Hablar
Escribir

Describe the day of Lorena and her dog Napoleón, according to the drawings. Use reflexive verbs when needed.

modelo: Lorena despierta a Napoleón.

1.  **2.**  **3.**

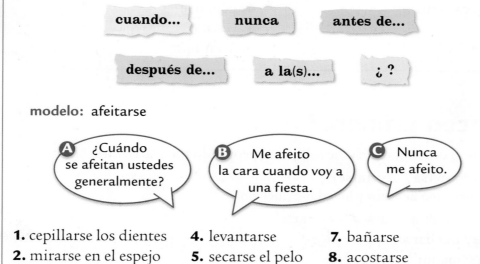

9 | ¿Cuándo lo hacen?

Hablar

Talk with classmates about when you generally do these activities.

cuando...   nunca   antes de...

después de...   a la(s)...   ¿ ?

modelo: afeitarse

A ¿Cuándo se afeitan ustedes generalmente?

B Me afeito la cara cuando voy a una fiesta.

C Nunca me afeito.

1. cepillarse los dientes   **4.** levantarse   **7.** bañarse
2. mirarse en el espejo   **5.** secarse el pelo   **8.** acostarse
3. ducharse   **6.** maquillarse   **9.** lavarse las manos

10 | Mi rutina

Escribir

Write about your daily routine, starting with the time you wake up and ending with the time you go to sleep. Include as many reflexive verbs as you can.

| acostarse | cepillarse los dientes | despertarse |

| dormirse | ducharse | levantarse | ¿ ? |

modelo: Me despierto a las seis y media, pero me levanto a las siete menos cuarto. Me ducho y...

Comparación cultural

El paisaje de Costa Rica

How can a country's geography affect daily life? **Costa Rica's** varied landscape includes mountain ranges, volcanoes, tropical rain forests, rivers, and sandy beaches. Volcán Arenal is one of the ten most active volcanoes in the world. After a major eruption in 1968, the town of La Fortuna became the area's main village. The volcano heats several hot springs in the area and has become a major tourist attraction.

Volcán Arenal,
Costa Rica

Compara con tu mundo *How does the landscape of your area compare to Costa Rica? What features are similar or different?*

Más práctica   Cuaderno *pp. 151–153*   Cuaderno para hispanohablantes *pp. 152–154*

PARA
Y
PIENSA

Did you get it? Create sentences using the following information. Use reflexive pronouns only when necessary.

1. yo / lavar(se) / las manos
2. los chicos / secar(se) / el perro
3. Juana y yo / poner(se) / la mesa
4. mi abuelo / afeitar(se) / la cara

Get Help Online
ClassZone.com

Lección 1
doscientos treinta y siete   **237**

GRAMÁTICA *en contexto*

¡AVANZA! **Goal:** Focus on the reflexive verbs Susana, Jorge, and their father use to talk about their vacation schedules. Then use these reflexive verbs to talk about different routines. *Actividades 11–12*

Telehistoria escena 2

@HomeTutor VideoPlus
View, Read and Record
ClassZone.com

STRATEGIES

Cuando lees
Compare daily routines While reading, make a note of Jorge's regular daily routine. How do you think his routine will change when he is on vacation?

Cuando escuchas
Listen for persuasion Jorge repeatedly asks his father about going to the beach. Listen to how Jorge tries to persuade him and how his father responds each time. What persuasive techniques would you try?

VIDEO
DVD

AUDIO

Susana and Jorge are at home eating lunch with their father.

Susana: ¿Y mamá? ¿Dónde está?

Papá: En la oficina. Ahora ustedes tienen vacaciones, ¿no? ¿Qué planes tienen?

Jorge: Queremos ir a la playa el sábado. ¿Podemos?

Papá: Sí, pero el primer autobús a Playa Jacó sale a las nueve. Con tu rutina, Jorge, debes acostarte a las diez, para levantarte a las seis de la mañana. Necesitas tiempo para ducharte, lavarte el pelo, secarte el pelo, peinarte, ponerte la ropa...

Jorge: *(with a horrified look)* ¿Despertarme a las seis? Normalmente me levanto temprano y me visto rápidamente para ir a la escuela, pero ¡estoy de vacaciones! Papá, ¿podemos ir a la playa en carro?

Papá: No, tengo que ir a la oficina el sábado.

Jorge: *(mischievously)* ¿Puedo usar yo el carro?

Susana and their father look at Jorge in amazement.

Continuará... p. 244

También se dice

Costa Rica To ask his father about using the car, Jorge says **el carro.** In other Spanish-speaking countries you might hear:
• **España** el coche
• **México** la nave
• **Venezuela, Cuba** la máquina
• **muchos países** el auto, el automóvil, el vehículo

11 | Planes para el sábado *Comprensión del episodio*

Escuchar
Leer

Match phrases from the columns to create accurate sentences according to the episode.

1. La madre está
2. Jorge y Susana quieren ir
3. Normalmente Jorge
4. Jorge quiere despertarse
5. No pueden ir en coche

a. se levanta temprano.
b. en la oficina.
c. más tarde el sábado.
d. porque su padre tiene que trabajar.
e. a la playa.

12 | La rutina de Susana

Escuchar
Escribir

Susana is talking about what she does on Saturdays. Listen to her description and put the photos in order according to what she says. Then write a paragraph describing her routine.

a.

b.

c.

d.

e.

f.

AUDIO

Pronunciación Los diptongos

In Spanish, vowels are divided into two categories: strong and weak. **A, e,** and **o** are the strong vowels; **i** and **u** are weak. A weak vowel with another vowel forms one sound, called a diphthong.

igualmente   demasiado   afeitarse   ciudad

If there are two consecutive vowels, and one has an accent mark, then each vowel is pronounced separately. The same is true for two strong vowels.

día   país   frío   leí   toalla   zoológico   peor   leer

PARA
Y
PIENSA

Did you get it? Complete these sentences with the correct form of **acostarse** or **levantarse,** based on the Telehistoria.
1. Jorge debe _____ a las diez si quiere tomar el autobús a las nueve.
2. Cuando está de vacaciones, Jorge no _____ a las seis.

Get Help Online
ClassZone.com

Lección 1
doscientos treinta y nueve   **239**

Presentación de GRAMÁTICA

Goal: Learn how to form the present progressive tense of the verbs you know. Then practice this tense to talk about what people are doing right now. *Actividades 13–18*

 ¿Recuerdas? Chores p. 70, houses p. 42

English Grammar Connection: In both English and Spanish, the **present progressive** tense is used to say that an action is in progress at this moment.

Roberto **is skating** in the park.   Roberto **está patinando** en el parque.

Present Progressive

Animated Grammar
ClassZone.com

To form the present progressive in Spanish, use the present tense of **estar** + a **present participle.**

Here's how: To form the **present participle** of a verb, drop the ending of the infinitive and add **-ando** or **-iendo.**

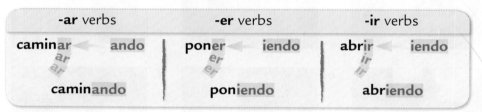

-ar verbs	**-er** verbs	**-ir** verbs
camin**ar** ← **ando**	pon**er** ← **iendo**	abr**ir** ← **iendo**
camin**ando**	pon**iendo**	abr**iendo**

Estamos poniendo** la mesa.   *We are setting the table.*

When the stem of an **-er** or **-ir** verb ends in a vowel, change the **-iendo** to **-yendo.**

l**e**er → le**y**endo   tra**e**r → tra**y**endo

The **e → i** stem-changing verbs have a vowel change in the stem.

p**e**dir → p**i**diendo   s**e**rvir → s**i**rviendo   v**e**stir → v**i**stiendo

Some other verbs also have a vowel change in the stem.

d**e**cir → d**i**ciendo   v**e**nir → v**i**niendo   d**o**rmir → d**u**rmiendo

Place **pronouns** before the conjugated form of **estar** or attach them to the end of the **present participle.** Add an **accent** when you attach a pronoun.

Me estoy vistiendo. *or* **Estoy vistiéndome.** *I'm getting dressed.*

before↰   attached↰

Más práctica

Cuaderno *pp. 154–156*

Conjuguemos.com

Cuaderno para hispanohablantes *pp. 155–158*

@HomeTutor
Leveled Practice
ClassZone.com

Práctica de GRAMÁTICA

13 | ¿De vacaciones o no? ¿*Recuerdas?* Chores p. 70

Hablar
Escribir

Complete the following sentences. Then decide whether these people are on vacation or not.

modelo: Jorge _____ la basura. (sacar)
Jorge **está sacando** la basura. No está de vacaciones.

1. Susana y Jorge _____ el sol en la playa. (tomar)
2. Nosotros _____ el autobús para ir a la escuela. (esperar)
3. Mi amigo _____ un viaje al campo. (hacer)
4. Tú _____ la mesa. (poner)
5. Yo _____ el suelo. (barrer)
6. Ustedes _____ un libro en la playa. (leer)

14 | ¿Qué están haciendo?

Escribir

Look at the drawings. Write what these people are doing.

> levantarse tarde
> hacer un viaje en barco
> nadar en la piscina
> hacer esquí acuático
> servir comida
> ponerse bloqueador de sol
> quedarse en un buen hotel

modelo: mi madre
Mi madre se está poniendo bloqueador de sol. (Mi madre está poniéndose bloqueador de sol.)

1. nosotros

2. yo

3. mis amigos

4. usted

5. el camarero

6. mi padre

15 | En el Hotel Central

Escribir

Look at the drawing and write sentences about what the people are doing right now.

modelo: Enrique está hablando por teléfono.

16 | ¿Dónde estoy? ♻ *¿Recuerdas?* Houses p. 42

Hablar

Describe what you are doing. Your partner will guess where you are.

modelo: cepillarse

Ⓐ Me estoy cepillando los dientes.

Ⓑ Estás en el baño.

Estudiante Ⓐ		Estudiante Ⓑ
		la sala
1. cocinar	**5.** ducharse	el baño
2. leer	**6.** vestirse	el cuarto
3. dormirse	**7.** jugar...	la cocina
4. mirar...	**8.** ¿ ?	el jardín
		¿ ?

17 | Por teléfono

Hablar

Comparación cultural

El uso de usted, tú y vos

How do forms of address differ among countries? Informal and formal address vary in the Spanish-speaking world. In both **Costa Rica** and **Uruguay**, *vos* is used rather than *tú*. In Costa Rica, family members often use *usted;* however, in Uruguay, *usted* is rarely used within a family. In **Ecuador,** some families may use *usted* as a sign of respect, but many families use *tú.*

Una tira cómica del costarricense Francisco Munguía

Compara con tu mundo *How does your language change depending on the situation you are in? How might you talk differently to a principal than to a classmate?*

You are from Costa Rica, and you are talking on the phone with your brother or sister. Use the **usted** form.

A Hola, Diego. ¿Qué está haciendo?

B Estoy estudiando. ¿Y usted?

18 | Una tarjeta postal

Escribir

You and five of your friends or family members have recently won the vacation of your dreams. While you are there, you write a postcard to your Spanish teacher. Tell your teacher about the trip and what each person in your group is doing at the moment.

> **modelo:** Mis amigos y yo estamos en la playa y hace calor.
> Yo estoy tomando el sol y mi amigo Jeff está...

Más práctica Cuaderno *pp. 154–156* Cuaderno para hispanohablantes *pp. 155–158*

PARA Y PIENSA

Did you get it? Complete each sentence with the correct present progressive form of the verb in parentheses.
1. Todos los días a las ocho de la mañana yo _____ . (ducharse)
2. Tú siempre _____ cuando queremos ir a la playa. (dormir)
3. Nosotros _____ para ir a la escuela. (vestirse)

Get Help Online
ClassZone.com

Todo junto

Goal: Show what you know Notice how Susana and Jorge use the present progressive in their conversation. Then use this tense and reflexive verbs to talk about your daily routine while on vacation. *Actividades 19–23*

 ¿Recuerdas? Telling time p. 14

Telehistoria completa

@HomeTutor VideoPlus
View, Read and Record
ClassZone.com

STRATEGIES

Cuando lees

Analyze differences in behavior
While reading, discover the differences in behavior between Jorge and Susana. How do they react to being late?

Cuando escuchas

Listen for attempts to control Listen for differences in intonation as Jorge and Susana each try to gain control over the situation. How does each person sound? Why? What is their father's role?

Escena 1 *Resumen*
Susana va a hacer un viaje con su familia, pero su hermano, Jorge, es imposible.

Escena 2 *Resumen*
Jorge y Susana quieren ir a la playa en coche el sábado, pero su padre tiene que ir a la oficina.

Escena 3

 VIDEO DVD

 AUDIO

Susana and Jorge are finishing breakfast in the kitchen. Their father waits in the car.

Susana: *(impatiently)* Jorge, estás comiendo y comiendo. ¡Por favor! ¿Quieres ir al centro comercial o no? Papá nos está esperando. Tiene que ir a la oficina.

Jorge keeps eating and ignores his sister.

Susana: Jorge, ¿no me escuchas? ¡Nos está llamando papá!

Jorge: Pero estoy comiendo el desayuno...

Susana wraps up his breakfast.

Susana: ¡Vamos, ahora! ¿No me estás escuchando? Papá está esperando. ¡Toma la mochila!

Jorge: Un momento, hay algo... Necesito algo importante. Pero, ¿qué puede ser?

Jorge unknowingly leaves Alicia's T-shirt behind.

19 | ¿Cierto o falso? *Comprensión de los episodios*

Escuchar
Leer

Tell whether these sentences are true or false. Correct the false ones.

1. Susana va a hacer un viaje con sus amigas.

2. Jorge y Susana quieren ir a la playa el sábado.

3. Su padre piensa que Jorge debe levantarse temprano para hacer su rutina.

4. Susana y Jorge pueden ir en coche a la playa porque su padre no tiene que trabajar el sábado.

5. Susana y Jorge necesitan salir porque su padre los está esperando.

6. Jorge sabe qué necesita para ir al centro comercial.

20 | ¿Qué está pasando? *Comprensión de los episodios*

Escuchar
Leer

Tell what is happening in each photo, according to the episodes.

modelo: Susana está pensando en unas vacaciones.
No está escuchando a Jorge.

1.  **2.** **3.**

21 | ¿Quién está de vacaciones? ♻ *¿Recuerdas?* Telling time p. 14

Hablar

STRATEGY Hablar

Use clock faces to link times and activities Organize your drawings by including clock faces with your daily routine. Practice narrating your routine using the clocks, then get together with your partner to ask and answer questions.

On a piece of paper, draw your daily routine while you are on vacation. Your partner is going to draw his or her daily routine during a typical school day. Ask questions about the drawings.

A ¿A qué hora te levantas?

B Me levanto a las seis porque tengo que ir a la escuela.

22 | Integración

Leer
Escuchar
Hablar

Read Ignacio's e-mail and listen to Carmen's phone message. Decide if the three of you can be online together before school. Explain why or why not.

Fuente 1 Correo electrónico

Hola, ¿qué tal? Tenemos que decidir a qué hora vamos a estar en línea mañana. Normalmente me levanto a las siete menos veinte de la mañana. Me lavo la cara y luego me visto. Entonces voy a la sala para ver un programa de televisión a las siete. Termina a las siete y media. A las ocho menos cuarto me pongo los zapatos y la chaqueta y salgo para la escuela. ¿Y tú? ¿Qué haces antes de las clases?
Ignacio

Fuente 2 Mensaje telefónico

Listen and take notes
· ¿A qué hora se levantó hoy Carmen?
· ¿Cuándo está ocupada?
· ¿Cuándo puede estar en línea?

modelo: Ignacio, Carmen y yo podemos estar en línea a las... porque... (No podemos estar en línea porque...)

23 | Un viaje fenomenal

Escribir

You are on a great trip. Write diary entries to describe where you are, what your daily routine is, and what you are doing on your trip.

modelo: sábado, 12 de junio 10:00
Estoy en Guanacaste. Acabo de levantarme y estoy comiendo el desayuno y bebiendo jugo al lado de la playa. Voy a...

Writing Criteria	Excellent	Good	Needs Work
Content	Your diary includes a lot of information.	Your diary includes some information.	Your diary includes little information.
Communication	Most of your diary is organized and easy to follow.	Parts of your diary are organized and easy to follow.	Your diary is disorganized and hard to follow.
Accuracy	Your diary has few mistakes in grammar and vocabulary.	Your diary has some mistakes in grammar and vocabulary.	Your diary has many mistakes in grammar and vocabulary.

Más práctica Cuaderno *pp. 157–158* Cuaderno para hispanohablantes *pp. 159–160*

PARA Y PIENSA

Did you get it? Tell what Jorge and Susana are doing before going to the mall, using this information and the present progressive.
1. Jorge / peinarse
2. Susana / maquillarse
3. los hermanos / cepillarse los dientes
4. Jorge / ponerse la chaqueta

Get Help Online
ClassZone.com

Juegos y diversiones

Review vocabulary by playing a game.

TU RUTINA DIARIA

The Setup

Your teacher will bring in items that represent daily routines. The items will be put in a box at the front of the room. He or she will also write vocabulary words on index cards. Form two teams. Each team will form a line at the back of the room. Next to the first player in line for each team will be a desk. Each desk will have an empty box and a pile of index cards on it.

Materials

- items used in daily routine
- index cards with vocabulary words
- boxes

Playing the Game

The first player for each team will pick up a card from the team's pile, read the card, and then hurry to the box at the front of the room to find the item that represents the action or noun on the card.

When a player has correctly matched the two up, he or she must hurry back and place the card and the item in the team's box.

Play continues until both teams finish matching their cards with the corresponding items.

The Winner!

The team to finish first wins, provided that all of the matches are correct.

Lectura

¡AVANZA! **Goal:** Read the captions from the scrapbook of a student who went on vacation to Costa Rica. Then talk about her vacation and compare it with what you would like to do.

Mi viaje a Costa Rica

AUDIO

El año pasado Sara y su familia hicieron un viaje a Costa Rica. Cuando volvieron a Miami, Sara hizo un álbum con fotos y recuerdos de sus experiencias.

STRATEGY Leer

Use an "L" to link place and event Draw L's like the ones below. On the tall part, write the name of the place. On the low part, write events and activities.

L L L L

¡Papá nunca tiene miedo! Aquí está en un zip line. Aquí va de árbol en árbol en un cable de metal.

Fuimos todos al bosque nuboso[1] en Monteverde. Es una reserva biológica con muchos tipos de árboles[2] y pájaros[3]. Es un lugar ideal para caminar y tomar fotos.

¿Qué están mirando mi mamá y mis hermanos? No es un pájaro y no es un avión... Es Papá.

Vimos un tucán. Es un pájaro bonito de muchos colores. Es típico de Costa Rica. Allí hay más de 850 especies de pájaros.

---

[1] **bosque...** cloud forest [2] trees [3] birds

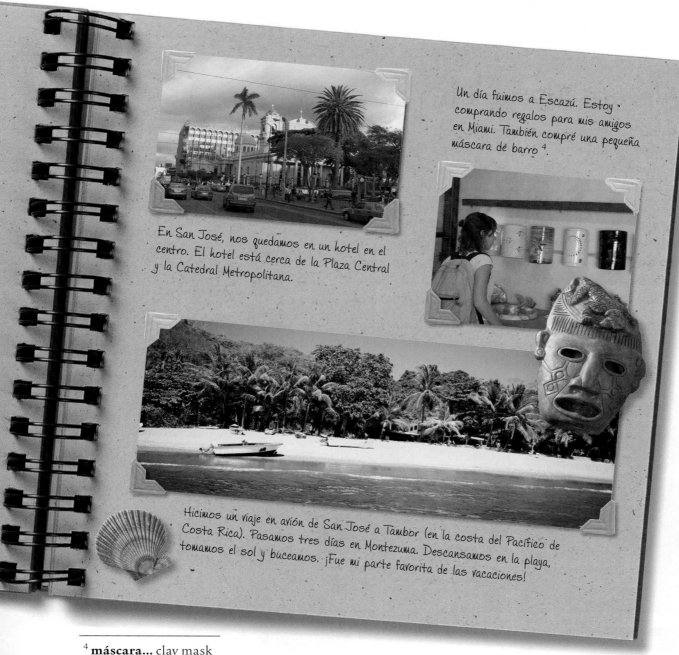

Un día fuimos a Escazú. Estoy comprando regalos para mis amigos en Miami. También compré una pequeña máscara de barro.[4]

En San José, nos quedamos en un hotel en el centro. El hotel está cerca de la Plaza Central y la Catedral Metropolitana.

Hicimos un viaje en avión de San José a Tambor (en la costa del Pacífico de Costa Rica). Pasamos tres días en Montezuma. Descansamos en la playa, tomamos el sol y buceamos. ¡Fue mi parte favorita de las vacaciones!

---

[4] **máscara...** clay mask

PARA Y PIENSA

¿Comprendiste?

1. ¿Adónde fueron Sara y su familia en Monteverde? Si te gusta ver pájaros, ¿es Costa Rica un buen lugar? ¿Por qué?

2. ¿Dónde está el hotel donde se quedaron Sara y su familia?

3. ¿Qué hizo Sara en Escazú?

4. ¿Está Tambor cerca o lejos de San José? ¿Cómo lo sabes?

¿Y tú?

¿Qué te gustaría hacer de vacaciones en Costa Rica?

Conexiones *Las ciencias*

¡Vamos al museo!

In addition to outdoor activities, visitors at **Parque La Sabana** in Costa Rica can enjoy **el Museo de Ciencias Naturales La Salle,** a museum dedicated to nature and science located in the southwest corner of the park. The museum is divided into various sections: **minerales y rocas, paleontología, invertebrados, malacología, artrópodos, insectos, vertebrados, ornitología, mamíferos,** and **esqueletos.** There are more than 55,000 exhibits on permanent display.

Choose five sections of the museum and find their meanings in a dictionary. Then make a list of two or three items you might see on exhibit for each of the five sections.

Museo de Ciencias Naturales La Salle

¡Ve el esqueleto de un mamut enorme en la exhibición de paleontología!
lunes a sábado, 8 a.m.–4 p.m.
domingo, 9 a.m.–5 p.m.
adultos ₡400, niños ₡300

Para más información llama:
Teléfono: 232-4876 **Fax:** 231-1920
o visita nuestro sitio Web

Proyecto 1 *Las matemáticas*

Your Spanish class has taken a trip to Costa Rica. Calculate how much it will cost in **colones** (symbol ₡) for everyone in your class to visit the museum. Then use a current exchange rate to calculate the cost in U.S. dollars. Write out your calculations in Spanish.

Proyecto 2 *El lenguaje*

Many scientific terms in Spanish and English are similar due in part to their common Latin and Greek roots. Research the Latin and Greek roots of the following words:

zoología   paleontología   ornitología

Proyecto 3 *El arte*

Make a list of six to ten animals or insects that may be found in **Parque La Sabana** or **el Museo de Ciencias Naturales La Salle.** If you need more animal names, see page R4. Make a poster containing illustrations of each with captions in Spanish.

Una mariposa

Vocabulario

Talk About a Daily Routine

acostarse (ue)	to go to bed	lavarse la cara	to wash one's face
afeitarse	to shave oneself	levantarse	to get up
bañarse	to take a bath	maquillarse	to put on makeup
cepillarse los dientes	to brush one's teeth	peinarse	to comb one's hair
despertarse (ie)	to wake up	ponerse (la ropa)	to put on (clothes), to get dressed
dormirse (ue)	to fall asleep	secarse	to dry oneself
ducharse	to take a shower	secarse el pelo	to dry one's hair
lavarse	to wash oneself	vestirse (i)	to get dressed

Talk About Grooming

el cepillo (de dientes)	brush (toothbrush)	el peine	comb
el champú	shampoo	el secador de pelo	hair dryer
el jabón	soap	la toalla	towel
la pasta de dientes	toothpaste		

Talk About a Typical Day

generalmente	generally
normalmente	normally
la rutina	routine

Other Words and Phrases

el campo	the country, countryside
la ciudad	city
esperar	to wait (for)
hacer un viaje	to take a trip
en avión	by plane
en barco	by boat
en tren	by train
el hotel	hotel
quedarse en	to stay in
las vacaciones	vacation
de vacaciones	on vacation

Gramática

Reflexive Verbs

Use **reflexive pronouns** with **reflexive verbs** when the subject in a sentence is the same as its object.

lavarse	to wash oneself
me lavo	**nos** lavamos
te lavas	**os** laváis
se lava	**se** lavan

Present Progressive

To form the present progressive in Spanish, use the present tense of **estar** + **present participle**.

-ar verbs	-er verbs	-ir verbs
caminar ← ando	poner ← iendo	abrir ← iendo
caminando	poniendo	abriendo

Some verbs have a spelling change or a stem change in the present participle.

Repaso de la lección

¡LLEGADA!

@HomeTutor
ClassZone.com

Now you can
- talk about a typical day
- talk about what you are doing
- talk about your daily routine while on vacation

Using
- reflexive verbs
- present progressive

To review
- reflexive verbs p. 234
- present progressive p. 240

1 Listen and understand

AUDIO

Listen to Silvia and her brothers and sisters as they get ready for school. Tell what they need and why.

a.

b.

c.

d.

e.

f.

1. Silvia   **3.** Anita   **5.** Tomás
2. Roberto   **4.** Juan   **6.** Laura

To review
- reflexive verbs p. 234

2 Talk about a typical day

Write when the following people do these activities.

modelo: Pancho / acostarse / 10:00 p.m.
Pancho se acuesta a las diez de la noche.

1. yo / dormirse / 10:50 p.m.
2. nosotros / cepillarse los dientes / 9:15 p.m.
3. papá / afeitarse / 6:40 a.m.
4. mi hermana / ducharse / 8:20 a.m.
5. Ignacio y Pablo / levantarse / 7:10 a.m.
6. tú / peinarse / 8:45 a.m.

To review
• reflexive verbs
p. 234

3 | Talk about your daily routine while on vacation

Julia is describing her vacation. Complete her letter with the correct form of the appropriate verb.

Hola, Beatriz.

¿Qué pasa? Estoy en un hotel bonito en San José. Mi rutina es muy diferente aquí. Mis padres prefieren __1.__ (maquillarse / levantarse) temprano para ir de compras. Yo __2.__ (ponerse / despertarse) más tarde, a las diez de la mañana. Después mi hermana y yo __3.__ (acostarse / vestirse). Luego salimos a conocer la ciudad.

Mis padres __4.__ (acostarse / despertarse) a las diez y media de la noche. Mi hermana y yo __5.__ (cepillarse / levantarse) los dientes, y después ella siempre __6.__ (ducharse / lavarse) el pelo. Yo leo mi libro y __7.__ (dormirse / ponerse) a las doce. ¿Y tú? ¿También __8.__ (quedarse / ponerse) en un hotel cuando vas de vacaciones?

To review
• present progressive p. 240

4 | Talk about what you are doing

These people can't go out because they are busy. Write what they are doing right now.

modelo: Alberto / correr
Alberto está corriendo.

1. mamá y papá / comer
2. Adriana / hablar por teléfono
3. tú / hacer la tarea
4. ustedes / escribir correos electrónicos
5. yo / cocinar
6. nosotros / envolver un regalo

To review
• **carretas**
p. 225
• **Tabacón**
p. 225
• Comparación cultural pp. 237, 243

5 | Costa Rica, Ecuador, and Uruguay

Comparación cultural

Answer these culture questions.

1. What are **carretas**? Describe them.
2. Where are the Tabacón hot springs and what can you do there?
3. What types of land features are found in Costa Rica?
4. How do family members address each other in Costa Rica, Ecuador, and Uruguay?

Get Help Online
ClassZone.com

Más práctica Cuaderno *pp. 159–170* Cuaderno para hispanohablantes *pp. 161–170*

Lección

2

Tema:

¡Vamos de vacaciones!

♦AVANZA!

In this lesson you will learn to
- talk about buying souvenirs on vacation
- talk about vacation activities

using
- indirect object pronouns
- demonstrative adjectives

♻ ¿Recuerdas?
- family, classroom objects
- numbers from 200 to 1,000,000
- **gustar** with an infinitive
- present progressive

Comparación cultural

In this lesson you will learn about
- transportation and marketplaces
- the coffee industry and desserts from Costa Rica and Uruguay
- travel destinations in Costa Rica, Ecuador, and Uruguay

Compara con tu mundo
This shop has several items depicting tropical birds, such as the **quetzal** and the **tucán.** Costa Rica is home to about five percent of the world's plant and animal species, making it an ideal place for ecotourism. *Where do you like to go and what do you like to do during vacation?*

¿Qué ves?

Mira la foto
¿Están enojados Susana y Jorge?

¿De qué color es la tienda?

¿Qué pueden comprar aquí?

Una tienda de artesanías y recuerdos
San José, Costa Rica

Costa Rica
doscientos cincuenta y cinco   **255**

Presentación de VOCABULARIO

Goal: Learn about the activities Susana likes to do on vacation. Then practice what you have learned to talk about buying souvenirs. *Actividades 1–2*

VIDEO
DVD

AUDIO

A Estoy comiendo **al aire libre** con mi amiga. Es divertido, pero yo **quisiera** hacer un viaje al campo o al mar.

comer al aire libre

Más vocabulario

el tiempo libre *free time*	**¿Me deja ver...?** *May I see . . . ?*
Le dejo... en... *I'll give . . . to you for . . .*	**¡Qué caro(a)!** *How expensive!*
Le puedo ofrecer... *I can offer you . . .*	**¿Qué es esto?** *What is this?*

Expansión de vocabulario p. R5

hacer surfing

hacer una parrillada

dar una caminata

acampar

montar a caballo

hacer surf de vela

B Me gustaría hacer surfing, hacer surf de vela, acampar o montar a caballo.

Continuará...

Presentación de VOCABULARIO
(continuación)

C Cuando estoy de vacaciones siempre compro **recuerdos** en **el mercado**. Allí puedes **regatear** y las cosas son más **baratas**.

el mercado

D Hay **artesanías** y **joyas** de buena **calidad**. Quiero comprar **un anillo de oro** pero cuesta **demasiado**. Hay **unos aretes de plata** menos **caros**.

las artesanías

la cerámica

el artículo de madera

las joyas

el anillo

el arete

el collar

¡A responder! Escuchar

Listen to the list of activities that Susana wants to do while on vacation. Point to the photo on the previous pages for each activity she mentions.

@HomeTutor VideoPlus
Interactive Flashcards
ClassZone.com

Práctica de VOCABULARIO

1 | ¿Qué hay en la tienda?

Hablar
Escribir

Indicate what items the store has, according to the ad.

> **modelo:** collares de plata
>   No hay collares de plata en la tienda.

1. artículos de madera
2. joyas
3. cerámica
4. anillos de oro
5. collares de madera
6. aretes de plata
7. artesanías
8. anillos de plata

2 | Unos aretes de plata

Leer
Escribir

Susana wants to buy something at the market. Complete the conversation.

le dejo	me deja ver	caro
demasiado	quisiera	ofrecer

Susana: Buenas tardes. __1.__ comprar un regalo para mi madre.
¿ __2.__ los aretes de plata?

Vendedor: Sí, claro. Son muy bonitos.

Susana: ¿Cuánto cuestan?

Vendedor: __3.__ los aretes en quince mil quinientos colones.

Susana: ¡Quince mil quinientos! ¡Qué __4.__! Le puedo __5.__ trece mil quinientos.

Vendedor: Lo siento. Son de buena calidad. Le dejo los aretes en catorce mil.

Susana: ¿Catorce mil? Es __6.__, pero me gustan mucho. Los compro.

Más práctica   Cuaderno *pp. 171–173*   Cuaderno para hispanohablantes *pp. 171–174*

PARA Y PIENSA

Did you get it? Ask to see the following items.
1. earrings
2. silver necklace
3. gold ring
4. wooden handicrafts

Get Help Online
ClassZone.com

VOCABULARIO *en contexto*

Goal: Pay attention to the words Susana uses to talk about items in a store. Then practice these words to talk about shopping and what you would and would not like to do in your free time. *Actividades 3–4*

Telehistoria escena 1

@HomeTutor VideoPlus
View, Read and Record
ClassZone.com

STRATEGIES

Cuando lees
Find the hidden reasons Read between the lines to understand hidden reasons. Why does Susana ask her father to buy a blue car?

Cuando escuchas
Identify teasing Susana is embarrassed twice in this scene. Identify who says things to embarrass her, when it happens, and what the differences are.

VIDEO
DVD

AUDIO

Vendedora

Susana

Susana and Jorge's father drops them off at a store in his red car that looks like a taxi. One of Susana's classmates is standing outside.

Susana: Gracias, Papi. Pero, ¿por qué no compras un carro nuevo? ¿Un carro azul?

Amiga: Eh, Susanita, ¡qué divertido viajar en taxi todos los días!

Embarrassed, Susana smiles, and she and Jorge enter the shop quickly.

Vendedora: ¿Quiere usted ver algo en especial?

Susana: A ver... ¿este anillo de oro?

Vendedora: Claro que sí.

Susana tries on the ring.

Susana: ¿Cuánto cuesta?

Vendedora: Veinte mil colones.

Susana: ¡Qué caro! Tengo diez mil colones, nada más.

Vendedora: Señorita, no estamos en el mercado. Aquí no regateamos.

A little embarrassed, Susana leaves.

Continuará... p. 266

3 | En una tienda *Comprensión del episodio*

Escuchar
Leer

Answer the questions about the episode.

1. ¿A Susana le gusta el coche de su papá? ¿Por qué?
2. ¿Con quién va Susana a la tienda?
3. ¿Qué anillo quiere ver Susana?
4. ¿Cuánto cuesta el anillo?
5. ¿Cuánto dinero tiene Susana?
6. ¿Por qué no regatea la vendedora?

4 | ¡Qué divertido!

Hablar

Ask if your partners would like to do the following activities.

A ¿Te gustaría acampar en tu tiempo libre?

B Sí, me gustaría acampar.

C No, no me gustaría acampar.

1.

2.

3.

4.

5.

6.

PARA Y PIENSA

Did you get it? Create logical sentences by choosing the correct word.

1. Susana está contenta porque el collar es muy (caro / barato).
2. A ella le gustan (la cerámica / los aretes) de madera.
3. Ella puede regatear en (las artesanías / el mercado).

Get Help Online
ClassZone.com

Presentación de GRAMÁTICA

¡AVANZA! **Goal:** Learn how to use indirect object pronouns. Then practice using these pronouns to talk about buying things for people. *Actividades 5–11*

♻ **¿Recuerdas?** Family p. 21, numbers from 200 to 1,000,000 p. 21

English Grammar Connection: In both English and Spanish, **indirect objects** are nouns or pronouns that tell *to whom* or *for whom* the action takes place in a sentence.

Aunt Lola sends **us** gifts.   Tía Lola **nos** manda regalos.

⬆   **indirect object pronoun**   ⬆   **indirect object pronoun**

Indirect Object Pronouns

Animated Grammar
ClassZone.com

Use **indirect object pronouns** to clarify to whom or for whom an action takes place.

Here's how: **Indirect object pronouns** use the same words as direct object pronouns except for **le** and **les**.

Singular		Plural	
me	*me*	**nos**	*us*
te	*you (familiar)*	**os**	*you (familiar)*
le	*you (formal), him, her*	**les**	*you, them*

The pronouns **le** and **les** can refer to a variety of people. To clarify what they mean, they are often accompanied by **a** + **noun** or **pronoun**.

Le doy las joyas.   **Le** doy las joyas **a Juana**.
*I'm giving the jewelry **to him/her/you**.*   *I'm giving the jewelry **to Juana**.*

When a conjugated verb is followed by an infinitive, the same rules for placement apply as for direct object pronouns. The **pronoun** can be placed before the **conjugated verb** or attached to the end of the **infinitive**.

Les voy a **comprar** recuerdos a mis amigos.

or Voy a **comprarles** recuerdos a mis amigos.

I'm going to buy souvenirs for my friends.

Más práctica
Cuaderno *pp. 174–176*
Cuaderno para hispanohablantes *pp. 175–177*

@HomeTutor
Leveled Practice
ClassZone.com

Práctica de GRAMÁTICA

5 | De compras ♻ *¿Recuerdas?* Family p. 21

Leer Susana is explaining to Jorge what their parents are buying. Choose the appropriate indirect object pronoun.

> **modelo:** Mamá y papá (te / le) compran un sombrero a nuestra tía.
> Mamá y papá **le** compran un sombrero **a nuestra tía.**

1. Mamá y papá (nos / les) compran un DVD a nosotros.
2. (Le / Les) compran aretes a nuestra abuela.
3. A nuestros primos (le / les) compran un disco compacto.
4. (Me / Te) compran un collar de madera a ti.
5. A mí también (me / les) compran un collar, pero es de plata.
6. (Le / Les) compran artículos de cerámica a su amigo.

6 | Una tarjeta postal

Leer Complete the postcard that Luis sent his friend Ana about his trip to Costa Rica by adding the correct indirect object pronouns.

¡Hola, Ana!

Estoy en San José, Costa Rica. Hoy fuimos a un mercado. Yo __1.__ compré unos aretes a mi madre y también __2.__ compré un regalo a ti. Mi madre __3.__ dice a mí que mañana vamos a visitar una de las playas bonitas. Después, su amiga Isa __4.__ va a preparar a nosotros una cena tradicional en su casa. Ahora, yo __5.__ voy a escribir una tarjeta postal a mis abuelos.

Luis

Ana Morelos
4508 Sandcastle Dr.
Miami, Florida 33010
USA

7 | ¿Qué les compró?

Escribir

While on vacation, Susana bought souvenirs. Write sentences indicating for whom she bought the following things.

> **modelo:** artículo de madera / padre
> **Le** compró un artículo de madera **a su padre.**

1. collar de madera / madre
2. aretes de plata / yo
3. cerámica / nosotros
4. anillo de oro / tú
5. joyas / amigas
6. aretes de oro / abuelas

8 | La vendedora ♻ ¿Recuerdas? Numbers from 200 to 1,000,000 p. 21

Yesterday a salesclerk sold a lot of things at the market. Indicate to whom she sold these items, based on the amount each person paid.

modelo: Tú pagaste dieciséis mil cuatrocientos colones.
Ella **te** vendió **un collar de plata.**

1. Jorge pagó quince mil seiscientos colones.
2. Mis amigos y yo pagamos cinco mil novecientos colones.
3. Susana y su madre pagaron dos mil colones.
4. Yo pagué treinta mil ochocientos colones.
5. La maestra de español pagó veinte mil colones.
6. Ustedes pagaron nueve mil trescientos colones.

Ventas, el 6 de junio

	Artículo	Precio	
1	aretes de oro	20.000	
2	recuerdos de madera	15.600	
3	collar de plata	16.400	
4	platos de cerámica	5.900	
5	libro de Costa Rica	2.000	
6	anillo de plata	9.300	
7	collares de oro	30.800	
8			
9			
10			
11			

Comparación cultural

El transporte

How is transportation important to a country? In **Costa Rica**, taxis are generally inexpensive and easy to find, especially in larger cities. You can recognize Costa Rican taxis by their color: airport taxis are orange, while all other taxis are red. Traveling by bus is also common. The capital, San José, has extensive bus lines and almost all areas of the country can be reached by bus. Many travelers also use local airlines to reach popular destinations, such as coastal cities and beaches.

Taxis en el Parque Central en San José

Compara con tu mundo *How does transportation in your area compare to Costa Rica? How do you and your friends usually get to school or to places around town?*

9 | ¿Qué les das a otros?

Hablar

Tell a partner to whom you are giving each gift.

 **A** ¿A quién le das artesanías?

B Le doy artesanías a mi abuela.

1. 2. 3.

4. 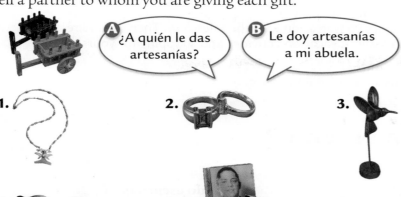 5. 6.

10 | ¿A quién?

Hablar

Ask a partner to whom or for whom he or she does the following things.

A ¿A quién le compras regalos de cumpleaños?

B Le compro regalos de cumpleaños a mi mejor amigo.

modelo: comprar regalos de cumpleaños

1. decir secretos
2. escribir correos electrónicos
3. dar tu número de teléfono
4. hacer llamadas

5. dar propinas
6. preparar la comida
7. dejar mensajes
8. dar una fiesta

11 | Muchos regalos

Escribir

You have just won a contest with a big cash prize. You decide to buy presents for your friends and family. Write about what gifts you are going to give, using indirect object pronouns.

modelo: Les voy a dar un coche nuevo a mis padres. Voy a comprarle unos discos compactos a mi amiga Diahanne...

Más práctica Cuaderno *pp. 174–176* Cuaderno para hispanohablantes *pp. 175–177*

PARA Y PIENSA

Did you get it? Give the correct indirect object pronoun.
1. Nosotros _____ damos los recuerdos a nuestros hermanos.
2. A ti _____ quiero comprar un collar de oro.
3. Carlos _____ pide 2.000 colones a nosotros.

Get Help Online
ClassZone.com

GRAMÁTICA en contexto

¡AVANZA! **Goal:** Listen to Susana's conversation with the salesclerk. Then use indirect object pronouns to talk about vacation activities and shopping for yourself and others. *Actividades 12–13*

♻ *¿Recuerdas?* **gustar** with an infinitive p. 8

Telehistoria escena 2

@HomeTutor VideoPlus
View, Read and Record
ClassZone.com

STRATEGIES

Cuando lees
Focus on shopping expressions
While reading, notice at least four expressions normally used in stores. Reread the scene, then write these expressions in new sentences.

Cuando escuchas
Listen for "turn-taking" tactics
Listen for how the salesclerk greets Susana and how Susana asks for something. How does Jorge enter the conversation?

VIDEO
DVD

AUDIO

Jorge

Vendedor

Susana

Susana and Jorge enter another shop.

Susana: ¡A mí me gustan los collares de madera! *(She looks at a price tag.)* ¡Qué caro!

Vendedor: ¡Buenos días! ¿Los puedo ayudar?

Susana: ¿Me deja ver esa joya? ¿Cuánto cuesta?

Vendedor: Cuesta cincuenta mil colones. Es un poco cara, ¿verdad?

Jorge: A ti te gustan todas las cosas caras.

Vendedor: *(to Susana)* ¿A usted le gustan los aretes de plata?

As Susana looks at the earrings, Jorge turns to see who has just entered the store.

Jorge: Susana...

Susana: *(impatiently)* Y ahora, ¿qué te pasa a ti?

Continuará... p. 272

También se dice

Costa Rica To ask Susana if she likes the earrings, the salesclerk uses **los aretes.** In other Spanish-speaking countries you might hear:
· **Argentina** los aros
· **España** los pendientes, los zarcillos
· **Puerto Rico** las pantallas

12 | Unas joyas *Comprensión del episodio*

All of these sentences are false. Correct them, according to the episode.

1. A Susana le gustan mucho los aretes de madera.
2. Los collares son muy baratos.
3. Susana quiere ver un recuerdo.
4. El vendedor dice que la joya no es cara.
5. Jorge dice que a Susana le gustan las cosas baratas.

13 | El viaje ideal ♻ *¿Recuerdas?* gustar with an infinitive p. 8

Hablar

Role-play with a partner. Tell a travel agent who likes to do these activities.
He or she will offer an ideal trip.

modelo: hacer un viaje en barco

A A mi hermano le gusta hacer un viaje en barco.

B A él le puedo ofrecer un viaje al mar.

Estudiante **A**	
1. hacer surfing	**4.** dar caminatas
2. montar a caballo	**5.** acampar
3. ir de compras	**6.** ¿ ?

Estudiante **B**	
la ciudad	el mar
la playa	¿ ?
el campo	

AUDIO

Pronunciación   Unir las palabras

Native speakers may seem to speak quickly when they link their words in breath groups. Instead of pronouncing each word separately, they run some words together. This is common in all languages.

¿A qué hora empieza el almuerzo?

Listen and repeat.

Quisiera el anillo de oro y el artículo de madera.

Ella no puede acampar porque está ocupada.

PARA
Y
PIENSA

Did you get it? Complete each sentence with the correct indirect object pronoun, based on the Telehistoria.
1. A Susana _____ gustan los collares de madera.
2. El vendedor _____ pregunta a Jorge y a Susana si los puede ayudar.
3. Susana quiere saber qué _____ pasa a Jorge.

Get Help Online
ClassZone.com

Presentación de GRAMÁTICA

Goal: Learn how to point out specific things by using demonstrative adjectives. Then use these words to identify objects. *Actividades 14–19*

♻ *¿Recuerdas?* Present progressive p. 240, classroom objects p. 12

English Grammar Connection: Demonstrative adjectives indicate the location of a person or thing in relation to the speaker. They go before the noun in both English and Spanish.

This necklace is expensive.   **Este** collar es caro.

↑   ↑

demonstrative adjective   demonstrative adjective

Demonstrative Adjectives

Animated Grammar
ClassZone.com

In Spanish, **demonstrative adjectives** must match the nouns they modify in gender and number.

Here's how:

Masculine

Singular		Plural	
este anillo	*this ring*	**estos** anillos	*these rings*
ese anillo	*that ring*	**esos** anillos	*those rings*
aquel anillo	*that ring (over there)*	**aquellos** anillos	*those rings (over there)*

Feminine

Singular		Plural	
esta camiseta	*this T-shirt*	**estas** camisetas	*these T-shirts*
esa camiseta	*that T-shirt*	**esas** camisetas	*those T-shirts*
aquella camiseta	*that T-shirt (over there)*	**aquellas** camisetas	*those T-shirts (over there)*

No sé si debo comprar **estos** aretes de aquí o **esos** aretes de allí.
*I don't know if I should buy **these** earrings here or **those** earrings there.*

Aquellas cerámicas son muy baratas.
***Those** ceramics **(over there)** are very inexpensive.*

Más práctica
Cuaderno *pp. 177–179*
Cuaderno para hispanohablantes *pp. 178–181*

@HomeTutor
Leveled Practice
ClassZone.com

Práctica de GRAMÁTICA

14 | En el mercado

Leer
Escribir

Susana is at the market. Choose the correct demonstrative adjectives to complete the conversation. Then write a list of the jewelry items in order from the closest to the farthest in relation to Susana.

Susana: Me gustan las joyas de plata. ¿Me deja ver __1.__ (aquella / aquel) collar?

Vendedora: Sí, le dejo __2.__ (aquel / aquellos) collar en treinta mil colones.

Susana: Es caro. ¿Y __3.__ (estas / estos) aretes de aquí? ¿Cuánto cuestan?

Vendedora: __4.__ (Esos / Esas) aretes de plata cuestan veinticinco mil colones. Son de buena calidad.

Susana: Me gustan __5.__ (esas / esos) joyas de allí, pero cuestan demasiado.

Vendedora: ¿Le gustaría __6.__ (ese / esa) anillo de plata? Sólo cuesta dieciocho mil colones.

Susana: ¡Está bien! Quisiera comprar __7.__ (esa / ese) anillo.

15 | ¿Qué están haciendo? ♻ *¿Recuerdas?* Present progressive p. 240

Escuchar
Escribir

There are a lot of people at the market today. Listen to the sentences about what the people are doing. Tell whether each sentence is true or false, according to the drawing.

16 ¿Cuánto cuestan?

Hablar

You and a friend are at a souvenir store in Costa Rica. Use demonstrative adjectives to ask a partner how much the various items cost.

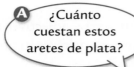

A ¿Cuánto cuestan estos aretes de plata?

B Cuestan quince mil colones.

17 En la clase

Hablar

Ask a partner questions about objects and people in your classroom, using demonstrative adjectives.

¿Cómo es...?   ¿De qué color es...?

¿De quién es...?   ¿Qué lleva...?   ¿ ?

A ¿De qué color es esa mochila?

B Esa mochila es roja.

18 | Hablando del café

Hablar

Comparación cultural

El café

How does Costa Rica's climate impact its leading exports? Coffee is one of **Costa Rica's** leading exports. It grows well due to the country's high altitudes, rich soils, and warm temperatures. The coffee harvest takes place between November and January. Workers carefully handpick and sort the berries of the coffee plants, placing only the ripe, red ones in their baskets. The berries are then brought to mills so that the beans can be removed and processed.

Coffee plantation, Costa Rica

Compara con tu mundo

What is an important industry in your area? Do you know anyone who works in that industry?

Completa el diálogo usando los adjetivos demostrativos apropiados.
(Complete the conversation with the appropriate demonstrative adjectives.)

Elena: __1.__ café de Costa Rica me gusta más que __2.__ café que toma Daniel, que es de Indonesia.

Rodrigo: Mi favorito fue __3.__ café que nos sirvió Alejandra la semana pasada.

Alicia: Estoy de acuerdo con Elena. En casa estamos tomando __4.__ cafés que nos compraron mis padres en San José el año pasado, y creo que los de Costa Rica son más sabrosos.

19 | ¡A jugar! Veo, veo ♻ **¿Recuerdas?** Classroom objects p. 12

Hablar

Describe to a partner objects that you see in the classroom. He or she is going to guess what they are, using demonstrative adjectives.

A — Veo una cosa roja.

B — ¿Es esta mochila?

No.

Sí.

¿Es aquella mochila?

Más práctica   Cuaderno *pp. 177–179*   Cuaderno para hispanohablantes *pp. 178–181*

PARA Y PIENSA

Did you get it? Complete each sentence with the correct demonstrative adjective: **esas, aquellos,** or **este.**

1. _____ aretes son más bonitos que esos aretes.
2. _____ anillo es de oro.
3. La calidad de _____ artesanías es muy buena.

Get Help Online
ClassZone.com

Lección 2
doscientos setenta y uno   **271**

Todo junto

¡AVANZA!

Goal: Show what you know Identify the demonstrative adjectives used to indicate items in a store. Then practice using demonstrative adjectives and indirect object pronouns to bargain and describe vacations.
Actividades 20–24

Telehistoria completa

@HomeTutor VideoPlus
View, Read and Record
ClassZone.com

STRATEGIES

Cuando lees
Find the dramatic turn Read the scene slowly, trying to discover the dramatic "turn" or change. Why do the teens stop paying attention to the salesclerk? What happens after that?

Cuando escuchas
Listen to problems and imagine solutions Listen to and observe the problems. What are they? How does Jorge respond? What are the possible solutions, if any?

Escena 1 *Resumen*
Jorge y Susana llegan al centro comercial. Susana quiere comprar un anillo, pero es muy caro.

Escena 2 *Resumen*
Susana está hablando con el vendedor en la tienda cuando Jorge ve a alguien.

VIDEO
DVD

AUDIO

Escena 3

Vendedor: ¿Y a usted no le gustan aquellos aretes de oro? ¿Ese collar de plata? ¿Estos anillos?

The salesclerk sees that Jorge and Susana have stopped paying attention and leaves.

Jorge: *(excited)* Susana, ¡allí está Trini Salgado, la jugadora de fútbol! Es ella, ¿no? ¿Qué está haciendo?

Susana: Sí, sí, es ella. Está comprando unos aretes.

Jorge: ¡Vamos! Necesito su autógrafo para Alicia. *(He opens his backpack but can't find the T-shirt.)* ¿Dónde está la camiseta de Alicia?

Susana: No sé...

While he looks through his backpack, Trini leaves the store.

20 | ¿En qué orden? *Comprensión de los episodios*

Escuchar
Leer

To describe the episodes, put these sentences in order.

a. Susana empieza a regatear, pero ella no está en el mercado.

b. Jorge no puede encontrar la camiseta.

c. Jorge le dice a Susana que a ella le gustan las cosas caras.

d. A Susana no le gusta llegar en el coche de su papá.

e. Jorge le dice a Susana que ve a Trini Salgado.

f. Susana le pregunta a Jorge qué le pasa a él.

21 | ¿Qué pasó? *Comprensión de los episodios*

Escuchar
Leer

Look at the photos and write what happened in the episodes.

1.
2.

3.
4.

22 | ¡A regatear!

Hablar

STRATEGY Hablar

Be realistic Make your drawings of items as clear as possible. Add details and colors, so that the bargaining can be realistic. If you have time to prepare in advance, bring actual items from home to use while you bargain.

Bargain with a classmate. Draw the articles that you want to sell, and try to get the best possible prices for them. Change roles.

A Buenas tardes. ¿Me deja ver aquel tocadiscos compactos?

B Sí. Es de buena calidad. Le dejo este tocadiscos compactos en treinta dólares...

23 | Integración

Leer
Escuchar
Hablar

Read the guide and listen to the ad. Then tell what you would like to do there and what you are going to buy for your family and friends.

Fuente 1 Guía turística

Tamarindo Playa Tamarindo Playa

De compras en
Playa Tamarindo

Mercado Costeño En este mercado al aire libre, encuentras ropa, artículos de madera, joyas de madera y café orgánico. Puedes regatear.

Artesanías Iguana Verde Esta tienda tiene artesanías de buena calidad, pero son un poco caras. Venden cerámica, platos de madera y joyas de oro.

Librería Sol Tico Aquí venden libros, discos compactos y mapas decorativos.

Tienda Colibrí En esta tienda hay anillos y aretes de plata, y collares de madera. También venden camisetas y sombreros. Precios baratos.

Fuente 2 Anuncio de radio

Listen and take notes
• ¿Qué actividades hay en la playa?
• ¿Qué puedes hacer si no te gusta el mar?

modelo: En Playa Tamarindo me gustaría...
A... le voy a comprar...

24 | ¡Ya llegan las vacaciones!

Escribir

Write an article for a Web site comparing two trips. Tell who would like each trip, what people do during their free time, and what people can buy and for whom.

modelo: Tenemos dos viajes fenomenales. Si a usted le gusta el mar, le podemos ofrecer un viaje a Playa del Coco. Usted puede...

Writing Criteria	Excellent	Good	Needs Work
Content	Your article includes a lot of information.	Your article includes some information.	Your article includes little information.
Communication	Most of your article is organized and easy to follow.	Parts of your article are organized and easy to follow.	Your article is disorganized and hard to follow.
Accuracy	Your article has few mistakes in grammar and vocabulary.	Your article has some mistakes in grammar and vocabulary.	Your article has many mistakes in grammar and vocabulary.

Más práctica   Cuaderno *pp. 180–181*   Cuaderno para hispanohablantes *pp. 182–183*

PARA Y PIENSA

Did you get it? Complete each sentence with the correct indirect object pronoun and demonstrative adjective, based on the Telehistoria.
1. Jorge _____ pregunta a Susana si _____ mujer allí es Trini Salgado.
2. El hombre _____ quiere vender a Jorge y a Susana _____ anillos de aquí.

Get Help Online
ClassZone.com

Juegos y diversiones

Review vocabulary by playing a game.

El mercado

The Setup

Your classroom has been transformed into a market. Your teacher will prepare play money and cards with pictures representing the items you would find in the market. Some of you will be asked to be vendors. The rest of you will be on teams trying to bargain with the vendors for specific items.

Playing the Game

There should be at least five teams as well as five vendors. Each team will have play money and a scavenger hunt list of items. Each team will ask the vendors for items on its list. As in a real Latin American market, the teams will have to bargain for the items. The bargaining must be conducted in Spanish. Players should take turns doing the bargaining.

The Winner!

The team that gets the most scavenger items on its list with the money it has wins.

Materials

- index cards with pictures representing vocabulary words
- index cards with lists of vocabulary words
- play money

¿Tiene usted un collar de plata?

Sí, lo tengo.

¿Cuánto cuesta?

Cuesta trece mil colones.

Lectura cultural

Comparación cultural

AUDIO

Mercados en Costa Rica y Uruguay

STRATEGY Leer
Diagram comparisons
Use a Venn diagram to compare markets and bargaining in Costa Rica, Uruguay, and the U.S.

Costa Rica

Uruguay   Estados Unidos

En Latinoamérica, muchas ciudades tienen mercados al aire libre, donde puedes ir de compras y encontrar artículos interesantes y de buena calidad. Es muy común regatear en los puestos[1] de estos mercados. Si quieres regatear, hay algunas recomendaciones. Cuando escuchas el primer precio, puedes contestar: «¡Es demasiado!» También es importante ir a varios puestos para encontrar el precio más barato.

———
[1] stalls

Costa Rica

Representación de un mercado, San José, Costa Rica

Mercado de fruta,
Montevideo, Uruguay

Uruguay

El Mercado Central de San José, Costa Rica, se fundó en el año 1880. En los puestos, venden una variedad de cosas, como café, frutas, verduras, pescado, carne, flores[2] y plantas medicinales. También puedes comprar recuerdos. Hay camisetas, joyas y artículos de madera y de cuero[3]. Si tienes hambre, hay restaurantes pequeños que se llaman sodas.

El Mercado del Puerto está cerca del mar en Montevideo, la capital de Uruguay. Se inauguró[4] en 1868. Allí hay artistas locales que venden sus artículos y puedes comprar artesanías en las tiendas. También puedes comer en los restaurantes, donde sirven carne y pescado. La parrillada, un plato con diferentes tipos de carne, es muy popular. Los sábados, muchas personas van a este mercado para almorzar y escuchar música.

[2] flowers   [3] leather   [4] opened

PARA Y PIENSA

¿Comprendiste?
1. ¿Qué puedes comprar en el Mercado Central? ¿En el Mercado del Puerto?
2. ¿Cuál de los mercados es más viejo?
3. ¿Qué recuerdos hay en el Mercado Central?
4. ¿En qué mercado es popular la parrillada?

¿Y tú?
¿Hay un mercado donde tú vives? Si hay, ¿cómo es? ¿Puedes regatear allí? ¿Dónde puedes regatear en Estados Unidos?

Proyectos culturales

Postres en Costa Rica y Uruguay

How can foods from other Spanish-speaking countries be enjoyed here in the U.S.? Desserts in Spanish-speaking countries may appear to be different from the desserts that you are used to, but if you read the ingredients you'll see that these recipes from **Costa Rica** and **Uruguay** contain foods you could find in your own kitchen or the supermarket. **Plátanos horneados** and **dulce de leche** are prepared in slightly different ways throughout Latin America.

Proyecto **1** *Plátanos horneados*

Costa Rica **Plátanos,** or plantains, grow in abundance in Latin America and are a dietary staple. This fruit resembles a banana, but it is typically not eaten raw. You know a plantain is ripe when its outer skin has turned from green to black. Ripe plantains are called **maduros.**

Ingredients for plátanos horneados
6 ripe plantains
1 stick of butter
1/2 cup honey
1/4 teaspoon ground cloves

Instructions
Preheat a toaster oven to 300 degrees. Remove the peels of the plantains and cut them in half lengthwise. Place them in a rectangular glass pan and pour the honey over them. Cut the butter into six pieces and place them on top of every other plantain, then sprinkle with the cloves. Cover the pan with aluminum foil and bake for 30 minutes or until the plantains are golden brown.

Optional: Once you remove the plantains from the oven, sprinkle them with cinnamon.

Proyecto **2** *Dulce de leche*

Uruguay **Dulce de leche** has a sweet, caramel flavor and a texture that resembles fudge. It is often used as a filling for pastries and desserts, but can also be eaten by itself.

Ingredients for dulce de leche
4 cups whole milk
2 cups sugar
1 teaspoon baking soda
1/2 teaspoon vanilla extract

Instructions
Place all the ingredients in a heavy-bottomed saucepan. Bring the liquid to a boil and then reduce to medium heat, stirring frequently until the mixture thickens and turns caramel in color. Cool to room temperature.

Optional: Serve with cookies, bread, or fruit.

En tu comunidad

The work of a professional chef often brings him or her in contact with foods and people from other countries. How would knowing about other languages and cultures help you to be a better chef?

Vocabulario

Talk About Vacation Activities

acampar	to camp	hacer surf de vela	to windsurf
comer al aire libre	to picnic, to eat outside	hacer surfing	to surf
dar una caminata	to hike	montar a caballo	to ride a horse
hacer una parrillada	to barbecue	el tiempo libre	free time

Indicate Position

aquel(aquella)	that (over there)
aquellos(as)	those (over there)
ese(a)	that
esos(as)	those
este(a)	this
estos(as)	these
¿Qué es esto?	What is this?

Talk About Buying Souvenirs

barato(a)	inexpensive
la calidad	quality
caro(a)	expensive
demasiado	too much
el mercado	market
el recuerdo	souvenir

Jewelry and Handicrafts

el anillo	ring
el arete	earring
las artesanías	handicrafts
los artículos	goods
de madera	wood
de oro	gold
de plata	silver
la cerámica	ceramics
el collar	necklace
las joyas	jewelry

Bargaining

Le dejo... en...	I'll give . . . to you for . . .
Le puedo ofrecer...	I can offer you . . .
¿Me deja ver...?	May I see . . . ?
¡Qué caro(a)!	How expensive!
Quisiera...	I would like . . .
regatear	to bargain

Gramática

Indirect Object Pronouns

Indirect object pronouns use the same words as direct object pronouns except for **le** and **les**.

Singular		Plural	
me	me	**nos**	us
te	you (familiar)	**os**	you (familiar)
le	you (formal), him, her	**les**	you, them

Demonstrative Adjectives

In Spanish, **demonstrative adjectives** must match the nouns they modify in gender and number.

Masculine

Singular	Plural
este anillo	**estos** anillos
ese anillo	**esos** anillos
aquel anillo	**aquellos** anillos

Feminine

Singular	Plural
esta camiseta	**estas** camisetas
esa camiseta	**esas** camisetas
aquella camiseta	**aquellas** camisetas

Repaso de la lección

¡AvanzaRap!
DVD
Sing and Learn

¡LLEGADA!

Now you can
• talk about buying souvenirs on vacation
• talk about vacation activities

Using
• indirect object pronouns
• demonstrative adjectives

@HomeTutor
ClassZone.com

To review
• indirect object pronouns p. 262
• demonstrative adjectives p. 268

AUDIO

1 | Listen and understand

Listen to the conversation between César and a vendor. Then choose the correct word to complete each sentence.

1. César busca (un recuerdo / un artículo de madera) para su amiga.
2. La amiga prefiere (las artesanías / las joyas).
3. César piensa que el anillo de (oro / plata) es bonito.
4. El anillo es muy (caro / barato).
5. La amiga de César prefiere las joyas de (oro / plata).
6. La vendedora le deja (los aretes / los anillos) en quince mil.

To review
• indirect object pronouns p. 262

2 | Talk about buying souvenirs on vacation

Soledad and her friend Ana are bargaining at a market. Complete the conversation with the appropriate indirect object pronoun.

Soledad: Buenos días, señor. ¿ __1.__ deja ver los collares de oro?

Vendedor: ¡Claro que sí! A usted __2.__ dejo el collar más bonito en quince mil colones.

Soledad: ¡Qué caro! Mi amiga también quiere comprar un collar. ¿ __3.__ deja ver a nosotras los collares de plata?

Vendedor: Sí, señoritas. A ustedes __4.__ dejo dos collares en veinticinco mil colones.

Soledad: Todavía son caros.

Vendedor: Está bien. A usted __5.__ dejo los dos collares en veinticuatro mil.

Ana: ¡Gracias, Soledad! ¿Quieres ir al café? __6.__ invito.

To review
• demonstrative adjectives p. 268

3 | Talk about vacation activities

You see many people at the beach while you are on vacation. Use demonstrative adjectives to indicate who is doing the following activities.

modelo: acampar
Estos chicos están acampando.

1. hacer surfing
2. montar a caballo
3. comer al aire libre
4. vender refrescos

5. caminar en la playa
6. hacer surf de vela
7. hacer una parrillada
8. comprar un refresco

To review
• Comparación cultural pp. 254, 264, 271
• Lectura cultural pp. 276–277

4 | Costa Rica and Uruguay

Comparación cultural

Answer these culture questions.

1. Why is Costa Rica a good destination for ecotourism?
2. What are some transportation options in Costa Rica? Describe them.
3. How is coffee harvested in Costa Rica? Why does it grow well there?
4. Where are **el Mercado Central** and **el Mercado del Puerto** located? What foods can you buy at these markets?

Más práctica   Cuaderno *pp. 182–193*   Cuaderno para hispanohablantes *pp. 184–193*

Get Help Online
ClassZone.com

Costa Rica

Ecuador

Uruguay

AUDIO

¡De vacaciones!

Lectura y escritura

WebQuest
ClassZone.com

① **Leer** Travel destinations vary around the world. Read and compare where and how Ernesto, Isabel, and Osvaldo are spending their vacations.

② **Escribir** Using the three descriptions as models, write a short paragraph about a real or imaginary vacation.

STRATEGY Escribir
Use three boxes Use three boxes to help you describe the vacation.

| Lugar | Actividades | Opinión |

Step 1 Complete the boxes. In the first box write information about the place, in the second box write details about what you usually do there, and in the third box give your opinion about the location.

Step 2 Write your paragraph. Make sure to include all the information from the boxes. Check your writing by yourself or with help from a friend. Make final corrections.

Compara con tu mundo

Use the paragraph you wrote to compare your vacation with a vacation described by *one* of the three students. How are they similar? How are they different?

Cuaderno *pp. 194–196*   Cuaderno para hispanohablantes *pp. 194–196*

Uruguay   *Ernesto*

¡Hola! Me llamo Ernesto y vivo en Montevideo. Es febrero, y mis padres y yo estamos de vacaciones en Punta del Este. Generalmente nos quedamos con mi abuela. Su casa está muy cerca de Playa Mansa. Es una playa donde el mar es muy tranquilo. Es ideal para nadar o tomar el sol. Yo prefiero ir a Playa Brava porque tiene más olas[1] y es perfecta para hacer surfing. En las tardes me gusta pasear por el Mercado de los Artesanos. Allí les compro recuerdos a mis amigos.

[1] waves

Ecuador   *Isabel*

¿Qué tal? Me llamo Isabel y soy de Quito. Mi familia y yo estamos pasando unos días de vacaciones en Baños, una ciudad que está en un valle[2], al lado de un volcán. Nos estamos quedando en un hotel que está muy cerca de las cascadas[3] y de las aguas termales[4]. Aquí puedes hacer muchas actividades al aire libre: montar a caballo, dar caminatas por la ruta de las cascadas y montar en bicicleta. ¡Es un lugar fenomenal!

[2] valley   [3] waterfalls   [4] hot springs

Costa Rica   *Osvaldo*

¡Hola! Me llamo Osvaldo y soy de Costa Rica. Estoy pasando las vacaciones de julio en el Parque Nacional Manuel Antonio. El hotel está en un bosque tropical lluvioso[5] pero también tiene una playa en la costa del océano Pacífico. Todas las mañanas, mis padres y yo nos levantamos muy temprano y salimos a dar caminatas en el parque. Allí hay plantas y animales muy exóticos. ¡Me gusta estar en la naturaleza[6]!

[5] **bosque...** tropical rain forest   [6] nature

Repaso inclusivo
♻ Options for Review

¡AvanzaRap!
DVD
Sing and Learn

1 | Listen, understand, and compare

Escuchar

Listen to the telephone conversation between Mrs. Daza and her husband. Then answer the following questions.

1. ¿Dónde está la señora Daza y qué está haciendo? ¿Por qué va a llegar tarde?
2. ¿Qué hizo el señor Daza después de trabajar?
3. ¿Qué está haciendo él ahora?
4. ¿Dónde están Luisa y David? ¿Qué están haciendo?
5. ¿Qué va a hacer la familia Daza este sábado? ¿Cuál es el problema?

Does your family eat dinner together? At what time? What do you do as a group on weekends?

2 | Mingle at a party

Hablar

In a group of six, role-play a dinner party in which you mingle with other guests. Walk around and introduce yourself to others. Talk about the people that you know in common, what you are studying, what you like to do in your free time, and anything else you find out about the person you are talking to, such as plans for summer vacation. You should spend at least one minute talking to each person.

3 | Interview a potential roommate

Hablar

Work in a group of four. Three of you room together at soccer camp and the fourth is a potential roommate. Ask questions to find out about your new roommate's personality, likes, dislikes, and daily routine. The potential roommate should give as much detail as possible about himself or herself and also ask questions. Each person should speak for at least one minute.

¿A qué hora te acuestas?

Me acuesto a las diez y media.

4 | Create a tourist booklet

Escribir

You are an intern at a travel agency and have been asked to plan a one-week trip for a family of four to a Spanish-speaking country. Research a destination and map out a route. Create a booklet describing places of interest along the route, transportation, and costs. Include other tourist information, such as cuisine, festivals, or souvenirs that can be bought there. Copy this chart on a piece of paper and use it to organize your information. Use illustrations and at least eight sentences.

Lugares	Información

5 | Talk about your health

Hablar

You are at the doctor's office for a checkup. You should tell your partner about your general health routine, including when you go to bed, what time you get up, what you eat and drink throughout the day, and what your activities are. Your partner will make recommendations about what you should do differently. Your conversation should be about four minutes long.

6 | Decide where to study

Leer
Escribir

This summer you want to study Spanish. Your Spanish teacher gave you this information to help you decide on a program. Read the descriptions and write a note to your teacher, explaining where you would like to study and why. Offer comparisons of the two programs.

Estudia en
¡Costa Rica!

Jacó

En esta ciudad muy pequeña no hay muchas tiendas, pero hay varias playas en el Océano Pacífico. Puedes vivir en una residencia de la escuela, con un(a) compañero(a) de cuarto.

Durante los fines de semana es muy popular hacer surf de vela o esquí acuático. También puedes nadar o tomar el sol en la playa.

Horario
Clases: 7:00–2:30
Almuerzo: 12:00–1:00

Heredia

Heredia es una ciudad pequeña cerca de San José, la capital. Puedes vivir en una casa con una familia con hijos. Las familias con hijos normalmente se acuestan a las diez de la noche. Se levantan a las seis y media para comer el desayuno.

Durante los fines de semana puedes dar caminatas en las áreas verdes y ver muchos animales exóticos. También hay volcanes cerca de la ciudad.

Horario
Clases: 8:00–4:30
Almuerzo: 1:00–3:00

¿? Entre dos

Pair Activities

Unidad 5 288

Unidad 6 290

Unidad 7 292

Unidad 8 294

Un hogar para las vacaciones

Estudiante A

Imagine that you and your family are going to rent a vacation home. You and your partner each found a home that would be available. First, answer your partner's questions about the home you found. Then, ask your partner at least five questions about the home you found. Decide which one you would select and why.

Estudiante A: **¿La casa tiene dos pisos?**

Estudiante B: **Sí/No...**

Estudiante A: **¿Tiene comedor?**

Estudiante B: **Sí/No...**

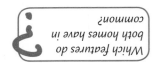

Which features do both homes have in common?

Un hogar para las vacaciones

Estudiante B

Imagine that you and your family are going to rent a vacation home. You and your partner each found a home that would be available. First, ask your partner at least five questions about the home he or she found. Then, answer your partner's questions about the home you found. Decide which one you would select and why.

Estudiante A: **¿La casa tiene dos pisos?**

Estudiante B: **Sí/No...**

Estudiante A: **¿Tiene comedor?**

Estudiante B: **Sí/No...**

Which features do both homes have in common?

Entre dos • Lección 2

Antes de celebrar, hay que limpiar

Estudiante A

Imagine that you and a family member (your partner) want to have a party. You are allowed to have the party as long as you both complete your chores. Take turns asking each other what you are going to do today. First, ask your partner if he or she plans to set the table, wash the dishes, make the bed, cook, and mow the lawn. Then, answer your partner's questions based on the images and clues below.

Estudiante A: **¿Vas a hacer la cama?**

Estudiante B: **Sí/No...**

What are two chores you and your partner still need to do tomorrow?

Antes de celebrar, hay que limpiar

Estudiante B

Imagine that you and a family member (your partner) want to have a party. You are allowed to have the party as long as you both complete your chores. Take turns asking each other what you are going to do today. First, answer your partner's questions based on the images and clues below. Then, ask your partner if he or she plans to sweep, feed the cat, take out the trash, iron, and vacuum.

Estudiante A: **¿Vas a planchar la ropa?**

Estudiante B: **Sí/No...**

What are two chores you and your partner still need to do tomorrow?

Los deportes

Estudiante A

Enrique

You and your partner are talking about what sports Enrique and Carolina like to play. Look at Enrique's equipment to see the sports he enjoys. With a partner, talk about what sports Enrique and Carolina do.

Estudiante A: **Enrique juega al fútbol americano. ¿Y Carolina?**

Estudiante B: **Ella no juega al fútbol americano, pero patina.**

Which sports do Carolina and Enrique have in common?

Los deportes

Estudiante B

Carolina

You and your partner are talking about what sports Enrique and Carolina like to play. Look at Carolina's equipment to see the sports she enjoys. With a partner, talk about what sports Carolina and Enrique do.

Estudiante A: **Enrique juega al fútbol americano. ¿Y Carolina?**

Estudiante B: **Ella no juega al fútbol americano, pero patina.**

Which sports do Carolina and Enrique have in common?

Entre dos • Lección 2

¡Ay, me duele… !

Estudiante A

You and your partner are doctors. Each of you has information about some patients. Ask each other about patients on your charts. Use the images to tell your partner what the medical problems are. Then, imagine what each patient did to cause that problem.

Estudiante A: **¿Qué le duele a Ana?**
Estudiante B: **Le duele el tobillo. Ayer caminó mucho.**

	Le duele…	¿Por qué?
Patricia		
Esteban		
Mario		

Sarita

Carlos

Daniela

What would you advise these patients to do to get better?

ENTRE DOS UNIDAD 6

¡Ay, me duele… !

Estudiante B

You and your partner are doctors. Each of you has information about some patients. Ask each other about patients on your charts. Use the images to tell your partner what the medical problems are. Then, imagine what each patient did to cause that problem.

Estudiante A: **¿Qué le duele a Ana?**
Estudiante B: **Le duele el tobillo. Ayer caminó mucho.**

	Le duele…	¿Por qué?
Daniela		
Carlos		
Sarita		

What would you advise these patients to do to get better?

Patricia

Esteban

Mario

El proyecto

Estudiante A

Roberto

Rita

Luisa y Andrea

You and your partner are in charge of a class project and you want to make sure that all your team members have completed their tasks. Ask your partner who did the tasks listed below. Answer your partner's questions based on the images. Take turns doing this activity.

> Use instant messaging
> Burn compact discs
> Surf the Internet
> Buy a new mouse

Estudiante A: **¿Quién habló con el profesor?**
Estudiante B: **... habló con el profesor./ Nadie.**

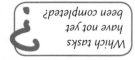

Which tasks have not yet been completed?

El proyecto

Estudiante B

You and your partner are in charge of a class project and you want to make sure that all your team members have completed their tasks. Ask your partner who did the tasks listed below. Answer your partner's questions based on the images. Take turns doing this activity.

> Take photos
> Send photos
> Look for books in the library
> Send e-mails

Estudiante A: **¿Quién habló con el profesor?**
Estudiante B: **... habló con el professor./ Nadie.**

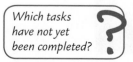

Which tasks have not yet been completed?

Juan y Cristina

Marcelo

Teresa y yo

Entre dos • Lección 2

El fin de semana pasada

Estudiante A

You and your partner are talking about what you did last weekend. Take turns asking and telling each other where you went and whether it was fun or boring.

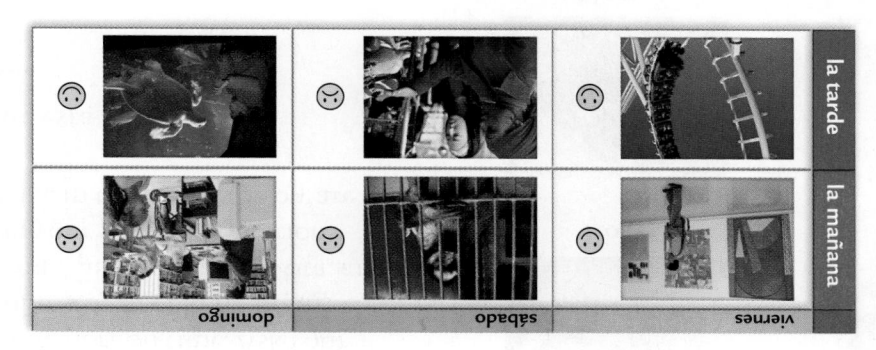

Estudiante A: **¿Adónde fuiste el viernes pasado?**

Estudiante B: **Por la mañana, ... y por la tarde...**

Estudiante A: **¿Cómo fue?**

Estudiante B: **... divertido(a)/aburrido(a). Y tú, ¿qué hiciste?**

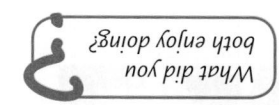
What did you both enjoy doing?

El fin de semana pasada

Estudiante B

You and your partner are talking about what you did last weekend. Take turns asking and telling each other where you went and whether it was fun or boring.

Estudiante A: **¿Adónde fuiste el viernes pasado?**

Estudiante B: **Por la mañana, ... y por la tarde...**

Estudiante A: **¿Cómo fue?**

Estudiante B: **... divertido(a)/aburrido(a). Y tú, ¿qué hiciste?**

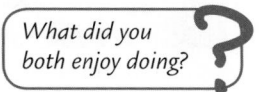
What did you both enjoy doing?

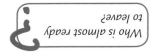

¿Who is almost ready to leave?

 Diego

 Isabel

 Sergio

 Mateo

 Sofía

 Rosa

Estudiante A

Your class is leaving for a trip to Spain today. You and your partner are trying to make sure that everyone gets to the airport on time. Ask your partner what the following people are doing: el Sr. Costas, Cris, la Sra. Vásquez, Rafael, Rita, and Elena. Then, answer your partner's questions about what the people in the images below are doing.

Estudiante A: **¿Qué está haciendo...?**

Estudiante B: **Está...**

¡Date prisa!

Your class is leaving today for a trip to Spain. You and your partner are trying to make sure that everyone gets to the airport on time. Answer your partner's questions about what the people in the images are doing. Then, ask your partner what these people are doing: Rosa, Sofía, Mateo, Sergio, Isabel, and Diego.

Estudiante A: **¿Qué está haciendo...?**

Estudiante B: **Está...**

 Who is almost ready to leave?

Estudiante B

 el Sr. Costas

 Cris

 la Sra. Vásquez

 Rita

 Rafael

 Elena

Entre dos • Lección 2

De vacaciones

Estudiante A

Ana   Gabi

Juan   Rosa

 (Ana / Raquel / Paloma images)
Raquel   Paloma

You and your partner are organizing a summer camp and are trying to decide what activities to include. Ask your partner what the teens on your list would like to do. Answer your partner's questions based on the images. Take turns doing the activity.

Estudiante A: **¿Qué le gustaría hacer a Miguel?**
Estudiante B: **A Miguel le gustaría...**

Miguel	Pablo
Susana	Jorge
María	Carlos

What are the two activities that more than one person would like? ¿?

De vacaciones

You and your partner are organizing a summer camp and are trying to decide what activities to include. Ask your partner what the teens on your list would like to do. Answer your partner's questions based on the images. Take turns doing the activity.

Estudiante A: **¿Qué le gustaría hacer a Miguel?**
Estudiante B: **A Miguel le gustaría...**

Gabi	Ana
Rosa	Juan
Paloma	Raquel

What are the two activities that more than one person would like? ?

Estudiante B

Miguel   Pablo

Susana   Jorge

María   Carlos

Recursos

Expansión de vocabulario

Unidad 5 . . . . **R2**

Unidad 6 . . . . **R3**

Unidad 7 . . . . **R4**

Unidad 8 . . . . **R5**

Para y piensa   Self-Check Answers   **R6**

Resumen de gramática **R9**

Glosario

Español-inglés **R18**

Inglés-español **R28**

Índice **R37**

Créditos **R45**

Lección 1
Vivimos aquí

Describe A House

el garaje	garage
la pared	wall
el traspatio	back yard
antiguo(a)	old, ancient
la cerca	fence

Describe Household Items

el congelador	freezer
la estufa	stove
el refrigerador	refrigerator
el lavaplatos	dishwasher
el microondas	microwave
la videograbadora	VCR
el teléfono celular	cellular phone
los audífonos	headphones

Lección 2
Una fiesta en casa

Plan a Party

sorprender	to surprise
el aniversario	anniversary
el confeti	confetti
la celebración	celebration
el día festivo	holiday
el ponche	punch
los juegos	games
los premios	prizes

Holidays/Celebrations

el bautizo	baptism
la graduación	graduation
la Navidad	Christmas
la Nochebuena	Christmas Eve
la Pascua Florida	Easter
el Ramadán	Ramadan
Rosh Hashaná	Rosh Hashanah
la Jánuca	Hanukkah
la Nochevieja	New Year's Eve
el día de Año Nuevo	New Year's Day
la confirmación	confirmation
el bar / bat mitzvá	bar / bat mitzvah

Talk About Gifts

la tarjeta de cumpleaños	birthday card
la tarjeta de regalo	gift card
el certificado de regalo	gift certificate

Talk About Chores and Responsibilities

quitar la mesa	to clear the table
el estipendio	allowance

Unidad 6

Expansión de vocabulario

Lección 1
¿Cuál es tu deporte favorito?

Sports

esquiar	to ski
hacer snowboard	to snowboard
el gol	goal
el hockey	hockey
el golf	golf
la gimnasia	gymnastics
el jonrón	homerun
los deportes de pista y campo	track and field
correr a campo traviesa	to run cross country
el (la) porrista	cheerleader
la carrera	race
las artes marciales	martial arts
caerse	to fall
saltar	to jump
hacer trucos	to do tricks
Locations and People	
la pista	track
el (la) entrenador(a)	coach
el (la) capitán del equipo	team captain
el árbitro	referee, umpire

Lección 2
La salud

Talking About Staying Healthy

el (la) doctor(a)	doctor
el (la) paciente	patient
el consultorio	doctor's office
tener una cita	to have an appointment
la alergia	allergy
la gripe	flu
el resfriado	cold
estornudar	to sneeze
toser	to cough
la medicina	medicine
Parts of the Body	
el dedo	finger
el dedo de pie	toe
el cuello	neck
la espalda	back
la garganta	throat
el hombro	shoulder
el oído	inner ear
la muñeca	wrist
Outdoor activities	
las máquinas para hacer ejercicio	exercise machines
remar	to row
hacer aeróbicos	to do aerobics
The Beach	
la arena	sand
el traje de baño	bathing suit
el tiburón	shark
el delfín	dolphin
la toalla	towel
las olas	waves
el (la) salvavidas	lifeguard

Unidad 7

Expansión de vocabulario

Lección 1
En el cibercafé

Talk About Technology

el apodo	screen name
la contraseña	password
cortar y pegar	to cut and paste
borrar	to delete
el archivo adjunto	attachment
la sonrisa, la carita feliz (emoticono)	smiley face (emoticon)
escribir a máquina	to type
charlar en línea	to chat
la cadena de e-mail	e-mail chain (forward)
arroba	@ (at)
punto com	.com (dot com)
el enlace	link
el blog	blog
bajar música	to download music
el tocador de mp3 (eme pe tres)	mp3 player
comenzar / terminar la sesión	to log on / to log off

Lección 2
Un día en el parque de diversiones

At the Amusement Park

el carrusel	carousel
el tobogán acuático	water slide
el espectáculo	show

Places of Interest

At the Aquarium	
la ballena	whale
el pez (pl. los peces)	fish
la tortuga	turtle
la foca	seal
At the Fair	
los juegos mecánicos	rides
el algodón de azúcar	cotton candy
los animales de peluche	stuffed animals
At the Zoo	
el león	lion
el tigre	tiger
el oso	bear
el canguro	kangaroo
el pingüino	penguin
el mono	monkey
el hipopótamo	hippopotamus
la jirafa	giraffe
la jaula	cage

Extend Invitations

Decline	
¿Quizás otra vez?	Maybe another time?

Make a Phone Call

¿De parte de quién?	Who's calling?
¿Puedo tomar un mensaje?	Can I take a message?
Puedo llamar más tarde.	I can call back later.

Unidad 8

Expansión de vocabulario

Lección 1
Pensando en las vacaciones

Talk About a Daily Routine

el despertador	alarm clock
rizarse el pelo	to curl one's hair
alisarse el pelo	to straighten one's hair

Talk About Grooming

el desodorante	deodorant
la seda dental	dental floss
el acondicionador	conditioner
la loción	lotion
el gel	hair gel
el lápiz labial	lipstick
el rímel	mascara
la sombra de ojos	eye shadow
el perfume	perfume
la colonia	cologne

Discussing a Vacation

el lago	lake
el río	river
hacer / tener una reservación	to make / have a reservation
el aeropuerto	airport

Lección 2
¡Vamos de vacaciones!

Talk About Vacation Activities

la tienda de campaña	tent
la cabaña	cabin
ver las atracciones	to go sightseeing
pescar	to go fishing
mandar tarjetas postales	to send postcards
el (la) turista	tourist

Talk About Shopping

el dinero en efectivo	cash
la tarjeta de crédito	credit card
probarse la ropa	to try on clothing
el probador	fitting room
el recibo	receipt
la moneda	coin
la talla	(clothing) size
la vitrina	store window
gastar	to spend
la caja	cash register
la billetera	wallet
el cajero automático	automatic teller machine

Jewelry and Handicrafts

la pulsera	bracelet
la joyería	jewelry store
brillante	shiny
el diamante	diamond

Bargaining

¿Tiene otros(as)?	Do you have others?

Para y piensa
Self-Check Answers

Unidad 5 Ecuador

Lección 1

p. 45 Práctica de vocabulario
Answers may vary but can include:
1. el sillón, el sofá, el televisor, la alfombra
2. la cama, el armario, la lámpara, la cómoda

p. 47 Vocabulario en contexto
Answers may vary but can include:
1. el disco compacto, el tocadiscos compactos, un radio
2. la lámpara, el sillón
3. el sofá, el televisor

p. 51 Práctica de gramática
1. estamos
2. estoy
3. es
4. son

p. 53 Gramática en contexto
1. es
2. están
3. está

p. 57 Práctica de gramática
1. Estoy en el sexto piso.
2. Estoy en el noveno piso.
3. Estoy en el segundo piso.
4. Estoy en el tercer piso.

p. 60 Todo junto
1. es; está
2. séptimo

Lección 2

p. 73 Práctica de vocabulario
Answers may vary but can include:
Cocinar, poner la mesa, decorar, limpiar la cocina

p. 75 Vocabulario en contexto
1. la basura
2. el césped
3. la aspiradora

p. 79 Práctica de gramática
1. pongo
2. dice
3. traigo

p. 81 Gramática en contexto
1. dice; viene
2. trae

p. 85 Práctica de gramática
1. Decora la sala. Acabo de decorarla. (La acabo de decorar.)
2. Haz los quehaceres. Acabo de hacerlos. (Los acabo de hacer.)
3. Corta el césped. Acabo de cortarlo. (Lo acabo de cortar.)

p. 88 Todo junto
Answers may vary but can include:
Pasa la aspiradora. Lava los platos. Limpia la cocina.

Unidad 6 República Dominicana

Lección 1

p. 107 Práctica de vocabulario
1. una cancha, una bola
2. un campo, un bate, un guante, un casco, una pelota
3. una cancha, una pelota, una raqueta

p. 109 Vocabulario en contexto
1. la ganadora
2. la natación
3. un casco

p. 113 Práctica de gramática
1. Ana y yo jugamos al béisbol.
2. Ustedes juegan al básquetbol.
3. El hermano de Rosa juega al voleibol.
4. Yo juego al tenis.

p. 115 Gramática en contexto
1. juega
2. juegan
3. jugar

p. 119 Práctica de gramática
1. Saben
2. conozco a
3. sabemos

p. 122 Todo junto
sabe; conocen; saben

Lección 2

p. 135 Práctica de vocabulario
Answers may vary but can include:
1. la boca, la nariz, los ojos, las orejas
2. el tobillo, el pie, la rodilla

p. 137 Vocabulario en contexto
1. le duele
2. le duelen

p. 141 Práctica de gramática
1. buceamos
2. tomaste
3. levantaron

p. 143 Gramática en contexto
1. Isabel y Mario llevaron cascos.
2. Mario no montó en bicicleta muy bien.
3. El señor de las frutas caminó delante de Mario.

p. 147 Práctica de gramática
1. llegué
2. jugaron
3. comenzó
4. practiqué

p. 150 Todo junto
1. comenzó
2. encontraron

Unidad 7 Argentina

Lección 1

p. 169 Práctica de vocabulario
Answers may vary but can include:
1. la pantalla, el ratón, el teclado
2. usar el mensajero instantáneo, navegar por Internet, mandar fotos, buscar un sitio Web

p. 171 Vocabulario en contexto
1. Primero, Trini llega a San Antonio.
2. Luego, Trini está en Puebla, México.
3. Más tarde, Trini va a Puerto Rico y a España.
4. Por fin, Trini está en Buenos Aires.

p. 175 Práctica de gramática
1. comí
2. Recibiste

p. 177 Gramática en contexto
1. recibió
2. compartieron
3. salieron

p. 181 Práctica de gramática
1. Nunca recibo ningún correo electrónico.
2. Alguien escribe algo con el mensajero instantáneo.
3. A Beatriz no le gusta ni navegar por Internet ni estar en línea.

p. 184 Todo junto
1. No, Mariano no perdió nada.
2. No, Florencia no recibió ni la fecha ni la hora.
3. No, Mariano no le escribió ningún correo electrónico a Alicia.

Lección 2

p. 197 Práctica de vocabulario
Answers may vary but can include:
1. la vuelta al mundo, la montaña rusa, los autitos chocadores
2. el zoológico, el museo, el acuario, el parque de diversiones

p. 199 Vocabulario en contexto
1. ¡Qué divertido!

2. ¡Qué pequeña!
3. ¡Qué interesante!
4. ¡Qué grandes!

p. 203 Práctica de gramática
1. hicimos; fue (ser)
2. fui (ir); Hice
3. Fueron (ir); hicieron

p. 205 Gramática en contexto
1. ¿Adónde fueron Florencia, Luciana y tú?
2. ¿Qué hiciste?
3. ¿Cómo fue el día?

p. 209 Práctica de gramática
1. nosotros
2. ti
3. ellos

p. 212 Todo junto
1. Florencia hizo una cena para él.
2. Las empanadas fueron para ellos.
3. Mariano fue con ella a los autitos chocadores.

Unidad 8 Costa Rica

Lección 1

p. 231 Práctica de vocabulario
Answers may vary but can include:
1. levantarse, lavarse la cara, maquillarse, lavarse el pelo, secarse el pelo, ducharse, afeitarse, cepillarse los dientes, vestirse
2. en barco, en tren, en avión

p. 233 Vocabulario en contexto
1. unas vacaciones
2. la ciudad
3. un hotel

p. 237 Práctica de gramática
1. Yo me lavo las manos.
2. Los chicos secan al perro.
3. Juana y yo ponemos la mesa.
4. Mi abuelo se afeita la cara.

p. 239 Gramática en contexto
1. acostarse
2. se levanta

p. 243 Práctica de gramática
1. me estoy duchando (estoy duchándome)
2. estás durmiendo
3. nos estamos vistiendo (estamos vistiéndonos)

p. 246 Todo junto
1. Jorge se está peinando. (Jorge está peinándose.)
2. Susana se está maquillando. (Susana está maquillándose.)
3. Los hermanos se están cepillando los dientes. (Los hermanos están cepillándose los dientes.)
4. Jorge se está poniendo la chaqueta. (Jorge está poniéndose la chaqueta.)

Lección 2

p. 259 Práctica de vocabulario
1. ¿Me deja ver los aretes?
2. ¿Me deja ver el collar de plata?
3. ¿Me deja ver el anillo de oro?
4. ¿Me deja ver las artesanías de madera?

p. 261 Vocabulario en contexto
1. barato
2. los aretes
3. el mercado

p. 265 Práctica de gramática
1. les
2. te
3. nos

p. 267 Gramática en contexto
1. le
2. les
3. le

p. 271 Práctica de gramática
1. Aquellos
2. Este
3. esas

p. 274 Todo junto
1. le; esa
2. les; estos

Resumen de gramática

Nouns, Articles, and Pronouns

Nouns

Nouns identify people, animals, places, and things. All Spanish nouns, even if they refer to objects, are either **masculine** or **feminine.** They are also either **singular** or **plural.**

Nouns ending in **-o** are usually masculine; nouns ending in **-a** are usually feminine.

To form the **plural** of a noun, add **-s** if the noun ends in a vowel; add **-es** if it ends in a consonant.

Singular Nouns		Plural Nouns	
Masculine	**Feminine**	**Masculine**	**Feminine**
abuelo	abuela	abuelos	abuelas
chico	chica	chicos	chicas
hombre	mujer	hombres	mujeres
papel	pluma	papeles	plumas
zapato	blusa	zapatos	blusas

Articles

Articles identify the class of a noun: masculine or feminine, singular or plural. **Definite articles** are the equivalent of the English word *the.* **Indefinite articles** are the equivalent of *a, an,* or *some.*

Definite Articles				Indefinite Articles		
	Masculine	**Feminine**			**Masculine**	**Feminine**
Singular	**el** chico	**la** chica		**Singular**	**un** chico	**una** chica
Plural	**los** chicos	**las** chicas		**Plural**	**unos** chicos	**unas** chicas

Pronouns

Pronouns take the place of nouns. The pronoun used is determined by its function or purpose in a sentence.

Subject Pronouns

yo	nosotros(as)
tú	vosotros(as)
usted	ustedes
él, ella	ellos(as)

Direct Object Pronouns

me	nos
te	os
lo, la	los, las

Indirect Object Pronouns

me	nos
te	os
le	les

Pronouns After Prepositions

mí	nosotros(as)
ti	vosotros(as)
usted	ustedes
él, ella	ellos(as)

Reflexive Pronouns

me	nos
te	os
se	se

Adjectives

Adjectives describe nouns. In Spanish, adjectives match the **gender** and **number** of the nouns they describe. To make an adjective plural, add **-s** if it ends in a vowel; add **-es** if it ends in a consonant. The adjective usually comes after the noun in Spanish.

Adjectives

	Masculine	Feminine
Singular	el chico alto	la chica alta
	el chico inteligente	la chica inteligente
	el chico joven	la chica joven
	el chico trabajador	la chica trabajadora
Plural	los chicos altos	las chicas altas
	los chicos inteligentes	las chicas inteligentes
	los chicos jóvenes	las chicas jóvenes
	los chicos trabajadores	las chicas trabajadoras

Adjectives (continued)

Sometimes adjectives are shortened when they are placed in front of a masculine singular noun.

Shortened Forms

alguno	**algún** chico
bueno	**buen** chico
malo	**mal** chico
ninguno	**ningún** chico
primero	**primer** chico
tercero	**tercer** chico

Possessive adjectives indicate who owns something or describe a relationship between people or things. They agree in number with the nouns they describe. **Nuestro(a)** and **vuestro(a)** must also agree in gender with the nouns they describe.

Possessive Adjectives

	Masculine		Feminine	
Singular	**mi** amigo	**nuestro** amigo	**mi** amiga	**nuestra** amiga
	tu amigo	**vuestro** amigo	**tu** amiga	**vuestra** amiga
	su amigo	**su** amigo	**su** amiga	**su** amiga
Plural	**mis** amigos	**nuestros** amigos	**mis** amigas	**nuestras** amigas
	tus amigos	**vuestros** amigos	**tus** amigas	**vuestras** amigas
	sus amigos	**sus** amigos	**sus** amigas	**sus** amigas

Demonstrative adjectives describe the location of a person or a thing in relation to the speaker. Their English equivalents are *this, that, these,* and *those.*

Demonstrative Adjectives

	Masculine	Feminine
Singular	**este** chico	**esta** chica
	ese chico	**esa** chica
	aquel chico	**aquella** chica
Plural	**estos** chicos	**estas** chicas
	esos chicos	**esas** chicas
	aquellos chicos	**aquellas** chicas

Comparatives

Comparatives are used to compare two people or things.

Comparatives

más (+)	menos (−)	tan, tanto (=)
más serio **que...**	**menos** serio **que...**	**tan** serio **como...**
Me gusta leer **más que** pasear.	Me gusta pasear **menos que** leer.	Me gusta hablar **tanto como** escuchar.

There are a few irregular comparative words. When talking about the age of people, use **mayor** and **menor.** When talking about qualities, use **mejor** and **peor.**

Age	Quality
mayor	mejor
menor	peor

Affirmative and Negative Words

Affirmative or **negative** words are used to talk about indefinite or negative situations.

Affirmative Words	Negative Words
algo	nada
alguien	nadie
algún/alguno(a)	ningún/ninguno(a)
o... o	ni... ni
siempre	nunca
también	tampoco

Verbs: Present Tense

Regular Verbs

Regular verbs ending in **-ar, -er,** or **-ir** always have regular endings in the present tense.

-ar Verbs		-er Verbs		-ir Verbs	
hablo	hablamos	vendo	vendemos	comparto	compartimos
hablas	habláis	vendes	vendéis	compartes	compartís
habla	hablan	vende	venden	comparte	comparten

Verbs with Irregular yo Forms

Some verbs have regular forms in the present tense except for the **yo** form.

conocer		dar		hacer	
conozco	conocemos	doy	damos	hago	hacemos
conoces	conocéis	das	dais	haces	hacéis
conoce	conocen	da	dan	hace	hacen

poner		saber		salir	
pongo	ponemos	sé	sabemos	salgo	salimos
pones	ponéis	sabes	sabéis	sales	salís
pone	ponen	sabe	saben	sale	salen

traer		ver	
traigo	traemos	veo	vemos
traes	traéis	ves	veis
trae	traen	ve	ven

Verbs: Present Tense (continued)

Stem-Changing Verbs

e → ie

quiero	queremos
quieres	queréis
quiere	quieren

Other **e → ie** stem-changing verbs are **cerrar, comenzar, despertarse, empezar, entender, pensar, perder,** and **preferir.**

o → ue

puedo	podemos
puedes	podéis
puede	pueden

Other **o → ue** stem-changing verbs are **acostarse, almorzar, costar, doler, dormir, encontrar, envolver,** and **volver.**

e → i

sirvo	servimos
sirves	servís
sirve	sirven

Other **e → i** stem-changing verbs are **pedir** and **vestirse.**

u → ue

juego	jugamos
juegas	jugáis
juega	juegan

Jugar is the only verb with a **u → ue** stem change.

Irregular Verbs

The following verbs are irregular in the present tense.

decir

digo	decimos
dices	decís
dice	dicen

estar

estoy	estamos
estás	estáis
está	están

ir

voy	vamos
vas	vais
va	van

ser

soy	somos
eres	sois
es	son

tener

tengo	tenemos
tienes	tenéis
tiene	tienen

venir

vengo	venimos
vienes	venís
viene	vienen

Verbs: Present Participles

Present participles are used with a form of **estar** to say that an action is in progress at this moment.

Regular Participles

-ar Verbs	-er Verbs	-ir Verbs
caminando	haciendo	abriendo
hablando	poniendo	compartiendo
jugando	vendiendo	saliendo

Stem Changes

decir	diciendo
dormir	durmiendo
pedir	pidiendo
servir	sirviendo
venir	viniendo
vestir	vistiendo

y Spelling Change

leer	leyendo
traer	trayendo

Verbs: Affirmative tú Commands

Affirmative tú commands are used to tell a friend or family member to do something. Regular affirmative **tú** commands are the same as the **él/ella forms** in the present tense.

Regular Affirmative tú Commands

-ar Verbs	-er Verbs	-ir Verbs
lava	barre	abre
cierra	entiende	duerme
almuerza	vuelve	pide

Irregular Affirmative tú Commands

Infinitive	Affirmative tú Command
decir	**di**
hacer	**haz**
ir	**ve**
poner	**pon**
salir	**sal**
ser	**sé**
tener	**ten**
venir	**ven**

Verbs: Preterite Tense

Regular Verbs

Regular preterite verbs ending in **-ar, -er,** or **-ir** have regular endings.

-ar Verbs

nad**é**	nad**amos**
nad**aste**	nad**asteis**
nad**ó**	nad**aron**

-er Verbs

vend**í**	vend**imos**
vend**iste**	vend**isteis**
vend**ió**	vend**ieron**

-ir Verbs

escrib**í**	escrib**imos**
escrib**iste**	escrib**isteis**
escrib**ió**	escrib**ieron**

Verbs with Spelling Changes

-car Verbs

bus**qu**é	buscamos
buscaste	buscasteis
buscó	buscaron

-gar Verbs

ju**gu**é	jugamos
jugaste	jugasteis
jugó	jugaron

-zar Verbs

almor**c**é	almorzamos
almorzaste	almorzasteis
almorzó	almorzaron

Note: The verb **leer** also has a spelling change in the preterite. You will learn about this in Level 2.

Irregular Verbs

hacer

hice	hicimos
hiciste	hicisteis
hizo	hicieron

ir

fui	fuimos
fuiste	fuisteis
fue	fueron

ser

fui	fuimos
fuiste	fuisteis
fue	fueron

Note: The verbs **dormir, pedir, preferir,** and **servir** have a stem change in the preterite tense. The verbs **dar, decir, estar, poner, querer, saber, tener,** and **traer** are irregular in the preterite tense. You will learn about the preterite of these verbs in Level 2.

Glosario
español-inglés

This Spanish-English glossary contains all the active vocabulary words that appear in the text as well as passive vocabulary lists. **LP** refers to the Lección preliminar.

A

a to, at
> **A la(s)...** At... o'clock. **2.1**
> **a pie** on foot **4.2**
> **¿A qué hora es/son...?** At what time is/are...? **2.1**

abril April **3.2**
abrir to open **5.2**
la abuela grandmother **3.2**
el abuelo grandfather **3.2**
los abuelos grandparents **3.2**
aburrido(a) boring **2.2**
acabar de... to have just... **5.2**
acampar to camp **8.2**
acompañar to go *or* come with
> **¿Quieres acompañarme a...?** Would you like to come with me to...? **7.2**

acostarse (ue) to go to bed **8.1**
la actividad activity **1.1**
el acuario aquarium **7.2**
Adiós. Goodbye. **LP**
adivinar to guess
adjunto(a) attached
adónde (to) where **2.2**
> **¿Adónde vas?** Where are you going? **2.2**

afeitarse to shave oneself **8.1**
el (la) aficionado(a) fan, sports fan **6.1**
agosto August **3.2**
el agua (fem.) water **1.1**
> **las aguas termales** hot springs

ahora now **3.1**
el aire air
> **al aire libre** outside; open-air **8.2**

al to the **2.2**
> **al aire libre** outside; open-air **8.2**
> **al lado (de)** next to **2.2**

alegre happy; upbeat
la alfombra rug **5.1**

algo something **7.1**
alguien someone **7.1**
alguno(a) some, any **7.1**
allí there **4.2**
almorzar (ue) to eat lunch **4.2**
el almuerzo lunch **3.1**
¿Aló? Hello? (on telephone) **7.2**
alquilar to rent **1.1**
> **alquilar un DVD** to rent a DVD **1.1**

alto(a) tall **1.2**
amarillo(a) yellow **4.1**
el (la) amigo(a) friend **1.2**
anaranjado(a) orange (color) **4.1**
andar en patineta to skateboard **1.1**
el anillo ring **8.2**
anoche last night **6.2**
anteayer the day before yesterday **7.1**
antes (de) before **1.1**
la antorcha torch
el anuncio advertisement; announcement
el año year **3.2**
> **el Año Nuevo** New Year
> **el año pasado** last year **7.1**
> **¿Cuántos años tienes?** How old are you? **3.2**
> **tener... años** to be... years old **3.2**

el apartamento apartment **5.1**
aprender to learn **1.1**
> **aprender el español** to learn Spanish **1.1**

los apuntes notes **2.1**
> **tomar apuntes** to take notes **2.1**

aquel (aquella) that (over there) **8.2**
aquellos (as) those (over there) **8.2**
aquí here **4.2**
el árbol tree
> **el árbol de Navidad** Christmas tree

el archivo file

el arete earring **8.2**
el armario closet; armoire **5.1**
el arrecife de coral coral reef
el arroz rice **4.2**
el arte art **2.1**
> **las artes marciales** martial arts

las artesanías handicrafts **8.2**
el artículo article
los artículos goods **8.2**
> **los artículos deportivos** sporting goods

artístico(a) artistic **1.2**
la aspiradora vacuum cleaner **5.2**
el (la) atleta athlete **6.1**
atlético(a) athletic **1.2**
los autitos chocadores bumper cars **7.2**
el autobús (*pl.* los autobuses) bus **4.2**
> **en autobús** by bus **4.2**

avanzar to advance, to move ahead
> **¡Avanza!** Advance!, Move ahead!
> **avancemos** let's advance, let's move ahead

el avión (*pl.* los aviones) airplane **8.1**
> **en avión** by plane **8.1**

ayer yesterday **6.2**
el aymara indigenous language of Bolivia and Peru
ayudar to help **5.2**
azul blue **4.1**

B

bailar to dance **5.2**
el (la) bailarín(ina) (*pl.* los bailarines) dancer
el baile dance
bajar to descend **5.1**
bajo(a) short (height) **1.2**
la balsa raft
la banana banana **3.1**
la banda musical band

la bandera flag
bañarse to take a bath **8.1**
el baño bathroom **2.2**
barato(a) inexpensive **8.2**
el barco boat **8.1**
  en barco by boat **8.1**
barrer to sweep **5.2**
  barrer el suelo to sweep the
    floor **5.2**
el básquetbol basketball (the
  sport) **6.1**
la basura trash, garbage **5.2**
la batalla battle
el bate (baseball) bat **6.1**
beber to drink **1.1**
la bebida beverage, drink **3.1**
el béisbol baseball (the sport) **6.1**
la biblioteca library **2.2**
la bicicleta bicycle **1.1**
bien well, fine **LP**
  Bien. ¿Y tú/usted? Fine. And you?
    (familiar/formal) **LP**
  Muy bien. ¿Y tú/usted? Very well.
    And you? (familiar/formal) **LP**
el bistec beef **4.2**
blanco(a) white **4.1**
el bloqueador de sol sunscreen **6.2**
la blusa blouse **4.1**
la boca mouth **6.2**
el boleto ticket **7.2**
bonito(a) pretty **1.2**
el borrador eraser **2.2**
el bosque forest
  el bosque nuboso cloud forest
  el bosque tropical lluvioso
    tropical rain forest
el brazo arm **6.2**
el brindis celebratory toast
el brócoli broccoli **4.2**
bucear to scuba-dive **6.2**
bueno(a) good **1.2**
  Buenos días. Good morning. **LP**
  Buenas noches. Good evening;
    Good night. **LP**
  Buenas tardes. Good
    afternoon. **LP**
buscar to look for **5.2**

el caballo horse
  montar a caballo to ride
    horses **8.2**
la cabeza head **6.2**

cada each; every
el café coffee; café **3.1, 4.2**
la cafetería cafeteria **2.2**
la calavera skull
el calcetín (*pl.* **los calcetines**)
  sock **4.1**
la calculadora calculator **2.2**
la calidad quality **8.2**
caliente hot
la calle street **4.2**
el calor heat
  Hace calor. It is hot. **LP**
  tener calor to be hot **4.1**
la cama bed **5.1**
  hacer la cama to make the
    bed **5.2**
la cámara camera **7.1**
  la cámara digital digital
    camera **7.1**
el cambio change
caminar to walk **6.2**
la caminata hike **8.2**
  dar una caminata to hike **8.2**
la camisa shirt **4.1**
la camiseta T-shirt **4.1**
el campeón (*pl.* **los campeones**)**, la**
  campeona champion **6.1**
el campo field (sports) **6.1**; the
  country, countryside **8.1**
la cancha court (sports) **6.1**
cansado(a) tired **2.2**
cantar to sing **5.2**
Carnaval Carnival
la carne meat **4.2**
caro(a) expensive **8.2**
  ¡Qué caro(a)! How expensive! **8.2**
la carrera (sports) race
la carreta horse-drawn carriage
el carro car
la casa house **5.1**
la cascada waterfall
el casco helmet **6.1**
el cascarón (*pl.* **los cascarones**)
  confetti-filled egg
la caseta small house or tent
casi almost **2.1**
castaño(a) brown (hair) **1.2**
catorce fourteen **2.1**
celebrar to celebrate **5.2**
el cementerio cemetery
la cena dinner **3.1**
el centro center, downtown **4.2**
  el centro comercial shopping
    center, mall **4.1**

cepillar to brush **8.1**
  cepillarse los dientes to brush
    one's teeth **8.1**
el cepillo brush **8.1**
  el cepillo de dientes
    toothbrush **8.1**
la cerámica ceramics **8.2**
cerca (de) near (to) **2.2**
el cereal cereal **3.1**
cero zero **LP**
cerrar (ie) to close **4.1**
el césped grass, lawn **5.2**
el champú shampoo **8.1**
la chaqueta jacket **4.1**
la chica girl **1.2**
el chico boy **1.2**
cien one hundred **2.1**
las ciencias science **2.1**
cierto(a) true
cinco five **LP**
cincuenta fifty **2.1**
el cine movie theater; the movies **4.2**
la ciudad city **8.1**
¡Claro que sí! Of course! **7.2**
la clase class, classroom **LP**; kind,
  type
el coche car **4.2**
  en coche by car **4.2**
la cocina kitchen **5.1**
cocinar to cook **5.2**
el colegio high school
el collar necklace **8.2**
el color color
  ¿De qué color es/son...? What
    color is/are...?
el comedor dining room **5.1**
comenzar (ie) to begin **6.2**
comer to eat **1.1**
  comer al aire libre to picnic, to
    eat outside **8.2**
cómico(a) funny **1.2**
la comida meal; food **1.1, 3.1**
como as, like
¿Cómo...? How...? **3.1**
  ¿Cómo eres? What are you
    like? **1.2**
  ¿Cómo estás? How are you?
    (familiar) **LP**
  ¿Cómo está usted? How are you?
    (formal) **LP**
  ¿Cómo se llama? What's his/her/
    your (formal) name? **LP**
  ¿Cómo te llamas? What's your
    name? (familiar) **LP**
la cómoda dresser **5.1**

comparar to compare
compartir to share **3.1**
comprar to buy **1.1**
comprender to understand **6.1**
   ¿Comprendiste? Did you
      understand?
la computadora computer **2.1**
común common
con with **7.2**
el concierto concert **4.2**
conectar to connect **7.1**
   conectar a Internet to connect
      to the Internet **7.1**
conmigo with me **7.2**
conocer (conozco) to know, to be
   familiar with; to meet **6.1**
contento(a) happy **2.2**
contestar to answer **2.1**
contigo with you **7.2**
contra against
la contraseña password
el corazón (*pl.* **los**
   corazones) heart **6.2**
corregir to correct
el correo electrónico e-mail **1.1**
correr to run **1.1**
cortar to cut **5.2**
   cortar el césped to cut the
      grass **5.2**
la cortina curtain **5.1**
la cosa thing **5.1**
costar (ue) to cost **4.2**
   ¿Cuánto cuesta(n)? How much
      does it (do they) cost? **4.1**
   Cuesta(n)... It (They) cost... **4.1**
la Cremà burning of papier-mâché
   figures during Las Fallas
el cuaderno notebook **2.2**
el cuadro painting
¿Cuál(es)? Which?; What? **3.1**
   ¿Cuál es la fecha? What is the
      date? **3.2**
   ¿Cuál es tu/su número de
      teléfono? What is your phone
      number? (familiar/formal) **LP**
cuando when **2.2**
¿Cuándo? When? **2.2**
cuánto(a) how much **3.2**
   ¿Cuánto cuesta(n)? How much
      does it (do they) cost? **4.1**
cuántos(as) how many **3.2**
   ¿Cuántos(as)...? How
      many...? **2.1**
   ¿Cuántos años tienes? How old
      are you? **3.2**

cuarenta forty **2.1**
cuarto quarter **2.1**
   ... y cuarto quarter past... (the
      hour) **2.1**
el cuarto room; bedroom **5.1**
cuarto(a) fourth **5.1**
cuatro four **LP**
cuatrocientos(as) four
   hundred **3.2**
la cuenta bill (in a restaurant) **4.2**
el cuero leather
el cuerpo body **6.2**
el cumpleaños birthday **3.2**
   ¡Feliz cumpleaños! Happy
      birthday! **3.2**

dar (doy) to give **5.2**
   dar una caminata to hike **8.2**
   dar una fiesta to give a
      party **5.2**
   darle de comer al perro to feed
      the dog **5.2**
los datos information
de of, from **1.1**
   de madera wood (made of
      wood) **8.2**
   de la mañana in the morning
      (with a time) **2.1**
   De nada. You're welcome. **LP**
   de la noche at night (with a
      time) **2.1**
   de oro gold (made of gold) **8.2**
   de plata silver (made of
      silver) **8.2**
   ¿De qué color es/son...? What
      color is/are...?
   de la tarde in the afternoon
      (with a time) **2.1**
   de vacaciones on vacation **8.1**
   de vez en cuando once in a
      while **2.1**
debajo (de) underneath, under **2.2**
deber should, ought to **5.2**
décimo(a) tenth **5.1**
decir to say **5.2**
   también se dice... you can
      also say...
la decoración (*pl.* **las decoraciones**)
   decoration **5.2**
decorar to decorate **5.2**

dejar to leave
   dejar un mensaje to leave a
      message **7.2**
   Le dejo... en... I'll give... to you
      for... (a price) **8.2**
   ¿Me deja ver...? May I see...? **8.2**
del (de la) of *or* from the **2.2**
delante (de) in front (of) **2.2**
demasiado too much **8.2**
dentro (de) inside (of) **2.2**
los deportes sports **1.1**
deprimido(a) depressed **2.2**
derecho(a) right
el desayuno breakfast **3.1**
descansar to rest **1.1**
descargar to download
desde from
el desfile parade
desorganizado(a) disorganized **1.2**
despertarse (ie) to wake up **8.1**
después (de) afterward; after **1.1**
destruir to destroy
detrás (de) behind **2.2**
el día day **LP**
   Buenos días. Good
      morning. **LP**
   ¿Qué día es hoy? What day is
      today? **LP**
   todos los días every day **2.1**
dibujar to draw **1.1**
el dibujo drawing
diciembre December **3.2**
diecinueve nineteen **2.1**
dieciocho eighteen **2.1**
dieciséis sixteen **2.1**
diecisiete seventeen **2.1**
diez ten **LP**
diferente different
difícil difficult **2.1**
el difunto deceased
el dinero money **4.1**
la dirección (*pl.* **las**
   direcciones) address **7.1**
   la dirección electrónica e-mail
      address **7.1**
el (la) director(a) principal **2.2**
el disco compacto compact
   disc **5.1**
   quemar un disco compacto to
      burn a CD **7.1**
el disfraz (*pl.* **los disfraces**)
   costume
divertido(a) fun **2.2**
   ¡Qué divertido! How fun! **7.2**

doce twelve **2.1**
el (la) doctor(a) doctor
el dólar dollar **4.1**
doler (ue) to hurt, to ache **6.2**
domingo Sunday **LP**
donde where
¿Dónde? Where? **2.2**
    ¿De dónde eres? Where are you from? (familiar) **LP**
    ¿De dónde es? Where is he/she from? **LP**
    ¿De dónde es usted? Where are you from? (formal) **LP**
dormir (ue) to sleep **4.2**
dormirse (ue) to fall asleep **8.1**
dos two **LP**
doscientos(as) two hundred **3.2**
ducharse to take a shower **8.1**
durante during **4.1**
el DVD DVD **1.1**

el ecoturismo ecotourism
el ejercicio exercise
el ejército army
él he **1.1**; him **7.2**
ella she **1.1**; her **7.2**
ellos(as) they **1.1**; them **7.2**
emocionado(a) excited **2.2**
emparejar to match
empezar (ie) to begin **4.1**
en in **2.1**; on
    en autobús by bus **4.2**
    en avión by plane **8.1**
    en barco by boat **8.1**
    en coche by car **4.2**
    en línea online **7.1**
    en tren by train **8.1**
Encantado(a). Delighted; Pleased to meet you. **LP**
encima (de) on top (of) **2.2**
encontrar (ue) to find **4.2**
la encuesta survey
enero January **3.2**
enfermo(a) sick **6.2**
enojado(a) angry **2.2**
la ensalada salad **4.2**
enseñar to teach **2.1**
entender (ie) to understand **4.1**
entonces then, so **7.1**
la entrada ticket **4.2**
la entrevista interview

entrevistar to interview
envolver (ue) to wrap **5.2**
el equipo team **6.1**
la escalera stairs **5.1**
la escena scene
escribir to write **1.1**
    escribir correos electrónicos to write e-mails **1.1**
el escritorio desk **2.2**
la escritura writing
escuchar to listen (to) **1.1**
    escuchar música to listen to music **1.1**
la escuela school **1.1**
    la escuela secundaria high school
ese(a) that **8.2**
esos(as) those **8.2**
el español Spanish **2.1**
especial special
el espejo mirror **5.1**
esperar to wait (for) **8.1**
el esqueleto skeleton
la estación (pl. las estaciones) season **4.1**
el estadio stadium **6.1**
la estancia ranch
estar to be **2.2**
    ¿Está...? Is... there? **7.2**
    ¿Está bien? OK?
    estar en línea to be online **7.1**
    No, no está. No, he's/she's not here. **7.2**
este(a) this **8.2**
el estómago stomach **6.2**
estos(as) these **8.2**
el (la) estudiante student **1.2**
estudiar to study **1.1**
estudioso(a) studious **1.2**
el euro euro **4.1**
el examen (pl. los exámenes) test, exam **2.1**

fácil easy **2.1**
las fallas displays of large papier-mâché figures
el (la) fallero(a) celebrant of Las Fallas
falso(a) false
la familia family **3.2**
favorito(a) favorite **6.1**
febrero February **3.2**

la fecha date **3.2**
    ¿Cuál es la fecha? What is the date? **3.2**
    la fecha de nacimiento birth date **3.2**
feliz happy
    ¡Feliz cumpleaños! Happy birthday! **3.2**
feo(a) ugly **4.1**
la feria fair **7.2**
la fiesta party; holiday
    la fiesta de sorpresa surprise party **5.2**
    la fiesta nacional national holiday
    la fiesta patria patriotic holiday
el fin end
    el fin de semana weekend **7.2**
    por fin finally **7.1**
la flor flower
la foto photo, picture **7.1**
    tomar fotos to take photos **7.1**
el (la) francés(esa) (pl. los franceses) French
los frijoles beans **4.2**
el frío cold
    Hace frío. It is cold. **LP**
    tener frío to be cold **4.1**
la fruta fruit **1.1**
los fuegos artificiales fireworks
la fuente source; fountain
fuerte strong **6.2**
el fútbol soccer **1.1**
el fútbol americano football (the sport) **6.1**

la galleta cookie **1.1**
ganador(a) winning
el (la) ganador(a) winner **6.1**
ganar to win **6.1**
el (la) gato(a) cat **3.2**
generalmente generally **8.1**
el gimnasio gymnasium **2.2**
el globo balloon **5.2**
el gorro winter hat **4.1**
Gracias. Thank you. **LP**
    Muchas gracias. Thank you very much. **LP**
la gramática grammar
grande big, large; great **1.2**
el grito shout
el guante glove **6.1**
guapo(a) good-looking **1.2**

la guitarra guitar **1.1**
gustar
   Me gusta... I like... **1.1**
   Me gustaría... I would like... **7.2**
   No me gusta... I don't like... **1.1**
   ¿Qué te gusta hacer? What do you like to do? **1.1**
   ¿Te gusta...? Do you like...? **1.1**
   ¿Te gustaría...? Would you like...? **7.2**
el gusto pleasure
   El gusto es mío. The pleasure is mine. **LP**
   Mucho gusto. Nice to meet you. **LP**

hablar to talk, to speak **1.1**
   hablar por teléfono to talk on the phone **1.1**
   ¿Puedo hablar con...? May I speak with...? **7.2**
hacer (hago) to make, to do **3.1**
   Hace calor. It is hot. **LP**
   Hace frío. It is cold. **LP**
   Hace sol. It is sunny. **LP**
   Hace viento. It is windy. **LP**
   hacer la cama to make the bed **5.2**
   hacer clic en to click on **7.1**
   hacer esquí acuático to water-ski **6.2**
   hacer una parrillada to barbecue **8.2**
   hacer surf de vela to windsurf **8.2**
   hacer surfing to surf **8.2**
   hacer la tarea to do homework **1.1**
   hacer un viaje to take a trip **8.1**
   ¿Qué hicieron ustedes? What did you do? (pl.) **6.2**
   ¿Qué hiciste tú? What did you do? (sing., familiar) **6.2**
   ¿Qué tiempo hace? What is the weather like? **LP**
hacerse to become
el hambre hunger
   tener hambre to be hungry **3.1**
la hamburguesa hamburger **3.1**

hasta until
   Hasta luego. See you later. **LP**
   Hasta mañana. See you tomorrow. **LP**
hay... there is/are... **2.1**
   hay que... one has to..., one must... **5.2**
el helado ice cream **1.1**
herido(a) hurt **6.2**
la hermana sister **3.2**
el hermano brother **3.2**
los hermanos brothers, brother(s) and sister(s) **3.2**
la hija daughter **3.2**
el hijo son **3.2**
los hijos children, son(s) and daughter(s) **3.2**
la hispanidad cultural community of Spanish speakers
la historia history **2.1**
Hola. Hello; Hi. **LP**
el hombre man **1.2**
la hora hour; time **2.1**
   ¿A qué hora es/son...? At what time is/are...? **2.1**
   ¿Qué hora es? What time is it? **2.1**
el horario schedule **2.1**
horrible horrible **3.1**
el hotel hotel **8.1**
hoy today **LP**
   ¿Qué día es hoy? What day is today? **LP**
   Hoy es... Today is... **LP**
el huevo egg **3.1**

el icono icon **7.1**
ideal ideal **5.1**
el idioma language
Igualmente. Same here; Likewise. **LP**
importante important **3.1**
   Es importante. It's important. **3.1**
los incas Incas, an indigenous South American people
la independencia independence
la información information
el inglés English **2.1**
inteligente intelligent **1.2**
interesante interesting **2.2**

Internet Internet **7.1**
   conectar a Internet to connect to the Internet **7.1**
   navegar por Internet to surf the Web **7.1**
el invierno winter **4.1**
los invitados guests **5.2**
invitar to invite **5.2**
   invitar a to invite (someone) **5.2**
   Te invito. I invite you; I'll treat you. **7.2**
ir to go **2.2**
   ir a... to be going to... **4.2**
   ir de compras to go shopping **4.1**
   Vamos a... Let's... **4.2**
izquierdo(a) left

el jabón (*pl.* **los jabones**) soap **8.1**
el jamón (*pl.* **los jamones**) ham **3.1**
el jardín (*pl.* **los jardines**) garden **5.1**
los jeans jeans **4.1**
joven (*pl.* **jóvenes**) young **1.2**
las joyas jewelry **8.2**
jueves Thursday **LP**
el (la) jugador(a) player **6.1**
jugar (ue) to play (sports or games) **6.1**
   jugar al fútbol to play soccer **1.1**
el jugo juice **1.1**
   el jugo de naranja orange juice **3.1**
julio July **3.2**
junio June **3.2**

el lado side
   al lado (de) next to **2.2**
la lámpara lamp **5.1**
el lápiz (*pl.* **los lápices**) pencil **2.2**
largo(a) long
lavar to wash **5.2**
   lavar los platos to wash the dishes **5.2**
   lavarse to wash oneself **8.1**
   lavarse la cara to wash one's face **8.1**

la lección (*pl.* **las lecciones**) lesson
la leche milk **3.1**
el lector DVD DVD player **5.1**
la lectura reading
leer to read **1.1**
  leer un libro to read a book **1.1**
lejos (de) far (from) **2.2**
las lentejas lentils
levantar to lift **6.2**; to raise
  levantar pesas to lift weights **6.2**
levantarse to get up **8.1**
el libertador liberator
el libro book **1.1**
limpiar to clean **5.2**
  limpiar la cocina to clean the kitchen **5.2**
limpio(a) clean **5.2**
la llamada phone call **7.2**
llamar to call (by phone) **7.2**
llamarse to be called
  ¿Cómo se llama? What's his/her/your (formal) name? **LP**
  ¿Cómo te llamas? What's your name? (familiar) **LP**
  Me llamo... My name is... **LP**
  Se llama... His/Her name is... **LP**
la llegada arrival
llegar to arrive **2.1**
llevar to wear **4.1**
llover (ue) to rain
  Llueve. It is raining. **LP**
Lo siento. I'm sorry. **6.2**
luego later, then **7.1**
  Hasta luego. See you later. **LP**
el lugar place **4.2**
lunes Monday **LP**

la madera wood **8.2**
  de madera wood (made of wood) **8.2**
la madrastra stepmother **3.2**
la madre mother **3.2**
el (la) maestro(a) teacher **LP**
malo(a) bad **1.2**
  Mal. ¿Y tú/usted? Bad. And you? (familiar/formal) **LP**
mandar to send **7.1**
la mano hand **6.2**
la manzana apple **3.1**

mañana tomorrow **LP**
  Hasta mañana. See you tomorrow. **LP**
  Mañana es... Tomorrow is... **LP**
la mañana morning **2.1**
  de la mañana in the morning (with a time) **2.1**
el mapa map **2.2**
maquillarse to put on makeup **8.1**
el mar sea **6.2**
marrón (*pl.* **marrones**) brown **4.1**
martes Tuesday **LP**
marzo March **3.2**
más more **1.1**
  Más o menos. ¿Y tú/usted? So-so. And you? (familiar/formal) **LP**
  más que... more than... **3.2**
  más... que more... than **3.2**
  más tarde later (on) **7.1**
la máscara mask
la mascletà firecracker explosions during Las Fallas
las matemáticas math **2.1**
mayo May **3.2**
mayor older **3.2**
la medianoche midnight
medio(a) half
  ...y media half past... (the hour) **2.1**
mejor better **3.2**
menor younger **3.2**
menos less
  ...menos (diez) (ten) to/before... (the hour) **2.1**
  menos que... less than... **3.2**
  menos... que less... than **3.2**
el mensaje message **7.2**
  dejar un mensaje to leave a message **7.2**
el mensaje instantáneo instant message
el mensajero instantáneo instant messaging **7.1**
el menú menu **4.2**
el mercado market **8.2**
  el mercado al aire libre open-air market
el mes month **3.2**
la mesa table **4.2**
  poner la mesa to set the table **5.2**
el metro meter
mí me **7.2**
mi my **3.2**

el miedo fear
  ¡Qué miedo! How scary! **7.2**
  tener miedo to be afraid **7.2**
miércoles Wednesday **LP**
mil thousand, one thousand **3.2**
un millón (de) million, one million **3.2**
el minuto minute **2.1**
mirar to watch **1.1**; to look at
  mirar la televisión to watch television **1.1**
mismo(a) same
la mochila backpack **2.2**
el momento moment
  Un momento. One moment. **7.2**
la montaña rusa roller coaster **7.2**
montar to ride **1.1**
  montar a caballo to ride a horse **8.2**
  montar en bicicleta to ride a bike **1.1**
mucho a lot **2.1**
  Mucho gusto. Nice to meet you. **LP**
muchos(as) many **2.1**
  muchas veces often, many times **2.1**
los muebles furniture **5.1**
la mujer woman **1.2**
el mundo world
el museo museum **7.2**
la música music **1.1**
  la música folklórica folk music
  la música rock rock music **4.2**
el (la) músico(a) musician
muy very **1.2**
  Muy bien. ¿Y tú/usted? Very well. And you? (familiar/formal) **LP**

nada nothing **7.1**
  De nada. You're welcome. **LP**
nadar to swim **6.1**
nadie no one, nobody **7.1**
la naranja orange (fruit) **3.1**
la nariz (*pl.* **las narices**) nose **6.2**
la natación swimming **6.1**
la naturaleza nature
navegar por Internet to surf the Web **7.1**
la Navidad Christmas
necesitar to need **2.1**
negro(a) black **4.1**

nervioso(a) nervous **2.2**
nevar (ie) to snow
　Nieva. It is snowing. **LP**
ni... ni neither... nor **7.1**
ninguno(a) none, not any **7.1**
el ninot (*pl.* **los ninots**) large
　papier-mâché figure
no no **LP**
la noche night **2.1**; evening **LP**
　Buenas noches. Good evening;
　　Good night. **LP**
　de la noche at night (with a
　　time) **2.1**
la Nochebuena Christmas Eve
la Nochevieja New Year's Eve
el nombre name
normalmente normally **8.1**
nosotros(as) we **1.1**; us **7.2**
la nota grade (on a test) **2.1**
　sacar una buena/mala nota to
　　get a good/bad grade **2.1**
novecientos(as) nine hundred **3.2**
noveno(a) ninth **5.1**
noventa ninety **2.1**
noviembre November **3.2**
nuestro(a) our **3.2**
nueve nine **LP**
nuevo(a) new **4.1**
el número number **LP**
　el número de teléfono phone
　　number **LP**
nunca never **2.1**
nutritivo(a) nutritious **3.1**

o or **1.1**
　o... o either... or **7.1**
la obra work (of art)
ocho eight **LP**
ochocientos(as) eight hundred **3.2**
octavo(a) eighth **5.1**
octubre October **3.2**
ocupado(a) busy **2.2**
la oficina office **2.2**
　la oficina del (de la)
　director(a) principal's office **2.2**
ofrecer (ofrezco) to offer
　Le puedo ofrecer... I can offer
　　you... (a price) **8.2**
el ojo eye **6.2**
once eleven **2.1**
la oración (*pl.* **las oraciones**)
　sentence

la oreja ear **6.2**
organizado(a) organized **1.2**
el oro gold
　de oro gold (made of gold) **8.2**
el otoño autumn, fall **4.1**
otro(a) other **3.1**

el padrastro stepfather **3.2**
el padre father **3.2**
los padres parents **3.2**
pagar to pay **4.1**
la página page
el país country, nation **LP**
el pájaro bird
el pan bread **3.1**
　el pan de muertos special bread
　　made for Día de los Muertos
la pantalla screen **7.1**
los pantalones pants **4.1**
　los pantalones cortos
　　shorts **4.1**
la papa potato **1.1**
　las papas fritas French fries **1.1**
el papel paper **2.2**
　el papel de regalo wrapping
　　paper **5.2**
　el papel picado paper cutouts
para for; in order to **3.1**
parar to stop
　Para y piensa. Stop and think.
la pared wall
la pareja pair
el párrafo paragraph
la parrillada barbecue **8.2**
　hacer una parrillada to
　　barbecue **8.2**
el parque park **4.2**
　el parque de diversiones
　　amusement park **7.2**
la parte part
el partido game (in sports) **6.1**
pasado(a) past **7.1**
　el año pasado last year **7.1**
　la semana pasada last week **7.1**
pasar to happen
　pasar la aspiradora to
　　vacuum **5.2**
　pasar un rato con los amigos to
　　spend time with friends **1.1**
　¿Qué pasa? What's
　　happening? **LP**

¿Qué te pasa (a ti)? What's the
　matter (with you)?
pasear to go for a walk **1.1**
el paseo walk, stroll; ride
el pasillo hall **2.2**
la pasta de dientes toothpaste **8.1**
el pastel cake **4.2**
la patata potato **4.2**
patinar to skate **6.1**
　patinar en línea to in-line
　　skate **6.1**
los patines en línea in-line
　skates **6.1**
el patio patio **5.1**
pedir (i) to order, to ask for **4.2**
peinarse to comb one's hair **8.1**
el peine comb **8.1**
la película movie **4.2**
peligroso(a) dangerous **6.1**
pelirrojo(a) red-haired **1.2**
el pelo hair **1.2**
　el pelo castaño/rubio brown/
　　blond hair **1.2**
la pelota ball **6.1**
pensar (ie) to think; to plan **4.1**
peor worse **3.2**
pequeño(a) little, small **1.2**
perder (ie) to lose **6.1**
Perdón. Excuse me. **LP**
perezoso(a) lazy **1.2**
el periódico newspaper
　el periódico escolar student
　　newspaper
pero but **1.1**
el (la) perro(a) dog **3.2**
la persona person **1.2**
el pescado fish (as food) **4.2**
el pie foot **6.2**
　a pie on foot **4.2**
la piel skin **6.2**
la pierna leg **6.2**
la pintura painting
la piscina swimming pool **6.1**
el piso floor (of a building) **5.1**
　primer piso second floor (first
　　floor above ground floor) **5.1**
la pista track; clue
el pizarrón (*pl.* **los pizarrones**)
　chalkboard, board **2.2**
la pizza pizza **1.1**
planchar to iron **5.2**
la planta plant
la planta baja first floor, ground
　floor **5.1**

la **plata** silver
 de plata silver (made of silver) **8.2**
el **plato** plate; dish; course
 el plato principal main
 course **4.2**
la **playa** beach **6.2**
la **pluma** pen **2.2**
un **poco** a little **1.2**
pocos(as) few
poder (ue) to be able, can **4.2**
 Le puedo ofrecer... I can offer
 you... **8.2**
 ¿Puedo hablar con...? May I
 speak with...? **7.2**
el **pollo** chicken **4.2**
poner (pongo) to put, to place **5.2**
 poner la mesa to set the
 table **5.2**
ponerse (me pongo) to put on **8.1**
 ponerse la ropa to put one's
 clothes on, to get dressed **8.1**
por for, per
 Por favor. Please. **LP**
 por fin finally **7.1**
 ¿Por qué? Why? **3.1**
porque because **1.2**
el **postre** dessert **4.2**
 de postre for dessert **4.2**
practicar to practice **1.1**
 practicar deportes to play or
 practice sports **1.1**
el **precio** price **4.1**
preferir (ie) to prefer **4.1**
la **pregunta** question
preparar to prepare **1.1**
 preparar la comida to prepare
 food, to make a meal **1.1**
presentar to introduce **LP**
 Te/Le presento a... Let me
 introduce you to... (familiar/
 formal) **LP**
la **primavera** spring **4.1**
primero(a) first **5.1**
 el primero de... the first of...
 (date) **3.2**
el (la) **primo(a)** cousin **3.2**
los **primos** cousins **3.2**
el **problema** problem **2.2**
la **procesión** (*pl.* **las procesiones**)
 procession
proclamar to declare
la **propina** tip (in a restaurant) **4.2**
proteger (protejo) to protect
el **pueblo** town
la **puerta** door **2.2**

¿Qué? What? **3.1**
 ¿De qué color es/son...? What
 color is/are...?
 ¡Qué bárbaro! How cool!
 ¡Qué caro(a) How expensive! **8.2**
 ¡Qué divertido! How fun! **7.2**
 ¡Qué lástima! What a shame! **7.2**
 ¡Qué miedo! How scary! **7.2**
 ¿Qué día es hoy? What day is
 today? **LP**
 ¿Qué es esto? What is this? **8.2**
 ¿Qué hicieron ustedes? What did
 you do? (pl.) **6.2**
 ¿Qué hiciste tú? What did you
 do? (sing., familiar) **6.2**
 ¿Qué hora es? What time is
 it? **2.1**
 ¿Qué pasa? What's
 happening? **LP**
 ¿Qué tal? How's it going? **LP**
 ¿Qué te gusta hacer? What do
 you like to do? **1.1**
 ¿Qué tiempo hace? What is the
 weather like? **LP**
el **quechua** indigenous language
 from South America
quedarse en to stay in **8.1**
los **quehaceres** chores **5.2**
quemar to burn
 quemar un disco compacto to
 burn a CD **7.1**
querer (ie) to want **4.1**
 ¿Quieres acompañarme a...?
 Would you like to come with
 me to...? **7.2**
 Quisiera... I would like... **8.2**
el **queso** cheese **3.1**
¿Quién(es)? Who? **3.1**
 ¿Quién es? Who is he/she/it? **LP**
quince fifteen **2.1**
quinientos(as) five hundred **3.2**
quinto(a) fifth **5.1**

el **radio** radio **5.1**
rápido(a) fast
la **raqueta** racket (in sports) **6.1**
un **rato** a while, a short time
el **ratón** (*pl.* **los ratones**) mouse **7.1**

la **raza** (human) race
la **razón** (*pl.* **las razones**) reason
 tener razón to be right **4.1**
recibir to receive **5.2**
la **reconstrucción** (*pl.* **las
 reconstrucciones**) reenactment
recordar (ue) to remember
 ¿Recuerdas? Do you remember?
el **recorrido** run, journey
el **recreo** recess
el **recuerdo** souvenir **8.2**
el **refresco** soft drink **1.1**
regalar to give (a gift)
el **regalo** present, gift **5.2**
regatear to bargain **8.2**
la **regla** rule
regular OK **LP**
 Regular. ¿Y tú/usted? OK. And
 you? (familiar/formal) **LP**
el **reloj** watch; clock **2.2**
el **repaso** review
responder to reply
la **respuesta** answer
el **restaurante** restaurant **4.2**
el **resultado** result
el **resumen** summary
 en resumen in summary
los **Reyes Magos** Three Kings
rico(a) tasty, delicious; **3.1**
la **rodilla** knee **6.2**
rojo(a) red **4.1**
la **ropa** clothing **4.1**
la **rosca de reyes** sweet bread eaten
 on January 6
rubio(a) blond **1.2**
la **rutina** routine **8.1**

sábado Saturday **LP**
saber (sé) to know (a fact, how
 to do something) **6.1**
sacar to take out
 sacar la basura to take out the
 trash **5.2**
 sacar una buena/mala nota to
 get a good/bad grade **2.1**
la **sala** living room **5.1**
salir (salgo) to leave, to go out **5.2**
la **salud** health **6.2**
¡Saludos! Greetings!
el **sándwich** sandwich **3.1**
 el sándwich de jamón y queso
 ham and cheese sandwich **3.1**

sano(a) healthy **6.2**
el santo saint
el secador de pelo hair dryer **8.1**
secar to dry
    secarse to dry oneself **8.1**
    secarse el pelo to dry one's hair **8.1**
el secreto secret **5.2**
la sed thirst
    tener sed to be thirsty **3.1**
según according to
segundo(a) second **5.1**
seguro(a) secure, safe
seis six **LP**
seiscientos(as) six hundred **3.2**
la semana week **LP**
    el fin de semana weekend **7.2**
    la semana pasada last week **7.1**
    Semana Santa Holy Week
Señor (Sr.) Mr. **LP**
Señora (Sra.) Mrs. **LP**
Señorita (Srta.) Miss **LP**
sentir to feel
    Lo siento. I'm sorry. **6.2**
septiembre September **3.2**
séptimo(a) seventh **5.1**
ser to be **1.1**
    Es de... He/She is from... **LP**
    Es el... de... It's the... of... (day and month) **3.2**
    Es la.../Son las... It is... o'clock. **2.1**
    Soy de... I'm from... **LP**
serio(a) serious **1.2**
servir (i) to serve **4.2**
sesenta sixty **2.1**
setecientos(as) seven hundred **3.2**
setenta seventy **2.1**
sexto(a) sixth **5.1**
si if **5.2**
sí yes **LP**
    ¡Claro que sí! Of course! **7.2**
    Sí, me encantaría. Yes, I would love to. **7.2**
siempre always **2.1**
siete seven **LP**
siguiente following
la silla chair **2.2**
el sillón (pl. los sillones) armchair **5.1**
simpático(a) nice, friendly **1.2**
sin without
el sitio Web Web site **7.1**
sobre about; on
el sofá sofa, couch **5.1**

el sol sun
    el bloqueador de sol sunscreen **6.2**
    Hace sol. It is sunny. **LP**
    tomar el sol to sunbathe **6.2**
el sombrero hat **4.1**
la sopa soup **3.1**
la sorpresa surprise **5.2**
su his, her, its, their, your (formal) **3.2**
subir to go up **5.1**
    subir a la vuelta al mundo/la montaña rusa to ride the Ferris wheel/roller coaster **7.2**
sucio(a) dirty **5.2**
el suelo floor (of a room) **5.1**
la suerte luck
    tener suerte to be lucky **4.1**

T

tal vez perhaps, maybe **4.2**
también also, too **1.1**
    también se dice... you can also say...
tampoco neither, not either **7.1**
tan... como as... as **3.2**
tanto como... as much as... **3.2**
tanto(a) so much
tantos(as) so many
tarde late **2.1**
la tarde afternoon **2.1**
    Buenas tardes. Good afternoon. **LP**
    de la tarde in the afternoon (with a time) **2.1**
    más tarde later (on) **7.1**
la tarea homework **1.1**
la tarjeta postal postcard
el teatro theater **4.2**
el teclado keyboard **7.1**
el teléfono telephone **7.2**
    ¿Cuál es tu/su número de teléfono? What is your phone number? (familiar/formal) **LP**
    Mi número de teléfono es... My phone number is... **LP**
    el teléfono celular cellular telephone **7.2**
la televisión television **1.1**
el televisor television set **5.1**
el tema theme

temprano early **2.1**
tener to have **2.1**
    ¿Cuántos años tienes? How old are you? **3.2**
    tener... años to be... years old **3.2**
    tener calor to be hot **4.1**
    tener frío to be cold **4.1**
    tener ganas de... to to feel like... **3.1**
    tener hambre to be hungry **3.1**
    tener miedo to be afraid **7.2**
    tener que... to have to... **2.1**
    tener razón to be right **4.1**
    tener sed to be thirsty **3.1**
    tener suerte to be lucky **4.1**
el tenis tennis **6.1**
tercero(a) third **5.1**
terminar to end **6.2**
ti you (sing., familiar) **7.2**
la tía aunt **3.2**
el tiempo weather **LP**; time **8.2**
    el tiempo libre free time **8.2**
    ¿Qué tiempo hace? What is the weather like? **LP**
la tienda store **4.1**
el tío uncle **3.2**
los tíos uncles, uncle(s) and aunt(s) **3.2**
típico(a) typical
el tipo type
la tiza chalk **2.2**
la toalla towel **8.1**
el tobillo ankle **6.2**
el tocadiscos compactos CD player **5.1**
tocar to play (an instrument) **1.1**
    tocar la guitarra to play the guitar **1.1**
todavía still; yet **5.2**
todo junto all together
todos(as) all **1.2**
    todos los días every day **2.1**
tomar to take **4.2**
    tomar apuntes to take notes **2.1**
    tomar fotos to take photos **7.1**
    tomar el sol to sunbathe **6.2**
el tomate tomato **4.2**
trabajador(a) hard-working **1.2**
trabajar to work **1.1**
traer (traigo) to bring **5.2**
el traje costume
tranquilo(a) calm **2.2**
trece thirteen **2.1**
treinta thirty **2.1**

treinta y uno thirty-one **2.1**
el tren train **8.1**
  en tren by train **8.1**
tres three **LP**
trescientos(as) three hundred **3.2**
triste sad **2.2**
tu your (sing., familiar) **3.2**
tú you (sing., familiar) **1.1**
el turismo tourism
el turrón (*pl.* **los turrones**) almond nougat candy

último(a) last
la unidad unit
uno one **LP**
usar to use **2.1**
  usar la computadora to use the computer **2.1**
usted you (sing., formal) **1.1**, **7.2**
ustedes you (pl.) **1.1**
la uva grape **3.1**
  las doce uvas twelve grapes eaten on New Year's Eve

las vacaciones vacation **8.1**
  de vacaciones on vacation **8.1**
el valle valley
varios(as) various
veinte twenty **2.1**
veintiuno twenty-one **2.1**
el (la) vendedor(a) salesclerk
vender to sell **3.1**

venir to come **5.2**
la ventana window **2.2**
la ventanilla ticket window **4.2**
ver (veo) to see **4.2**
  ¿Me deja ver...? May I see...? **8.2**
el verano summer **4.1**
la verdad truth
  ¿Verdad? Really?; Right? **LP**
verde green **4.1**
las verduras vegetables **4.2**
el vestido dress **4.1**
vestirse (i) to get dressed **8.1**
la vez (*pl.* **las veces**) time
  a veces sometimes
  de vez en cuando once in a while **2.1**
  muchas veces often, many times **2.1**
  tal vez maybe **4.2**
el viaje trip, journey
  hacer un viaje to take a trip **8.1**
la vida life
el videojuego video game **5.1**
viejo(a) old **1.2**
el viento wind
  Hace viento. It is windy. **LP**
viernes Friday **LP**
el villancico seasonal children's song
visitar to visit
vivir to live **3.2**
el vocabulario vocabulary
el voleibol volleyball (the sport) **6.1**
volver (ue) to return, to come back **4.2**
vosotros(as) you (pl. familiar) **1.1**, **7.2**
la vuelta al mundo Ferris wheel **7.2**
vuestro(a) your (pl. familiar) **3.2**

y and
  ...y (diez) (ten) past... (the hour) **2.1**
  ...y cuarto quarter past... (the hour) **2.1**
  ...y media half past... (the hour) **2.1**
  ¿Y tú? And you? (familiar) **LP**
  ¿Y usted? And you? (formal) **LP**
ya already **3.2**
yo I **1.1**
el yogur yogurt **3.1**

el zapato shoe **4.1**
el zoológico zoo **7.2**

Glosario
inglés-español

This English-Spanish glossary contains all the active vocabulary words that appear in the text as well as passive vocabulary lists. **LP** refers to the Lección preliminar.

A

about sobre
to accompany acompañar **7.2**
according to según
to ache doler (ue) **6.2**
activity la actividad **1.1**
address la dirección (*pl.* las direcciones) **7.1**
   e-mail address la dirección electrónica **7.1**
to advance avanzar
advertisement el anuncio
afraid: to be afraid tener miedo **7.2**
after después (de) **1.1**
afternoon la tarde **2.1**
   Good afternoon. Buenas tardes. **LP**
   in the afternoon de la tarde **2.1**
afterward después **1.1**
against contra
air el aire
airplane el avión (*pl.* los aviones) **8.1**
   by plane en avión **8.1**
all todos(as) **1.2**
all together todo junto
almost casi **2.1**
already ya **3.2**
also también **1.1**
always siempre **2.1**
and y
angry enojado(a) **2.2**
ankle el tobillo **6.2**
announcement el anuncio
answer la respuesta
to answer contestar **2.1**
any alguno(a) **7.1**
   not any ninguno(a) **7.1**
apartment el apartamento **5.1**
apple la manzana **3.1**
April abril **3.2**

aquarium el acuario **7.2**
arm el brazo **6.2**
armchair el sillón (*pl.* los sillones) **5.1**
armoire el armario **5.1**
arrival la llegada
to arrive llegar **2.1**
art el arte **2.1**
   martial arts las artes marciales
article el artículo
artistic artístico(a) **1.2**
as como
   as... as tan... como **3.2**
   as much as... tanto como... **3.2**
to ask for pedir (i) **4.2**
at a
   at night de la noche **2.1**
   At... o'clock. A la(s)... **2.1**
   At what time is/are...? ¿A qué hora es/son...? **2.1**
athlete el (la) atleta **6.1**
athletic atlético(a) **1.2**
attached adjunto(a)
August agosto **3.2**
aunt la tía **3.2**
autumn el otoño **4.1**

B

backpack la mochila **2.2**
bad malo(a) **1.2**
   Bad. And you? (familiar/formal) Mal. Y tú/usted? **LP**
ball la pelota **6.1**
balloon el globo **5.2**
banana la banana **3.1**
barbecue la parrillada **8.2**
to barbecue hacer una parrillada **8.2**
to bargain regatear **8.2**
baseball el béisbol **6.1**
   (baseball) bat el bate **6.1**
basketball el básquetbol **6.1**

bathroom el baño **2.2**
to be ser **1.1**; estar **2.2**
   to be able poder (ue) **4.2**
   to be afraid tener miedo **7.2**
   to be called llamarse
   to be cold tener frío **4.1**
   to be familiar with conocer (conozco) **6.1**
   to be hot tener calor **4.1**
   to be hungry tener hambre **3.1**
   to be lucky tener suerte **4.1**
   to be online estar en línea **7.1**
   to be right tener razón **4.1**
   to be thirsty tener sed **3.1**
   to be... years old tener... años **3.2**
beach la playa **6.2**
beans los frijoles **4.2**
because porque **1.2**
to become hacerse
bed la cama **5.1**
   to go to bed acostarse (ue) **8.1**
   to make the bed hacer la cama **5.2**
bedroom el cuarto **5.1**
beef el bistec **4.2**
before antes (de) **1.1**; menos (with a time) **2.1**
to begin empezar (ie) **4.1**, comenzar (ie) **6.2**
behind detrás (de) **2.2**
better mejor **3.2**
beverage la bebida **3.1**
bicycle la bicicleta **1.1**
big grande **1.2**
bill (in a restaurant) la cuenta **4.2**
bird el pájaro
birth date la fecha de nacimiento **3.2**
birthday el cumpleaños **3.2**
   Happy birthday! ¡Feliz cumpleaños! **3.2**
black negro(a) **4.1**
blond rubio(a) **1.2**
blouse la blusa **4.1**
blue azul **4.1**

board el pizarrón (*pl.* los pizarrones) **2.2**
boat el barco **8.1**,
    by boat en barco **8.1**
body el cuerpo **6.2**
book el libro **1.1**
boring aburrido(a) **2.2**
boy el chico **1.2**
bread el pan **3.1**
breakfast el desayuno **3.1**
to bring traer (traigo) **5.2**
broccoli el brócoli **4.2**
brother el hermano **3.2**
brown marrón (*pl.* marrones) **4.1**
    brown hair el pelo castaño **1.2**
brush el cepillo **8.1**
to brush cepillar
    to brush one's teeth cepillarse los dientes **8.1**
bumper cars los autitos chocadores **7.2**
burn: to burn a CD quemar un disco compacto **7.1**
bus el autobús (*pl.* los autobuses) **4.2**
    by bus en autobús **4.2**
busy ocupado(a) **2.2**
but pero **1.1**
to buy comprar **1.1**

café el café **4.2**
cafeteria la cafetería **2.2**
cake el pastel **4.2**
calculator la calculadora **2.2**
call la llamada **7.2**
to call llamar **7.2**
calm tranquilo(a) **2.2**
camera la cámara **7.1**
    digital camera la cámara digital **7.1**
to camp acampar **8.2**
can (to be able) poder (ue) **4.2**
    I can offer you... Le puedo ofrecer... **8.2**
car el coche **4.2**; el carro
    by car en coche
cat el (la) gato(a) **3.2**
CD player el tocadiscos compactos **5.1**
to celebrate celebrar **5.2**
cellular phone el teléfono celular **7.2**
center el centro **4.2**
ceramics la cerámica **8.2**
cereal el cereal **3.1**

chair la silla **2.2**
chalk la tiza **2.2**
chalkboard el pizarrón (*pl.* los pizarrones) **2.2**
champion el campeón (*pl.* los campeones), la campeona **6.1**
change el cambio
cheese el queso **3.1**
chicken el pollo **4.2**
children los hijos **3.2**
chores los quehaceres **5.2**
Christmas la Navidad
    Christmas tree el árbol de Navidad
city la ciudad **8.1**
class la clase **LP**
classroom la clase **LP**
clean limpio(a) **5.2**
to clean limpiar **5.2**
to click on hacer clic en **7.1**
clock el reloj **2.2**
to close cerrar (ie) **4.1**
closet el armario **5.1**
clothing la ropa **4.1**
clue la pista
coffee el café **3.1**
cold el frío
    It is cold. Hace frío. **LP**
    to be cold tener frío **4.1**
color el color
    What color is/are...? ¿De qué color es/son...?
comb el peine **8.1**
    to comb one's hair peinarse **8.1**
to come venir **5.2**
    to come back volver (ue) **4.2**
    to come with acompañar **7.2**
common común
compact disc el disco compacto **5.1**
to compare comparar
computer la computadora **2.1**
concert el concierto **4.2**
to connect conectar **7.1**
    to connect to the Internet conectar a Internet **7.1**
to cook cocinar **5.2**
cookie la galleta **1.1**
coral reef el arrecife de coral
to correct corregir
to cost costar (ue) **4.2**
    How much does it (do they) cost? ¿Cuánto cuesta(n)? **4.1**
    It (They) cost... Cuesta(n)... **4.1**
costume el disfraz (*pl.* los disfraces), el traje
couch el sofá **5.1**

country el campo **8.1**; el país **LP**
course plato
    main course el plato principal **4.2**
court la cancha **6.1**
cousin el (la) primo(a) **3.2**
curtain la cortina **5.1**
to cut cortar **5.2**
    to cut the grass cortar el césped **5.2**

dance el baile
to dance bailar **5.2**
dangerous peligroso(a) **6.1**
date la fecha **3.2**
    birth date la fecha de nacimiento **3.2**
    What is the date? ¿Cuál es la fecha? **3.2**
daughter la hija **3.2**
day el día **LP**
    the day before yesterday anteayer **7.1**
    every day todos los días **2.1**
    What day is today? ¿Qué día es hoy? **LP**
December diciembre **3.2**
to decorate decorar **5.2**
decoration la decoración (*pl.* las decoraciones) **5.2**
delicious rico(a) **3.1**
Delighted. Encantado(a). **LP**
depressed deprimido(a) **2.2**
to descend bajar **5.1**
desk el escritorio **2.2**
dessert el postre **4.2**
    for dessert de postre **4.2**
to destroy destruir
different diferente
difficult difícil **2.1**
dining room el comedor **5.1**
dinner la cena **3.1**
dirty sucio(a) **5.2**
dish el plato
    main dish el plato principal **4.2**
disorganized desorganizado(a) **1.2**
to do hacer (hago) **3.1**
doctor el (la) doctor(a)
dog el (la) perro(a) **3.2**
dollar el dólar **4.1**
door la puerta **2.2**
to download descargar
downtown el centro **4.2**
to draw dibujar **1.1**

drawing el dibujo
dress el vestido **4.1**
dresser la cómoda **5.1**
drink la bebida **3.1**
to drink beber **1.1**
to dry secar
    to dry one's hair secarse el
      pelo **8.1**
    to dry oneself secarse **8.1**
during durante **4.1**
DVD el DVD **1.1**
    DVD player el lector DVD **5.1**

each cada
ear la oreja **6.2**
early temprano **2.1**
earring el arete **8.2**
easy fácil **2.1**
to eat comer **1.1**
    to eat lunch almorzar (ue) **4.2**
    to eat outside comer al aire
      libre **8.2**
ecotourism el ecoturismo
egg el huevo **3.1**
eight ocho **LP**
eight hundred ochocientos(as) **3.2**
eighteen dieciocho **2.1**
eighth octavo(a) **5.1**
either
    either... or o... o **7.1**
    not either tampoco **7.1**
eleven once **2.1**
e-mail el correo electrónico **1.1**
    e-mail address la dirección (*pl.*
      las direcciones) electrónica **7.1**
to end terminar **6.2**
English el inglés **2.1**
eraser el borrador **2.2**
euro el euro **4.1**
evening la noche **LP**
    Good evening. Buenas
      noches. **LP**
every cada
    every day todos los días **2.1**
exam el examen (*pl.* los
    exámenes) **2.1**
excited emocionado(a) **2.2**
Excuse me. Perdón. **LP**
exercise el ejercicio

expensive caro(a) **8.2**
    How expensive! ¡Qué caro(a)! **8.2**
eye el ojo **6.2**

fair la feria **7.2**
fall el otoño **4.1**
to fall asleep dormirse (ue) **8.1**
false falso(a)
family la familia **3.2**
fan el (la) aficionado(a) **6.1**
far (from) lejos (de) **2.2**
fast rápido(a)
father el padre **3.2**
favorite favorito(a) **6.1**
February febrero **3.2**
to feed darle(s) de comer **5.2**
    to feed the dog darle de comer
      al perro **5.2**
to feel sentir (ie)
    to feel like... tener ganas
      de... **3.1**
Ferris wheel la vuelta al mundo **7.2**
few pocos(as)
field el campo **6.1**
fifteen quince **2.1**
fifth quinto(a) **5.1**
fifty cincuenta **2.1**
file el archivo
finally por fin **7.1**
to find encontrar (ue) **4.2**
fine bien **LP**
    Fine. And you? (familiar/
      formal) Bien. Y tú/usted? **LP**
fireworks los fuegos artificiales
first primero(a) **5.1**
    the first of... el primero de... **3.2**
fish el pescado **4.2**
five cinco **LP**
five hundred quinientos(as) **3.2**
flag la bandera
floor el piso; el suelo **5.1**
    first *or* ground floor la planta
      baja **5.1**
    **second floor (first above
      ground)** el primer piso **5.1**
flower la flor
following siguiente
food la comida **1.1, 3.1**
food server el (la) camarero(a) **4.2**
foot el pie **6.2**
    on foot a pie **4.2**

football el fútbol americano **6.1**
for para **3.1**; por
forest el bosque
    cloud forest el bosque nuboso
    tropical rain forest el bosque
      tropical lluvioso
forty cuarenta **2.1**
fountain la fuente
four cuatro **LP**
**four
    hundred** cuatrocientos(as) **3.2**
fourteen catorce **2.1**
fourth cuarto(a) **5.1**
free time el tiempo libre **8.2**
French fries las papas fritas **1.1**
Friday viernes **LP**
friend el (la) amigo(a) **1.2**
    to spend time with friends
      pasar un rato con los amigos **1.1**
from de **1.1**; desde
front: in front (of) delante
    (de) **2.2**
fruit la fruta **1.1**
fun divertido(a) **2.2**
    How fun! ¡Qué divertido! **7.2**
funny cómico(a) **1.2**
furniture los muebles **5.1**

game el partido **6.1**
garbage la basura **5.2**
garden el jardín (*pl.* los
    jardines) **5.1**
generally generalmente **8.1**
to get
    to get dressed vestirse (i) **8.1**
    to get up levantarse **8.1**
gift el regalo **5.2**
girl la chica **1.2**
to give dar (doy) **5.2**; regalar
    to give a party dar una fiesta **5.2**
glove el guante **6.1**
to go ir **2.2**
    to be going to... ir a... **4.2**
    to go for a walk pasear **1.1**
    to go out salir (salgo) **5.2**
    to go shopping ir de
      compras **4.1**
    to go to bed acostarse (ue) **8.1**
    to go up subir **5.1**
    to go with acompañar **7.2**

gold el oro
  (made of) gold de oro **8.2**
good bueno(a) **1.2**
  Good afternoon. Buenas tardes. **LP**
  Good evening. Buenas noches. **LP**
  Good morning. Buenos días. **LP**
  Good night. Buenas noches. **LP**
Goodbye. Adiós. **LP**
good-looking guapo(a) **1.2**
goods los artículos **8.2**
  sporting goods los artículos deportivos
grade la nota **2.1**
  to get a good/bad grade sacar una buena/mala nota **2.1**
grammar la grámatica
grandfather el abuelo **3.2**
grandmother la abuela **3.2**
grandparents los abuelos **3.2**
grape la uva **3.1**
grass el césped **5.2**
  to cut the grass cortar el césped **5.2**
green verde **4.1**
Greetings! ¡Saludos!
to guess adivinar
guests los invitados **5.2**
guitar la guitarra **1.1**
gymnasium el gimnasio **2.2**

hair el pelo **1.2**
  blond hair pelo rubio **1.2**
  brown hair pelo castaño **1.2**
hair dryer el secador de pelo **8.1**
half medio(a)
  half past... ... y media **2.1**
hall el pasillo **2.2**
ham el jamón (*pl.* los jamones) **3.1**
hamburger la hamburguesa **3.1**
hand la mano **6.2**
handicrafts las artesanías **8.2**
to happen pasar
  What's happening? ¿Qué pasa? **LP**
happy contento(a) **2.2**; feliz **3.2**; alegre
  Happy birthday! ¡Feliz cumpleaños! **3.2**
hard-working trabajador(a) **1.2**
hat el sombrero **4.1**
  winter hat el gorro **4.1**

to have tener **2.1**
  one has to... hay que... **5.2**
  to have just... acabar de... **5.2**
  to have to... tener que... **2.1**
he él **1.1**
head la cabeza **6.2**
health la salud **6.2**
healthy sano(a) **6.2**
heart el corazón (*pl.* los corazones) **6.2**
Hello. Hola. **LP**
  Hello? ¿Aló? **7.2**
helmet el casco **6.1**
to help ayudar **5.2**
her su **3.2**; ella **7.2**
here aquí **4.2**
Hi. Hola. **LP**
high school el colegio, la escuela secundaria
hike la caminata **8.2**
to hike dar una caminata **8.2**
him él **7.2**
his su **3.2**
history la historia **2.1**
homework la tarea **1.1**
  to do homework hacer la tarea **1.1**
horrible horrible **3.1**
horse el caballo **8.2**
  to ride a horse montar a caballo **8.2**
hot caliente
  It is hot. Hace calor. **LP**
  to be hot tener calor **4.1**
hotel el hotel **8.1**
hour la hora **2.1**
house la casa **5.1**
How...? ¿Cómo...? **3.1**
  How are you? ¿Cómo estás? (familiar); ¿Cómo está usted? (formal) **LP**
  How cool! ¡Qué bárbaro!
  How expensive! ¡Qué caro(a)! **8.2**
  How fun! ¡Qué divertido! **7.2**
  How many...? ¿Cuántos(as)...? **2.1**
  How old are you? ¿Cuántos años tienes? **3.2**
  How scary! ¡Qué miedo! **7.2**
  How's it going? ¿Qué tal? **LP**
how many cuántos(as) **3.2**
how much cuánto(a) **3.2**
  How much does it (do they) cost? ¿Cuánto cuesta(n)? **4.1**
hungry: to be hungry tener hambre **3.1**

hurt herido(a) **6.2**
to hurt doler (ue) **6.2**

I yo **1.1**
  I'm sorry. Lo siento. **6.2**
ice cream el helado **1.1**
icon el icono **7.1**
ideal ideal **5.1**
if si **5.2**
important importante **3.1**
  It's important. Es importante. **3.1**
in en **2.1**
  in front (of) delante (de) **2.2**
  in order to para **3.1**
  in the afternoon de la tarde **2.1**
  in the morning de la mañana **2.1**
inexpensive barato(a) **8.2**
information la información; los datos
in-line skates los patines en línea **6.1**
to in-line skate patinar en línea **6.1**
inside (of) dentro (de) **2.2**
instant message el mensaje instantáneo
instant messaging el mensajero instantáneo **7.1**
intelligent inteligente **1.2**
interesting interesante **2.2**
Internet Internet **7.1**
  to connect to the Internet conectar a Internet **7.1**
interview la entrevista
to interview entrevistar
to introduce presentar **LP**
  Let me introduce you to... Te/Le presento a... (familiar/formal) **LP**
to invite invitar **5.2**
  I invite you. Te invito. **7.2**
to iron planchar **5.2**
its su **3.2**

J

jacket la chaqueta **4.1**
January enero **3.2**
jeans los jeans **4.1**
jewelry las joyas **8.2**
juice el jugo **1.1**
  orange juice el jugo de naranja **3.1**

July julio **3.2**
June junio **3.2**

keyboard el teclado **7.1**
kind amable
kitchen la cocina **5.1**
knee la rodilla **6.2**
to know
   (a fact; how to do
     something) saber (sé) **6.1**
   (a person) conocer
   (conozco) **6.1**

lamp la lámpara **5.1**
language el idioma, el lenguaje
large grande **1.2**
last último(a)
   last night anoche **6.2**
   last week la semana pasada **7.1**
   last year el año pasado **7.1**
late tarde **2.1**
later luego **7.1**
   See you later. Hasta luego. **LP**
later (on) más tarde **7.1**
lawn el césped **5.2**
lazy perezoso(a) **1.2**
to learn aprender **1.1**
   to learn Spanish aprender el
   español **1.1**
leather el cuero
to leave salir (salgo) **5.2**; dejar **7.2**
left izquierdo(a)
leg la pierna **6.2**
less menos
   less than... menos que... **3.2**
   less... than menos... que **3.2**
lesson la lección
Let's... Vamos a... **4.2**
library la biblioteca **2.2**
life la vida
to lift levantar **6.2**
   to lift weights levantar pesas **6.2**
like como
to like
   Do you like...? ¿Te gusta...? **1.1**
   I don't like... No me gusta... **1.1**
   I like... Me gusta... **1.1**
   I would like... Me gustaría... **7.2**;
   Quisiera... **8.2**

What do you like to do? ¿Qué
   te gusta hacer? **1.1**
   Would you like...? ¿Te
   gustaría...? **7.2**
Likewise. Igualmente **LP**
to listen (to) escuchar **1.1**
   to listen to music escuchar
   música **1.1**
little pequeño(a) **1.2**
   a little un poco **1.2**
to live vivir **3.2**
living room la sala **5.1**
long largo(a)
to look (at) mirar
   to look for buscar **5.2**
to lose perder (ie) **6.1**
a lot mucho **2.1**
luck la suerte
   to be lucky tener suerte **4.1**
lunch el almuerzo **3.1**
   to eat lunch almorzar (ue) **4.2**

to make hacer (hago) **3.1**
   to make the bed hacer la
   cama **5.2**
mall el centro comercial **4.1**
man el hombre **1.2**
many muchos(as) **2.1**
   many times muchas veces **2.1**
map el mapa **2.2**
March marzo **3.2**
market el mercado **8.2**
   open-air market el mercado al
   aire libre
to match emparejar
math las matemáticas **2.1**
May mayo **3.2**
maybe tal vez **4.2**
me mí **7.2**
meal la comida **1.1, 3.1**
meat la carne **4.2**
to meet conocer (conozco) **6.1**
   Nice to meet you. Mucho
   gusto. **LP**
menu el menú **4.2**
message el mensaje **7.2**
   instant message el mensaje
   instantáneo **7.1**
   to leave a message dejar un
   mensaje **7.2**
meter el metro
milk la leche **3.1**
million un millón (de) **3.2**

minute el minuto **2.1**
mirror el espejo **5.1**
Miss Señorita (Srta.) **LP**
moment el momento **7.2**
   One moment. Un
   momento. **7.2**
Monday lunes **LP**
money el dinero **4.1**
month el mes **3.2**
more más **1.1**
   more than... más que... **3.2**
   more... than más... que **3.2**
morning la mañana **2.1**
   Good morning. Buenos días. **LP**
   in the morning de la
   mañana **2.1**
mother la madre **3.2**
mouse el ratón (pl. los ratones) **7.1**
mouth la boca **6.2**
movie la película **4.2**
movie theater el cine **4.2**
the movies el cine **4.2**
Mr. Señor (Sr.) **LP**
Mrs. Señora (Sra.) **LP**
museum el museo **7.2**
music la música **1.1**
   folk music la música folklórica
   rock music la música rock **4.2**
must: one must... hay que... **5.2**
my mi **3.2**

name el nombre
   His/Her name is... Se
   llama... **LP**
   My name is... Me llamo... **LP**
   What's his/her/your (formal)
   name? ¿Cómo se llama? **LP**
   What's your (familiar) name?
   ¿Cómo te llamas? **LP**
nature la naturaleza
near (to) cerca (de) **2.2**
necklace el collar **8.2**
to need necesitar **2.1**
neither tampoco **7.1**
   neither... nor ni... ni **7.1**
nervous nervioso(a) **2.2**
never nunca **2.1**
new nuevo(a) **4.1**
   New Year el Año Nuevo
newspaper el periódico
   student newspaper el periódico
   escolar
next to al lado (de) **2.2**

nice simpático(a) **1.2**
  Nice to meet you. Mucho gusto. **LP**
night la noche **2.1**
  at night de la noche **2.1**
  Good night. Buenas noches. **LP**
  last night anoche **6.2**
nine nueve **LP**
nine hundred novecientos(as) **3.2**
nineteen diecinueve **2.1**
ninety noventa **2.1**
ninth noveno(a) **5.1**
no no **LP**
nobody nadie **7.1**
no one nadie **7.1**
none ninguno(a) **7.1**
normally normalmente **8.1**
nose la nariz (*pl.* las narices) **6.2**
notebook el cuaderno **2.2**
notes los apuntes **2.1**
  to take notes tomar apuntes **2.1**
nothing nada **7.1**
November noviembre **3.2**
now ahora **3.1**
number el número **LP**
  phone number el número de teléfono **LP**
nutritious nutritivo(a) **3.1**

o'clock: It is... o'clock. Es la.../Son las... **2.1**
October octubre **3.2**
of de **1.1**
  Of course! ¡Claro que sí! **7.2**
to offer ofrecer **8.2**
office la oficina **2.2**
  principal's office la oficina del (de la) director(a) **2.2**
often muchas veces **2.1**
OK
  OK? ¿Está bien?
  OK. And you? Regular. ¿Y tú/usted? (familiar/formal) **LP**
old viejo(a) **1.2**
  How old are you? ¿Cuántos años tienes? **3.2**
  to be... years old tener... años **3.2**
older mayor **3.2**
on en; sobre
  on foot a pie **4.2**
  on top (of) encima (de) **2.2**
  on vacation de vacaciones **8.1**

once: once in a while de vez en cuando **2.1**
one uno **LP**
one hundred cien **2.1**
one thousand mil **3.2**
online en línea **7.1**
to open abrir **5.2**
open-air al aire libre **8.2**
or o **1.1**
orange (color) anaranjado(a) **4.1**
orange (fruit) la naranja **3.1**
to order pedir (i) **4.2**
organized organizado(a) **1.2**
other otro(a) **3.1**
ought to deber **5.2**
our nuestro(a) **3.2**
outside al aire libre **8.2**

page la página
painting el cuadro, la pintura
pair la pareja
pants los pantalones **4.1**
paper el papel **2.2**
  wrapping paper el papel de regalo **5.2**
parade el desfile
paragraph el párrafo
parents los padres **3.2**
park el parque **4.2**
  amusement park el parque de diversiones **7.2**
part la parte
party la fiesta
  surprise party la fiesta de sorpresa **5.2**
password la contraseña
past pasado(a) **7.1**
  half past... ...y media **2.1**
  quarter past... ...y cuarto **2.1**
patio el patio **5.1**
to pay pagar **4.1**
pen la pluma **2.2**
pencil el lápiz (*pl.* los lápices) **2.2**
perhaps tal vez **4.2**
person la persona **1.2**
phone el teléfono **LP**
  phone call la llamada **7.2**
  What is your phone number? ¿Cuál es tu/su número de teléfono? (familiar/formal) **LP**
  My phone number is... Mi número de teléfono es... **LP**

photo la foto **7.1**
  to take photos tomar fotos **7.1**
to picnic comer al aire libre **8.2**
picture la foto **7.1**
pizza la pizza **1.1**
place el lugar **4.2**
to place poner (pongo) **5.2**
to plan pensar (ie) **4.1**
plant la planta
plate el plato
to play
  (an instrument) tocar **1.1**
  (games) jugar (ue) **6.1**
  (sports) jugar (ue) **6.1**, practicar **1.1**
player el (la) jugador(a) **6.1**
Please. Por favor. **LP**
  Pleased to meet you. Encantado(a). **LP**
pleasure el gusto **LP**
  The pleasure is mine. El gusto es mío. **LP**
postcard la tarjeta postal
potato la papa **1.1**; la patata **4.2**
to practice practicar **1.1**
to prefer preferir (ie) **4.1**
to prepare preparar **1.1**
  to prepare food/a meal preparar la comida **1.1**
present el regalo **5.2**
pretty bonito(a) **1.2**
price el precio **4.1**
principal el (la) director(a) **2.2**
problem el problema **2.2**
to protect proteger (protejo)
to put poner (pongo) **5.2**
  to put on (clothes) ponerse (me pongo) (la ropa) **8.1**
  to put on makeup maquillarse **8.1**

quality la calidad **8.2**
quarter (to) (menos) cuarto **2.1**
quarter past ...y cuarto **2.1**
question la pregunta

race la carrera
racket la raqueta **6.1**
radio el radio **5.1**

raft la balsa
to rain llover (ue)
   It is raining. Llueve. **LP**
to raise levantar
ranch la estancia
to read leer **1.1**
   to read a book leer un libro **1.1**
reading la lectura
Really? ¿Verdad?
to receive recibir **5.2**
recess el recreo
red rojo(a) **4.1**
red-haired pelirrojo(a) **1.2**
to rent alquilar **1.1**
   to rent a DVD alquilar un
   DVD **1.1**
to reply responder
to rest descansar **1.1**
restaurant el restaurante **4.2**
result el resultado
to return volver (ue) **4.2**
review el repaso
rice el arroz **4.2**
to ride montar **1.1**; subir a **7.2**
   to ride a bike montar en
   bicicleta **1.1**
   to ride a horse montar a
   caballo **8.2**
   **to ride the Ferris wheel/roller
   coaster** subir a la vuelta al
   mundo/la montaña rusa **7.2**
right derecho(a)
   Right? ¿Verdad? **LP**
   to be right tener razón **4.1**
ring el anillo **8.2**
roller coaster la montaña rusa **7.2**
room el cuarto **5.1**
routine la rutina **8.1**
rug la alfombra **5.1**
rule la regla **6.1**
to run correr **1.1**

S

sad triste **2.2**
safe seguro(a)
salad la ensalada **4.2**
salesclerk el (la) vendedor(a)
same mismo(a)
   Same here. Igualmente. **LP**
sandwich el sándwich **3.1**
   ham and cheese sandwich el
   sándwich de jamón y queso **3.1**
Saturday sábado **LP**

to say decir **5.2**
scary: How scary! ¡Qué miedo! **7.2**
scene la escena
schedule el horario **2.1**
school la escuela **1.1**
   high school el colegio, la escuela
   secundaria
science las ciencias **2.1**
screen la pantalla **7.1**
to scuba-dive bucear **6.2**
sea el mar **6.2**
season la estación (*pl.* las
   estaciones) **4.1**
second segundo(a) **5.1**
secret el secreto **5.2**
secure seguro(a)
to see ver (veo) **4.2**
   May I see...? ¿Me deja ver...? **8.2**
   See you later. Hasta luego. **LP**
   See you tomorrow. Hasta
   mañana. **LP**
to sell vender **3.1**
to send mandar **7.1**
sentence la oración (*pl.* las
   oraciones)
September septiembre **3.2**
serious serio(a) **1.2**
to serve servir (i) **4.2**
set: to set the table poner (pongo)
   la mesa **5.2**
seven siete **LP**
seven hundred setecientos(as) **3.2**
seventeen diecisiete **2.1**
seventh séptimo(a) **5.1**
seventy setenta **2.1**
shame: What a shame! ¡Qué
   lástima! **7.2**
shampoo el champú **8.1**
to share compartir **3.1**
to shave oneself afeitarse **8.1**
she ella **1.1**
shirt la camisa **4.1**
shoe el zapato **4.1**
shop: to go shopping ir de
   compras **4.1**
shopping center el centro
   comercial **4.1**
short (height) bajo(a) **1.2**
shorts los pantalones cortos **4.1**
should deber **5.2**
shower: to take a shower
   ducharse **8.1**
sick enfermo(a) **6.2**
silver la plata
   (made of) silver de plata **8.2**

to sing cantar **5.2**
sister la hermana **3.2**
six seis **LP**
six hundred seiscientos(as) **3.2**
sixteen dieciséis **2.1**
sixth sexto(a) **5.1**
sixty sesenta **2.1**
to skate patinar **6.1**
   to in-line skate patinar en
   línea **6.1**
to skateboard andar en
   patineta **1.1**
skin la piel **6.2**
to sleep dormir (ue) **4.2**
small pequeño(a) **1.2**
to snow nevar (ie)
   It is snowing. Nieva. **LP**
so entonces **7.1**
   so many tantos(as)
   so much tanto(a)
soap el jabón (*pl.* los jabones) **8.1**
soccer el fútbol **1.1**
sock el calcetín (*pl.* los
   calcetines) **4.1**
sofa el sofá **5.1**
soft drink el refresco **1.1**
some alguno(a) **7.1**
someone alguien **7.1**
something algo **7.1**
sometimes a veces
son el hijo **3.2**
sorry: I'm sorry. Lo siento. **6.2**
So-so. And you? Más o menos. ¿Y
   tú/usted? (familiar/formal) **LP**
soup la sopa **3.1**
source la fuente
souvenir el recuerdo **8.2**
Spanish el español **2.1**
to speak hablar **1.1**
   May I speak with...? ¿Puedo
   hablar con...? **7.2**
special especial
**to spend: to spend time with
   friends** pasar un rato con los
   amigos **1.1**
sports los deportes **1.1**
spring la primavera **4.1**
stadium el estadio **6.1**
stairs la escalera **5.1**
to stay in quedarse en **8.1**
stepfather el padrastro **3.2**
stepmother la madrastra **3.2**
still todavía **5.2**
stomach el estómago **6.2**
to stop parar

store la tienda **4.1**
street la calle **4.2**
strong fuerte **6.2**
student el (la) estudiante **1.2**
studious estudioso(a) **1.2**
to study estudiar **1.1**
summary el resumen
   in summary en resumen
summer el verano **4.1**
sun el sol
   It is sunny. Hace sol. **LP**
to sunbathe tomar el sol **6.2**
Sunday domingo **LP**
sunscreen el bloqueador de sol **6.2**
to surf hacer surfing **8.2**
   to surf the Web navegar por Internet **7.1**
surprise la sorpresa **5.2**
survey la encuesta
to sweep barrer **5.2**
   to sweep the floor barrer el suelo **5.2**
to swim nadar **6.1**
swimming la natación **6.1**
swimming pool la piscina **6.1**

table la mesa **4.2**
   to set the table poner la mesa **5.2**
to take tomar **4.2**
   to take a bath bañarse **8.1**
   to take a shower ducharse **8.1**
   to take a trip hacer un viaje **8.1**
   to take notes tomar apuntes **2.1**
   to take out the trash sacar la basura **5.2**
   to take photos tomar fotos **7.1**
to talk hablar **1.1**
   to talk on the phone hablar por teléfono **1.1**
tall alto(a) **1.2**
tasty rico(a) **3.1**
to teach enseñar **2.1**
teacher el (la) maestro(a) **LP**
team el equipo **6.1**
telephone el teléfono **7.2**
   cellular telephone el teléfono celular **7.2**
television la televisión **1.1**
television set el televisor **5.1**
ten diez **LP**
tennis el tenis **6.1**

tenth décimo(a) **5.1**
test el examen (*pl.* los exámenes) **2.1**
Thank you. Gracias. **LP**
   Thank you very much. Muchas gracias. **LP**
that ese(a) **8.2**
   that (over there) aquel (aquella) **8.2**
theater el teatro **4.2**
their su **3.2**
them ellos(as) **7.2**
theme el tema
then luego; entonces **7.1**
there allí **4.2**
   there is/are... hay... **2.1**
these estos(as) **8.2**
they ellos(as) **1.1**
thing la cosa **5.1**
to think pensar (ie) **4.1**
third tercero(a) **5.1**
thirst la sed
   to be thirsty tener sed **3.1**
thirteen trece **2.1**
thirty treinta **2.1**
thirty-one treinta y uno **2.1**
this este(a) **8.2**
those esos(as) **8.2**
   those (over there) aquellos(as) **8.2**
thousand mil **3.2**
three tres **LP**
three hundred trescientos(as) **3.2**
Thursday jueves **LP**
ticket la entrada **4.2**; el boleto **7.2**
time la hora **2.1**; la vez; el tiempo **8.2**
   At what time is/are...? ¿A qué hora es/son...? **2.1**
   free time el tiempo libre **8.2**
   What time is it? ¿Qué hora es? **2.1**
tip la propina **4.2**
tired cansado(a) **2.2**
to menos (with a time) **2.1**; a
today hoy **LP**
   Today is... Hoy es... **LP**
   What day is today? ¿Qué día es hoy? **LP**
tomato el tomate **4.2**
tomorrow mañana **LP**
   See you tomorrow. Hasta mañana. **LP**
   Tomorrow is... Mañana es... **LP**
too también **1.1**
too much demasiado **8.2**
toothbrush el cepillo de dientes **8.1**

toothpaste la pasta de dientes **8.1**
tourism el turismo
towel la toalla **8.1**
town el pueblo
track la pista
train el tren **8.1**
   by train en tren **8.1**
trash la basura **5.2**
tree el árbol
trip el viaje **8.1**
true cierto(a)
truth la verdad
T-shirt la camiseta **4.1**
Tuesday martes **LP**
twelve doce **2.1**
twenty veinte **2.1**
twenty-one veintiuno **2.1**
two dos **LP**
two hundred doscientos(as) **3.2**
type el tipo; la clase
typical típico(a)

ugly feo(a) **4.1**
uncle el tío **3.2**
under debajo (de) **2.2**
underneath debajo (de) **2.2**
to understand entender (ie) **4.1**; comprender **6.1**
   Did you understand? ¿Comprendiste?
unit la unidad
until hasta
us nosotros(as) **7.2**
to use usar **2.1**
   to use the computer usar la computadora **2.1**

vacation las vacaciones **8.1**
   on vacation de vacaciones **8.1**
to vacuum pasar la aspiradora **5.2**
vacuum cleaner la aspiradora **5.2**
valley el valle
various varios(as)
vegetables las verduras **4.2**
very muy **1.2**
   Very well. And you? Muy bien. ¿Y tú/usted? (familiar/formal) **LP**

video game el videojuego **5.1**
to visit visitar
vocabulary vocabulario
volleyball el voleibol **6.1**

to wait (for) esperar **8.1**
waiter el camarero **4.2**
waitress la camarera **4.2**
to wake up despertarse (ie) **8.1**
to walk caminar **6.2**
   to go for a walk pasear **1.1**
wall la pared
to want querer (ie) **4.1**
to wash lavar **5.2**
   to wash one's face lavarse la cara **8.1**
   to wash oneself lavarse **8.1**
   to wash the dishes lavar los platos **5.2**
watch el reloj **2.2**
to watch mirar **1.1**
   to watch television mirar la televisión **1.1**
water el agua (fem.) **1.1**
waterfall la cascada
to water-ski hacer esquí acuático **6.2**
we nosotros(as) **1.1**
to wear llevar **4.1**
weather el tiempo **LP**
   What is the weather like? ¿Qué tiempo hace? **LP**
Web site el sitio Web **7.1**
Wednesday miércoles **LP**
week la semana **LP**
   last week la semana pasada **7.1**
weekend el fin de semana **7.2**
welcome: You're welcome. De nada. **LP**
well bien **LP**
   Very well. And you? Muy bien. ¿Y tú/usted? (familiar/formal) **LP**
what qué
   What? ¿Qué?; ¿Cuál? **3.1**
   What a shame! ¡Qué lástima! **7.2**
   What are you like? ¿Cómo eres? **1.2**
   What color is/are...? ¿De qué color es/son...?

What day is today? ¿Qué día es hoy? **LP**
What did you do? (pl., formal) ¿Qué hicieron ustedes? **6.2**
What did you do? (sing., familiar) ¿Qué hiciste tú? **6.2**
What do you like to do? ¿Qué te gusta hacer? **1.1**
What is the date? ¿Cuál es la fecha? **3.2**
What is the weather like? ¿Qué tiempo hace? **LP**
What is this? ¿Qué es esto? **8.2**
What is your phone number? (familiar/formal) ¿Cuál es tu/su número de teléfono? **LP**
What time is it? ¿Qué hora es? **2.1**
What's happening? ¿Qué pasa? **LP**
What's his/her/your (formal) name? ¿Cómo se llama? **LP**
What's your (familiar) name? ¿Cómo te llamas? **LP**
when cuando **2.2**
   When? ¿Cuándo? **2.2**
where donde
   Where? ¿Dónde? **2.2**
   (To) Where? ¿Adónde? **2.2**
   Where are you from? ¿De dónde eres (familiar)/es usted (formal)? **LP**
   Where are you going? ¿Adónde vas? **2.2**
   Where is he/she from? ¿De dónde es? **LP**
Which? ¿Cuál(es)? **3.1**
a while un rato
   once in a while de vez en cuando **2.1**
white blanco(a) **4.1**
Who? ¿Quién(es)? **3.1**
   Who is he/she/it? ¿Quién es? **LP**
Why? ¿Por qué? **3.1**
to win ganar **6.1**
wind el viento
   It is windy. Hace viento. **LP**
window la ventana **2.2**
   ticket window la ventanilla **4.2**
to windsurf hacer surf de vela **8.2**
winner el (la) ganador(a) **6.1**
winning ganador(a)
winter el invierno **4.1**

with con **7.2**
   with me conmigo **7.2**
   with you contigo **7.2**
without sin
woman la mujer **1.2**
wood la madera **8.2**
   made of wood de madera **8.2**
work (of art) la obra
to work trabajar **1.1**
world el mundo
worse peor **3.2**
to wrap envolver (ue) **5.2**
wrapping paper el papel de regalo **5.2**
to write escribir **1.1**
   to write e-mails escribir correos electrónicos **1.1**
writing la escritura

year el año **3.2**
   last year el año pasado **7.1**
   New Year el Año Nuevo
   to be... years old tener... años **3.2**
yellow amarillo(a) **4.1**
yes sí **LP**
   Yes, I would love to. Sí, me encantaría. **7.2**
yesterday ayer **6.2**
   the day before yesterday anteayer **7.1**
yet todavía **5.2**
yogurt el yogur **3.1**
you
   (sing., familiar) tú **1.1**; ti **7.2**
   (sing., formal) usted **1.1**, **7.2**
   (pl., familiar) vosotros(as) **1.1**
   (pl.) ustedes **1.1**
young joven (*pl.* jóvenes) **1.2**
younger menor **3.2**
your
   (sing., familiar) tu **3.2**
   (pl., familiar) vuestro(a) **3.2**
   (formal) su **3.2**

zero cero **LP**
zoo el zoológico **7.2**

❈ Índice

A

a (personal), 117
abrir, affirmative tú command, 82, 93
acabar de, + infinitive, 84, 93
accent, consecutive vowels, 239
accented syllables, 56
adjectives
    comparative adjectives, 24
    demonstrative adjectives, 268, 279
    estar +, 18
    gender, 7
    noun-adjective agreement, 7, 199
    personal description, 3, 5, 7, 48
    possessive adjectives, 22
    qué + adjective, 199
    singular/plural, 7
affirmative tú commands, 82, 93
affirmative words, 178, 189
age
    birthday party, 68, 69
    date of birth, 21
    expressing, 16
agreement
    alguno and ninguno, 178, 189
    demonstrative adjectives, 268, 279
    noun-adjective agreement, 7, 199
    of ordinal numbers, 54, 65
    of possessive adjectives, 22
alberca, 108
alcoba, 46
alguno(a), 178, 189
almorzar
    present tense, 34
    preterite tense, 144, 155
Altar de la Patria (Dominican Republic), 101
amusement parks, 192–197, 217
Andes (mountains), 39
Año Nuevo, C12–C13
appearance, vocabulary, 3
–ar verbs
    present participle, 240, 251
    present progressive tense, 240, 251
    present tense, 10
    preterite tense, 144, 155
architecture, Inca, 64

Arenal Volcano (Costa Rica), 225, 237
aretes, 266
Argentina, 162–163
    amusement park, 192–193
    art of, 203
    Buenos Aires, 163, 203
    Casa Rosada, 165
    celebrations of, C10–C11
    famous persons from, 162
    foods of, 162, 209
    gauchos, 163
    geography of, 57
    jeringozo, 188
    location on map, 162
    lunfardo, 173
    map of, 162
    museums in, 214–215
    origin of name of country, 188
    Parque de la Costa, 192–193
    scenes of, 163, 165, 214
    tango, 163, 173
    vocabulary variations by country, 108, 170, 198, 204, 266
armario, 52
armario empotrado, 52
aros, 266
art
    of Argentina, 203
    carretas, 225
    of Dominican Republic, 119, 141
    of Ecuador, 39, 51
    textile art, 92
asado, 209
athletes
    Serie del Caribe, 112
auto, 238
automóvil, 238

B

bailes folklóricos, 90–91
balón, 114
bandoneón, 163
barrer, affirmative tú command, 82, 93
baseball
    Serie del Caribe, 112
    vocabulary, 104–105

beaches, 101, 130, 225
béisbol, 104
Beltrán, Carlos, 112
beverages
bife, 209
birthday party, 68, 69
birthdays, 21
bizcocho, 80
body, parts of, 133, 155
bola, 114
Bolívar, Simón, C24–C25
Bolivia
    celebrations of, C14–C15, C22–C23, C24–C25
    museums in, 215
bombilla, 164
Bosque escondido (Salazar), 141
Buenos Aires (Argentina), 163, 165, 203, 214–215
buscar, preterite tense, 144, 155

C

Cabrera, Miguel, 112
cake, vocabulary variations for, 80
calendar, 166
    date, 21, 23
    date of birth, 21
    days of the week, 12
car, expressions for, 238
–car verbs, preterite tense, 144, 155
Carnaval, C14–C15
carretas, 225
carro, 238
Casa Rosada (Argentina), 165
Castilla, Vinny, 112
celebrations
    Año Nuevo, C12–C13
    Carnaval, C14–C15
    Cinco de Mayo, C20–C21
    Día de Colón, C6–C7
    Día de la Hispanidad, C6–C7
    Día de la Independencia, C4–C5
    Día de la Raza, C6–C7
    Día de los Muertos, C8–C9
    Día de Simón Bolívar, C24–C25
    Día Nacional de España, C6–C7
    Las Fallas, C16–C17
    Feria de Málaga, C2–C3

Inti Raymi, C22–C23
Las Navidades, C10–C11
Semana Santa, C18–C19
cerrar, 27
che, 204
Chile
    celebrations of, C4–C5, C6–C7,
        C10–C11
    vocabulary variations by country,
        46, 170
chores, vocabulary, 70, 71, 93
Cinco de Mayo, C20–C21
class schedule, 15
classroom, 12–13
clóset, 52
clothing
    describing, 28
    shopping for clothes, 28
    vocabulary, 28
coche, 238
coffee, 271
cognates, 74
colega, 204
Colombia
    celebrations of, C12–C13, C14–C15,
        C24–C25
    vocabulary variations by country,
        198, 204
colors, expressing, 28, 30, 31, 33
commands, affirmative **tú** commands,
    82, 93
communication
    body language, 80
    gestures, 154
    See also language; vocabulary
Comparación cultural
    Argentina, 57, 164, 173, 181, 192,
        203, 209, 214–215
    art and music, 92, 119, 147, 203,
        214–215
    baseball in Dominican Republic,
        102
    beaches, 130, 181
    Bolivia, 215
    coffee, 271
    Costa Rica, 226, 237, 243, 250, 254,
        264, 271, 276–277, 278
    dessert in Costa Rica and Uruguay,
        278
    Dominican Republic, 102, 112,
        119, 141, 147, 152–153
    double last name, 216

Ecuador, 40, 51, 57, 77, 85, 90, 92,
    243
Festival del Merengue, 147
Fiestas de Quito, 77
foods, 278
gestures, 154
home styles, 40, 51
informal and formal address
    forms, 243
last names, 216
location of a country, 57
lunfardo, 173
markets, 276–277
mate, 164
Mexico, 112
musical instruments, 215
Panama, 90, 92
proverbs, 154
public transportation, 264
Puerto Rico, 112
Serie del Caribe, 112
slang, 173
sports, 152–153
textile art of Ecuador and Panama,
    92
traditional crafts, 85, 92
Uruguay, 243, 277, 278
usted, tú, y **vos,** 243
Venezuela, 112, 153
comparisons, 24
compartir, present tense, 25
computers
    components, 168
    virus protection questionnaire,
        186–187
    vocabulary, 166–169, 189
condition, expressing, 18
Conexiones
    Costa Rica, science museum, 250
    Dominican flag, 126
    jeringozo, 188
    ruins of Ingapirca, 64
conmigo, 206, 217
conocer, present tense, 116, 127
contigo, 206, 217
Costa Rica, 224–225
    celebrations of, C4–C5
    famous persons from, 224
    food of, 224, 278
    geography of, 237
    location on map, 224
    map of, 224

mercados in, 276–277
public transportation, 264
scenes of, 225, 226–227, 248–249,
    250, 254–255, 276
science museum, 250
surf kayaking, 225
tropical plants and birds, 226–227,
    254
vocabulary variations by country,
    238, 243, 266
costar, 34
Cotopaxi (Ecuador), 39
country of origin, expressing, 48
cuarto, 46
cuate, 204
Cuba, vocabulary variations by
    country, 238
culture. *See* **Comparación cultural**

D

daily routine, activities of, 228–230,
    251
daily schedule, 251
dance
    in celebrations, C3, C5, C13,
        C14–C15, C20, C23
    in Ecuador, 90
    flamenco, C2, C3
    indigenous culture, 90–91
    merengue, 147
    in Panama, 91
    sevillanas, C3
    tango, 163, 173
dar, present tense, 76, 93
date of birth, expressing, 21, 23
dates, expressing, 21, 23
days of the week, 2
de, 6, 18, 48
decir
    affirmative **tú** command, 82, 93
    present tense, 76, 93
definite article, 5
demonstrative adjectives, 268, 279
dessert, in Costa Rica and Uruguay,
    278
Día de Colón, C6–C7
Día de la Hispanidad, C6–C7
Día de la Independencia, C4–C5
Día de la Raza, C6–C7
Día de los Muertos, C8–C9
Día de Simón Bolívar, C24–C25

Día de trabajo (Quinquela Martín), 203

Día Nacional de España, C6–C7

diphthongs, 239

direct object, personal **a** after verb, 117

direct object nouns, 32

direct object pronouns, 32
    command used with, 82

direct objects, 32

dislikes, expressing, 2, 5, 8, 9

doler, 137

dominguero, 91

Dominican Republic, 100–101
    art of, 119, 141
    baseball, 101, 102, 103
    beaches, 101, 130–131
    famous persons from, 100
    Festival del Merengue, 147
    flag of, 100, 126
    food of, 100
    location on map, 100
    map of, 100
    scenes of, 101, 102, 126, 131
    Serie del Caribe, 112
    sports in, 101, 102, 124–125, 152–153
    vocabulary variations by country, 108, 136

dormir, 34

dormitorio, 46

double negative, 178

dulce de leche, 278

E

e→i stem-changing verbs
    present participle, 240
    present tense, 35

e→ie stem-changing verbs, present tense, 27

earthquakes, Inca ruins, 64

ecotourism, Costa Rica, 254

Ecuador, 38–39
    art of, 39, 51
    birthday party, 68–69
    celebrations of, C8–C9, C18–C19, C22–C23, C24–C25
    dance in, 90
    family traditions, 68, 69
    famous persons from, 38
    Fiestas de Quito, 77

food of, 38
    geography of, 57
    home styles, 40, 41, 62–63
    houses and apartments in, 62–63
    Inca ruins, 64
    indigenous language, 64
    location on map, 38
    map of, 38
    Otavalo, 39, 85, 92
    ruins of Ingapirca, 64
    scenes of, 39, 41, 62, 63, 69, 77, 85, 90
    textiles, 85, 92
    traditional crafts, 85
    traditional dress, 39
    vocabulary variations by country, 46, 52, 80, 170

education. See school

Egas, Camilo, 39

El Salvador, celebrations of, C4–C5, C18–C19

emotions, expressing, 13, 18

empezar, 27

encontrar, 34

entender, 27

–er verbs
    present participle, 240, 251
    present progressive tense, 240, 251
    present tense, 25
    preterite tense, 172, 189

es coser y cantar, 136

es fácil, 136

es pan comido, 136

es un guame, 136

escribir, preterite tense, 172, 189

está tirado, 136

estancias, 209

estar
    + adjectives, 18
    to express location, 18, 58
    + present participle, 240, 251
    present progressive formed with, 240, 251
    present tense, 18
    using, 18, 48, 58, 65
    vs. ser, 48

estrella, 198

excuses, making, 155

exercise activities, vocabulary, 132

expressing. See **También se dice;** vocabulary

extending invitations, 217

F

fácil, 136

factual information, expressing, 116

Las Fallas, C16–C17

families
    last names, 216
    members of, 21

family traditions
    birthday party, 68, 69

feelings, expressing, 13, 18

feminine. *See* gender

feminine nouns, 7
    form of numbers before, 15

Ferris wheel, expressions for, 198

Festival del Merengue, 147

Fiestas de Quito, 77

flamenco, C2, C3

Las floristas (Egas), 39

food
    of Argentina, 162, 209
    beverages, 164
    in celebrations, C3, C8, C9, C10, C12, C14, C19
    of Costa Rica, 224, 278
    dessert in Costa Rica and Uruguay, 278
    of Dominican Republic, 100
    of Ecuador, 38
    fruits, 20
    restaurants, 29
    snacks, 2
    of Uruguay, 278
    vocabulary variations for names of, 80

formal forms of address, 6, 243

frequency, expressions of, 13

furniture, 65

fútbol, 39

G

–gar verbs, preterite tense, 144, 155

Gardel, Carlos, 173

gauchos, 163

gender
    adjectives, 7
    demonstrative adjectives, 268, 279
    nouns, 7
    ordinal numbers, 54, 65

possessive adjectives, 22
gestures, 154
gifts
    in celebrations, C10, C11
    vocabulary, 93
greetings, expressions for, 204
grooming, 228–230, 251
Guatemala, celebrations of, C4–C5,
    C8–C9, C12–C13
gustar
    + infinitive, 8
    + noun, 8
    pronouns 8, 206

H

habitación, 46
hablar, present tense, 10
hacer
    affirmative **tú** command, 82, 93
    present tense, 26
    preterite tense, 200, 217
health, vocabulary, 132–134, 155
home
    rooms in, 45, 46
    styles, 40, 41, 62–63
Honduras, celebrations of, C4–C5
house, describing, 42–44, 52, 65
household tasks, vocabulary, 70–71,
    93

I

Inca ruins, 64
indefinite article, 5
indigenous cultures, 64, 85, 90–91,
    225
indigenous languages, 64
indirect object, 262
indirect object pronouns, 262, 279
infinitive
    acabar de +, 84
    gustar +, 8
    ir a +, 30
    pronouns placed after, 262
    saber +, 116, 127
    tener que +, 16
informal forms of address, 61, 243
Ingapirca (Ecuador), 64
Internet, vocabulary, 167–169, 186,
    189
interrogatives, 20

Inti Raymi, C22–C23
invitation, extending, 207–208, 217
ir
    a + infinitive, 30
    affirmative **tú** command, 82, 93
    present tense, 19
    preterite tense, 200, 217
–ir verbs
    present participle, 240, 251
    present progressive tense, 240, 251
    present tense, 25
    preterite tense, 172, 189
irregular verbs
    present participle, 240
    present progressive tense, 240
    present tense, 6, 16, 18, 19, 26, 76
    preterite tense, 200, 217
    stem of, 240

J

jeringozo, 188
jewelry, vocabulary, 258, 266, 279
juego de pelota, 104
jugar
    a + sport, 110, 127
    present tense, 110, 127
    preterite tense, 144, 155
    using, 110, 127

L

La Boca (Buenos Aires), 203
language
    gestures, 154
    jeringozo, 188
    language games, 188
    lunfardo, 173
    proverbs, 154
    Quechua, 64
    See also Spanish; vocabulary
Larreal, Daniela, 153
lavar, affirmative **tú** command, 82, 93
lavarse, present tense, 234, 251
leisure. See recreation
le(s), 262, 279
likes, expressing, 5, 9
listening strategies
    attempts to control, 244
    body language, 80
    cognates, 74
    commands, 86

comparing characters' approaches,
    210
drawing a map, 46
finding the real feelings, 52
implied meaning, 148
linking words and visual images,
    198
listen for goals, 120
listening for action, 136
listening for incomplete sentences,
    142
listening for sequences, 170
listening to problems and
    imagining solutions, 272
non–responses, listening for, 108
persuasion, 238
practicing what you hear, 182
reactions, 58
sort out the speakers, 204
stressed words, 114
teasing, 260
"turn–taking" tactics, 266
understanding the interruption,
    232
visual clues while listening, 176
llave, 204
location, expressing, 18, 48, 65, 268
lunfardo, 173

M

maduros, 278
making excuses, 155
maps
    Argentina, 162
    Costa Rica, 224
    Dominican Republic, 100
    Ecuador, 38
máquina, 238
Mar del Plata (Argentina), 181
masculine. See gender
masculine adjectives, 7
masculine nouns, 7
    form of numbers before, 15
mate, 164
meals
    restaurants, 29
    vocabulary, 20, 29
    See also food
Medina, Juan, 119
mercados, 276–277
merengue, 147
Mexico

celebrations of, C4–C5, C6–C7, C8–C9, C10–C11, C14–C15, C18–C19, C20–C21

Serie del Caribe, 112

vocabulary variations by country, 46, 108, 170, 198, 204, 238

mí, 206, 217

Mitad del Mundo monument (Ecuador), 57

molas, 92

money
  of Argentina, 162
  of Costa Rica, 224
  of Dominican Republic, 100
  of Ecuador, 38
  of Venezuela, C24

Montevideo (Uruguay), 277

months, 21

Museo al Aire Libre (Buenos Aires), 214–215

Museo de Ciencias Naturales La Salle (Costa Rica), 250

Museo de Instrumentos Musicales (Bolivia), 215

museums
  in Argentina, 214–215
  in Bolivia, 215
  in Costa Rica, 250

music
  in celebrations, C2, C3, C20
  Festival del Merengue, 147
  merengue, 147

musical instruments
  of Argentina, 163
  in celebrations, C2
  Museo de Instrumentos Musicales (Bolivia), 215

N

nadar, preterite tense, 138, 155

names, 216

native cultures, C6, C7, C8, C9, C22, C23, 64, 85

nave, 238

Las Navidades, C10–C11

negative words, 178, 180, 189

Nicaragua, celebrations of, C4–C5

ninguno(a), 178, 180, 189

Nochebuena (Toaquiza), 51

noria, 198

nouns
  definite articles for, 5

gender, 7

gustar +, 8

indefinite articles for, 5

noun–adjective agreement, 7, 199

possession, expressing, 22

singular/plural, 7

number
  agreement of demonstrative adjectives, 268, 279
  agreement of possessive adjectives, 22
  noun–adjective agreement, 7
  ordinal number agreement, 54, 65

numbers
  from 1 to 10, 12
  from 11 to 100, 12
  from 200 to 1,000,000, 21
  before masculine and feminine nouns, 15
  date of birth, 21, 23
  expressing age, 17
  ordinal numbers, 54–65

O

o→ue stem–changing verbs, present tense, 34

El Obelisco (Buenos Aires), 163

ordinal numbers, 54–55, 65

origin, expressing, 48, 65

Ortiz, David, 112

Otavalo (Ecuador), 39, 85, 92

P

pampas, 163

pana, 204

Panama
  celebrations of, C10–C11
  dance in, 91
  scenes of, 91
  textiles, 92

pantallas, 266

Paraguay, celebrations of, C14–C15

Parque de la Costa (Argentina), 192–193

Parque La Sabana (Costa Rica), 250

parrilla, 209

parts of the body, 133, 155

party planning, vocabulary, 72, 93

pastel, 80

pedir, 35

pendientes, 266

pensar, 27

Pérez, Oliver, 112

personal **a,** 117

personal description, 3, 5, 7, 48

personality, vocabulary, 3

Peru
  celebrations of, C10–C11, C12–C13, C18–C19, C22–C23
  Inca ruins, 64
  scenes of, 64
  vocabulary variations by country, 170, 198

pets, 21

phone. *See* telephone

pieza, 46

pileta, 108

piscina, 108

plátanos horneados, 278

Playa Caribe (Dominican Republic), 131

plural. *See* singular/plural

poder, present tense, 34

polleras, 91

poner
  affirmative **tú** command, 82, 93
  present tense, 76, 93

pool, expressions for, 108

porteños, 203

possession, expressing, 22

possessive adjectives, 22

preferir, 27

prepositions, pronouns placed after, 206, 217

present participle, 240, 251

present progressive tense, 240, 251

present tense
  –ar verbs, 10
  –er verbs, 25
  –ir verbs, 25
  irregular verbs, 6, 16, 18, 19, 76
  reflexive verbs, 234, 251
  stem-changing verbs **e→i,** 35
  stem-changing verbs **e→ie,** 27
  stem-changing verbs **o→ue,** 34
  stem-changing verbs **u→ue,** 110, 127

preterite tense, 138
  –ar verbs, 138, 155
  –car, –gar, and **–zar** verbs, 144, 155
  –er and **–ir** verbs, 172, 189
  irregular verbs, 200, 217

professions, expressing, 48
pronouns
  direct object pronouns, 32
  indirect object pronouns, 262, 279
  placed after infinitive, 262
  placed after prepositions, 206, 217
  placed after present participle, 240
  placed before conjugated form of
    estar, 240, 262
  reflexive pronouns, 234, 251
  subject pronouns, 6
pronunciation
  accented syllables, 56
  b and **v,** 79
  diphthongs, 239
  g before **a, o,** or **u,** 115
  g before **e** or **i,** 146
  j, 146
  ll and **y,** 205
  qu, 174
  running words together, 267
  y, 205
proverbs, 154
public transporation, 264
Puerto Rico
  Serie del Caribe, 112
  vocabulary variations by country,
    80, 136, 198, 204, 266

Q

qué
  + adjective, 199
  ¡Qué bacán!, 170
  ¡Qué bárbaro!, 170
  ¡Qué chévere!, 170
  ¡Qué guay!, 170
  ¡Qué padre!, 170
Quechua (language), C9, 64
queque, 80
querer, present tense, 27
question words, 20
quetzal, 254
Quinquela Martín, Benito, 203
Quito, **Fiestas de Quito,** 77

R

reading strategies
  brainstorming before reading, 108
  compare uses of the verb, 46
  cultural customs, 74

daily routines, 238
differences in behavior, 244
dramatic turn, 272
drawing and labeling, 136
excuses, 142
finding the topics, 148
grouping expressions, 232
hidden reasons, 260
information exchange, 182
key event, 86
key phrases, 176
know whether and where, 58
listing related words, 170
mapping the scene, 198
mindmap for related words, 114
predicting based on visuals, 80
recall and reason, 210
scanning for details, 120
setting, 52
shopping expressions, 266
verb forms in context, 204
recámara, 46
recreation, 2
  after-school activities, 2
  beaches, 101, 130, 225
  bicycle riding, 153
  healthy activities, 132, 134, 155
  sports, 102–106, 108, 127, 257
  vocabulary, 2
  See also entertainment; vacation
reflexive pronouns, 234, 251
reflexive verbs, 234, 251
refranes, 154
restaurants, 29
Rodríguez, Iván, 112
rueda de Chicago, 198
rueda de la fortuna, 198
ruins of Ingapirca (Ecuador), 64

S

saber, present tense, 116, 127
Salazar, Amaya, 141
salir
  affirmative **tú** command, 82, 93
  present tense, 76, 93
San Blas Islands, 92
San José (Costa Rica), 249
Sánchez, Félix, 152–153
sanjuanito, 90
Santana, Johan, 112
sayings (proverbs), 154
school

after-school activities, 2
class schedule, 15
classroom, 12–13
school subjects, 13
vocabulary for, 12–13
seasons, expressing, 28
Semana Santa, C18–C19
ser
  affirmative **tú** command, 82, 93
  de +, 6
  describing people, 6, 52
  present tense, 6
  preterite tense, 200, 217
  using, 6, 48, 58, 65
  vs. **estar,** 48, 65
serenatas quiteñas, 77
servir, present tense, 35
sevillanas, C3
shopping, 28, 279
singular/plural
  adjectives, 7
  demonstrative adjectives, 268, 279
  direct object pronouns, 32
  noun-adjective agreement, 7, 199
  nouns, 7
  ordinal number agreement, 54, 65
  possessive adjectives, 22
slang, Argentina, 173
snacks, 2
soccer, 39
souvenirs, 255, 259
Spain
  celebrations of, C2–C3, C6–C7,
    C10–C11, C12–C13, C14–C15,
    C16–C17
  vocabulary variations by country,
    46, 136, 170, 198, 204, 238, 266
speaking strategies
  being realistic, 273
  expanding and using the list, 211
  graphics, use of, 59
  imagination combined with
    organization, 87
  interesting topic, 183
  link times and activities with a
    clock, 245
  logical steps to meet the goal, 121
  Venn diagram for similarities and
    differences, 149
sports
  baseball, 101, 102, 104, 105, 112
  bicycle riding, 153
  in Dominican Republic, 101, 102,
    124–125, 152–153

in Ecuador, 39
equipment, 104–106
healthy activities, 132, 134, 155
soccer, 39
sports club, 124–125
surf kayaking, 225
vocabulary, 104–106, 108, 127, 257
See also athletes
sports equipment, 104–106, 127
stem-changing verbs
  e→i, 35, 240
  e→ie, 27
  o→ue, 34
  u→ue, 110, 127
present tense, 6, 10, 16, 18, 19, 25, 26, 27, 34, 35, 127
strong vowels, 239
subject pronouns, 6
swimming pool, expressions for, 105

T

Tabacón Hot Springs (Costa Rica), 225
talking on the phone, 217
También se dice
  ball, 114
  bedroom, 46
  cake, 80
  car, 238
  closet, 52
  Cool!, 170
  earrings, 266
  easy, 136
  Ferris wheel, 198
  greetings, 204
  jewelry, 266
  swimming pool, 108
tamborito, 91
tango, 163, 173
tapestries, Otavalo, 85, 92
tarta, 80
technology, vocabulary, 166–169, 186, 189
Tejada, Miguel, 112
telephone call, making, 217
telling time, 12, 14
tener
  + **que** + infinitive, 16
  affirmative **tú** command, 82, 93
  present tense, 16
  using, 16, 17

tener que, 16
textiles
  Ecuador, 85, 92
  Panama, 92
ti, 206, 217
time, 12, 14
  class schedule, 15
  expressions for, 12, 14, 189
  expressions of frequency, 13
  telling, 12, 14
tío(a), 204
Toaquiza, Targelia, 51
tocar, 110
torta, 80
traditional crafts, 85
traer, present tense, 76, 93
transportation, 29, 230, 264
tropical birds, 248, 254
tú, 6, 243
tú commands, 93
tucán, 248, 254

U

u→ue stem-changing verbs, present tense, 110, 127
United States, celebrations of, C6–C7, C8–C9, C20–C21
Uruguay
  food of, 278
  mercados in, 277
  vocabulary variations by country, 243
Ushuaia (Argentina), 57
usted(es), 6, 243

V

vacation, vocabulary, 230, 251, 256–258, 279
vehículo, 238
Vendedora de flores (Medina), 119
vender
  present tense, 25
  preterite tense, 172, 189
Venezuela
  celebrations of, C24–C25
  Serie del Caribe, 112
  vocabulary variations by country, 204, 238
venir
  affirmative **tú** command, 93

present tense, 76, 93
Venn diagram, 149, 276
verbs
  reflexive verbs, 234, 251
  See also specific tenses
virus protection questionnaire, computers, 186–187
vocabulary
  affirmative words, 178–189
  amusement park, 195–197, 217
  baseball, 104
  birthday party, 72
  body, parts of, 133
  classroom, 12–13
  clothing, 28
  colors, 28
  comparisons, 24
  computer, 166–169, 189
  condition, 13
  daily routine, 228–230, 251
  date of birth, 21
  dates, 21, 23
  days of the week, 2
  emotions, 13
  exercise activities, 132
  family members, 21
  feelings, 18
  foods, 2, 20, 29, 80
  frequency, 13
  furniture, 65
  gifts, 93
  health, 132–134, 155
  house and household items, 42–44, 52, 65
  household tasks, 70–71, 93
  interrogatives, 20
  invitations, 207, 217
  jewelry, 258, 266, 279
  likes and dislikes
  lists of, 2, 3, 12, 13, 20, 21, 28, 29, 44, 72, 104, 134, 167, 194
  making excuses, 155
  meals, 20, 29
  months, 21
  negative words, 178–179, 189
  numbers, 12, 21
  parts of the body, 133
  party planning, 93
  personal description, 48
  pets, 21
  possession, 22
  question words, 20
  recreation, 2
  school, 12–13

seasons, 28
shopping, 28
snacks, 2
something that has just happened, 84
sports, 104–106, 108, 127, 257
telephone call, 217
time, 12, 189
transportation, 29, 230, 264
vacation, 230, 251, 256–258, 279
variations by country, 104, 108, 114, 132, 136, 170, 204, 238, 266
words of location, 13, 268
See also expressing; **También se dice**
volver, 34
vos, 162, 243
vosotros(as), 6
vowels
noun–adjective agreement, 7

strong/weak, 239
vuelta al mundo, 198

W

weak vowels, 239
writing strategies
family vacation, 282
favorite sport, 158
party celebrations, 96
visiting a new place, 220

Z

–zar verbs, preterite tense, 144, 155
zarcillos, 266

 # Créditos

Photography

Cover *Background* Rodriguez Joseph/Gallery Stock Limited; *inset right* H. Sitton/zefa/Corbis; **i** *Title Page* Rodriguez Joseph/ Gallery Stock Limited; cover *bottom right* H. Sitton/zefa/Corbis; **iii** *Half Title Page* H. Sitton/zefa/Corbis; **Back Cover** *top left* Steve Dunwell/The Image Bank/Getty Images; *top center* Rodriguez Joseph/Gallery Stock Limited; *top right* Panoramic Images/Getty Images; *bottom left* Doug Armand/Getty Images; *bottom center* David Noton Photography; *bottom right* P. Pet/ zefa/Corbis; **iv** *bottom left* Jaime Puebla/AP Images; *bottom right* Alberto Martin/Agencia EFE; *top* Guy Jarvis/School Division/Houghton Mifflin Harcourt; **xxii** *top* Erich Lessing/Art Resource, New York; **xxiii** *top* Ann Summa/Holt McDougal/Houghton Mifflin Harcourt; *center, bottom* Ken Karp/Holt McDougal/Houghton Mifflin Harcourt; **xxv** *top* Jay Penni/Holt McDougal/Houghton Mifflin Harcourt; **xxvii** *both* Michael Goss/Holt McDougal/Houghton Mifflin Harcourt; **xxviii** *top left* Robert Galbraith/Reuters Pictures; *top right* Holt McDougal/Houghton Mifflin Harcourt; **xxix** *top left* Richard Wareham Fotografie/Alamy; *top right* Ann Summa; *center* Edward Hernandez/Edward H. Photos; *bottom* Philip Coblentz/Brand X Pictures/Getty Images; **C2** *banner, left to right 1* Jesus Dominguez/Agencia EFE; *2-4* Rafael Diaz/Agencia EFE; *all others* Rafael Diaz/Agencia EFE; **C3** *top left, top right* Rafael Diaz/Agencia EFE; *bottom right* Jesus Dominguez/Agencia EFE; **C4** *banner, left to right* Juan Carlos Ulate/Reuters Pictures; The Brownsville Herald/Anthony Padilla/AP Images; Jose Luis Magana/AP Images; Agencia EFE; *bottom left* Hector Lopez/Agencia EFE; *bottom right* Marco Ugarte/AP Images; **C5** *top right* Kent Gilbert/AP Images; *top left* Daniel LeClair/Reuters Pictures; *bottom right* Juan Carlos Ulate/Reuters Pictures; **C6** *banner, left to right* Greg Smith/Corbis; Eduardo Verdugo/AP Images; Claudia Daut/Landov/Reuters Pictures; Les Stone/ NewsCom/Zuma Press; *left* Laura Cano/NewsCom/Agence France Presse; *bottom right* Jacqueline Castellon/NewsCom/ Notimex; **C7** *center left* Dennis Callahan/NewsCom/Notimex; *bottom right* Susana Vera/Reuters Pictures; *top right* Claudia Daut/Reuters/Landov LLC; **C8** *banner, left to right* Ann Summa; © 2007 Robert Frerck/Odyssey/Chicago; Denis Defibaugh; Rodrigo Abd/AP Images; *bottom left* Juan Barreto/Getty Images; *bottom left, inset* Ann Summa; *center left* Charles Bennett/AP Images; *top right* Marco Ugarte/AP Images; **C9** *top left* Glen Allison/Alamy; *top right* Eduardo Verdugo/AP Images; *bottom left* Jaime Puebla/AP Images; **C10** *banner, left to right* Marcelo Del Pozo/NewsCom/Reuters; Enrique Marcarian/Reuters Pictures; Juan Martin/Agencia EFE; Blake Sell/NewsCom/Reuters; *top left* Alberto Lowe/NewsCom/Reuters; *bottom left* Viesti Associates, Inc.; *bottom right* Leo La Valle/epa/Corbis; **C11** *top* Silvia Izquierdo/AP Images; *bottom* Desmond Boylan/ NewsCom/Reuters; **C12** *banner, left to right* Dolores Ochoa R./AP Images; Marcou/Sipa Press; Denis Doyle/AP Images; Eric L. Weather/Lonely Planet Images; Luis Nereo Bueno Martinez/NewsCom/Reforma; *top left* Silvia Izquierdo/AP Images; *bottom right* Alberto Martin/Agencia EFE; *bottom center* Juanjo Martin/Agencia EFE; *bottom left* Olga Vasilkova/ ShutterStock; **C13** *top right* Kryzsztof Dydynki/Lonely Planet Images; *left* Richard I'Anson/Lonely Planet Images; **C14** *banner, left to right* Miguel Vidal/Reuters/Corbis; Pablo Aneli/EPA/Sipa Press; Miguel Menendez V./EPA/Sipa Press; Andres Leighton/AP Images; *left* Elvira Urquijo A./EPA/Sipa Press; *bottom right* Martin Crespo/EPA/Sipa Press; **C15** *top left* Juan Barreto/Staff/Getty Images; *right* David Mercado/Reuters Pictures; *bottom left* Javier Galeano/AP Images; *top center* Guy Jarvis/Holt McDougal/Houghton Mifflin Harcourt; **C16** *banner, left to right 1* Kai Forsterling/Agencia EFE; *2* Hannah Levy/ Lonely Planet Images; *3-5* Manuel Bruque/Agencia EFE; *bottom* Hannah Levy/Lonely Planet Images; *left* J.C. Cardenas/ Agencia EFE; **C17** *right* Heino Kalis/Reuters/Corbis; *left* Kai Forsterling/Agencia EFE; **C18** *banner, left to right* Jack Kurtz/ NewsCom/Zuma Press; Viesti Associates, Inc.; Viesti Associates, Inc.; Jack Kurtz/NewsCom/Zuma Press; *bottom right* Viesti Associates, Inc.; *left* Ann Summa; **C19** *top left* Pilar Olivares/Reuters Pictures; *bottom right* Viesti Associates, Inc.; *right* Dolores Ochoa R./AP Images; **C20** *banner, left to right* Tyler Hicks/New York Times; Joe Raedle/Getty Images; Jorge Uzon/ Getty Images; Damian Dovarganes/AP Images; *right, bottom left* Robert Galbraith/Reuters Pictures; **C21** *top right* Jose Luis Magana/AP Images; *center* Michael Springer/Zuma Press; **C22** *banner, left to right* © Keren Su/Corbis; Paolo Aguilar/Agencia EFE; *left* EPA/Corbis; *bottom right* Paolo Aguilar/Agencia EFE; **C23** *right* Guillermo Legaria/Agencia EFE; *left* Christian Lombardi/Agencia EFE; **C24** *banner, left to right* Dado Galdieri/AP Images; Tony Morrison/South American Pictures; Stuart Franklin/Magnum Photos; *left* Daniel Munoz/Reuters/Corbis; *bottom right* Jupiterimages/Comstock; **C25** *bottom* Pablo Corral V/Corbis; *top left* Stuart Franklin/Magnum Photos; *top right* "Simón Bolívar" (1830), José Gil de Castro. Oil on canvas, 237cm x 167cm (93 5/16" x 65 3/4"). Museo Nacional de Arqueología, Antropología, e Historia del Perú, Instituto Nacional de Cultura, Lima. Photograph by Mireille Vautier/The Art Archive; **4** *3* Shutterstock; *5* Myrleen Cate/Index Stock Imagery; **9** *1* Royalty-Free/Corbis; *modelo, 2* Comstock; *4* Michael Newman/PhotoEdit; *5* Guy Jarvis/School Division/ Houghton Mifflin Harcourt; *6* SuperStock; **11** *modelo* PhotoObjects/Jupiterimages; *1* Stockdisc/Getty Images; *2, 3* Jupiter Images/Comstock; *4* C Squared Studios/Getty Images; *5* PhotoObjects/Jupiterimages; *6* Don Farrall/Getty Images; **15** *2* Edyta Pawlowska/Shutterstock; *3, 5, 6* PhotoObjects/Jupiterimages; **16** *1* Mike Tolstoy/Shutterstock; *2, 6* PhotoObjects/